THE RISE AND FALL OF THE GERMAN
DEMOCRATIC REPUBLIC, 1945–1990

Pearson
Education

We work with leading authors to develop the
strongest educational materials in history,
bringing cutting-edge thinking and best learning
practice to a global market.

Under a range of well-known imprints, including
Longman, we craft high quality print and
electronic publications which help
readers to understand and apply their content,
whether studying or at work.

To find out more about the complete range of our
publishing please visit us on the World Wide Web at:
www.pearsoneduc.com

THE RISE AND FALL OF THE GERMAN DEMOCRATIC REPUBLIC, 1945–1990

MIKE DENNIS

Longman

An imprint of **Pearson Education**

Harlow, England · London · New York · Reading, Massachusetts · San Francisco
Toronto · Don Mills, Ontario · Sydney · Tokyo · Singapore · Hong Kong · Seoul
Taipei · Cape Town · Madrid · Mexico City · Amsterdam · Munich · Paris · Milan

Pearson Education Limited
Edinburgh Gate
Harlow
Essex CM20 2JE
England

and Associated Companies throughout the world

Visit us on the World Wide Web at:
http://www.pearsoneduc.com

First published 2000

ISBN 0 582 24562 1 PPR
ISBN 0 582 24561 3 CSD

British Library Cataloguing-in-Publication Data
A catalogue record for this book is available from the British Library

10 9 8 7 6 5 4 3 2 1
04 03 02 01 00

Typeset by 35 in 11/13.5pt Columbus
Produced by Pearson Education Asia Pte Ltd.
Printed in Singapore

CONTENTS

CONTENTS

LIST OF ABBREVIATIONS

CDU	Christlich-Demokratische Union (Christian Democratic Union)
COMECON	Council for Mutual Economic Aid
CPSU	Communist Party of the Soviet Union
DA	Democratic Awakening
DBD	Demokratische Bauernpartei Deutschlands (Democratic Farmers' Party of Germany)
DJ	Demokratie Jetzt (Democracy Now)
DSU	Deutsche Soziale Union (German Social Union)
DTSB	Deutscher Turn- und Sportbund der DDR (German Gymnastics and Sports Association of the GDR)
DVP	Deutsche Volkspolizei (German People's Police)
DWK	Deutsche Wirtschaftskommission (German Economic Commission)
EAC	European Advisory Commission
ESS	Economic System of Socialism
FDGB	Freier Deutscher Gewerkschaftsbund (Confederation of Free German Trade Unions)
FDJ	Freie Deutsche Jugend (Free German Youth)
FRG	Federal Republic of Germany
GDR	German Democratic Republic
GO	Grundorganisation (Basic Organisation)
GST	Gesellschaft für Sport und Technik (Society for Sport and Technology)
HVA	Hauptverwaltung Aufklärung (Main Reconnaissance Administration)
IFM	Inititiative Frieden und Menschenrechte (Initiative for Peace and Human Rights)

IM	Inoffizieller Mitarbeiter (Unofficial Collaborator)
K-5	Kommissariat-5
KB	Kulturbund der DDR (League of Culture of the GDR)
KoKo	Kommerzielle Koordinierung (Coordination of Commerce)
KPD	Kommunistische Partei Deutschlands (Communist Party of Germany)
KVP	Kasernierte Volkspolizei (People's Police in Barracks)
LDPD	Liberal-Demokratische Partei Deutschlands (Liberal Democratic Party of Germany)
LPG	Landwirtschaftliche Produktionsgenossenschaft (Agricultural Cooperative)
MfS	Ministerium für Staatssicherheit (Ministry of State Security – also Stasi)
NATO	North Atlantic Treaty Organisation
NES	New Economic System of Planning and Management
NDPD	Nationaldemokratische Partei Deutschlands (National Democratic Party of Germany)
NKVD	Narodny Kommissariat Vnutrennikh Del (People's Commissariat of Internal Affairs)
NSDAP	Nationalsozialistische Deutsche Arbeiterpartei (National Socialist German Workers' Party)
NVA	Nationale Volksarmee (National People's Army)
NVR	Nationaler Verteidigungsrat (National Defence Council)
OECD	Organisation for Economic Cooperation and Development
PDS	Partei des Demokratischen Sozialismus (Party of Democratic Socialism)
PGH	Produktionsgenossenschaften des Handwerks (Artisans' Cooperatives)
SED	Sozialistische Einheitspartei Deutschlands (Socialist Unity Party of Germany)
SMAD	Soviet Military Administration in Germany
SPD	Sozialdemokratische Partei Deutschlands (Social Democratic Party of Germany)
VE	Verrechnungseinheit (Unit of Account)
VEB	Volkseigener Betrieb (Nationalised Enterprise)
VM	Valuta Mark
VVB	Vereinigung volkseigener Betriebe (Association of National Enterprises)
ZAIG	Zentrale Auswertungs- und Informationsgruppe (Central Evaluation and Information Group)

LIST OF TABLES

Acknowledgements

We are grateful to the following for permission to reproduce copyright material:

Table 5.2 from Niemann, H. (1993) *Meinungsforschung in der DDR. Die geheimen Betrichte des Instituts fuer Meinungsforschung an das Politbuero der SED*, by permission of Edition Ost, Berlin.

While every effort has been made to trace the owners of copyright material, in a few cases this has proved impossible and we take this opportunity to offer our apologies to any copyright holders whose rights we have unwittingly infringed.

INTRODUCTION

The German Democratic Republic attracted a plethora of negative comments during its forty-year history. It was variously described as the state that ought not to be, Stalin's unloved child and an artificial construct of the cold war dependent on Soviet bayonets and raw materials for life support. Even the long-time Soviet ambassador to the GDR, Abrassimov, denigrated the GDR as a homonculus from the Soviet test tube. Western commentators, certainly until the late 1960s, tended to view it as a link in German history's chain of misery, a totalitarian state bearing a striking similarity to the National Socialist dictatorship and an unjust system which denied basic human rights to its own citizens and imprisoned them behind the monstrous Berlin Wall. This concrete rampart was depicted as the supreme symbol of the cold war and of Communism's failure to mobilise the levels of popular support achieved by its Western adversaries. Since the breakdown of the East German Communist state, revelations of a vast system of surveillance by the Ministry of State Security have served to underline the image of an illegitimate and repressive regime. And the sheer rapidity of that collapse has added fuel to those who see the history of the GDR in terms of a decline and fall in stages,[1] a consequence of the structural flaws inherent in the imposition of the Stalinist political and economic model on an unreceptive population.[2]

This negative portrayal was fiercely contested by the Socialist Unity Party of Germany (SED), the GDR's ruling party. The GDR represented, according to SED doctrine, an anti-fascist and socialist alternative to the capitalist Federal Republic and, rather than being part of German history's chain of misery, a progressive element in the struggle of working people and working-class organisations against oppression by imperial princes, capitalist barons and fascist thugs. One does not, however, have to subscribe to the canons of Marxism-Leninism to recognise that the GDR eventually acquired the reputation of a state that perhaps ought to be. It managed to overcome the heavy reparations burden of the immediate post-war period to launch what many observers regarded as a 'second German economic miracle' in the 1960s, and, though clearly inferior to those of West Germany, to enjoy the highest living standards in the Communist world. The paternalistic social welfare system of the 1970s appeared to have sealed a tacit social compact between regime and population. Even if the East German population was hardly enthusiastic in its support of the regime, most East Germans, in the absence of a realistic altern- ative, conformed at least outwardly and in varying degrees with the highly politicised structures of party, the official mass organisations and state institu- tions; simultaneously, they sought refuge in the semi-private niches of family and friends.

Confined for so many years to semi-isolation as a diplomatic leper and disdainfully placed within quotation marks as 'the so-called GDR', the coun- try started to emerge from the international cold towards the close of the 1960s, culminating in the conclusion of the Basic Treaty between the two Germanies in 1972 and entry into the United Nations one year later. When superpower détente broke down at the end of the decade, the GDR leader, Erich Honecker, enhanced his own reputation and that of his country by seeking to prevent a further deterioration in East–West relations. The near-normalisation of relations between the two Germanies was sealed by Honecker's visit to Bonn, the capital of the Federal Republic, in 1987. At this stage, the GDR, far from being on the verge of collapse, seemed, despite its many problems, to be relatively secure behind its protective barriers and the SED in full control of the reins of power.[3]

This perception proved to be flawed. Two years after his visit to Bonn, Honecker had been ejected from power, and on 3 October 1990, after a ser- ies of breathtakingly rapid developments, Germany was once more united, leaving Stefan Heym, one of the GDR's most distinguished writers, to lament that his country merited little more than a footnote in history. The ultimate failure of the East German Communists to create a viable alternative to, and the GDR's incorporation into, the FRG testifies to the enduring appeal among East Germans of West Germany's federal and social market system. The GDR's demise is also related to the vacuum created by the Soviet Union's retreat from empire after Gorbachev's arrival in power and the abandonment of the Brezhnev Doctrine of the limited sovereignty of the East European states. Whether a sovereign GDR could have survived the lifting of the Iron Curtain in 1989 by the introduction of appropriate reforms is most unlikely, but is one of the questions which will be examined in a later chapter. Yet it has proved easier to remove the GDR from the political map than to create a

[xii]   flourishing eastern economy and an all-German cultural identity. Four decades of GDR history have left a legacy of distinctive mentalities, expectations and socio-economic structures which has impeded a smooth transfer into the new Berlin republic. This has been compounded by easterners' resentment at what many believe to be a ruthless West German colonisation of the GDR's cultural and economic assets. Controversies over GDR history have exacerbated these problems of transition. Among these controversies, many of which form the subtext to this book, are: Was the GDR little more than a puppet of the Soviet Union? Was it essentially an unjust, totalitarian state which has little to contribute to the reconstruction of the new Germany? Why was Germany divided in 1949? Were the crises of 1953, 1961, 1968 and 1989 key moments in the decline and fall of an illegitimate entity? How was society pacified? Did West Germany's *Ostpolitik* prop up the ailing SED regime in the Honecker era? And why did Gorbachev abandon the GDR to its fate?

In seeking to answer these and many other questions, a mountain of new material is available to historians which makes GDR historiography one of the fastest growing areas of contemporary historical studies. Four years into a unified Germany, the number of research projects in German relating to the history of the GDR already numbered well over 700 and showed no sign of slackening. The main documentary sources are to be found in the Berlin branch of the Federal Archive, which houses the papers of the SED, the mass organisations and the organs of state, and in the *Behörde des Bundesbeauftragten für die Unterlagen der Staatssicherheit der ehemaligen DDR* (Authority of the Federal Agent for the State Security Files of the Former GDR) or, as it is popularly known, the Gauck Authority, after the name of its director, Joachim Gauck. A considerable volume of archival material has already been published from these archives; they constitute the main documentary sources used in this book.[4] These sources can be supplemented by the records of the nationalised enterprises, the files of the CDU and other political parties, the archives of opposition groups, interviews and memoirs. While some of the memoirs of former members of the SED elite are little more than retrospective expulcation,[5] others inject a level of criticality and provide valuable insights into the *modus operandi* of the top echelons of the party dictatorship.[6] Another crucial source is the vast amount of material collected by the first Commission of Enquiry set up by the Bundestag in 1992 to investigate the 'History and Consequences of the SED Dictatorship'. The public hearings, the contributions by expert witnesses and the primary documents were published in nine volumes in 1995 under the title of *Materialien der Enquete-Kommission 'Aufarbeitung von Geschichte und Folgen der SED-Diktatur in Deutschland'*.[7] The sources, while plentiful, often fail to provide neat 'solutions' to old and new historical controversies such as Stalin's German policy and the motives behind collaboration with the Ministry of State Security, partly because of the problems inherent in any historical document and partly because the pickings are not so rich from West German and Russian archives.

The new opportunites for studying the GDR have swept away many former research groups and institutes such as the Federal Office for All-German Affairs and spawned many fresh ones. Among the most prominent of the new foundations and institutes are the Hannah Arendt Institute for the Study of Totalitarianism in Dresden, the Centre for Contemporary Historical Research in Potsdam, the Gauck Authority's Department of Education and Research, the Institute for Military Research in Potsdam and the Centre for Research on the SED State at the Free University in Berlin. The Centre for Contemporary Historical Research is of particular interest as it has deliberately utilised ex-GDR academics who meet the criteria set by the Council on Scholarship (*Wissenschaftsrat*). Central to its mission is the development of a wide range of programmes, using a comparative approach, which delves into social and cultural history and everyday life in a 'thoroughly dominated society' (*durchherrschte Gesellschaft*). Encouraging a 'critical historisation' and seeking to avoid theories of totalitarianism, it opted for the conceptual umbrella of 'modern dictatorship'.[8] Its research trajectory raised the hackles of many historians. Not only did some, such as the Association of Independent Historians, a group of younger ex-GDR historians whose careers had been impeded by the SED authorities, take particular exception to the employment of historians who were reckoned to have been close to the SED regime, but many other critics objected to the abandonment of the totalitarian paradigm. Other controversies, often bitter and personalised, have surrounded that section of the old GDR research community in the West which, allegedly, helped to prop up the SED regime by failing to expose the intrinsically coercive nature of the system.[9] These debates, which sometimes include the 'settling of old scores', draw attention to the never-ending search in historical studies for methodologically appropriate paradigms.

The totalitarian paradigm exemplifies the contentious nature of the search. The GDR, like the other countries in the Soviet Union's condominium of Eastern European satellites, was viewed by the West through the prism of totalitarianism during the Stalin and Khrushchev eras. Totalitarianism was introduced into the vocabulary of politics in 1923 by a liberal critic of Mussolini and subsequently developed by a broad church of theorists, including Marxists such as Otto Bauer and Rudolf Hilferding. Of the many variants on

[xiv] the totalitarian theme, those by Carl J Friedrich and Hannah Arendt came to enjoy the greatest resonance, both reflecting and promoting the dichotomies of the cold war. Arendt's classic text, *Origins of Totalitarianism* (first published in 1951), captured, like Koestler's *Darkness at Noon*, the essence of the Nazi and Stalinist regimes. Unable to realise their goals because of the inherent contradiction between utopia and reality, totalitarian regimes, according to Arendt, resorted to an all-pervasive terror, including the concentration and death camps, in order to impose total control over an atomised society. Although the leader's position was impregnable and institutional autonomy non-existent, the system was not monolithic but characterised by confusion, flux and shapelessness. However, unlike Friedrich, Arendt was persuaded, after Stalin's death, that the totalitarian approach had become redundant in the Soviet Union with the establishment of a one-party dictatorship, the liquidation of the huge police empire and the end of the purges.[10] In their seminal text, *Totalitarian Dictatorship and Autocracy* (published in 1956), Friedrich and Brzezinski also insisted on a generic similarity between Communist and fascist totalitarian dictatorships. They classified totalitarian systems according to a syndrome, or pattern, of six interrelated features: a single mass party typically led by a dictator, a totalistic and revolutionary ideology, a system of terror directed against demonstrable or arbitrarily selected 'enemies' of the regime, a technologically conditioned near-complete monopoly of all means of effective communication, a weapons monopoly and a centrally directed economy.[11] The regimes' intent was to achieve total control and to prevent genuine subjectivity. Towards the end of the 1960s, Friedrich, in the light of economic and political change and the development of what he believed to be a substantial consensus in the Communist world, significantly modified some of the core traits, notably the replacement of a terroristic secret police by 'a fully developed secret police'. However, this reassessment failed to spare the syndrome from sustained attack as historians exposed a level of administrative chaos in the Third Reich which did not harmonise with the kind of structured polity depicted in Friedrich's model. Furthermore, as East–West relations eased in the era of détente and as physical terror began to slacken in Eastern Europe, totalitarianism also lost much of its value as a 'boo' word which Western statesmen such as Adenauer and Truman had utilised in order to discredit the Communist foe. Consequently, alternative paradigms were developed by Western social scientists to take account of the interplay of newly unearthed group pressures and of social and economic modernisation programmes. With regard to the former, Allen Kossof likened Soviet-type systems to an administered society and Jerry Hough opted for a limited

'institutional pluralism' perspective. Other Western scholars drew on the industrial society approach of Clark Kerr and Talcott Parsons and variants of modernisation theory to predict a convergence between capitalist and Communist societies. As far as the GDR was concerned, the main revisionists were the West German social scientists Peter Christian Ludz and Hartmut Zimmermann. Ludz, drawing on his studies of clashes between SED ideologists and experts, claimed that the GDR had largely abandoned terror and had moved from totalitarianism to a system of consultative authoritarianism. By the end of the 1970s, revisionism was so far advanced that one leading West German expert on Communism, Gerd Meyer, argued that it was time to pension off the totalitarian model.[12]

Yet the approach was far from obsolete, finding powerful support among distinguished scholars such as Karl Dietrich Bracher and those associated with the *Gesellschaft für Deutschlandforschung*, founded at the end of the 1970s. A centralised, monopolistic ideology, a rigorously restricted freedom of opinion and the striving for the greatest degree of control by a single party and its leaders testified, in Bracher's opinion, to the enduring relevance of totalitarianism.[13] Ironically, as the model was losing favour in many Western studies of Communism, East Europeans were endorsing its utility. The Pole Adam Michnik summed up the opinion of many fellow dissidents in his blunt statement: 'There is no such thing as nontotalitarian ruling communism. It either becomes totalitarian or ceases to be communism'.[14] Since the fall of the Berlin Wall, this perspective has received so powerful a boost from evidence of the deep penetration of East German society by the state security organs that one leading historian, Christoph Klessmann, is persuaded that George Orwell's negative utopia was realised to a greater extent in the GDR than was ever the case in the Third Reich.[15] A semi-official blessing arrived in 1994 when the German parliament's first Commission of Enquiry reaffirmed the validity of the totalitarian model for both the GDR and the Third Reich.[16]

This verdict was much contested. In its minority statement in the Bundestag commission's final report, the Party of Democratic Socialism (PDS), the successor party to the SED, objected that the commission's demonisation of the GDR obscured the complexity of life in the GDR and the positive features of the social welfare system.[17] The commission's verdict, so party representatives argued, was tantamount to creating an absolute symbolic wall between East and West. The PDS plea for a more flexible model strikes a chord among the many historians and social scientists who, while they might not share the party's political philosophy, wish to avoid what they see as the ideological and methodological flaws of older paradigms. 'Modern dictatorship', 'thoroughly dominated society', 'post-totalitarianism' and 'political religion' are but a few of the new terms. There is a broad consensus that the GDR was a form of dictatorship in that a monistic power centre enjoyed an extensive domination but, beyond that, opinions vary as to the ingredients of the dictatorship and the appropriate defining adjective. It is a common objection that the term 'dictatorship', which can be applied to a range of dissimilar autocratic regimes, runs the risk of trivialising the tyranny of a Hitler or Stalin. This kind of criticism may also be levelled with some justification at the term 'modern dictatorship' even though, by highlighting the modern methods of mass mobilisation, coercion, socialisation and enticement which both the NSDAP and the SED utilised, it seeks to draw a distinction with other forms of authoritarian and dictatorial rule.[18] Konrad Jarausch has picked up the theme of enticement by referring to the GDR as a 'welfare dictatorship' (*Fürsorgediktatur*) which, in his words, describes 'the particular blend of social provision and dictatorship that characterises the GDR'.[19] The difficulties inherent in finding an appropriate label are all too apparent in Eckhard Jesse's awkward hybrid, 'autalitarian dictatorship', which conflates the authoritarian and totalitarian features of the GDR in the second half of the 1980s.[20] Linz and Stepan's categorisation of the GDR under Honecker as a post-totalitarian system located along a continuum from totalitarianism to democracy is a more promising approach. Without constituting a conceptual Holy Grail, it offers a differentiated conceptual framework for further detailed historical research (see Chapter 10).

Finally, new work on the GDR's social history, together with a growing sensitivity to the complexity of life under a dictatorship, has fostered a series of new insights into the interaction between rulers and society under the rubric of 'domination as social practice'. According to this perspective, a system cannot operate on the principle of rule by *Diktat* but involves some elements of compromise and mutual interdependence. Drawing on the history of everyday life (*Alltagsgeschichte*), social history and a history of mentalities, the new approaches and concepts are clearly influenced by the 'critical historicisation' of the Third Reich pioneered by Martin Broszat at the Institute for Contemporary History in Munich. *Eigen-Sinn* ('a sense of one's own self'), *Resistenz* and *durchherrschte Gesellschaft* ('thoroughly dominated society') are but three of the concepts utilised by historians to try to capture the variety and complexity of patterns of life in the GDR. The notion of *Eigen-Sinn* is central to several recent investigations into those areas of life which, though by no means islands of political seclusion, enjoyed a certain breathing space from the all-encompassing institutions and mechanisms of SED domination. Located at the base of society – the work collective, the family, the agricultural collective and so forth – these areas constituted an arena for the unfolding of a wide range of attitudes and actions which demonstrate that society in the GDR had neither expired nor been immobilised.[21] This kind of perspective on society underlines the limits on the party-state's claim to exercise total control, and it is also highly revealing of what Mary Fulbrook has referred to as 'a symbiotic mode of life, a coming to terms with the parameters of the system and operating within often unwritten rules' and an 'often unthinking – even unconscious – conformity, of cooperation with the often implicit rules of the game'.[22]

This book adopts the kind of perspective encapsulated by notions of a ruthlessly and thoroughly dominated society in which the asymmetrical balance of power was weighted heavily in favour of the rulers. The term 'Stalinist dictatorship' best describes the ruthless domination of the later 1940s and the early 1950s before its gradual evolution into the thorough and comprehensive domination of the post-totalitarian dictatorship of the post-Wall period. This approach will involve what some readers may regard as a perhaps disproportionate emphasis on how the central organs of party and state, under varying degrees of Soviet control, sought to impose their vision of socialist society and to remove impediments to the authority of the central steering instruments. But account will also be taken of the restrictions on the regime's aspirations, with particular reference being made to the 1953 Uprising, the mass emigration of East Germans, the intrinsic defects of the centrally planned economy, the cultural and economic influence of West Germany, competing notions of socialism, the limited economic and financial resources of the regime and the population's capacity to carve out partial niches. In pursuing these and other issues, I would like to acknowledge the receipt of a Small Grant from the British Academy which enabled me to undertake research in Berlin at an early stage of this book. I also wish to record my appreciation of the financial assistance which I received at crucial times from the History Division and the Russian and East European Research Centre at the University of Wolverhampton.

References

1. The main work in this vein is Mitter A., Wolle S. 1993: 4

2. Weber H. 1991: 39

3. Dennis M. 1988: 197

4. Among the many examples are the records of the East German Communist leaders' meetings with Stalin and other top Soviet officials (Badstübner R., Loth W. 1994), Gorbachev's conversations with Honecker (Küchenmeister D. 1993) and the organisation and operations of the Ministry of State Security (Müller-Enbergs H 1996)

5. Memoirs of this ilk are Krenz E. 1990 and Mittag G. 1991

6. See Schabowski G. 1990 and Schürer G. 1996

7. Henceforth Deutscher Bundestag 1995

8. Kocka J. 1995: 102–5; Klessmann C., Sabrow M. 1997: 231

9. Hacker J. 1992

10. Arendt H. 1966: xix, xxi

11. Friedrich C. J., Brzezinski Z. K. 1956: 10

12. See Friedrich U.-W. 1994: 9

13. Bracher K. D. 1995: 146–50

14. Michnik A. 1985: 47

15. Klessmann C. 1998: 43

16. Deutscher Bundestag I 1995: 182, 743–4

17. Ibid., 719

18. Kocka J. 1995: 93

19. Jarausch K. H. 1997: 44

20. Jesse E. 1994: 23

21. Lindenberger T. 1999: 16–36; Lüdtke A. 1998: 3, 12–13

22. Fulbrook M. 1995: 273

PART ONE

THE ORIGINS OF THE GDR, 1945–49

CHAPTER ONE

AN ANTI-FASCIST DEMOCRATIC GERMANY

The military occupation of Germany

The German Democratic Republic emerged from the power vacuum in Germany after the comprehensive defeat and destruction of Hitler's Third Reich. It was created more by default than by design, a result in the first place of the failure of the victors to formulate a coherent strategy and to establish a *modus operandi* once the bond of a common enemy had lost its adhesive power. But the 'unloved country' was also born of the determination of the Soviet Union and its German Communist assistants to enforce policies in the Soviet zone of occupation in accordance with the Soviet Union's vital security and economic interests and its ideological assumptions when it became apparent that deep-seated East–West differences and mutual suspicion ruled out international agreement on the modalities of German unification.

The territorial configuration of the Soviet zone/GDR was determined not by any compelling economic, cultural or geographical logic but rather by the competing interests of the members of the Grand Alliance against Germany. Stalin, Roosevelt and Churchill all toyed, at times, with the idea of dismembering and partitioning Germany before they finally settled for a much reduced Germany divided into four zones of military occupation. There was, however, much disagreement over which parts of the country were to be allocated to the occupying powers and where the boundaries were to be drawn. The European Advisory Commission (EAC), based in London, was made responsible for drafting an occupation statute. The revised EAC protocol of November 1944 was confirmed in substance at the heads-of-government conference at Yalta in February 1945, with one major modification: it was decided to carve a French zone of occupation out of the two western ones. The mechanisms and principles for the occupation regime and a future peace treaty were laid down at the Potsdam Conference between 17 July and 2

[4] August 1945, the last of the Big Three meetings. It endorsed earlier plans to divide Germany within its 1937 borders into American, British, French and Soviet zones of occupation and Greater Berlin into four sectors. Agreement was reached on the dissolution of the NSDAP and the demilitarisation of Germany. A Council of Foreign Ministers was entrusted with the task of preparing a peace settlement for Germany. In the meantime, the four military governors were to form an Allied Control Council, in which the principle of unanimity prevailed, to deal with questions relating to Germany as a whole.

The Potsdam Agreements further stipulated that Germany be treated as a single economic unit, a principle which clashed with the supremacy of each zonal commander within his own sphere. This conflict would erupt most acutely over the highly controversial issue of reparations. The Americans had no wish for the Soviets to take what they wanted in reparations from the industrial areas of the three western zones and refused Soviet requests for a commitment to a fixed sum. However, as the western zones were the more highly industrialised, the Soviets were granted 10 per cent of the industrial capital equipment of these zones, which was considered unnecessary for the German peacetime economy, and a further 15 per cent in exchange for foodstuffs and other goods from the eastern zone. The question of exchange soon developed into a bone of contention between East and West.

Other issues discussed at Potsdam concerned the revival of political life, Germany's new borders and access to Berlin. Denazification and democratisation were accepted as desirable principles without, however, bridging the gulf between Western and Soviet understanding of the concept of democracy. The territories west of a line drawn along the rivers Oder and Western Neisse were subtracted from the Soviet zone and put under Polish administration pending a final peace settlement, thereby compensating Poland for land lost on its eastern border to the Soviet Union. Between 1945 and 1947, various administrative changes in the Soviet zone led to its restructuring into the five *Länder* of Brandenburg, Saxony, Saxony-Anhalt, Thuringia and Mecklenburg-Western Pomerania. Saxony and Thuringia were virtually restored on their pre-1933 basis but the other three had a hybrid composition.

Beyond the creation of an Allied Kommandatura to administer the German capital, with a sector allocated to each of the victors, arrangements for Berlin were highly unsatisfactory. Although American representatives on the European Advisory Commission had pressed their government to insist on binding Soviet guarantees of access by land and water across their zone to Berlin, only three air corridors were formally approved, in November 1945. The western sectors found themselves marooned deep inside the Soviet zone.

The historical antecedents of the Soviet zone [5]

The area which comprised the Soviet occupation zone had experienced a highly chequered and diverse history. Its much disputed and fluctuating eastern border was the product of the long struggle between Germans and Slavs. Like the other German territories, it had once consisted of a mosaic of secular and ecclesiastical territories deeply divided by dynastic and social conflicts. These fissures were widened by the Protestant Reformation, which had its origins in Electoral Saxony where Martin Luther was professor of theology at the University of Wittenberg.

After the Thirty Years War (1618–48), which left Germany economically devastated and more divided than ever, Frederick William, the Great Elector of Brandenburg-Prussia, began the process of reconstruction which culminated in Prussia's emergence as a major European power under its enlightened absolutist monarch, Frederick the Great, and in the creation of a powerful state which spearheaded German unification under the leadership of Otto von Bismarck. During the Second Reich (1871–1918), parts of the later Soviet zone underwent rapid industrialisation and urbanisation and became a stronghold of the German labour movement. The Social Democratic Party of Germany (SPD) was founded in Gotha in 1875. Saxony, one of Europe's great industrial centres, was dubbed 'Red Saxony' because of the SPD's strength in the region. Although both the SPD and the German Communist Party (KPD) scored relatively well there as late as the Reichstag election of July 1932, with 28.8 per cent and 17.5 per cent of the votes respectively, Hitler's extreme right movement penetrated this heartland during the calamitous final years of the Weimar Republic. With 40.8 per cent of the vote, the NSDAP was easily the most popular party, an achievement which was repeated in Thuringia, Brandenburg and Saxony-Anhalt. In these three areas, the KPD recorded around 16 per cent of the vote.[1]

The KPD, founded in 1919, was the predecessor of the ruling party of the GDR, the Socialist Unity Party of Germany. With its roots in the nineteenth-century German labour movement, the KPD's very existence and traditions testify that the GDR was not without links to specific sections of German society. KPD membership rose from 100,000 in 1919 to 300,000 in 1932. Its massive vote of 6 million in November 1932, the last free election in Germany before Hitler's accession to power, made it the third largest party in the Reichstag behind the SPD and the NSDAP. Many supporters were attracted by the KPD's emancipatory convictions and its aim to rid society of the exploitation and discrimination endemic in the capitalist order. A major weakness

[6]   was its narrow social base. About 80 per cent of its rapidly changing membership in the later 1920s came from the relatively young, male industrial working class. During the early 1930s, the vast majority of members stemmed from the ranks of the unemployed, for whom the party and its associations, like the Red Front, provided self-respect and refuge from the social deprivation of the economic depression. However, the radicalisation of the KPD's ideology and class rhetoric, its adventurism and its growing subservience to Moscow and the Comintern during the 1920s prevented it from attracting the broad social support enjoyed by the catch-all NSDAP.

The mutual and deep-seated hostility between the Communists and Social Democrats during the Weimar Republic culminated in the Communists' wholehearted support for the Comintern's 'social fascism' thesis of 1928, according to which Social Democracy was the main 'social prop' of the bourgeoisie and, thus, of the survival of capitalism. Not only did this doom to failure the KPD's belated overtures to the SPD in 1932 for a united front but it also reflected a fatal underestimation of the Nazi threat. Even after the Nazi dictatorship had revealed its iron fist and the 'social fascism' thesis had been abandoned in 1935, KPD calls for a popular front made little headway with a highly suspicious SPD leadership. The Communists' revolutionary professions and the substantial Stalinisation of the KPD since the mid-1920s were hardly conducive to cooperation. The Stalinisation process swept away the internal democratic tendencies of the original party of Rosa Luxemburg and replaced them with a high concentration of power in the hands of the party *apparat* and its Comintern controllers. Henceforth, the KPD was characterised by an intolerance of deviation from the party line and with the propagation of a crude Marxist-Leninist ideology. Such practices and structure were also endemic in the party's SED successor.

Stalin's brutal persecution of German Communists in Moscow during the 1930s and early 1940s and the secret protocol in the 1939 Nazi–Soviet pact, which divided the spoils of war in Poland and the Baltic states between Hitler and Stalin, were such politically sensitive aspects of a highly flawed heritage that they became taboo subjects for GDR historians. On the other hand, the German Communists' anti-fascist credentials were not without substance. The Communists were persecuted remorselessly during the Third Reich; by the end of the war, perhaps as many as 20,000 had been murdered by the Nazis, including the KPD leader, Ernst Thälmann. Communists were among the first victims of the severe repression carried out by the Nazis: about 60,000 were imprisoned in 1933–34 and a further 15,000 in 1935. It is estimated that about half of the party's 1932 members were incarcerated in the prisons and concentration camps of the Third Reich.[2] Although by 1935 Nazi terror [7] and persecution had decimated the party, to overlook the Communist resistance to National Socialism both before and after this date would, in the words of one historian, 'distort one's understanding of the GDR [and] . . . be blind to the historical roots and to present it as a mere rootless imposition of Soviet military occupation'.[3] Even as late as 1989, some East German intellectuals were still supportive of the GDR as 'the anti-fascist phoenix that rose from the ashes of the Nazi inferno'.[4]

East German society and economy

On the eve of the Second World War, the population of the later Soviet zone stood at 16,745,385. Despite the heavy losses suffered during the war, the zonal population rose to 19.1 million by 1947, a result of the return of prisoners of war and of the influx of refugees expelled from the territories east of the Oder–Western Neisse rivers line. An estimated 4.3 million settlers were living in the zone in December 1947, often without adequate shelter and food. By 1950, the population density ranged from 87 inhabitants per sq km in the predominantly agricultural *Land* of Mecklenburg-Western Pomerania to 334 inhabitants per sq km in industrialised Saxony. The age, sex and employment structure was distorted, primarily because of the heavy male casualty rate in the 18–40 age group during the war. In 1946, for every 100 persons of employment age there were 58.6 who did not fall into this category; the ratio of women to men stood at 135:100, declining one year later to 125:100. The population was predominantly Protestant (81.6 per cent in 1946), though with an appreciable Catholic minority of 12.2 per cent.

One persistent myth is that the Soviet zone's level of economic development was significantly inferior to that of the three western zones. Although it is true that the province of Brandenburg, parts of Saxony-Anhalt and, in particular, Mecklenburg-Western Pomerania were predominantly agrarian, Saxony was one of Germany's major industrial regions. In 1939, it had the highest level of employees in industry as a proportion of the total labour force in Germany, closely followed by Westphalia, parts of the Prussian provinces, Thuringia and Berlin. Overall, in 1936, the area of the Soviet zone accounted for 49.7 per cent of domestic production in machine-tools construction, 61.6 per cent in electrical engineering and 57.5 per cent in precision-instrument making and optics. As a percentage of the territory's domestic production,

[8]   industry and handicrafts constituted 57.8, agriculture 19.5 and trade, communications and services 22.7, as against 60.1, 16.2 and 23.1 respectively in the three western zones.[5]

One serious problem for future economic development was the Soviet zone's low share of basic raw materials industries and the shortage of raw materials. In 1936, the region had produced only a small percentage of Germany's total production of iron ore and hard coal. Although it possessed large deposits of brown coal (lignite), uranium and potassium salts, it was heavily dependent on supplies of hard coal, iron ore and steel from the western areas of Germany and from the eastern territories beyond the Oder–Western Neisse rivers line, notably Upper Silesia. This pattern of trade was so disrupted by the cold war that the GDR was obliged to develop its own basic materials and capital goods sectors to the disadvantage of other branches of the economy.

The future was bleak for the people of the Soviet zone as they emerged from the trauma of war. Anton Ackermann, a leading KPD functionary, recalled that the people 'were paralysed by the poison of despair equally weighed down by the traumatic experience of nightly air raids and the other horrors of war'.[6] The Battle for Berlin between 16 April and 2 May 1945 had been one of the bloodiest campaigns of the war and cost the conquering Red Army at least 200,000 dead, wounded and missing. The Germans may have suffered casualties of around 50,000, including over 20,000 civilians. Chaos and desolation reigned in the capital and most citizens of the zone were without adequate food and obliged to resort to the blackmarket and barter.

The war caused acute material distress and substantial destruction of production capacity, albeit less than in the western zones which had borne the brunt of the allied bombing campaign. The housing stock of the eastern zone was seriously depleted. About 433,000 houses were totally destroyed and 207,000 severely damaged. The loss was greatest in Berlin, where 500,000 houses had been destroyed, but cities like Magdeburg and Dresden were also badly affected, with 15 per cent and 12.1 per cent respectively of housing suffering total destruction.[7]

Although the heavy destruction towards the end of the war significantly reduced the economic potential of the zone, official GDR claims that the area had suffered a 40 per cent loss of industrial capacity were deliberately exaggerated, partly to disguise the extent of the damage caused by Soviet dismantling and requisitioning. Most large enterprises were able to resume production a few weeks after the end of the war. New archival evidence indicates that, in comparison to 1944 capacity, war-related damage did not exceed 15 per cent

in industry, 2 per cent in agriculture, 10 per cent in transport and communications, 15 per cent in commerce and 14 per cent in housing.[8]

The trauma of rape

As the Red Army swept across eastern and central Germany and into Berlin,
the German population suffered pillage and rape by Soviet troops. The brutal
war of annihilation between the Third Reich and the Soviet Union, Russian
envy of German wealth, a desire for revenge and the Russians' status of con-
queror all combined to produce a nightmare of rape for German girls and
women of all ages. Even women KPD activists were not spared. Although
Stalin neither forbade nor authorised the atrocities, his attitude is reflected
in his retort to Milovan Djilas's complaints against Soviet troops' raping of
Yugoslav women:

> *Well then, imagine a man who has fought from Stalingrad to Belgrade – over thousands of
> kilometres of his own devastated land, across the dead bodies of his comrades and dearest
> ones. How can such a man react normally? And what is so awful in his amusing himself
> with a woman, after such horrors?*[9]

One tragedy, which was not untypical, occurred in 1946 in a village near
Cottbus to a twenty-year-old girl, Angela B, who was raped by three Russians while on her way home from the cinema:

> *Later she noticed that she was pregnant. Although abortion in such cases is officially
> permitted, a medical examination could not be undertaken without danger to her life. The
> girl, who had been very strictly brought up, was afraid to confide in her parents, and when
> the child was born she was in such desperation that she strangled it with a handkerchief and
> subsequently appeared in court on a charge of infanticide.*[10]

In the immediate aftermath of war, it was the women of Berlin who had to
bear most of the physical and psychological shock and the humiliation of
sexual violence. Even when the situation in Berlin was brought under control, rape by Soviet troops continued on a widespread scale in Chemnitz, Frank-
furt/Oder and several other east German cities. Although it ceased to be a
major problem by the beginning of 1947, incidents continued until the
imposition of much harsher penalties in 1949. It is impossible to assess how
many German women were violated by Soviet troops, whether in the Soviet
zone or fleeing East Prussia, Silesia and the Sudetenland; according to recent
estimates, it may have been in the hundreds of thousands, possibly even 2
million.[11] When a memorial to the victorious Red Army was later erected in

[10]   East Berlin's Treptow Park, painful memories were reflected in references to it as the 'Tomb of the Unknown Rapist'.[12]

Communist plans for one Germany

The future of the Soviet zone would depend very much on Soviet and Western conceptions of a new political and economic order for Germany and on the compatibility of the security needs of Hitler's conquerors. At times, Stalin toyed with the idea of partitioning Germany to prevent a resurgence of militarism and Nazism. In the later stages of the war, Soviet planners in the Commissariat of Foreign Affairs and in the State Security agencies were directed to develop concepts for the deindustrialisation of Germany and its dismemberment into separate states.[13] However, Stalin and his advisers ultimately opted for preserving Germany intact, with the exception of substantial territorial excisions in eastern Germany, for fear lest a dismembered Germany fuel revanchism and fall prey to monopoly capitalism. A unified Germany within the Soviet orbit was the ultimate goal; the problem was how to achieve it.

In wartime Moscow, German Communists around the KPD's core leadership group of Wilhelm Pieck, Wilhelm Florin and Walter Ulbricht had also been busy devising plans for postwar Germany. The German Communists were not free agents; they had to take orders from the Kremlin and to coordinate their ideas with Stalin's representatives, notably the Bulgarian Georgi Dimitrov, the General Secretary of Comintern until its dissolution in 1943, and subsequently head of the Department for International Relations of the CPSU Central Committee. Other experienced Communist functionaries in exile in Moscow, who later became influential politicians in the GDR, included Anton Ackermann, Hermann Matern, Fred Oelssner and Rudolf Herrnstadt.

Wilhelm Pieck was born in 1876 in Guben in eastern Germany. A member of the SPD since 1895, he defected over the party's support for the Kaiser's war. He then went underground helping to organise the conspiratorial network which was to become the Spartacist League. A co-founder of the KPD, Pieck was one of the party's leading functionaries during the Weimar Republic. He served as a Comintern representative in Germany and as head of the KPD parliamentary group in the Reichstag, becoming party chairman after the imprisonment of Thälmann in 1933. Soon after Hitler's appointment as chancellor, Pieck fled to Paris before moving to Moscow in the following year. From there he helped to found the National Committee for a Free Germany, which consisted of German prisoners of war who, operating from the Soviet Union, worked for the liberation of Germany after the fall of Stalingrad in 1943. After the war, the white-haired, jovial and rotund Pieck appeared to embody everyone's friendly grandfather. In fact, he was a doctrinaire Marxist-Leninist, utterly devoted to Stalin and the Soviet Union. Florin, like Pieck, was closely associated with the Spartacist movement and the early KPD. He became a member of the KPD Politbüro in 1929 and held high office in the Comintern.

The other member of the triumvirate, Walter Ulbricht, would later become the head of party and state in the GDR. Born in 1893 in Leipzig, the son of a tailor, Ulbricht was a member of the SPD from 1912 to 1918, before joining the Spartacists and the KPD. With a thin, rasping voice, a pronounced Saxon dialect and devoid of personal charm, Ulbricht embodied the ambitious, intolerant but astute party bureaucrat. At the end of the 1980s, one expert on Eastern Europe and the GDR, Michael Simmons, depicted Ulbricht in unflattering terms:

> *He was more important for what he became – East Germany's chief defender and head of state and a major influence on the European stage – than for the sort of human being, or political animal, that he was, which was a cautious, usually centrist political schemer.*[14]

Ulbricht joined the KPD Politbüro in 1928 and headed the party's Berlin-Brandenburg regional organisation between 1929 and 1933, using his position to consolidate his own power and to push through the Stalinisation of the party. Exiled in Moscow for most of the Third Reich, he was a co-founder of the National Committee for a Free Germany. Wolfgang Leonhard, a member of the postwar Ulbricht 'initiative' group, provides an apt description of the qualities which enabled Ulbricht to become one of the leading figures in the early years of the German Communist movement:

> *His strong points were his talents as an organiser, his phenomenal memory for names, his skill in foreseeing each successive change in the Party line, and his tireless industry. He never seemed to be exhausted even after the longest day's work. I seldom saw him laugh . . . Being entirely innocent of theoretical ideas or personal feelings, to the best of my knowledge, he never failed to carry out the directives transmitted to him by the Soviet authorities with ruthlessness and skill.*[15]

Moscow was the main base of the exiled Communists. After the KPD Central Committee had moved there in 1935, other leading functionaries soon followed. The city proved to be a dangerous place: many comrades fell victim to the Stalinist terror campaigns and purges. Between 1,200 and 1,300

[12] German anti-fascists, including over 70 per cent of the KPD members in Soviet exile, were incarcerated by the NKVD (People's Commissariat of Internal Affairs); most of them were murdered.[16] Indeed, more top Communist cadres were caught up in Stalin's terror machine than in Hitler's: whereas five members and candidates of the KPD Politbüro of the Weimar era were murdered in Germany between 1933 and 1945, seven died in the Stalinist purges. Among Stalin's victims were Hermann Remmele, one of the leading KPD functionaries during the final days of the Weimar Republic, and Hugo Eberlein, a co-founder of the KPD and the father of Werner Eberlein, a member of the SED Politbüro during the 1980s.[17] Survivors such as Pieck and Ulbricht, unswervingly loyal to Stalin, must have collaborated with the NKVD, although it is known that Pieck did at least attempt to secure the release of some comrades. Exile in Moscow reinforced the surviving German Communists' dependence on the CPSU and familiarised them with the arbitrary and brutal elimination of political opponents. Furthermore, as true Marxist-Leninists, the experience strengthened their sense of party discipline and the Red Army's victory in the war against fascism reaffirmed their belief in the ultimate victory of the Soviet model and the demise of capitalism.

The KPD exiles' thinking on the nature of the postwar order in Germany assumed a sense of urgency when it became clear by spring 1944 that Hitler's fall was only a question of time. Important documents, only recently published, show that they favoured a socialist Germany on the Soviet model, dominated by a Marxist-Leninist party and enjoying close relations with the Soviet Union. They appreciated, however, that this had to be a long-term goal. Not only would the American and British governments vigorously oppose any move to introduce a Soviet-style socialist system but the KPD anticipated fierce competition from the SPD, the *Zentrum* and the other political parties.[18] An alternative scenario was devised: the progressive elimination of capitalism during an anti-fascist 'democratic' stage and the establishment of a 'bloc of militant democracy' under the leadership of the KPD. Drawing on notions of a popular front and a democratic republic propagated during the 1930s, this 'bloc' was conceived as a broad, anti-fascist and democratic mass movement for the mobilisation of groups hitherto beyond the reach of the KPD: Catholic workers, the non-socialist intelligentsia and all sections of the petty bourgeoisie. While the KPD exiles hoped to woo individual Social Democrats with their anti-fascist programme, their visceral hostility to the SPD ruled out an immediate fusion of the two left-wing parties. By outmanoeuvring the SPD leadership and exploiting divisions within the party, it was hoped to attract left-wing Social Democrats and to bring the entire

working-class movement, including the trade unions, under KPD control.
One crucial task of the 'bloc of militant democracy' was to create a state administration which would help to destroy the roots of fascism by the imprisonment of leading Nazis and by the removal of National Socialists from the state apparat. The KPD realised that it would have to dilute its radicalism, at least temporarily, for, as Pieck warned, too radical a socialist programme would weaken the party's mass appeal.

The KPD exiles had to modify their initial focus on the whole of Germany after the Big Three conference at Yalta agreed on the division of Germany into four zones of occupation. Without abandoning the creation of a 'bloc of militant democracy' for the whole country, the German Communists, under instructions from Dimitrov and Soviet officials, were obliged to concentrate on measures for the reconstruction of the Soviet zone. In early February 1945, Pieck received the green light to select and train 150 reliable cadres to support the occupying power. On instructions from the CPSU Central Committee, guidelines were drafted for the tasks of the three small 'initiative' groups which were to help the Soviet authorities in setting up administrative bodies in the zone and in organising the economy and media.[19] At this juncture, it was not intended to authorise other political parties.

Germany under four-power control

The failure at Potsdam to reach agreement on many basic issues reflected not only strong political and ideological differences between the occupying powers but also uncertainties within all countries as to the most appropriate way of dealing with Germany. Stalin, although attracted to the idea of dismemberment, came to favour an all-German solution as long as guarantees were provided for security against a future German threat and for the recovery of the Soviet economy. In 1945, Moscow probably believed that these basic goals could best be achieved for the present through the joint occupation of Germany. This would enable the Soviet Union to influence events in the western zones and to exact reparations from its own zone as well as from the western industrial areas, especially the Ruhr. Beyond these essential goals, Soviet plans for Germany were subject to change and fluctuation.

While the most desirable outcome from the point of view of the Soviet Union was the installation of a socialist system on the Soviet model, this could only be a long-term goal, conditional on a series of variables such as the popular

[14]   appeal of the German Communists. Stalin appreciated that the goal would be extremely difficult to attain for, as he told the leader of the London-based Polish exile government, Mikolajzyk, in 1944, 'Communism fits German like a saddle fits a cow'.[20] Another possible solution, perhaps more readily attainable, was the establishment of a united, neutral Germany, unattached to any bloc, but which might nevertheless be strongly influenced by a powerful Soviet Union. This was not an easy option, however. It contained the danger of a strong German orientation towards the West and it required a high level of cooperation with the Western powers on the whole postwar order.

Perhaps the second most undesirable alternative, after a united, capitalist Germany, was a divided Germany with a western state closely linked to the United States and hostile to Soviet aspirations and an eastern state with a population antipathetic to the Soviet model of society. Territorial revisionism and a resurgence of German nationalism were other potential drawbacks of this option. American willingness to retain a military presence in Europe and to provide economic assistance would be crucial to the final outcome.

In the meantime, the Soviets were determined to consolidate their own power and that of their German Communist assistants in the eastern zone. But this was a policy which, unless pursued in an adroit and flexible manner, ran the risk of bringing about one of the outcomes which Stalin and his associates wished to avoid, that is, the division of Germany into two antagonistic camps. Adroitness was not, however, a conspicuous feature of Soviet diplomacy given the leadership's underlying ideological assumption of an irreconcilable contradiction between Western imperialism and socialism and its belief in the efficacy of military power and threats.

What kind of system did Moscow wish to introduce into the Soviet zone which would best secure Soviet goals? The Kremlin rejected, at least initially, the implementation of a Soviet-style system; this would have prejudiced its broader all-German goals and it was simply not feasible at a time of economic and political chaos. Most Germans were primarily concerned about food, clothing and missing relatives. The withdrawal from politics – 'without me' being the typical attitude – was also driven by feelings of guilt and by the reaction against the intensity of Nazi political indoctrination. On the other hand, there did exist, both in eastern and western Germany, a strong ideological current in favour of fundamental social and political changes to extirpate the evils of National Socialism. This current was not inherently hostile to a Soviet Union whose system had proved its value in the defeat of fascism and whose planning model appeared to offer a real prospect of overcoming the recurrent crises experienced by capitalist states in the 1920s and 1930s. The pronounced authoritarian tradition in German political culture in the first half of the twentieth century was also conducive to the form of anti-fascism from above [15] favoured by Moscow and the KPD; it could be received, rather than actively learned. As one German expert on the topic has observed: 'It offered self-redemption instead of self-responsibility'.[21]

What the Soviet Union opted for was the anti-fascist 'democratic' system hatched in the latter stages of the war. This system would, it was hoped, boost the KPD's position in the Soviet zone, provide a model for the whole of Germany and enable the Communists to destroy the roots of Nazism and militarism. According to notes kept by Pieck of a meeting with Stalin in Moscow on 4 June 1945, the Soviet leader defined his key policy goals as, 'completion of the bourgeois-democratic revolution, bourgeois-democratic government, break the power of the estate owners, get rid of the remnants of feudalism'. His doubts about the chances of holding Germany together surfaced in the phrase, 'Perspective – there will be two Germanies – despite the unity of the allies'.[22] In order to prevent this outcome, he urged, 'Protection of unity by a unified KPD, a unified party of the working class'.[23] Why Germany might be divided was inherent in Stalin's own thinking, as illustrated by his famous statement to the Yugoslav Communist Milovan Djilas in April 1945, that 'this war is not as in the past; whoever occupies a territory also imposes on it his own social system'.[24] However, Stalin was too shrewd and experienced a leader to rush into such a course of action in Germany, particularly as the Red Army only occupied part of the country. Further light is shed on Stalin's strategy at his meeting with Ulbricht in February 1946. Stalin countered the German's definition of the KPD's maximum goal as the achievement of worker power and socialism in Germany with the warning that the transformation would have to be along the 'democratic path', not, as in Russia, by means of a dictatorship, because of the existence of parliamentary traditions in the West.[25] This and other statements by Stalin on democracy should not be interpreted as a commitment to the installation of a Western-type democratic, pluralistic system, but rather that the Communists' attainment of power in Germany must be pursued flexibly in accordance with national conditions and the fluctuating international 'correlation of forces'.

SMAD and the political direction of the zone

The body mainly responsible for the restoration of order and the implementation of policy in the Soviet zone of occupation was the Soviet Military Administration in Germany (SMAD), which operated in conjunction with experienced Communist cadres such as Ulbricht and Ackermann. Accompanied

[16]   by nine colleagues, Ulbricht returned to Berlin on 30 April 1945, the same day as Hitler committed suicide, to assist the Soviet authorities in the reconstruction of the Berlin region in the Soviet zone. Ulbricht rapidly emerged as the main German political figure in the zone. Trusted by the Soviets and responsive to their needs and priorities, he set about the task of administrative reconstruction with great vigour and ruthlessness. The activities of the Ulbricht group were parallelled by the other 'initiative' groups under the control of two other Moscow émigrés, Ackermann, in Saxony, and Gustav Sobottka, in Mecklenburg-Western Pomerania. Following orders issued from Moscow to set up a German civil administration, the three groups appointed mayors and established local and regional administrations. They selected personnel from a wide range of social and political backgrounds, such as Communists, Social Democrats and 'progressive' middle-class people, in line with the official Soviet policy to create a broadly based, anti-fascist democratic order. However, they took great care to place reliable Communists in charge of education, personnel and the police. The basic principle was laid down by Ulbricht as, '. . . it's got to look democratic, but we must have everything in our control'.[26]

The new political order precluded autonomous anti-fascist activities and sectarian Communists' wishes to launch a socialist revolution. Anti-fascist committees and grass-roots organisations had sprung up spontaneously in many towns and villages to cope with local needs immediately before and after the collapse of the Third Reich and initially provided support to the authorities in their efforts to restore order in the zone. However, their existence conflicted with SMAD and the German Communists' desire for political and ideological control: most of those who refused incorporation into the new administrative bodies were dismantled in May and June; a few managed to linger on until August in the less accessible areas.

The Soviet Military Administration was officially created on 9 June 1945. Marshal Zhukov, the Soviet war hero, was appointed commander-in-chief and V D Sokolovskii and I A Serov became his deputies. The former replaced Zhukov in April 1946. SMAD had responsibility for implementing Allied decisions and for the administration of the Soviet zone's economic, political, social and cultural order. Its strength fluctuated from 49,887 members, including 21 generals, in November 1946 to 31,500 in August 1948. In addition to SMAD's own troops, several hundred thousand Soviet occupation troops were stationed in the zone.[27]

SMAD was split up into four main administrative spheres – military affairs, the economy, civil administration and political questions – and subdivided into over twenty departments. It had close links to the security forces of the [17] Ministry of Internal Affairs and the Ministry of State Security. SMAD's central headquarters in Berlin-Karlshorst and its regional administrative organs issued a flood of orders, instructions and guidelines. Violation of an order could be treated as sabotage and, at least in the economic sphere, carried a sentence of fifteen years and, in serious cases, the death penalty. Despite its considerable administrative apparat and powers of enforcement, SMAD was far from being a monolithic organisation and did not function as smoothly as was formerly believed. Both Norman Naimark and Stefan Creuzberger have shown that it was bedevilled by internal rivalries and an overlapping of competencies. This was a consequence of the not infrequent ambiguity of policy directives emanating from Stalin, a shortage of high-calibre Soviet administrators in the zone and confusion over the respective responsibilities of the central Soviet state and party authorities in Moscow.[28]

One of SMAD's main tasks was to set up German administrative bodies to assist the Russians in the running of the zone. In July 1945, it authorised the creation of civilian provincial governments and eleven – later seventeen – central administrations to determine policy in areas such as health, education, agriculture, finance and justice. Essentially auxiliary bodies, these German administrations lacked the power to issue laws or decrees. By far the most significant central administration was the German Economic Commission (DWK). Established in 1947, it comprised the central German administrations for trade and supply, industry, transport and agriculture. In 1948, when Germany was beginning to split into two, the DWK was transformed into a proto-government; its membership was expanded from 36 to 101, and its powers were boosted by Sokolovskii's order giving it the right to issue decrees binding on all German bodies.[29]

An anti-fascist democratic programme

Denazification

The programme pursued by SMAD and its German Communist allies was anti-fascist democratic reconstruction. It was designed to resuscitate the revival of political life in the zone under strictly controlled conditions, to eliminate the socio-economic preconditions of militarism and Nazism, and to pave the way for radical social reform. The cauterising of Nazism served another purpose. Together with the heroicisation of the Communist resistance

[18]   in the Third Reich, it constituted the main component of the powerful anti-fascist myth which lay at the heart of the SED's political legitimation strategy. After the foundation of the GDR, the myth was underpinned by a comprehensive programme of remembrance: memorials, schools and streets were named after resistance fighters and martyrs; school textbooks portrayed the German resistance as a virtual monopoly of the KPD; and visits were organised to official memorial sites to the victims of fascism at the former Nazi concentration camps in Buchenwald and Sachsenhausen.

In the absence of central directives from SMAD, denazification measures were initially carried out in a somewhat haphazard manner and, until the end of 1945, varied considerably in scope from one province to another. It was a major undertaking as an estimated 1.5 million ex-Nazis remained in the zone. In Thuringia, 'old comrades' who had joined the NSDAP before April 1933 and party members in certain high-ranking positions were dismissed, whereas nominal Nazis were allowed to remain in public administration on condition they subjected themselves to political and ideological indoctrination. In Brandenburg and Mecklenburg-Western Pomerania, by contrast, all former NSDAP members were liable to dismissal. By late summer 1945, the removal of NSDAP members from top positions in the administration was virtually complete[30] and by the end of 1946, between 306,000 and 390,000, excluding Mecklenburg-Western Pomerania, are believed to have been either dismissed or not reinstated as a result of denazification.

In August 1947, SMAD order number 201 paved the way for the transfer of Nazi and war criminals to German courts and for the rehabilitation of nominal Nazis. Newly constituted denazification commissions now homed in on Nazi activists who had not committed an offence. The investigations focused on employees in the economy rather than, as before, on those in public administration. All commission heads and the majority of commission members belonged to the SED. Between September 1947 and March 1948, the overtaxed commissions examined and reached decisions on 140,645 cases before, in April 1948, yet another SMAD order closed them down and terminated formal denazification in the Soviet zone. By this date, the total number of persons either dismissed or not reinstated may have amounted to approximately 450,000.[31]

As the new rulers of the zone could not dispense lightly with skilled and experienced personnel, many former Nazis, primarily nominal members, survived in certain areas of the economy and public administration. For example, about 46 per cent of practising doctors, dentists and chemists and many highly trained engineers and technicians in industry and transport had once belonged to the NSDAP. Such pragmatism notwithstanding, denazification swept away most ex-Nazis from the schools, the judiciary and public administration. By the end of December 1946, only about 11 per cent of primary and secondary schoolteachers and 2.9 per cent of the judiciary were former Nazis. Yet, despite the relative thoroughness of denazification in the Soviet zone, a 1965 report of a group of West Berlin lawyers, the Investigating Committee of Free Jurists, managed to unearth the Nazi past of twelve SED Central Committee members, five government ministers and several *Volkskammer* deputies.[32] While the National Democratic Party, founded in 1948, was given major responsibility for the absorption of ex-Nazis, the SED itself also recruited minor Nazis. According to SED internal statistics, former National Socialists constituted 8.7 per cent of the party's membership at the end of 1953; a further 6 per cent of members and candidates had once belonged to a Nazi subsidiary organisation.

The authorisation of political parties

A crucial step along the self-styled anti-fascist democratic road was SMAD's unexpected authorisation of free trade unions and political parties in June 1945. The news was transmitted by Stalin to Pieck and other KPD leaders at a meeting in Moscow on 4 June.[33] The decision to license parties in the Soviet zone, before their authorisation in the western zones, was probably prompted by the Kremlin's wish to influence the development of political parties throughout Germany and to persuade the German population in its zone to assist in the work of reconstruction. This fitted in with the overall strategy of keeping options open for the eventual construction of socialism in Germany as a whole, if conditions were propitious, while at the same time strengthening Soviet control over its own zone. In addition to the two workers' parties, SMAD permitted the establishment of the Christian Democratic Union (CDU) and the Liberal Democratic Party (LDP). The SPD proclamation of 15 June, with its demand for large-scale nationalisation, contained more radical elements than that of the KPD. The CDU, too, was responsive to the new political climate for while it advocated protection for private enterprise, it called for public control over key industries and mineral resources. In contrast, the LDP, which aspired to heal the divisions in the old liberal camp, was unwilling to countenance such a high level of public control of economic policy.

The four parties agreed in July to form a bloc of anti-fascist democratic parties; a committee of five members constituted the main coordinating body.

[20]   The bloc system, which would be operated by SMAD and the SED as one of the main levers for transforming the political and social system of the zone, also included several large mass organisations founded between 1945 and 1947, notably the FDGB (Confederation of Free German Trade Unions), the FDJ (Free German Youth movement), the League of Culture, the Society for German–Soviet Friendship and the Farmers' Mutual Aid Association. Although at the time of their founding these organisations were by no means pliant transmission belts of the Communists, there was already a discernible trend in this direction. For example, while the FDGB, established in February 1945, attracted support from the SPD-orientated free trades unions and the liberal Hirsch-Duncker trades unions, the early spirit of cooperation soon foundered on the KPD's determination to use the organisation as a lever to strengthen its presence in the trade union movement. The Free German Youth, created in March 1946 as an all-German organisation and supposedly above party, was used by the KPD and the SED to bring the zone's 2 million young people aged 14 to 25 years under Communist influence.

The KPD programme

The programme of the KPD, issued on 11 June 1945, was crafted by its leaders and SMAD in accordance with the principles worked out before the fall of the Third Reich. The manifesto, which targeted all parts of Germany, proclaimed that it was wrong for the Soviet system to be imposed on Germany as it 'was not appropriate to the present circumstances of development in Germany' and that it was in the interests of the German people to establish 'an anti-fascist, democratic government, a parliamentary, democratic republic with all democratic rights and freedoms for the people'.[34] To this end, the programme stressed the need to complete the bourgeois revolution of 1848. While the KPD proposed the expropriation of the Nazi bosses and war criminals and state ownership of public utilities, it pledged its support for the development of trade and private enterprise on the basis of private ownership. Although the silence on the construction of socialism and on the creation of the dictatorship of the proletariat caused, as predicted, consternation among many veteran Communists, the KPD's appeal for an anti-fascist bloc of democratic parties was tailored to the immediate postwar situation. Its determination to root out the preconditions of fascism and to punish the Nazi big-wigs was shared by the other parties and it could claim a linkage to proposals in the 1930s for a broad alliance of anti-fascist groups. The publication, in February 1946, of Anton Ackermann's article 'Is there a Special

German Road to Socialism?' with its emphasis on a non-Soviet, peaceful transition to socialism along national lines, was designed to make *rapproche-ment* more palatable to broad sections of the population. While the thesis was an integral part of official policy, its author represented a less doctrinaire line than that espoused by Ulbricht and Matern.

References

1. Lapp P. J. 1990: 42, 45, 49, 53

2. Weber H. 1991: 29

3. Merson A. 1985: 311

4. Torpey J. C. 1995: xi

5. Details from Staritz D. 1995: 47

6. Cited in Heitzer H. 1981: 11

7. Karlsch R. 1993: 46–7

8. Ibid., 44–6. The percentages for the western zones read 22, 2, 10, 15 and 24 respectively.

9. Djilas M. 1952: 102

10. Löwenthal F. 1950: 244

11. Naimark N. M. 1995: 132–3

12. Richie A. 1998: 617

13. Filitov A. M. 1995: 133–5

14. Simmons M. 1989: 65

15. Leonhard W. 1979: 288

16. Erler P., Laude H., Wilke M. 1994: 108, 250

17. Weber H. 1990: 19–20

18. See the important documents and discussion in Erler P., Laude H., Wilke M. 1994: 68–70, 125–8

19. Ibid., 116–18, 369–74, 378–9; Keiderling G. 1993: 30–1

20. Cited in McElvoy A. 1992: 2

[22]   21. Gruneberg A. 1997: 80

22. Badstübner R., Loth W. 1994: 50. The notes which Pieck kept of his meetings with Stalin and other members of the Soviet elite are an essential source for the study of Soviet and KPD policy. They do, however, have a number of limitations in that they are rough notes, not a stenographic record and, while reproducing Stalin's thoughts, can provide only a partial insight into the Soviet decision-making process.

23. Ibid., 50–1

24. Djilas M. 1962: 104

25. Badstübner R., Loth W. 1994: 68

26. Leonhard W. 1979: 303

27.   Naimark N. M. 1995: 23–4

28. Ibid., 24–32; Creuzberger S. 1996: 29, 40–3

29. Naimark N. M. 1995: 52–3

30. Wille M. 1993: 65

31. Staritz D. 1995: 108; Wille M. 1993: 206, 210

32. Herf J. 1997: 187

33. Badstübner R., Loth W. 1994: 50–1

34. Cited in Thomaneck A. K. A., Mellis J. 1989: 13

CHAPTER TWO

THE STALINISATION OF THE EASTERN ZONE

The founding of the SED

The Ackermann thesis was intended as a contribution to a merger between the KPD and the SPD. Initially, in June 1945, Ulbricht had rejected the SPD leaders' proposal for a united party on the grounds that 'organisational unity must be preceded by a process of ideological clarification'.[1] This contrasted with the willingness of Otto Grotewohl, Max Fechner and other leaders on the SPD's Berlin Central Committee to form a united party of the working class with socialist credentials. Their attitude was influenced by vivid memories of persecution and imprisonment under the Nazis and by the realisation that the internecine strife on the left had seriously weakened opposition to Hitler. The leading SPD politician in the Soviet zone, Otto Grotewohl, had been chairman of a workers' and soldiers' council in 1918 and had held several ministerial posts in Brunswick during the Weimar Republic. He joined an illegal SPD resistance group after Hitler came to power. Imprisoned during 1938 and 1939, he subsequently spent most of the war as manager of a small business in Berlin.

Outside the capital many regional officials were too suspicious of the German Communists and the Russians to follow the Central Committee's chosen path. The restoration of the SPD along traditional lines was favoured by Social Democrats in Magdeburg and Leipzig, while in Thuringia the Minister President, Hermann Brill, advocated a broadly based League of Democratic Socialists to overcome what he regarded as the historically outmoded SPD and KPD. Encouraged by the expansion of party membership and sensitive to the opposition in the provinces to a merger, the Berlin Central Committee began to change tack. It declared itself in favour of a gradual fusion with the KPD, but only after the SPD had reconstituted itself on an all-German basis.

Ironically, as SPD ardour for union cooled, that of the KPD grew. In accordance with Soviet preferences, the KPD had originally confined itself to a 'unity of action' agreement with the SPD on 19 June which committed the two parties to regular meetings and to joint action committees for the construction of a new democratic republic in Germany. This kind of joint activity would, it was envisaged, make the SPD more amenable to Soviet wishes. SMAD and the Communist leaders judged a merger inopportune until they had restructured the KPD, integrated new members into the party and overcome comrades' opposition to cooperation with the 'old enemy'.

From September 1945 onwards, SMAD and the KPD set in motion a campaign for a speedy amalgamation and the elimination of the SPD as an effective political force. Pressure intensified in November when the setbacks suffered by Communists in elections in Austria and Hungary highlighted Communism's weak electoral appeal. The growth of SPD membership, the Social Democrats' aspiration to become the leading political force in the bloc and the ineffectiveness of the 'unity of action' for binding the SPD to the KPD were other major considerations prompting the KPD to press ahead with unification. The moment was well chosen. The unequivocal rejection of a merger by the leader of the SPD in the western zones, the bitterly anti-Communist Kurt Schumacher, destroyed Grotewohl's claim to speak for Social Democrats throughout Germany and rendered an increasingly isolated Berlin Central Committee vulnerable to Soviet and KPD pressure.

The first conference of sixty on 20 and 21 December, at which the SPD and KPD were equally represented, exposed the political enfeeblement of the SPD Central Committee and proved to be a watershed in the unification process. Despite Grotewohl's protestations that a fusion of the two parties in the Soviet zone would destroy the unity of the workers' movement, the SPD representatives succumbed to intensified KPD pressure and agreed to work towards a merger.[2] Last-ditch attempts to delay the process by making it conditional on unification on an all-German basis proved abortive. The Social Democrats in the western zones withheld their support for the manoeuvre, and the KPD and SMAD refused to tolerate further obstruction.

The Berlin Central Committee finally surrendered on 11 February 1946. Its endorsement of amalgamation was upheld by the chairmen of the party's five provincial organisations. A fortnight later, a second conference of sixty agreed on a draft statute for the new party. Then, after a series of local and regional conferences had met to ratify a merger, a joint KPD-SPD Party Congress, held in Berlin on 21 and 22 April 1946, voted unanimously in favour of the formation of the Socialist Unity Party of Germany. The new party

declared its support for a 'democratic' road to socialism and to the unity of [25]
Germany as an anti-fascist, parliamentary, democratic system. It promised to
safeguard the right to strike and the democratic rights of the people, including 'Freedom to express opinions in words, pictures and writing, subject to
the preservation of democratic government from reactionary attacks. Freedom of thought and religion. Equality of all citizens before the law irrespect-
ive of race or sex'.[3] The principle of parity of office-holding between former
KPD and former SPD members was accepted, and Grotewohl and Pieck were
elected joint chairmen.

The popular portrayal of the fusion of the KPD and SPD as a forced merger
was firmly rejected by East German historians as a legend concocted by 'right-
wing Social Democrats' and other enemies of the GDR. And even since the
collapse of SED rule in 1989, the merger remains a highly controversial
issue, with the SPD and the PDS disagreeing, often bitterly, over its significance to each party's place in Germany's socialist heritage. This is under-
standable, especially as some members of the CDU seek to exploit the merger
by pinning a charge of collusion and collaboration on Social Democrats. On
balance, the interpretation of the merger as a shotgun marriage is far more
convincing than the notion of union by consent, even though some members
of the family of the SPD bride were not unhappy with the match. The SPD
had come under intense pressure, especially from November 1945 onwards:
from above by SMAD and KPD officials and from below by Communist activists among factory groups. SPD leaders such as Dahrendorf and Klingelhöfer
were justifiably aggrieved at SMAD's preferential treatment of the KPD. SMAD
openly favoured the KPD in the printing and distribution of its literature and
in placing Communists in key administrative and economic posts. Recalcitrant SPD leaders and members were targeted by SMAD; for some, this led to
the loss of office, surveillance, intimidation, threats and imprisonment in a
Soviet 'special' camp.[4]

Despite the blatant discrimination against the SPD, the principle of cooperation retained its appeal among some of the SPD's rank and file. Local groups
sometimes took the initiative in pushing for a merger and the desire for union
was alive in many factories. An important indicator of party opinion is provided by the March 1946 plebisciste of SPD members conducted in the western
sectors of Berlin. SMAD banned a similar plebiscite in the Soviet sector. Out
of a total membership of 33,247, the vote cast was 23,775. In response to the
question, 'Are you for the immediate merger of both workers' parties?' 2,940
voted for and 19,529 against. On the other hand, this apparently decisive
rejection of a merger was qualified by a high level of support for the notion of

[26] cooperation: 14,763 members expressed themselves in favour and 5,559 against the question, 'Are you for the alliance that would guarantee cooperative effort and exclude fratricidal support?' Some Social Democrats, while accepting the inevitability of a merger, hoped to exert influence inside the SED in order to preserve a Social Democratic tradition in the Soviet zone. Others were attracted by the opportunities for personal advancement and privileges associated with membership of the SED. A combination of these motives seems to have persuaded Otto Grotewohl to abandon his original opposition to unification, the first of many such compromises on the path to becoming the GDR's first Minister President. He was severely criticised in the West for an alleged lack of moral fibre, as is illustrated in the following extract from the mid-1950s:

> . . . this ugly, rangy man, with the thick myopic glasses, is regarded in the rest of Germany as more fool than rogue. He depends entirely on Russian support for his dubious position, and the constant humiliations of his present post are regarded by many as sufficient punishment for his sins.[5]

The SED was by far the largest party in the zone. At the time of the merger in April 1946, it numbered 619,256 Communists and 679,159 Social Democrats. By mid-1948, membership had risen to almost 2 million. The SED was essentially a workers' party: 59 per cent of members in the Soviet zone and 50 per cent in the Soviet sector of Berlin were classified as workers against the 19 per cent and 25 per cent respectively of white-collar employees, the second largest category.[6] A party executive (*Parteivorstand*) of 80 members was elected by the Party Congress and a Central Secretariat became the party's leading organ. The fourteen positions on the Central Secretariat were split equally between Communists and Social Democrats, including Grotewohl, Fechner and Gniffke from the SPD and Pieck, Ulbricht and Ackermann from the KPD.

The SED's legitimation crisis

The popularity of the new party was put to the test in local elections in September 1946 and in the provincial elections (*Landtagwahlen*) held one month later. It fought its campaign on the basis of the new anti-fascist order. In the local elections, where SMAD frequently intervened to prevent the electoral registration of CDU and LDP local groups, the SED polled 57.1 per cent of the vote. Although emerging as the largest party in the provincial elections

with 4.7 million out of the 9.9 million votes cast, the SED failed to achieve [27]
50 per cent of the votes in a single province. Its 249 seats in the provincial
parliaments were slightly less than the combined total of the CDU (133) and
the LDP (121) and other organisations (16). The SED only secured a majority in Magdeburg and Chemnitz among the ten largest cities in the zone. The
results undoubtedly flattered the SED as the other parties suffered discrimination both with regard to technical resources and the right to hold campaign meetings. In Greater Berlin, where the SED and the SPD campaigned
separately, the SED (19.8 per cent) came in a poor third behind the SPD
(48.7 per cent) and the CDU (22.2 per cent). It recorded 29.7 per cent in the
Soviet sector as against 13.7 per cent in the three western sectors. The party's
poor performance was attributable not only to its own policies but also to its
close identification with the Soviet Union.

The SED was in a weak condition. After a period of rapid growth in 1946,
membership stagnated in 1947 and ideological and political conflicts per-
sisted between its SPD and KPD wings. Not only were former Social Democrats disillusioned with the autocratic methods of SMAD officers and
ex-German Communists but many also remained faithful to their traditional
political values and ideas. The latter was particularly true of the party in the
smaller towns and rural areas. Furthermore, the party experienced serious
problems in accommodating 'ultraleftist' Communists who accused the
Soviet Union of betraying socialism and of exploiting German workers in line
with an alleged state capitalist philosophy. Numerous Soviet and SED internal reports on party meetings and the mood of members revealed high levels
of dissatisfaction with the Soviets' ruthless dismantling procedures, food shortages, black market activities, rampant corruption among party officials, the
loss of the eastern territories and the lack of information about German POWs.
Many SED functionaries and leaders simply lacked the experience and skills
to cope with this barrage of criticism. A mood of disillusionment and resignation pervaded the party.[7]

The SED's disappointing election results highlighted one of the problems
inherent in political legitimation. The SED, like other ruling parties in the
Communist bloc, would come to use elections for reasons of political mobilisation and indoctrination, not for democratic legitimation. Other modes of
legitimation – the propagation of the Soviet Union as an external model and
the Communist nirvana as an end goal – although exercising an undeniable
appeal among Communists and many anti-fascists, was counterproductive in
other circles. Another problem in the early postwar years concerned the tentative nationalism propounded by Ackermann. Not only did his thesis of

[28] 'socialism in one country' soon fall foul of a policy shift in Moscow but the national question would bedevil the SED for over forty years. With the democratic legitimation of SED rule so problematic, coercion became a structural feature of the Soviet zone and the GDR.

The bloc succumbs

The other two parties in the zone, boosted by their electoral successes in 1946 and a growing membership, proved to be troublesome associates of the dominant party in the anti-fascist democratic bloc. In 1948, membership of the CDU and the LDPD peaked at 231,000 and 197,000 respectively. Both parties vigorously resisted the SED offensive in 1947 to increase its authority in the bloc. The CDU chairman, Jakob Kaiser, boldly proclaimed his party to be the 'breakwater of dogmatic Marxism and its totalitarian tendencies'[8] and he urged the inclusion of the zone in the Marshall Plan. In addition, the CDU refused to accept the SED proposal for a National Congress designed to support the Soviet negotiating position at the Foreign Ministers' Conference in November 1947; the party was anxious not to appear to be a pliant instrument of the SED to the detriment of its appeal in the eastern and western zones. SMAD's response to CDU obduracy was to dismiss two of its leaders, Kaiser and Lemmer, in December 1947. The position of the CDU and LDP was further undermined in 1948 with the foundation, on Stalin's prompting, of two additional 'bourgeois' parties, the National Democratic Party of Germany (NDPD) and the Democratic Farmers' Party of Germany (DBD). The new parties were highly amenable to SED wishes and served as a counterattraction to the CDU and LDPD among the urban middle classes and farmers. The NDPD targeted resettlers, former nominal Nazis and POWs who had returned home. Its chairman, Lothar Bolz, like his DBD counterpart, Goldenbaum, had once belonged to the KPD. The two new parties entered the multi-party bloc system in 1948, thereby further weakening the LDP and the CDU. SED control over the bloc system was sealed by the creation of the National Front in 1949.

The FDGB, which also joined the bloc, had come under great pressure since 1947 when the SED intensified its efforts to transform it into one of its transmission belts. At the crucial Bitterfeld meeting of FDGB functionaries in November 1948, the leadership placed plan fulfilment before trade union activity, the troublesome enterprise councils were *de facto* dissolved and their

rights of worker representation transferred to the more accommodating [29]
enterprise trade union executives. In 1950, the FDGB Congress recognised
the leading role of the SED and accepted democratic centralism as its basic
organisational principle. Workers' rights in the self-styled workers' and peasants' state had thus been drastically curtailed.

The SED as a party of a new type

Creeping Stalinisation

Meanwhile, the SED itself was undergoing a fundamental transformation. A
'creeping Stalinisation' between late 1946 and 1948 culminated in the adoption of the Bolshevik model in January 1949. The main components of the
model are well known: a highly centralised and disciplined political entity
based on the organisational principle of hierarchic centralism; the personality cult of the leader; a uniform Marxist-Leninist ideology; the intensive ideological and political training of members; the enforcement of the party's
claim to the leading role in society; and the banning of internal party factions.
Other features include the elimination of opposition through purges and
expulsion and a vast bureaucracy responsible for controlling all aspects of
social, cultural, economic and political life. At the apex of the party stood a
small inner circle of leaders not accountable to the broad party membership.

A powerful impetus to the Stalinisation of the SED was given in September 1947 by Stalin's counter to the Truman Doctrine, that is, the unveiling
by Zhdanov, the leading Soviet ideologue, of the thesis of the division of
the world into two hostile camps and of a sharpening of the class struggle.
Together with the Communist coup in Czechoslovakia in February 1948 and
Yugoslavia's expulsion from Cominform (the successor to Comintern), the
thesis was used to justify the persecution of alleged traitors, imperialist agents,
heretics and Titoists throughout Stalin's East European empire. The death
knell of any notions of a special road to socialism had been sounded. With
bloc uniformity prevailing over divergence, Communist parties throughout
Eastern Europe were obliged to bring their party system into line with that of
the CPSU and to recognise the Soviet Union as their model. In the Soviet
zone Anton Ackermann was compelled, in September 1948, to retract his
thesis of a special German road to socialism.

While the timing of the official adoption of the Bolshevik model was an
immediate result of the Soviet–Yugoslav conflict, its implementation was

[30] primarily determined by the Marxist-Leninist conception of power, according to which fundamental political and economic change in the zone was most effectively carried out by a highly centralised party. The KPD exiles in wartime Moscow had regarded a 'party of a new type' as the most desirable form but tactical and organisational considerations had dictated a different course in 1945–46. With the cold war intensifying, the SED leaders became less inhibited. For example, at a party executive meeting in September 1947, Walter Ulbricht identified the total elimination of capitalist elements in town and country as constituting the task of 'socialist construction',[9] a task for which a Stalinist-type party was deemed to be essential.

Yet in 1948, on the eve of the Stalinisation of the SED, the party was far from being a highly centralised and cohesive party. Soviet officers such as Tiul'panov were particularly concerned about 'contamination by Schumacher ideology' and left-wing sectarianism and they were critical of the lack of firm central leadership. In a memorandum of May 1948, Tiul'panov advocated a rapid restructuring of the SED for two reasons: the Soviet zone was drawing closer to the kind of system characteristic of the People's Democracies of Eastern Europe and the SED bore special responsibilities on account of the zone's location on the border between capitalism and socialism.[10] His arguments met with a mixed reception in Moscow where serious differences of opinion existed over whether the Soviet model should be implemented quickly or according to the gradual course advocated by Semyonov, the Foreign Ministry's representative in Germany.[11] Despite the uncertainty in Moscow, a series of decisions by the SED executive in June, July and September 1948 prepared the way for the reorganisation of the party on the basis of democratic centralism. Party control commissions were to be established at central, regional and district level to remove 'hostile' and 'degenerate' elements and to ensure the unity and purity of the party through purges and other disciplinary measures.

Stalinisation complete

The First SED Party Conference from 25 to 28 January 1949 completed the organisational and ideological transformation of the SED which would later enable it to function as the governing party of an East German state. Preparations for the conference were made in December at a meeting between Stalin, Pieck, Grotewohl, Ulbricht and Oelssner. While agreement was reached on the restructuring of the SED, the Soviet dictator, unwilling to abandon his zig-zag policy on Germany, rejected the SED leaders' eagerness to press ahead with transferring the zone into a People's Democracy.[12] From their point of view, recognition as a People's Democracy would have the virtue of bolstering their power and of enhancing the status of the new political formation. The Party Conference ratified far-reaching changes to the party: the replacement of the SED's Central Secretariat by a nine-man Politbüro, the abolition of parity of status between former Communists and former Social Democrats and the creation of a Small Secretariat of the Politbüro. Consisting of five members, the latter body, under Walter Ulbricht's direction, was earmarked to assist the Politbüro in conducting its day-to-day business. Democratic centralism was recognised as the basic organisational principle of the newly constituted Marxist-Leninist party. Ulbricht's emergence as the leading political figure in the zone was confirmed by his election, at the Third Party Congress in 1950, as General Secretary of the Central Committee, the pivotal office in the party.

The restructuring of the party was accompanied by a series of expulsions and purges which were launched in July 1948 and continued until 1953. They were carried out in close cooperation with Soviet officials and were part of the Stalinist terror which was inflicted on Eastern Europe during those years. The purges were crucial to the creation of a disciplined and ideologically pure party more in tune with the Bolshevik model than the original hybrid of Social Democracy and Communism. Not only were they intended to 're-educate' and mobilise members behind the party's goals, but they also strengthened the position of old Communists such as Ulbricht and Pieck who had spent much of the Nazi period in exile in Moscow. The main targets for expulsion from the party, as implemented by the main investigative body, the Central Party Control Commission, were former Social Democrats, alleged agents of the SPD's Eastern Bureau and non-conformist Communists. Among the latter were those who had been associated with small splinter groups, such as the KAPD and KPD (Opposition), which had been critical of the suppression of inner-party pluralism before 1933 and had joined the KPD after 1945. They were accused of sectarianism and Trotskyism. Social Democrats at all levels of the party were targeted if, unlike Grotewohl, they remained loyal to their original political convictions. The flight in October 1948 of Erich Gniffke, a member of the Central Secretariat, was used to whip up an atmosphere of hysteria over alleged agents and sabotage. Gniffke, the second most important former Social Democrat in the SED, warned in a letter of 28 October 1948 that the SED was intent on the destruction of all democratic rights and on imposing a totalitarian system.[13]

[32]   The expulsions reached a peak in 1951. By this date, only about 200,000 erstwhile Social Democrats remained in the party and between 15 January and 30 September the SED lost about 320,000 members and candidates. *In toto*, between 1948 and 1952, party membership fell from 2 million to 1.2 million as a result of expulsions and the imposition of more exacting entry requirements. A fall in the proportion of working-class members, from 41 per cent to 38 per cent, reflected the shift from the party's roots in the working-class movement to its position as the hegemonic state party.[14]

The purges claimed top functionaries such as Paul Merker, a member of the Politbüro, Lex Ende, the editor-in-chief of the party organ, *Neues Deutschland*, and Leo Bauer, editor-in-chief of the *Deutschlandsender*. All were accused of collaboration with an alleged American agent, Noel Field. The death sentence passed on Bauer by a Soviet military tribunal in 1952 was commuted to 25 years' forced labour; he was allowed to leave the GDR three years later. Ende, an exile in Prague, Paris and Mexico during the Third Reich, was dismissed from his editorial position. Merker, an orthodox Communist who had spent much of the war in Mexico, was targeted as the victim of a GDR version of the show trials of Slansky in Czechoslovakia and Rajk in Hungary. He was arrested in 1952 and the preparations for his trial were accompanied by strong anti-semitic overtones. He refused, despite intensive interrogation, to make a public confession. Although Stalin's death spared him from the fate of his East European counterparts, he received an eight-year prison sentence at a secret political trial in 1955, only to be released one year later.

The purge of Bauer, Ende and other Jewish Communists, such as Bruno Goldhammer and Willy Kreikemeyer, was symptomatic of the widespread anti-semitism in the upper echelons of the SED, which seriously undermined the anti-fascist credentials of the new system. Merker, though not a Jew himself, was committed to the equality of status between Jewish victims of fascism and Communist resistance fighters. He was convinced of the justice of Jewish claims to restitution and of the need to combat anti-semitism in the zone. His solidarity with the Jewish victims of Nazism brought him into conflict with the SED's prioritisation of the Communist resistance and with the outburst of attacks against 'cosmopolitanism' in the Soviet Union and Eastern Europe. 'Anti-cosmopolitanism' was fostered by Stalin's paranoia, by the Moscow émigrés' distrust of Communists in the Western emigration and by the Communist association of Jewry with capitalism and American imperialism.[15] While East German anti-semitism cannot be equated with the biological racism and mass murder of the Third Reich, its insidious influence

permeated the 'Lessons from the Trial against the Slansky Conspiracy Cen-   [33]
tre', a document written by Hermann Matern, which attacked efforts to use
'the poison of chauvinism and cosmopolitanism . . . to contaminate the workers
with the most reactionary bourgeois ideology'.[16]

The emergence of a political police system

The Soviet role

SMAD and other Soviet agencies conducted their own independent security
operations in the zone as well as exercising firm control over the German
political police. The main Soviet agencies, with offices in every district and
Land, were the NKVD and the NKGB (People's Commissariat for State
Security), both renamed in 1946 as the MVD (Ministry of Internal Affairs)
and the MGB (Ministry for State Security) respectively. The latter concentrated on undercover work and spying and the MVD on internal security
issues. One of the most influential officials was an unsavoury character,
Lieutenant General Ivan Serov, who, though a SMAD officer, was responsible in his capacity as a NKVD/MVD officer only to his superiors in Moscow.
One of Serov's main jobs was to create a system of operations groups consisting of Soviet officers, troops and interpreters which drew on Germans as
informers and *agents provocateurs*. The initial targets were former Nazis, the
so-called young Werewolves and anyone who engaged in the catch-all
category of anti-Soviet activities. As the new political and economic system
evolved, Social Democrat opponents of the merger with the KPD, right-
wing 'reactionaries' and Western agents were all caught in the Soviet net.
Intimidation, detention, arrests and internment were a common occurrence.

German agencies

The east German security forces developed under strict Soviet supervision:
appointments and dismissals required Soviet approval; senior officers had to
report directly to Soviet intelligence agents; and much of the police force's
budget was financed by the Soviets. Fundamental to the development of an
east German security force was the establishment, in the summer of 1945, of
Kommissariat-5 (K-5) of the Saxon police force; on Soviet orders, other K-5
agencies soon followed in other police administrations. Their functions included providing support for the KPD/SED, protecting the new economic

[34] order, combating fascist gangs, uncovering ex-Nazi functionaries and the surveillance of Interior Ministry personnel. Later, in 1948, K-5 was separated from other criminal police activities and became the core of a centralised political police with additional powers for crushing political opponents.[17] A second important development was the creation of a German police force (*Deutsche Volkspolizei* – DVP) in 1945 for restoring public order. Initially subordinate to the *Länder* Ministries of the Interior, it was transferred one year later to the German Administration of the Interior (DVdI) as part of a centralisation drive designed to improve efficiency and to combat corruption in the police force. In addition to the reorganisation of the police, the DVdI was entrusted with the establishment of Alert Police units. Later called the People's Police in Barracks (KVP), they were in effect paramilitary units and served as the basis of the National People's Army founded in 1955. Such developments lend support to Norman Naimark's contention that 'from the very beginning, security concerns within the German party [SED] and the Soviet military government helped create an East German state that was inseparable from its internal police function'.[18]

Another crucial structural element in the zonal security system was the Main Division for Intelligence and Information under Erich Mielke. Officially constituted as an organ of the DVdI in November 1947, the new body was flanked by the existing regional information offices; it carried out counter-intelligence, controlled the media and collected and disseminated information. Informers and confidants were recruited to meet Mielke's aim 'to know everything and to report on everything worth knowing'.[19] Such duties anticipated the kind of work conducted by the Ministry of State Security throughout the history of the GDR. Measures were introduced in the DVdI to improve the political indoctrination and reliability of security staff, notably the launching of the Main Department Political Culture (HA-PK) in the autumn of 1948. The department's highly trained political cultural officers – with a ratio of one to every 100 to 110 police officers by mid-1948 – conducted regular political training courses for members of the security organs and sought to ensure that appointments conformed with SED priorities.[20] This resulted in the mass ejection of police officers who had belonged to the NSDAP – although 'valued' individuals might be exempted – and of those who, in Mielke's words, had 'ties to the enemies of the democratic order'.[21]

As part of a general overhaul of security, the protection of the economy was transferred in the first half of 1949 into the hands of the Main Department for the Protection of the National Economy (*Hauptverwaltung zum Schutz der Volkswirtschaft* – HVzSV) in the Ministry of the Interior. This department

also assumed many of the political police functions of K-5 and enjoyed wide- [35]
ranging powers for combating the class enemy and anti-democratic activities. By late 1948, the Soviet zone disposed of a large police force of 80,971,
including K-5 and the Administrative, Criminal, Civil, Railway, Alert and
Border police forces.[22] Yet more organisational changes led to the dissolution of K-5 in August 1949 and the transfer of numerous functions to
Department D of the criminal police, a precursor of the Ministry of State Security. The new ministry, whose creation was approved unanimously by the
Volkskammer in February 1950, consisted of the HVzSV, sections of the former
Department for Intelligence and Information, the criminal police and the Main
Department Political Culture. Its brief was to protect the new 'democratic'
order and the economy against hostile agents, subversives, spies, saboteurs
and bandits. Wilhelm Zaisser was appointed minister and Mielke became one
of his deputies with the rank of State Secretary. Zaisser, who had fought in
the Spanish Civil War under the pseudonym of General Gomez, had conducted political propaganda among German POWs in the later stages of the
Second World War and had held various security and military posts in the
zone. Like Mielke, he enjoyed the trust of key members of the Soviet intelligence service.

The Soviet 'special' camps

One of the darkest chapters in East German history is the development of a
system of Soviet 'special' camps, that is, the eleven internment camps modelled on the Gulag Archipelago. The camp system in the Soviet zone was
initiated by an order from Beria on 18 April 1945, based on an earlier direct-
ive in January. Under Serov's command, camps were established at Bautzen,
Sachsenhausen, Ketschendorf, Jamlitz, Frankfurt/Oder, Weesow, Berlin-
Hohenschönhausen, Fünfeichen and, after the Western Allies had evacuated
their troops from the Soviet zone, Buchenwald, Torgau and Mühlberg.
These permament camps were all functioning by the autumn of 1945. Most
of them had served a similar purpose during the Third Reich: for example,
Sachsenhausen and Buchenwald had been concentration camps, Mühlberg a
POW camp, and Bautzen and Torgau state prisons.

Beria's order of 18 April 1945 identified the various categories of internees or, in the dehumanised language of the bureaucrats, so reminiscent of the
Nazis, 'special contingents': spies, terrorists, partisans, NSDAP activists, leaders

[36] of fascist youth organisations and members of the Gestapo and other agencies of terror.[23] Most of the internees were not guilty in a legal sense. The wave of arrests in the first few months after the end of the war affected not only ex-Nazis but also members of the bourgeoisie and the intelligentsia, Junkers, capitalists, Social Democrats and Communists. About 400 Social Democrats and 200 Communists were held in Buchenwald in 1946. Even members of the resistance were interned. Justus Delbrück and Ulrich Freiherr von Sell, who had been involved in the July Bomb Plot, both died in Jamlitz.[24]

From 1946 onwards, the camps were used increasingly to intern opponents of the SED and extended far beyond what might be termed denazification or the elimination of militarism and the 'remnants' of feudalism. Arrests were made by Soviet operations groups in 'night and fog' actions at the workplace, on the streets and during house searches; usually, no reason was given and the slightest suspicion of being a 'fascist' or 'dangerous' could lead to arrest. Before being sent to a camp, victims were interrogated by the NKVD in cellars, small prisons, even garages. Forced confessions were obtained during interrogation, often through beatings and sleep deprivation or under threat of deportation to Siberia. The whole process – arrest, interrogation, arbitrary sentencing, often without the right of defence, and internment – was typical of the Stalinist system. Whereas only a small number of internees were actually tried by Soviet Military Tribunals in the early stage of the camps' existence (10 per cent in November 1946), the proportion may have risen to over 50 per cent by late 1949. Where a sentence was passed, it was normally for 25 years or longer and the 'trial' was conducted without witnesses and in Russian.[25] The system left its legacy in the politicisation of justice in the GDR. In some cases the legacy was also physical: the Berlin-Hohenschönhausen camp passed into the hands of the Ministry of State Security in 1951 and was used as one of the ministry's two central detention and interrogation centres.

Conditions in the camps

Conditions in the 'special' camps, especially from 1945 to 1947, were often primitive, the death rate was high, and inmates were subjected to harsh and sometimes brutal treatment.[26] Malnutrition, appalling hygiene and totally inadequate medical care were the main causes of death, particularly after the reduction by the Soviet authorities in November 1946 of the already meagre rations. In the Mühlberg camp the main type of warm food was a kind of pulp, a by-product of potato starch, without nutritional value and causing the body to bloat. Most camps were overcrowded and without basic toilet

facilities; prisoners were poorly clad, rarely able to wash properly, not [37]
allowed to work and deprived of physical exercise. The result was lassitude,
a loss of memory, skin complaints, dysentery and intestinal diseases, followed
by pneumonia, tuberculosis and outbreaks of typhus. Tuberculosis was the
main cause of death. One former prisoner in the Torgau camp recalled:

> In Torgau up to eighteen prisoners were crowded into one small room with only three plank
> beds. There were no straw sacks or mattresses, and not all the prisoners had blankets. Three
> to four stools formed the whole of the rest of the furniture. The windows were barred and
> painted over, and it was strictly forbidden to open them. The camp was separated from the
> outside world by a high wooden fence topped with barbed wire.
>
> Every form of intellectual occupation – reading, discussion, lectures, etc. – was strictly
> prohibited. The 'Unity Party' officials in charge of the camp administration saw to it that
> all the camp rules were strictly obeyed. They browbeat and bullied us and swindled us out
> of the little food we were allowed . . .
>
> We were badly undernourished, and the result was hunger oedema. The worst of the
> sick cases were sent for a few days into the lazaret, where they were not given food, but
> injections. No one was allowed in the lazaret for more than four days at a time. Whoever
> couldn't stand up after that just had to die.[27]

In the early days of the Berlin-Hohenschönhausen camp, beatings by
fellow-inmates who helped the Soviets run the camp were not infrequent
and women were raped by Soviet guards. The roll-call, which was held in
the camp courtyard, usually lasted for about three hours. Bodies were buried
by prisoner commandos in mass graves some distance from the camps. The
burials usually took place late at night or in the early morning; in some camps,
the special commandos of prisoners responsible for burying internees were
shot in order to prevent them from disclosing details.[28]

Despite the availability of new material from the Russian archives, it is still
impossible to calculate exactly how many people were interned and died
in the camps. According a report issued in July 1990 by the Soviet Interior
Ministry,[29] 122,671 Germans were incarcerated in the 'special' camps in the
Soviet zone/GDR between 1945 and 1950, of whom 45,262 were released,
42,889 died there, 12,770 Germans were sent to the USSR and a further
6,690 were transferred to POW camps. In addition, several thousand internees were handed over to the German authorities and 756 were sentenced to
death by military courts. Several years later, these figures were revised after
the discovery of the reports compiled by the medical branch of the Soviet
Department Special Camps. These records provide the most reliable, though
not definitive, guide to the whole issue as they contain a virtually complete
record of deaths in the camps. Based on these and other sources now available

[38]   to historians, it has been estimated by a specialist Russian–German research group that at least 154,000 Germans and about 35,000 non-Germans were interned and that about 43,000 Germans died in the special camps.[30]

Most of the deaths occurred between late spring 1945 and the beginning of 1948. The severe winters of 1945–46 and 1946–47 took a particularly heavy toll. Several camps were closed during these years because of the high death rate, leaving only Buchenwald, Sachsenhausen, Bautzen, Mühlberg and Fünfeichen as functioning camps. In the summer of 1948, a combination of Western pressure to close the camps and the decision to terminate the denazification programme led to the closure of Mühlberg and Fünfeichen and the transfer of their inmates to the remaining three camps. In 1950, these camps, too, were shut down. Not all prisoners were released: 3,432 were transferred for sentencing by GDR courts and a further 10,513 for a review of their sentences. The former were incarcerated in the Waldheim prison in Saxony and sentenced in a series of lightning trials, mostly *in camera*, between April and June 1950. Sentences were passed on 3,392 of the accused, including the death penalty on 33 and a life sentence on over 130. Twenty-four were executed in the cellar of the Waldheim prison on 3 and 4 November. Although the SED used the trials as part of its anti-fascist propaganda, only about 160 of those sentenced were actually war or Nazi criminals; most were opponents of the Stalinist system or Nazi fellow-travellers.[31]

The death toll in the special camps has prompted speculation that the Soviets were pursuing a policy of organised murder, a claim which historians working on Soviet sources have been unable to corroborate. While the physical well-being of internees was so grievously neglected that some historians are persuaded that the Soviet camps can be likened to death camps,[32] it seems, for example, that the high death rate and the reduction in rations in 1946 were primarily the consequence of bureaucratic confusion and mismanagement. Instead of internees being released, as was planned, new arrivals compounded a dire situation at a time when responsibility for supplies had been transferred unexpectedly to an ill-prepared SMAD.[33] Terrible though the camps undoubtedly were, they should not be equated with the Nazi death camps. Systematic inhuman and barbaric torture was not the norm; unlike Auschwitz, Treblinka, Sobibor and other Nazi death camps, the Soviet camps were not centres for the mass extermination of racial and other enemies of the Third Reich. However, the new findings on the administration of the camps should not lead historians to lose sight of the fact that terror was intrinsic to the Stalinist system and that Beria's orders on the isolation and treatment of inmates determined the fate of tens of thousands of victims.[34] And it should be remembered that although there may not have been an explicit order-to-kill, the Soviet [39] authorities were fully aware of the fatal consequences of malnutrition, inadequate medical care and forced inactivity.

The social and economic transformation of the zone

Social reconstruction

As was seen in Chapter 1, the Soviet authorities and the German Communists were determined to erase what they regarded as the socio-economic preconditions of fascism and militarism. Among the earliest measures were the land and educational reforms (1945), the nationalisation of industrial property belonging to former Nazis and war criminals (1945–46) and the restructuring of the judiciary and the police. The popularity of some of these measures and their absence in the western zones lends some weight to the claim that an anti-fascist order, though not yet a full-scale social revolution, was being implemented in the zone.

The expropriation of the Junkers and the large landowners with Nazi connections was supported by all four political parties in the Soviet zone, although the Liberal Democrats and some of the CDU leaders, notably Hermes and Schreiber, had reservations about the lack of compensation for those dispossessed owners who were untainted by Nazism. The SPD Chairman, Otto Grotewohl, defended expropriation on the grounds that the Junkers had been the backbone of reaction in Germany. In the land reform of September 1945, all landowners with holdings exceeding 100 hectares, former Nazi activists and war criminals were expropriated without compensation, sometimes in a brutal and demeaning manner. Over 3.3 million hectares, about one-third of useful agricultural land, were affected and almost 2 million hectares were redistributed among about 300,000 landless peasants, agricultural labourers and smallholders. The major beneficiaries were former manual workers and salaried employees who constituted 32.7 per cent of the total number of recipients; however, the average size of their plots was a meagre 0.6 hectares. A shortage of livestock and machines and mandatory and arbitrary Soviet requisitions disrupted agriculture. Some of the new farmers left their fields untilled and thousands abandoned their farms.

In October 1945, SMAD authorised the confiscation of the property of the German state, the armed forces and the NSDAP. Some of this property,

[40] mainly the strategic heavy industrial concerns, was converted into Soviet joint stock companies; the remainder was put at the disposal of the German provincial administrative organs in March 1946. Although opposed by influential bourgeois politicians, such as Kaiser and Lemmer of the CDU, SMAD and its SED allies decided to hold a carefully managed referendum in July 1946 in Saxony, where about two-fifths of the zone's industrial potential was located: 77.6 per cent expressed their approval of a law expropriating without compensation the enterprises owned by former National Socialists and war criminals. Legitimised by the Saxon precedent, the other regional firms, accounting for a relatively high level of total industrial production, were confiscated by the state or municipal authorities.[35] Although these measures represented a significant shift from the KPD's original programme, SED leaders assiduously avoided reference to any association with 'socialism' for fear of antagonising the middle classes; instead, they concentrated propaganda on the expropriation of fascists and war criminals.

Socio-economic reconstruction and denazification created many new opportunities for social advancement: 54.2 per cent of the managers of the new public enterprises in 1947 were recruited from the working class and white-collar employees, and Communist cadre policy ensured that SED members enjoyed a disproportionately higher share of administrative posts. In 1948, 43.6 per cent of all employees in the state apparat belonged to the SED. Workers also derived concrete benefits from the educational reforms and the 'Sovietisation' of higher education. Whereas in 1945 only 3 per cent of university students were from working-class families, by 1960 their share had risen to about 58 per cent. This helped to create a distinctively different intelligentsia which was obligated to the regime for its status and privileges. Yet, although the landowning aristocracy and the big industrialists were swept away and the smaller producers lost their former significance as part of the SED's attack on the 'bourgeoisie', the social revolution was not complete. The traditional educated middle class managed to retain its hold on the Churches[36] and the tenacity of sections of the old elites can also be seen in higher education where, in 1954, over one-quarter of university professors were former Nazis.[37]

The burden of reparations

The zone's economic development was hit extremely hard by various types of Soviet exactions: the dismantling of plant and equipment to help rebuild the shattered Soviet economy, reparation payments out of current production and contributions to the costs of the Soviet occupation regime. According to [41] investigations by Rainer Karlsch, the total losses from reparation payments and occupation costs between 1945 and 1953 amounted to at least 54 billion Reichsmarks (RM) at current prices.[38] The major items were dismantling (6.1 billion RM), occupation costs (16.8 billion RM), the Wismut uranium mining company (7.3 billion RM) and deliveries from current production (11.5 billion RM). However, the final balance sheet cannot be drawn up as too many statistical uncertainties surround categories such as the loss of German 'know-how' and the 'trophies' plundered by special Soviet 'trophy' brigades. The 'trophies' included gold and silver objects, furniture, clothes, paintings and sculptures.

Reparations policy passed through three phases. From March 1945 to the summer of 1946, the zone suffered from the depredations of 'trophy' hunters and from the rapid and often indiscriminate dismantling in the consumer goods industries and the armaments-related branches of industry. The Soviet authorities reassessed their policy once it was appreciated that the Soviet economy was not reaping the anticipated benefits from the dismantling programme and that it was not in their interest to preside over economic chaos in their zone. Factories from the zone were often not reassembled and machine parts were allowed to rust when they reached the Soviet Union. The second phase commenced with the transfer of large German-owned enterprises into Soviet joint stock companies and with improvements in the organisation of dismantling activities. After dismantling was terminated in 1948, efforts were concentrated on deliveries from current output. By 1949, three-quarters of all such deliveries came from mechanical engineering firms. The damage inflicted by dismantling operations on the zone's economy is illustrated by the following figures: by March 1947, 11,800 km of railway track, that is almost half of total track in 1938, had been removed, and between 2,000 and 2,400 enterprises were partially or totally dismantled. The most serious losses were suffered in Berlin and in machine-building centres such as Gera, Chemnitz, Leipzig and Dresden. Demolition resulted in the loss of at least 29 per cent of the level of industrial capacity in 1944.[39] The third and final phase extended from 1951 to 1953. Although the overall burden in these years was considerably lighter than in 1946 and 1947, it remained onerous since East German contributions to occupation costs continued at a high level.

Some indication of the impact of Soviet reparations on the East German economy can be obtained from calculations based on current payments as a percentage of gross national product at 1944 prices. The payments – including occupation costs, losses on foreign trade and the repurchasing of the

[42]   Soviet joint stock companies – amounted to 48.1 per cent of GNP in 1946, 38.4 per cent in 1947, 31.1 per cent in 1948 and 12.9 per cent in 1953. The lower percentage losses suffered by the western zones/FRG of 14.6, 12.8, 9.0 and 3.8 respectively contrasted sharply with the bleeding of the eastern economy.[40] The heavy burden of reparations and the negative impact on living standards contributed significantly to undermining whatever goodwill the Red Army had earned in overthrowing the Third Reich. Popular hostility towards the Soviet Union was also compounded by its role in the loss of the eastern territories to Poland, by the maltreatment of German workers engaged in dismantling operations and by the 'special' camps. The horrors of rape committed by Soviet troops during the invasion of Germany not only traumatised many Germans but also reinforced the stereotyping of Russians as cultural inferiors.

Economic planning

The coordination and planning of economic policy was boosted by the restructuring of the German Economic Administration (DWK) in March 1948, a development which reflected the emergence of two different types of economic management systems in the eastern and western zones. In 1948, the planned economy concept of the Soviet zone was described by Fritz Selbmann, the Deputy Chairman of the German Economic Commission, as: 'We will plan down to the last machine, down to the last production unit of state-owned industry, and then we will see who is the stronger – the planned state-owned industry or the non-planned free market economy'.[41] Central direction of the economy was tightened with the introduction of a central economic plan for the second half of 1948 and of a two-year plan for 1949–50. In 1950, a State Planning Commission was created as the supreme planning authority and the GDR's first five-year economic plan was introduced. An activist movement was launched in 1948, modelled on the Stakhanovite movement in the Soviet Union. To promote the initiative, a specially chosen miner, Adolf Hennecke, managed to increase his daily output of coal by 380 per cent and was toasted by the SED as a hero of labour. Both the activist movement and tighter economic planning were clear indications of the growing influence of the Soviet economic mechanism on the zonal economy. Another sign was the relatively high share of the publicly owned sector of the economy, accounting for 61 per cent of gross zonal product in 1948.[42]

Although it would be several years before a Soviet-style economic mechanism was fully implemented in East Germany, the foundations were laid in

this early period. The main characteristics of the mechanism are state ownership of almost all the large factories, mines and banks; an extensive central
bureaucracy responsible for the elaboration of plans; the central determination of allocations and most prices; the strict regulation of foreign trade; and
central planning of the economy through detailed short- and medium-term
economic plans for production goods. Other features include: narrow income
differentials; administered prices, which performed an administrative function rather than providing signals as in a market-type economy; and intensive investment in heavy industry. This kind of system undoubtedly had some
value in the period of extensive growth and reconstruction in the late 1940s
and early 1950s when resources had to be mobilised to develop the area's
own basic materials and capital goods sectors. And it should be remembered
that planning was in vogue in Western Europe, too. However, the Communist variant would prove to be a serious impediment to innovation and to
keeping pace with West German levels of labour productivity once the Federal Republic had launched its social market system.

Germany divided

While the socio-economic and political restructuring of the zone was drawing it ever closer to the Soviet model, the deterioration in relations between
the Western powers and the Soviet Union was also rapidly reducing the likelihood of Germany reunification. A major quarrel occurred over reparations.
Indignant at the Soviets' refusal to supply food and other commodities to the
western zones and at their insistence on the delivery of an additional 10 per
cent of reparations in the form of industrial capital equipment from the West,
General Lucius Clay unilaterally suspended dismantling operations and reparations deliveries from the American zone in May 1946. For their part, the
Russians were angered by Washington's failure to accommodate the Soviet
request for a loan to assist economic reconstruction, by American disengage-
ment from various commitments entered into at Yalta and by attempts to
circumscribe Soviet power in Eastern Europe. In truth, the United States and
the Soviet Union were both eager to take advantage of the opportunities
and ambiguities of the wartime agreements and to readjust their policies to
containment of each other's power rather than continuing a cooperative
approach to postwar reconstruction.

The crumbling of Allied unity in Germany doomed to failure the deliberations of the four powers in Moscow in March 1947. Soon after the

[44] commencement of the conference, President Truman enunciated his 'Doctrine' in which he promised American support to the 'free peoples' of the world and vilified the Communist way of life as one based on the will of a minority forcibly imposed upon the majority. The economic prop of the Truman Doctrine, the European Recovery Programme or Marshall Plan, was announced in June 1947. The western zones were targeted as the main beneficiaries of Marshall Aid to Germany; the United States never seriously intended to include the Soviet zone or the People's Democracies of Eastern Europe. However, much to the chagrin of SMAD, Jakob Kaiser of the CDU proposed the inclusion of the Soviet zone in the programme. Many private entrepreneurs, too, would have welcomed such a move.

In order to spur economic recovery in their zones, the Western powers finally decided to replace the worthless Reichsmark with the new Deutschmark on 18 June 1948. In the deteriorating political climate the Soviet representative had withdrawn from the Allied Control Council three months earlier, thus removing a major obstacle to a reform of the currency. The Western Allies pressed ahead at the same time with plans for the creation of a separate West German state: the six-nation London conference agreed on 7 June 1948 that the West Germans could draft a constitution for a separate state and on 1 September the Parliamentary Council started work on a Basic Law. The Western powers, rather than Stalin, were taking the initiative in cutting Germany into two. Although from early 1947 SED leaders were pressing Stalin and SMAD officials to enhance their powers and although bodies like the German Economic Commission were taking shape as part of an embryonic state structure, Stalin remained reluctant to abandon the idea of German unity. Even as late as their visit to Moscow in March 1948, Pieck and Grotewohl failed to obtain an unambiguous mandate from Stalin to launch the construction of an eastern 'counter-state formation'.[43] Stalin was still unwilling to declare his hand, particularly as the London talks were broken off on 6 March, albeit temporarily, and the French were known to be unenthusiastic about the emergence of a West German state. Given his procrastination, it is a reasonable assumption that Stalin, rather than working to a blueprint, was becoming increasingly uncertain as to what kind of hand he should be playing.

When the London conference reached the decision in June on a draft constitution for a separate state and on a Western currency reform, the Soviet Union abandoned caution: it severed all road, rail and canal links to the Western sectors of Berlin on 24 June 1948. West Berlin was regarded as the Western powers' Achilles heel as it was situated a hundred miles inside the Soviet zone without any written guarantees of right of access by land. After some discussion of the proposal of the American military governor, Lucius Clay, to call [45] the Russians' bluff by sending an armed convoy to Berlin and also of the alternative favoured by the Joint Chiefs of Staff to withdraw from Berlin, Washington, with the full backing of the British Foreign Minister, Ernest Bevin, decided to relieve West Berlin's population of over 2 million by means of an airlift. The Soviet blockade was eventually called off in May 1949. Western perceptions of the aggressive side of Soviet behaviour in the Berlin crisis hastened the final establishment of a West German state. A constitution – the Basic Law – came into force in May 1949, the first elections to the Bundestag took place on 14 August and a government was formed under Chancellor Konrad Adenauer in the following month.

Despite the availability of much new archival evidence, it is still difficult to determine whether Stalin regarded Berlin as a lever or a prize. The most likely interpretation is that Stalin was pursuing a dual-track policy: on the one hand, in a last throw of the diplomatic dice, to force the Western powers to abandon their plan for a separate West German state and to undermine the German people's confidence in the West, but, on the other hand, if no concessions were forthcoming, to remove the West from Berlin and incorporate the city into the Soviet zone. That Stalin was keen to remove the Western powers from Berlin can be seen in his response to Pieck's observation, at a meeting on 26 March, that the SED would welcome the departure of the Western powers from Berlin. Stalin commented, 'Let's try with all our might, and maybe we'll drive them out'.[44]

Stalin's plans came to nought as a result of the relief of the Western sectors of Berlin by the famous airlift. And as East–West relations deteriorated further with the rapid advance of Western plans to found a West German state, Soviet and SED officials began to finalize their own arrangements for a separate East German state. On 18 December 1948, Pieck, Ulbricht, Grotewohl and Oelssner held talks with Stalin and other top Soviet leaders on the SED paper 'German government for the Soviet zone of occupation'. This government was to be created out of the German Economic Commission, the Central Administration for Justice and other bodies. Characterising the current system in the zone as a 'higher democratic order' rather than a People's Democracy on the grounds that capitalist forces still controlled sections of the economy and reactionary elements in the bourgeois parties had not yet been eradicated, the SED leaders proposed a transition to a People's Democracy after a further strengthening of the SED and the state.[45]

But even at this late stage, Stalin was not for turning. The SED was not allowed to join Cominform and he refused to raise the zone to the status of a

[46] People's Democracy on the grounds that a state had not been founded and SED rule was not yet secure. He insisted, once more, that the SED leaders adhere to a zig-zag course, an 'opportunistic policy to socialism'. The difference in tactics was highlighted by his comparison of the SED leaders to their predecessors, the 'Teutons', who, though courageous, had suffered defeat at the hands of the Romans because they had waged war 'bare-chested' and with 'open visor'.[46] However, Stalin could not remain inactive: he endorsed the final arrangements for the transformation of the SED into a party of a new type and, in anticipation of the establishment of a West German government in February or March, he agreed to the creation of a provisional 'German' government and a People's Chamber (*Volkskammer*), although only after the Western powers had taken the critical steps. Stalin, it would appear, wished to avoid being depicted as one of Germany's partitioners; furthermore, his perception of the Soviet Union's global interests caused him to restrain the SED leaders, especially Ulbricht, from pushing ahead with the zone's entry into the community of People's Democracies, a development which they saw as vital to securing their own domestic political position.[47] Stalin's hesitation, together with Soviet initiatives on German unity in 1952, suggests that Moscow had not finally ruled out other alternatives to the German question and that the imposition of a uniform model on Eastern Europe, including the GDR, had not been pre-ordained.

A People's Congress movement was set up to carry out the zig-zag course decreed by Stalin. A German People's Congress for Unity and a Just Peace had been founded in late 1947. The First People's Congress numbered 2,215 representatives, including 464 West German members, mostly from the KPD. The movement performed a dual role: it professed commitment to national unity, thus ostensibly absolving Stalin and the SED from responsibility for the division of Germany, but in the event of a failure of its all-German aspirations it was expected to deliver the institutional framework for an East German state. This was reinforced by the creation, on Stalin's orders, of a National Front to mobilise Germans in all four zones behind a 'national front for independence' against American imperialists and their German helpers.[48] The SED was required to square the political circle. It was supposed to uphold national unity while simultaneously building a party of a new type on the Soviet model and constructing a provisional state structure in the eastern zone.

The key pronouncements on the creation of a separate East German state emanated from the Third People's Congress in May 1949. In the elections to this body, voters were asked whether they were in favour of German unity and a just German peace treaty. A vote in favour was interpreted as a vote for the single-list of bloc candidates. This was the first time that a single list was used for elections in the zone, a practice which was to become the standard method by which the SED controlled the outcome of elections in the GDR. People could only vote 'yes' or 'no'. From the point of view of the authorities, the 66.1 per cent in favour was a disappointing vote; it certainly discredited SED claims that the Congress enjoyed a popular mandate. The 2,016 delegates then elected a People's Council of 330 members, which agreed upon a draft constitution for the German Democratic Republic on 30 May 1949. The Council, which was only allowed to issue statements with Moscow's approval, proclaimed the foundation of the GDR on 7 October.

The point of no return was probably reached at some stage between the Bundestag election on 14 August and Konrad Adenauer's election as chancellor. The arrangements for the new East German state were completed at a top-level meeting in Moscow on 16 September between East German and Soviet representatives and the Soviet seal of approval was delivered eleven days later. Agreement was reached on the creation of a People's Chamber, the promulgation of a constitution, the election of Pieck as President of the new state and the formation of a provisional government headed by Grotewohl as Minister President. The government was to assume all the administrative tasks hitherto exercised by SMAD and the latter was to be transformed into a Soviet Control Commission. While the East German delegation preferred the title of a 'German government' in the Soviet zone, they had to bow to the Soviet wish for the new state formation to be called a provisional government of the 'German Democratic Republic'.[49] Stalin's sickly and 'unwanted' child had been born.

References

1. Cited in Leonhard W. 1979: 350

2. Krusch H.-J., Malycha A. 1990: 67–70, 72–3

3. Thomaneck J. K. A., Mellis J 1989: 21

4. Malycha A. 1996: 51–2

5. Connell B. 1957: 188

6. Hurwitz H. 1997: 106

7. Bordjugow G. 1998: 291–3; Naimark N. M. 1995: 294–7; Mählert U. 1998b: 361–4

[48]   8. Staritz D. 1995: 154

9. Malycha A. 1996: 93

10. Badstübner R., Loth W. 1994: 128–9, 150–1, 171, 216–17

11. Malycha A. 1996: 93

12. Badstübner R., Loth W. 1994: 248–9, 260–1; Malycha A. 1993: 281–2

13. Gniffke E. W. 1966: 369

14. Malycha A. 1996: 133; Mählert U. 1998b: 417–18, 428

15. Herf J. 1997: 158–60

16. Cited in ibid., 127

17. Wegmann B. 1997: 17

18. Naimark N. M. 1995: 334–5

19. Ibid., 366

20. Wegmann B. 1997: 21

21. Naimark N. M. 1995: 367

22. Ibid., 374

23. Kilian A. 1997: 539–40

24. Klonovsky M., von Flocken J. 1991: 22–3; Kilian A. 1993: 1145

25. Finn G. 1995: 360

26. Klonovsky M., von Flocken J. 1991: 37–40; Kilian A. 1993: 1156; Oleschinski B., Pampel B. 1997: 30–2

27. Löwenthal F. 1950: 258–9

28. Erler P. 1995: 40, 42; Prieß B. 1992: 54

29. Klonovsky M., von Flocken J. 1991: 18

30. Neske N. 1998: 189–92; von Plato A. 1998: 54–5

31. Finn in Deutscher Bundestag IV 1995: 348, 355; Wendel E. 1996: 42

32. Naimark N. M. 1995: 377

33. Neske N. 1998: 197–201; von Plato A. 1998: 38, 55–6

34. Finn G. 1998: 6

35. Weber H. 1985: 114–15

36. Staritz D. 1995: 109–10; Wille M. 1993: 206, 210

37. Jessen R. 1994: 241

38. Karlsch R. 1993: 230–1

39. Ibid., 81, 85–9, 225, 233

40. Ibid., 234

41. Cited in Roesler J. 1991: 48

42. Staritz D. 1995: 196

43. See Pieck's report in Badstübner R., Loth W. 1994: 189–202

44. Cited in Narinskii M. N. 1996: 65

45. Badstübner R., Loth W. 1994: 247, 249, 253

46. Ibid., 261, 167–8

47. Loth W. 1995: 294–5

48. Badstübner R., Loth W. 1994: 281

49. Ibid., 302–5

PART TWO

CONSTRUCTING STATE SOCIALISM, 1949–61

CHAPTER THREE

PARTY AND SOCIETY IN CONFLICT

The GDR, at the time of its founding on 7 October, appeared to be little more than a provisional structure or, in Ernst Richert's apt phrase, 'the state that ought not to be'. Only the Soviet Union, the People's Democracies of Eastern Europe and North Korea entered into diplomatic relations with the new republic. Moreover, the mass exodus of the population only served to reinforce Western condemnation of the GDR as a Stalinist clone without a popular mandate and to justify treating it as a political leper. The prospects for survival were bleak and the country would face existential crises in 1953 and 1961 arising from widespread opposition to the imposition of Soviet-style socialism. These crises and the construction of the socialist system constitute the main themes of Chapters 3 and 4.

The ruling party

After the foundation of the GDR, the People's Council turned itself into a Provisional People's Chamber (*Volkskammer*) and approved a constitution for the new republic. In accordance with SED wishes for a delay of one year, the Kremlin permitted elections to the People's Chamber to be postponed until October 1950. The elections were organised by the National Front of Democratic Germany, which was utilised by the SED as the main instrument for breaking CDU and LDP opposition to the single list of candidates and for arranging the allocation of seats in advance of the election. Voting, which in many places did not take place in the secrecy of the polling booths, produced a rigged 99.7 per cent vote in favour of the National Front list. The SED claimed 100 seats in the People's Chamber, the CDU and LDP 60 each, and the NDPD and DBD 30 each. The FDGB obtained 40, the FDJ 20 and the

[54] remaining mass organisations 60 seats. As most of the delegates of the mass organisations belonged to the SED, the party commanded an inbuilt majority in what was anyhow a compliant and supine body. The SED was dominant, too, in the state system: the Council of Ministers, the main organ of government, was obliged to comply with decisions taken by the party's central bodies, and senior party members like Grotewohl, Ulbricht and Rau occupied key positions on the Council.

Unchallenged in central government, the SED was easily the dominant force in public administration and the economy. During the 1950s, the party came to exercise a virtual monopoly on all leading positions in the state and the economy and newly appointed public employees – whether teachers or judges, enterprise managers or government officials – were given a stake in the new system. By the end of the 1940s, about 46 per cent had a working-class background and approximately 14 per cent came from white-collar and 11 per cent from civil servant families.[1] This development was accelerated by the introduction, at the beginning of the 1950s, of quotas of 60 per cent for working-class and peasant children at secondary school and university. Special courses were provided by university workers' and peasants' departments (*Arbeiter- und Bauernfakultäten*) which enabled young people from these social groups to obtain the requisite qualifications for a place in higher education. Servants of the state were first and foremost servants of the party. The *sine qua non* of any position was ideological and required political conformity and strict compliance with party decisions. Special cadre departments were responsible for the selection and training of suitable personnel, especially the so-called *nomenklatura* cadres who occupied the leading positions in the political parties, the state system, the mass organisations and the economy. A *nomenklatura*, which is a list of these key posts, was devised in 1949 and was utilised by the SED as part of its domination of the political system.

The SED's leading role in state and society and the centralisation of the party were boosted by the Third Party Congress held in July 1950. A new party statute unequivocally committed the SED to Stalinist norms: it described the SED as the 'conscious and organised vanguard' of the German labour movement and as the 'highest form of class organisation of the working class' guided by the theory of Marx, Engels, Lenin and Stalin. By subscribing to Marxist-Leninist ideology, the SED claimed, spuriously, to have access to the scientific laws of history which made it uniquely qualified to take charge of the transition to a new social formation. Not only did Marxism-Leninism provide a justification for the party's leading role but it was also employed as the basis for the political socialisation and motivation of members. One major

organisational change was the replacement of the party executive by a Cent- [55]
ral Committee. Although the new body was assigned responsibility for the
management of the party, this function was in fact exercised by the Politbüro
and the Central Committee Secretariat. As was discussed in Chapter 2, purges
of the party membership during the early 1950s, especially of ex-Social Democrats, helped to create a more disciplined and tightly organised party in which
opposition and factions were officially banned.

A state without a future?

Despite the tightening of SED rule, the GDR's political future looked bleak.
Although greeted by Stalin as a turning-point in the history of Europe, the
new republic did not enjoy sovereign rights. It had been severed from its
natural hinterland, onerous reparations had been exacted and the emphasis
on heavy industry hit the consumer hard. The standard of living was low,
meat, fat and sugar were rationed, and many other goods were in short supply. With the average monthly income a mere DM 256 in 1950, workers and
white-collar employees were unable to afford the high prices charged in the
state retail outlets; a kilo of butter, for example, cost DM 36.[2] The Federal
Republic, with about three times the population, unencumbered by Stalinist
excesses, better endowed with resources and enjoying a higher standard of
living, proved to be an irresistible magnet for East Germans. In 1950,
197,788 fled to West Germany; by the end of 1959 the cumulative total had
escalated to 2.3 million.

Even the SED's German policy appeared to have as its goal the eventual
withering away of the GDR as a separate state. Not only did President Pieck
refer to 'the fact that the struggle of the national front of all Germans for
German unity and a just peace treaty has entered a new phase with the foundation of the German Democratic Republic',[3] but also Stalin, in his congratu-
latory telegram, hailed the new state as the foundation stone for a united,
democratic, peace-loving Germany. Furthermore, the GDR anthem, penned
by Johannes Becher, who later became Minister of Culture, looked forward
to the end of division:

Our faces turned towards the future
Let us serve you for the good
Germany, one fatherland

[56]   Indeed, the very existence of the GDR appeared to be under threat from the Soviet dictator's diplomatic manoeuvring. In his famous note of 10 March and a subsequent one on 9 April to the other three occupying powers, Stalin proposed negotiations on German unification and the signing of a peace treaty with an all-German government. He dangled the bait of freedom of activity for democratic parties and associations, free elections to an all-German parliament under the supervision of the four occupying powers, and a neutral Germany with armed forces in relation to its defence requirements.

There is general agreement among historians that the notes were designed to forestall the impending rearmament of the Federal Republic and its entry into the European Defence Community, then at a delicate negotiating stage. But whether Stalin was sincere in seeking an all-German solution based on ostensibly generous concessions to the West is a matter which continues to divide scholars, partly because the new documentary evidence is fragmentary and the recollections of contemporary witnesses often unreliable. Wilfried Loth, one of Germany's leading authorities on the cold war, contends that Stalin's diplomatic offensive provides yet one more example of his long-standing commitment to a united Germany based on Western democratic principles as the most effective safeguard for Soviet security. A commitment to political pluralism is, however, difficult to associate with Stalin and Loth is obliged to concede that the parliamentary-democratic route was intended to lead to a socialist destination.[4] Loth's interpretation has been fiercely contested by Gerhard Wettig, an expert on Soviet foreign and security policy. Utilising documents from the Russian archives, Wettig argues that Stalin's notes did not represent a genuine offer of reunification; they were essentially part of a carefully coordinated campaign by the Soviet Control Commission, the SED and the party's West German KPD adjunct to bring down Chancellor Adenauer's government and to mobilise West German popular opinion behind the Soviet concept of an anti-fascist democratic Germany. Adenauer's fall, it was anticipated, would spell the end to the integration of the FRG into the Western system and hasten the withdrawal of American forces from Europe.[5] An examination of Wilhelm Pieck's notes on the two high-level Soviet–GDR meetings in Moscow, on 1 and 7 April 1952, tends to favour the view that Stalin was continuing his old 'zig-zag' course on Germany. Still trying to keep his options open, he wanted to sow confusion among his opponents and to use the unification issue to obstruct the formation of an anti-Western bloc. This course was becoming increasingly difficult to pursue as the drawing of the GDR into the Soviet orbit was reducing the value of unification as an instrument of diplomacy. The record of the two meetings offers no sign of any fear among SED leaders that Stalin was about to abandon the GDR. Asserting that the 'pacifist period' was over since his proposals in March had failed to impress the West, Stalin urged Ulbricht and Pieck to build up the GDR's armed forces and to press ahead with the organisation of their own state.[6] However, while he favoured the introduction of socialist measures such as the collectivisation of agriculture, he preferred to await the outcome of the current diplomatic negotiations. Hence, he instructed the SED leaders to delay the start of collectivisation until autumn; with regard to unification, he advised 'Unity, peace treaty – carry on agitating'.[7]

The so-called 'battle of the notes' between Stalin and the Western powers, which dragged on throughout the summer, indicates that Soviet policymakers were not finally reconciled to the partition of Germany and that Stalin, albeit fleetingly, toyed with the idea of a neutral, unified Germany as the lesser of two evils. On the other hand, he was too ambivalent about a reunified Germany to enter into serious negotiations with Western statesmen who, not unreasonably, were sceptical about his motives. In the final analysis, neither Stalin nor the three Western powers were prepared to run the risk of a united Germany aligning itself, at some time in the future, with the rival bloc and all harboured fears of an eventual resurgence of German power. It was better to keep – and control – what each had rather than risk losing all.

The planned construction of socialism

With the Soviet initiative on Germany stalling, the Soviet and GDR leaders prepared the ground for the final transition from an anti-fascist democratic polity to a Soviet-style socialist system. After the SED delegation's meeting with Stalin in April, measures were introduced which would pave the way for the formal announcement in July of the construction of socialism and drive a further wedge between East and West Germany. In late May, work began on a five-kilometres-wide prohibited zone between the GDR and the FRG. In an operation known as 'action vermin', hundreds of families who were deemed to be a threat to the regime were forcibly evicted from their homes and villages in night-and-fog manoeuvres in the border zone. Nobody was allowed to enter this zone without official permission.

The People's Police in Barracks (KVP – *Kasernierte Volkspolizei*) was created on 1 July and plans were laid to increase the size of the armed forces, including naval and airforce units of the People's Police, to a total strength of

[58]   200,000. By December 1952, these units already exceeded 90,000 troops and the GDR possessed an army in all but name. A further impetus to the militarisation of society was given by a decision in August to set up a new mass organisation, the Society for Sport and Technology (GST), to prepare young people for military service. Finally, after prior consultation with the Soviet Control Commission, the SED Politbüro decided, on 3 June, to bite the bullet and proceed with the collectivisation of agriculture. However, given the controversial nature of a programme so closely associated with the Stalinist model of socialism and the millions of victims during the famine of 1932–33, the Control Commission did not finally authorise its commencement until after the SED Party Conference in July 1952.[8]

The proclamation of the 'planned construction of socialism'

Only when it became clear in late May, with West Germany's signing of the European Defence Community treaty and the conclusion of the *Deutschlandvertrag* by the USA, France, Great Britain and the FRG, that Stalin's diplomatic offensive had finally run out of steam were the major external impediments to the socialist project removed. On the pretext that the tasks of the 'bourgeois-democratic revolution' had been completed, the Politbüro decided, on 1 July, to seek Stalin's approval for the initiative. The SED leaders' request was buttressed by much wishful thinking. They claimed that socialism would boost East Germans' work performance and make the GDR more attractive to the West German working class. Whether or not Stalin was convinced by these arguments, the CPSU Politbüro finally gave the go ahead on 8 July.[9] The Soviet Union's hesitation before finally committing itself to a socialist course for the GDR should be seen in the context of the need to strike a balance between its various interests in Germany and Europe rather than as an instance of any fundamental antagonism between the SED and Soviet elites. Even so, tension between GDR and Soviet interests could not be ruled out.

In his address to the SED Party Conference, Ulbricht placed the construction of socialism within the Stalinist context of the intensification of the class struggle. He called for a strengthening of the power of the state to protect the GDR against implacable adversaries both at home and in the imperialist West. The tasks of the state were identified as: breaking the resistance of expropriated big capitalists and large landowners, the establishment of an army and the 'organisation of the construction of socialism with the help of all working people united around the working class'.[10] In addition, he announced a series

of other policy initiatives: the collectivisation of agriculture, discrimination   [59]
against the Churches, the reorganisation of administration and the elimination of private business.

Constructing socialism

At the end of July, the five *Länder* were dissolved and replaced by fifteen regional administrations (*Bezirke*) as part of a concerted attack on federalism
and regional traditions. The regional council (*Bezirksrat*) became the most
important organ at regional level and the post of council secretary – the leading executive office – was turned into a monopoly of the SED. Functionaries
of the ruling party were obliged to undergo an intensive training programme
to equip them for the struggle against 'hostile forces' and the leadership
judged that the party must be purged of real or alleged enemies. At the end of
December, the Central Committee formulated a series of 'Lessons from the
Trial against the Slansky Conspiracy Centre' in Czechoslovakia. This was
the pretext for the SED to expel many ordinary members from the party and
to prepare a show trial against leading East German Communists. Ulbricht
seized the opportunity to accuse an old rival, Franz Dahlem, of capitulation
at the time of the outbreak of the Second World War and to remove him from
the Central Committee in May 1953. Dahlem, a survivor of the Mauthausen
camp, was the leading figure in the SED among former Nazi concentration
camp victims.

The construction of socialism had profound implications for the education system. On 29 July 1952, a Politbüro resolution sought to raise the level
of party control over education by improving the quality of party work in
schools, by educating young people as 'all-round personalities' committed to
the construction of socialism and by establishing Marxism-Leninism as the
basis of their education and upbringing. This policy led to an intensification
of repression against the Evangelical Churches in 1952 and 1953. With 92
per cent of East Germans adhering to the Christian faith, the Churches constituted a major cultural obstacle to the SED's ambitious political socialisation
programme. As part of the *Kirchenkampf*, the Churches were forbidden to conduct religious education in schools, politically active ministers were dismissed
and Church officials were imprisoned. A vigorous campaign was launched
against the *Junge Gemeinden*, the Evangelical Churches' organisation for young
people and a serious rival to the FDJ. The *Junge Gemeinden* was falsely accused
of conducting espionage on behalf of Western imperialists and 300 pupils
who belonged to the organisation were expelled from secondary school.

[60]   The July Conference gave renewed impetus to the implementation of the Soviet economic mechanism. In 1950, the GDR had been accepted into COMECON, the Soviet bloc's economic organisation, and the country's first five-year economic plan was put into operation one year later. SED leaders predicted that the plan, which targeted high levels of growth in production and labour productivity, would enable the GDR to outstrip capitalist countries in industrial development and to overtake West German living standards. The results at the end of the first year were encouraging: the party organ *Neues Deutschland* reported an overfulfilment of targets and a 21.9 per cent increase in industrial production. At the Party Conference, Ulbricht stressed the need to introduce technically based work norms in order to reduce production costs and raise labour productivity. When these norms were introduced, they immediately provoked fierce worker opposition.

Ulbricht sought to sugar the pill of collectivisation in agriculture by assuring farmers that it would be a voluntary process. This proved to be an empty promise. By 1952, there were about 889,000 agricultural enterprises, of which 95 per cent were in private hands. According to the SED definition of size, 'small' peasants with farms of up to ten hectares constituted 73 per cent of the peasantry and worked less than 50 per cent of the land. 'Large' farmers, with 20 to 100 hectares, owned about 20 per cent of the land, the same proportion as 'medium-sized' peasants. Collectivisation of agriculture, which commenced in a modest way in 1950, was promoted by offering peasants tax relief, by the manipulation of obligatory deliveries to the state and by the provision of modern equipment and seed. Three types of agricultural production cooperatives (LPGs – *Landwirtschaftliche Produktionsgenossenschaften*) were developed according to the degree of socialisation of the means of production. The dominant form, type III, encompassed the collectivisation of all means of production (land, livestock, machinery, buildings). The number of LPGs rose rapidly from 1,900 with 37,000 members and 200,000 hectares of land in 1952 to 6,000 with 190,000 members and 1.2 million hectares in 1955.[11]

Private farmers were not the only target of discrimination, for private property in general was, according to Marxist-Leninist ideology, linked inextricably with capitalist exploitation and the breeding of saboteurs against the new order. The collectivisation of handicrafts commenced with the introduction of artisans' production cooperatives. Private retailers, craftsmen, traders and self-employed businessmen had for many years suffered higher rates of taxation and restrictions on credits. This kind of discrimination was accelerated in 1953 as part of the general campaign against the old social order.

On the eve of the June Uprising [61]

The SED leaders were guilty of self-delusion, overestimating both the capacity of the GDR to outstrip the FRG economically and the appeal of the new socialist system to East and West Germans alike. At the July Party Conference, Ulbricht had assured his listeners that 'working people from West Germany who come to visit the German Democratic Republic can only be agreeably surprised at future elections and they will state: We, too, want such a construction of socialism'.[12] Even on the eve of the June Uprising, internal documents show that neither Ulbricht nor Stasi officials foresaw the ferocity of the impending political storm.[13]

The package of measures introduced in the summer of 1952 was far too ambitious and overstretched the GDR's limited means.[14] Little allowance had been made in the five-year plan to finance the restructuring of agriculture and the expansion of the armed forces. The Kremlin, anticipating that the latter would absorb about 1.5 billion Marks, recommended it be subsidised by social security and social welfare savings, by an increase in income and property taxes, and by cuts in consumption. This proved to be a serious underestimate as expenditure amounted to 2 billion Marks by mid-1953. There was also a long list of other commitments: heavy occupation costs and reparations obligations; payments for Soviet weaponry with products from the GDR's chemical and machine-building industries; and 1.5 billion Marks for the reorganisation of agriculture. The state budget closed in 1952 with a deficit of 700 million Marks and the country had a negative balance of 600 million Marks in trade with its Communist allies.

A further burden was imposed by the accelerated development of heavy industry, a programme which aimed to make the GDR independent of capitalist countries and to support the expansion of the armed forces. Between 1951 and 1953, it is estimated that about 60 per cent of the growth of the capital stock of centrally managed industry occurred in mining, iron and steel and energy, whereas light industry accounted for a mere 2 per cent. The neglect of consumer goods production and the rapid expansion of heavy industry distorted economic development and caused dissatisfaction among consumers. This imbalance was not simply the consequence of the unstable political and economic situation in the early 1950s; it was also a development inherent in an economic system which prioritised heavy industry over the consumer goods industry.

Opposition to collectivisation mounted rapidly. Farmers resented the absence of consultation and the imposition of more stringent administrative

[62] controls. District councils and mayors, themselves under pressure from higher bodies, forced farmers to meet centrally determined targets for sowing and harvesting and seized the assets of insolvent farmers. Although the plan targets were unrealistic, failure to attain them was treated by state officials as evidence of opposition and sabotage and farms were confiscated. Many private farmers saw little future in the GDR and left the country. The disruption to farming was widespread: by mid-1953, about 750,000 hectares, that is, about 13 per cent of agriculturally useful land, lay fallow, mainly as a result of SED policy.

In order to relieve the pressure on public finances, severe cuts were made in the social budgets in early 1953. The monthly household day for single working mothers was cancelled, as were cheap fares for journeys to work or school for workers, pupils and apprentices. The decline in agricultural imports and output and the neglect of the consumer goods sector created bottlenecks in the supply situation. In the first half of 1953, a shortfall in plan targets was recorded in shoes, paper, bricks, textiles and clothes. Shortages also occurred in foodstuffs, particularly of sugar, fruit, vegetables, potatoes, rice and butter. The refusal of Stalin's successors to provide significant relief prompted the SED in April and May to make deeper cuts. On 9 April, the Council of Ministers decided to withdraw food ration cards from independents, the owners of rented property and other groups from 1 May onwards; about two million people were affected. Many had to shop in state-run retail outlets, where goods were dear. Price increases were decreed for jam, confectionery and bread. Wages were caught up in the general squeeze: bonuses were reduced and workers were transferred into lower wage categories.

One of the most controversial attempts to reduce wages and boost productivity was the campaign to introduce the new technically determined work norms, which supposedly represented targets realisable under optimal work organisation. A case could be made out for some adjustment to existing norms as they were frequently overfulfilled, in heavy machine building by as much as 120 per cent to 150 per cent. It was decided to enforce by fiat a 10 per cent increase in the norms. The date for their introduction was set for 30 June by the Council of Ministers. Increases on this scale threatened many workers with a cut in real wages of between 25 per cent and 30 per cent as the overfulfilment of norms was crucial to the bonus payments which boosted low rates of pay. The whole situation was exacerbated by the need for frequent repairs and maintenance work and by difficulties in obtaining material supplies, thereby making the fulfilment of the new norms an unattainable target.

The arbitrary treatment of state factory workers and the wave of repression against large farmers, independent businessmen and the religious community

added to the climate of fear and uncertainty at a time when the SED was [63]
seeking to unearth enemy agents and saboteurs, Trotskyists and freemasons,
Zionists and 'morally depraved persons' as part of the party's intensification
of the class struggle. A harsher enforcement of the penal code was an integral
aspect of the offensive against 'internal enemies' and 'capitalist' producers. In
1952 and 1953, cases against economic criminals, saboteurs and agents rose
sharply. Some penalties were extremely harsh: the death sentence was imposed for certain types of crime against property. In April 1953, a Leipzig
court sentenced two workers to four and six years' imprisonment respectively
for belittling Stalin. The number of prison inmates mushroomed from 30,092
in July 1952 to 61,377 in May 1953. The upsurge in proceedings against
public property offences in early 1953 caused the GDR public prosecutor,
Dr Melsheimer, to predict that 40,000 would be imprisoned for this offence,
a level which he regarded as unacceptable.[15]

The growing popular unrest worried Soviet and SED officials. In the
autumn of 1952, the Soviet Control Commission set up a special team to monitor popular opinion and, in the spring of 1953, the Central Committee and
the East German government conducted their own surveys of the mood of
the population. These reports revealed worker hostility towards the tough
measures taken by the SED and the government as well as despondency and
apathy among functionaries in the party's factory and district branches.[16] One
indicator of the high level of social unrest was the swelling numbers of émigrés.
Whereas about 165,648 left the GDR in 1951 and 182,393 in 1952, a record
331,390 fled during 1953, including 120,000 in the first fourth months of
the year.[17] The loss of 20,000 independent farmers disrupted the supply situation and the republic lost considerable intellectual and business potential through the exodus of teachers, doctors and scientists. Members of the
SED, the FDJ and the People's Police in Barracks also fled to the West. The
motives for the mass exodus, ranging from socio-economic grievances to a
mixture of political and personal reasons, amounted to a broad rejection of
the SED's societal strategy and its harsh methods.

The New Course

After Stalin's death in March 1953, his successors granted some relief to the
hard-pressed SED regime by easing the GDR's reparations and export
obligations. But as Moscow itself was in no position to provide a major
transfusion of aid and was also alarmed at the symptoms of crisis in Poland

[64]   and Czechoslovakia, the new Soviet leadership opted for a New Course. Their recommendations for a change of direction were set out in a CPSU Politbüro document of 27 May entitled 'Measures for restoring the political situation in the German Democratic Republic'. A GDR delegation, consisting of Ulbricht, Grotewohl and the Central Committee Secretary for Propaganda, Oelssner, was called to Moscow to receive and discuss the Soviet proposals. On 2 and 3 June, they met Beria, Khruschchev and other high-ranking Soviet politicians. The CPSU document, while highly critical of the acceleration of socialism in the GDR, conceded that the SED did not bear sole responsibility for the policy. Without wishing the SED to abandon the socialist project entirely, the Kremlin urged the East Germans to pursue a more conciliatory policy towards farmers, small business, the consumer and the Churches.[18] Several fundamental preconditions of the crisis, such as Ulbricht's excessive personal power and the negative impact of democratic centralism on party life, were not tackled; surprisingly, the work norms were not even mentioned. Of the stunned SED representatives, Ulbricht was the most affected as he was the one most closely associated with the rapid construction of socialism.

    The decision to proceed with the New Course was taken at the SED Politbüro meeting and endorsed by the Council of Ministers two days later. The communiqué of 11 June, mainly drafted by Herrnstadt, was based on the Soviet recommendations. The Politbüro announced the withdrawal of the price increases introduced in April and the restoration of the intelligentsia's ration cards. It promised to end discrimination against young Christians, to discontinue the collectivisation programme and to restore the property of farmers and enterprise owners if they returned to the GDR. The expansion of heavy industry was to be slowed down and more foodstuffs and consumer goods were to be made available. Many East Germans were astonished at this admission of fallibility. The internal reports which the East German CDU gathered on opinion within the party convey a sense of satisfaction with the New Course but also a well-justified suspicion of the SED's motives.[19] By contrast, some SED members felt that the cause of Communism had been betrayed and others demanded that the party leaders be forced to account for their actions. Calls were heard among former SPD members for the dissolution of the SED and the restoration of the SPD and KPD as separate parties.[20]

    While many groups welcomed the SED's concessions, the industrial workers were aggrieved at the failure to rescind the work norms. Astonishingly, the Politbüro meeting on 13 June denied that the norms had been a mistake and reaffirmed the leadership's commitment to socialism. This was a fatal error in

view of the inflammatory nature of the norms issue and the precarious political situation. In May and early June, lightning strikes and the downing of
tools had been multiplying in enterprises in East Berlin, Karl-Marx-Stadt (formerly Chemnitz), Leipzig and many other provincial towns. On the evening
of 15 June, a rally of about 1,000 protesters was held in Johanngeorgenstadt
and on the morning of 16 June an appeal for the rescinding of the work norms
and for free and secret elections appeared on the notice board of the shipyard
in Warnemünde.[21] A survey of the popular mood conducted by the FDGB
executive revealed that unrest in the factories was not limited to social and
economic demands; it also had a political dimension in that some workers
were calling for the dissolution of the SED.[22] Opposition to SED rule was rife
in the countryside, too. In some villages the proclamation of the New Course
was celebrated by farmers as proof of the bankruptcy of the political order;
agricultural cooperatives began to collapse. The political stakes were being
raised: on 13 June, about 200 farmers in Eckolstadt, in the Apolda district,
agreed on a resolution calling for the resignation of the government.[23]

The June Uprising

While mass unrest was already widespread before the major explosion on
16 June, it was essentially spontaneous and localised. It was the mass demonstration against work norms by construction workers on the prestigious
Stalinallee building project in East Berlin on 16 June which proved to be the
trigger for a wave of strikes and demonstrations elsewhere in the country and
ushered in the first full-scale rebellion against Communist rule in the Soviet
Union's Eastern European empire. Party and state functionaries were taken
by surprise at the scale of the revolt. According to a highly placed SED official in East Berlin, 'Something incomprehensible was taking place before
their eyes: the workers were rising in revolt against the "Workers and Peasants State". Victims of their own mass deception, they had taken the fiction
for reality'.[24]

On 16 June, the workers on the Stalinallee drew up a petition and decided
to submit it personally to the head of government, Otto Grotewohl. Inflamed
by an article in the FDGB organ, *Tribüne*, confirming the work norms, the
workers marched to the House of the Council of Ministers. As they marched
through the streets of East Berlin, they were joined by other workers. About
2,000 gathered outside the Council of Ministers building in Leipzigerstrasse,

calling for Grotewohl and Ulbricht to appear before them and for a lowering of the work norms and prices. An ill-judged Politbüro announcement that the decree on the work norms would not be implemented by ordinance but only on a voluntary basis antagonised the crowd further. After formulating demands for the resignation of the government and the disbanding of the KVP, it was decided to call a general strike for the following day.

The uprising reached a climax on 17 June. Thousands of protesters gathered in East Berlin and unrest escalated elsewhere in the republic. In the capital, about 20,000 construction workers assembled in Strausbergerplatz on the Stalinallee; during the morning, workers from large enterprises such as Kabelwerk Oberspree and Bergmann-Borsig joined the demonstration. By about 09.00 hours, approximately 25,000 protesters had gathered outside the Council of Ministers. Their demands were both political and socio-economic: the withdrawal of the new norms, an immediate reduction in the cost of living, free and secret elections, the resignation of the government and no punishment of strikers. Violent clashes occurred between the demonstrators and the security forces throughout the centre of East Berlin; the first shots were fired around midday to prevent the storming of the Council of Ministers building.

State and party were ill-equipped to quell the uprising. The party organisation had already been thrown into disarray by the New Course. Party bodies in the factories were rudderless and unable to prevent members from taking part in the demonstrations and abandoning the party. The FDGB and the FDJ, too, were in turmoil; many of their members and officials also joined in the strikes and demonstrations. The armed forces – the KVP – were only deployed in small numbers for fear that the troops would be unwilling to use force against fellow citizens. Once it became apparent that the GDR authorities had lost control of the situation, the Soviet military commander in Greater Berlin gave the command, at about 12.30 hours, for Soviet units to restore law and order in East Berlin. Tanks were used to disperse the demonstrations and to seal off the sectoral borders. A state of emergency was imposed by the Soviet Military Administration at 13.00 hours. All public gatherings of more than three people were banned and anyone disobeying the order could be punished according to martial law. Many Berliners fled the streets and squares; others, outraged by the deployment of Soviet troops, resisted. Cars were overturned and burned, some demonstrators died of bullet wounds, and people on both sides were injured. Gradually, the Soviet forces, with the assistance of KVP units, were able to clear the streets and restore public order by the evening of 17 June 1953.[25]

The villages and other East German towns were also centres of revolt, [67]
although it was the unrest in East Berlin on 16 and 17 June which ignited the
flame of open rebellion. In particular, workers in the large cities and the industrial centres gathered behind the demands formulated by the Berlin construction workers. However, few links were established between individual
strike committees and the whole protest movement lacked effective coordination and leadership. Only in the towns of Görlitz and Bitterfeld were supra-
regional strike executives able to influence the general development of the
movement. The central areas of the country – the highly industrialised and
essentially working-class *Bezirke* of Halle, Leipzig and Magdeburg – were
the scenes of the most violent clashes. While the outcome of so shortlived an
uprising cannot be predicted with certainty, the widespread demand for free
and secret elections, popular opposition to the SED's socialist programme
and cries for the resignation of the government would in all probability have
led to the dismantling of the central elements of the socialist order and to the
reunification of the country.[26]

According to GDR archival materials,[27] 373 towns and places, including
113 out of 181 district towns (*Kreisstädte*) and eight of the regional capitals
(*Bezirksstädte*), were affected by disturbances between 17 and 23 June. Estimates based on official reports suggest that about 497,000 employees went
out on strike and about 418,000 took part in demonstrations on 17 June. On
the following day, the number fell to 106,000 and 44,000 respectively. The
Halle *Bezirk*, with 148,681 strikers and about 94,000 demonstrators, was
the region most affected by the mass protests of 17 June. The Berlin figures
read 25,500 and 90,000 respectively. Although such numbers represent a
minority of the population, non-participation was primarily a reflection of a
fear of reprisals and of a wait-and-see attitude rather than one of support for
the regime.

While the events of 16 and 17 June primarily involved the urban working class, other groups were heavily involved, notably the rural community.
Although far more is known about urban than rural disaffection, research continues to uncover instances of unrest in the villages. The deliberate refusal to
meet delivery targets set by state organs and the mass withdrawals from the
LPGs were among the main types of protest. In some villages, SED and LPG
officials were beaten up and local authority buildings occupied. Open protests occurred in the district town of Jessen in the Cottbus *Bezirk*, where a
demonstration by about 200 farmers attracted several hundred sympathisers
from factories and had to be dispersed by Soviet tanks.[28] Larger demonstrations took place on the following day in Mühlhausen and Zossen. Stasi reports

[68] indicate that not only did opposition continue well into July but that the unrest also had a strong political element, with farmers calling for the imprisonment of Ulbricht and the resignation of the government.[29] Concerted action was rare. Communications in the countryside made it even more difficult than in the towns to organise opposition to the regime, protests were quickly crushed by Soviet tanks and harsh sentences were imposed by Soviet and GDR courts.

Most members of the middle class and the intelligentsia, especially university lecturers, kept their distance from the revolt. Many had been appeased by the concessions granted by the government as part of the New Course and, in the case of white-collar employees in administration, by the social and career advantages offered by the state. The technical intelligentsia in the factories, above all in the central areas of the country, were less passive: some engineers sat on strike committees and took an active role in directing the strike movement.[30] Although some craftsmen and independents protested against the regime, the intelligentsia and the middle classes contributed neither large-scale support nor intellectual leadership to the uprising.

The uprising crushed

After initial hesitation, the Soviet authorities crushed the uprising in a ruthless manner.[31] A state of emergency was imposed on all but one of the fifteen *Bezirke*. Soviet tanks cleared the streets and in some enterprises the entire workforce was locked up for days inside their factory. At least fifty demonstrators were killed during clashes with Soviet and GDR troops. By 22 June, nineteen demonstrators had been sentenced to death; with one exception, execution was by firing squad. By the end of August, about 13,000 had been arrested; about two-thirds were workers and 13 per cent were white-collar employees. Arrests were intended not simply to punish direct participants but also to intimidate the population and root out opposition to the regime. Sentences were often extremely harsh: a lawyer from Görlitz was sentenced to five years' imprisonment for providing legal assistance to inmates released from prison by demonstrators. Even the Minister of Justice, a former SPD member, Max Fechner, was imprisoned for an interview published in *Neues Deutschland* on 2 July in which he defended the right to strike and advocated a milder policy towards protesters. *In toto*, 1,400 people received life sentences and 200 were executed.

Despite the harshness and scale of the repression, the grievances against the SED regime were so deep-seated that popular protests continued until mid-July; however, with the streets under the control of the security forces, they were mainly confined to the factories. Reports on the mood of its party rank-and-file, collected by the East German CDU general secretariat between 20 June and 15 July, reveal that East Germans rejected outright the authorities' interpretation of the uprising as the work of *agents provocateurs*. The surveys also showed that the political demands of 17 June still commanded much support.[32] Visits to factories by SED dignatories to propagate the New Course and the thesis of the counterrevolutionary nature of the events of 17 June failed to mollify the workforce. The protests in the factories and institutions ebbed and flowed for about four weeks after 17 June. They took various forms: verbal criticism of the SED leadership, strikes and demands for improvements in wages and living conditions. On a visit to the Leuna Works on 24 June, Ulbricht was obliged to listen to the workforce's demands for freedom of speech and the separation of party and unions. One engineer protested, 'If I make a mistake ... I end up in prison. If the Government makes mistakes ... ?'[33] The unrest peaked in mid-July when several thousand workers went out on strike in Carl-Zeiss-Jena and the Buna Works in Schkopau. The Buna workers' demands ranged from free, all-German elections to the release of all political prisoners. The crushing of the two strikes finally brought to an end the second and final wave of unrest.[34]

As a wide range of social groups – independent farmers, LPG workers, some white-collar workers and sections of the intelligentsia – participated in the protests of June–July 1953, it would be misleading to categorise the events simply as an uprising of the industrial workers. Nevertheless, recent work on the social composition of the rebels has confirmed earlier findings that industrial workers formed the mass base of the uprising and that the main centres of revolt, such as East Berlin, Dresden and the industrial regions around Halle, Leipzig, Bitterfeld and Magdeburg, had a heavy concentration of construction workers and workers in large enterprises.[35] Other activists included workers in steel, machine building and the chemical industry; on the other hand, workers in the smaller state enterprises and those in the cooperative or private production enterprises were less involved, partly because they were less affected by the norm increases.

The failure of the June–July Uprising can be attributed to a series of factors: the lack of supra-regional organisational networks; the determination of the Soviet Union and the SED authorities to crush public unrest; and the feeble response of the West. The acquiesence of the Western powers and the

[70]   FRG to the Soviets' use of force deflated East Germans' hopes of change.[36] Both Chancellor Adenauer and the West German Minister for All-German Affairs, Jakob Kaiser, counselled the East Germans to stay calm and the three Western powers held back from direct intervention for fear of provoking Soviet retaliation against West Berlin. The British Premier, Churchill, was less passive than most Western politicians. His willingness to explore opportunities for a settlement of the German question extended to a reconsideration of West Germany's incorporation into the Western military alliance. His advisers and ministers, however, were unwilling to take any risk. Selwyn Lloyd's comment epitomises this attitude:

> To unite Germany while Europe is divided even if practicable, is fraught with danger for all. Therefore everyone – Mr Adenauer, the Russians, the Americans, the French and ourselves – feel in our hearts that a divided Germany is safer for the time being. But none of us dare say so openly because of the effect on German public opinion.[37]

Once the SED leaders had recovered their nerve, they devised their own version of events. The main responsibility was placed on fascist *agents provocateurs* and on the roll-back policy of President Eisenhower and his Secretary of State, John Foster Dulles. It was claimed, on the flimsiest of evidence, that plans had been laid for a counterrevolutionary coup. On 16–17 June, armed fascist bands from the West, it was alleged, were intending to provoke a general strike, incite the workers and overthrow the GDR government by force. Although this was a crude fabrication, it is undeniable that many West Berliners joined in the demonstrations in East Berlin and that West German organisations were engaged in undercover activities in the GDR. In addition, RIAS, the American radio station in the American sector of Berlin, contributed to the spread of strikes by disseminating news of the events. However, the fundamental determinant of the uprising was worker opposition to the policies of the SED leadership. In fact, in the SED's initial response to the uprising, the Central Committee meeting on 21 June 1953 had admitted as much: 'if masses of workers do not understand the party, then the party is guilty, not the workers'.[38] Bertolt Brecht, who sympathised with the workers' frustration while remaining loyal to the regime, penned his own typically cryptic remarks in a poem:

> *After the uprising of the 17th June*
> *The Secretary of the Writers' Union*
> *Had leaflets distributed in the Stalinallee*
> *Stating that the people*

Had forfeited the confidence of the government
And could win it back only
by redoubled efforts. Would it not be easier
In that case for the government
To dissolve the people
And elect another?

Ulbricht's survival

Ulbricht's fate was inextricably linked to the outcome of the uprising. Since 1951, many of his colleagues had been growing increasingly restless at the concentration of so much power in his hands, in particular his domination of the Central Committee Secretariat. This key body was responsible for the organisation and management of the party. Rudolf Herrnstadt, an astute party intellectual who had edited *Neues Deutschland* since 1949, emerged as Ulbricht's most persistent critic. A candidate member of the Politbüro since 1950, Herrnstadt attracted the support, in varying degrees, of most of his Politbüro colleagues, in particular the Minister of State Security, Wilhelm Zaisser, and Friedrich Ebert. The latter was a former SPD member and the son of the Weimar Republic's first president. Ulbricht's policies and autocratic style of leadership came under fire at a series of Politbüro and Central Committee meetings after he and other top leaders had returned from their highly embarassing refuge in the Soviet military headquarters during the night of 17 to 18 June. Until the fall of Beria, it appeared probable that he would have to resign, particularly as there were indications that the Soviet Union, the crucial player, was contemplating Herrnstadt as his successor.[39]

On 7 July, the day before Ulbricht and Grotewohl were due to fly to Moscow, a full-scale attack was mounted against Ulbricht. In his memoirs, Herrnstadt recalls that out of thirteen members and candidates present, only the arch-Stalinist Matern and a wavering Honecker wanted Ulbricht to remain as General Secretary, while Oelssner and Mückenberger were undecided. Zaisser, arguing that Ulbricht was unsuitable for implementing the New Course, proposed Herrnstadt as General Secretary.[40] In rejecting Zaisser's proposal, Herrnstadt showed a lack of self-confidence in his own ability and too deferential an attitude to Ulbricht. He preferred, it appears, to control Ulbricht by means of collective decision-making structures, a policy which he failed to pursue with sufficient determination.[41] Although he was anxious to curtail Ulbricht's power, to mobilise greater popular support and to revive

[72] trust in the SED, it is doubtful whether he offered a fundamental alternative to Ulbricht. He did not question the central elements of Communist rule, that is, the party's leading role and its monopoly on power. Too detached from the people, he deluded himself that the party could represent their interests. And, like Ulbricht's other critics, he was too constrained by party ideology and discipline to stage an effective palace coup.

Although Ulbricht launched his own counteroffensive, accusing his domestic critics of factionalism and a betrayal of the class character of the SED, the fate of Herrnstadt and Zaisser was ultimately determined by developments in the Kremlin. On their return from Moscow, Ulbricht and Grotewohl brought with them not only news of Beria's arrest on 26 June but also reassurances that Ulbricht would not be deposed.[42] Despite its dissatisfaction with Ulbricht, Moscow had decided that power was safer in his hands, particularly as events in Hungary were reinforcing the dangers inherent in reform and a relaxation of party control. The General Secretary struck quickly against Herrnstadt and Zaisser, charging them, unjustly, of forming a separate platform characterised by defeatism and a Social Democratic orientation. Zaisser, like Beria, was accused of plotting to raise the security forces above the party, and he was criticised for his ministry's failure to prevent the June Uprising.[43] Although Zaisser and Herrnstadt defended themselves against the charges, their Politbüro colleagues deserted them, even though, like the weak and typically vacillating Grotewohl, they had originally supported Herrnstadt's diagnosis of the SED's errors. On 8 July, Zaisser was relieved of his ministerial post and five days later he, Herrnstadt, Hans Jendretzky, Elli Schmidt and Ackermann, despite the latter's last-minute self-criticism, were removed from the Politbüro. The reins of power were firmly in Ulbricht's hands.

Beria's plans for Germany

As the SED regime tottered under the weight of popular opposition, the survival of the GDR as a separate state came under renewed threat as a result of the Kremlin's reassessment of the Soviet Union's strategic interests. After Stalin's death, the new leadership was anxious to strike a more conciliatory note in its relations with the West as it was concerned about American nuclear superiority and the possibility of West German rearmament. Furthermore, it wished to acquire breathing space for urgently needed economic recovery and regime consolidation at home. The more flexible approach found expression in Beria's thinking on Germany. Newly released evidence in the form of memoirs, oral testimonies and Russian archival materials lends some support to an earlier interpretation that Beria, the brutal, long-serving head of Soviet security, was not averse to a Soviet withdrawal from its unstable East German satellite and the creation of a neutral, democratic Germany. The veteran Soviet statesman Andrei Gromyko recalled in his memoirs that Beria was scornfully dismissive of the GDR: 'It's not even a real state. It's only kept in place by Soviet troops . . .'[44] This kind of thinking was anathema to the Foreign Minister, Molotov, who argued that the termination of socialism in the GDR would so discourage the East German and other East European Communists that their states would eventually defect to the West.[45]

The evidence has to be handled with the utmost care as much of it derives from the accounts of Beria's rivals in the vicious struggle to succeed Stalin. One of the main sources for Beria's ideas on Germany is the stenographic record of the proceedings of the CPSU Central Committee meeting in July 1953, held shortly after Beria's arrest.[46] The statements by Bulganin and others that Beria planned to incorporate the GDR into a bourgeois German state cannot be accepted at face value as they were part of the general campaign to discredit Beria.[47] There are, however, other materials which also indicate that a retreat from the GDR was indeed a possibility. One of Beria's top security agents, Pavel Sudaplatov, has testified that he was authorised by Beria, without the knowledge of the other Soviet leaders, to appoint two agents to test the opinion of West German and American politicians on the creation of an all-German state under a coalition government.[48]

If Sudaplatov's version is correct, then it is reasonable to assume that Beria was motivated by a wish to relieve the Soviet Union of the burden of an ailing GDR and by the attraction of Western financial and economic aid for the Soviet Union. Soviet security interests, it could be argued, were being damaged rather than furthered by maintaining a Soviet presence in an economically stricken and politically volatile East German state. Beria's ideas may have attracted the sympathy, at least initially, of Malenkov. Like Beria, the pragmatic Malenkov was concerned about the burden of Soviet subsidies to the GDR and feared that the use of force in the GDR would undermine peaceful coexistence with the West. But whatever Malenkov's original stance on German unification, he soon joined in the general condemnation of Beria's policy at the decisive May Presidium meeting. If the record is accurate, Molotov insisted that only a Communist system could guarantee peace and Khrushchev denounced those who wished to abandon 18 million East Gemans to the Soviet Union's implacable American foe.[49] The New Course was regarded as a more

[74] appropriate alternative. While, on balance, it seems that Beria did at least en-
tertain the idea of a neutral and democratic Germany, it is highly doubtful
whether his interpretation of democracy would have met Western criteria or
whether he would have been able to extract satisfactory guarantees for Soviet
security. Whatever the truth behind the episode, it does at least indicate that
the GDR was expendable if Soviet goals could be attained through an appropriate reconfiguration of Germany. But perhaps more significantly, it demon-
strates that most of the top leaders were unwilling to sacrifice their East
German outpost given the intensity of the struggle with Western 'imperialism' and given their memory of the losses suffered by the Soviet Union in the
war against the Third Reich.

The East German dictatorship: a contested domination

Despite Soviet wavering on the future of the GDR, there was no disputing
that the country had acquired most of the basic characteristics of the standard
Stalinist societal model or what Hermann Weber has called the broader
version of Stalinism.[50] That is to say, the SED led and directed society,
the majority of mass organisations had been reduced to little more than
transmission belts of the party, an economic planning system had been introduced, private ownership in industry and, though to a lesser extent, trade had
been superseded by public ownership. The social structure was undergoing a
radical transformation, too. The Junkers had been swept away, the status and
privileges of the traditional middle classes had been eroded and the supporters of the SED enjoyed new opportunities for social mobility. The terroristic
and repressive features of the Stalinist system, which Weber has designated
Stalinism in the narrow sense of the concept, were also present: the political
police and security forces were integral elements of the system, physical force
had been used to crush the June Uprising, and Marxism-Leninism provided
the compass for ideological indoctrination and social change in the self-
proclaimed first workers' and peasants' state on German soil. This thoroughly ruthless system of domination can, with justice, be classified as a
dictatorship and, the many later changes notwithstanding, would remain so
until the demise of the SED. But as the term 'dictatorship' can be applied to so
many diverse regimes, should the adjective 'totalitarian' be added, as Friedrich and Brzezinski insisted, in order to distinguish both the Communist and

fascist dictatorships from other forms of autocracy? As indicated in the introduction, they held that totalitarian dictatorships were markedly different
from earlier autocracies in that modern technology afforded them greater
opportunities for control, they pursued a more radical restructuring of the
social order in accordance with ideological goals and they were intrinsically
hostile to human dignity and freedom. However, while the developments in
the Soviet zone and the GDR outlined above afford some support to the
application of the totalitarian label to the Stalinist period between 1945 and
1953, reality's match with the model was far from complete. For example,
many impediments obstructed the party dictatorship's claim to total power:
other political parties, such as the CDU, exercised a modicum of influence;
the Churches, which had managed to frustrate the regime's efforts to transform them into transmission belts, represented an alternative *Weltanschauung*
to Marxism-Leninism; and the Federal Republic loomed large as a source of
countervalues and an alternative destination for dissaffected citizens. The
existence of the 'other' German state rendered emotional as well as functional
support for the GDR a perennial problem for its Communist rulers. Other
constraints were also significant. Many 'bourgeois' doctors and engineers
had survived the reshaping of society; collectivisation in agriculture had
made chequered progress; and many lesser Nazis had escaped denazification.
The June Uprising underlined the palpable failure of the SED to mobilise
mass support behind the slogan of the workers' and peasants' state. Indeed,
the main steering instruments, such as the SED, the police and the Stasi, were
by no means monolithic and efficient; they had all been found wanting in
1953. And the SED did not enjoy full control over its own internal affairs
as it was so heavily dependent on Moscow, and its leaders were necessarily
ultra-sensitive to developments in the Soviet Union. Destalinisation would
soon present an unwelcome reminder of this dependency as the Kremlin
strove to come to terms with the Communist world after Stalin.

References

1. Staritz D. 1996: 67; Weber H. 1985: 191

2. Staritz D. 1996: 54–9

3. Cited in Steele J. 1977: 71

4. Loth W. 1994: 223–5

[76] 5. Wettig G. 1994: 816–29

6. Otto W. 1991: 389

7. Ibid.

8. Scherstjanoi E. 1994: 357–60

9. Staritz D. 1996: 96–7; Stöckigt R. 1990: 652

10. Ulbricht W. 1968: 206

11. Weber H. 1991: 63

12. Ulbricht W. 1968: 210

13. Mitter A., Wolle S. 1993: 49

14. Details in Diedrich T. 1991: 13, 19, 25, 34–5, 46; Hagen M. 1992: 24; Schulz D. 1993: 14

15. Mitter A., Wolle S. 1993: 47; Hagen M. 1992: 26; Diedrich T. 1991: 44

16. Loth W. 1994: 196

17. Wendt H. 1991: 390

18. Stöckigt R. 1990: 651–4

19. Wengst U. 1993: 281

20. Mitter A., Wolle S. 1993: 281

21. Hagen M. 1992: 36

22. Mitter A., Wolle S. 1993: 72

23. Ibid., 74–6

24. Brandt H. 1970: 208

25. Diedrich T. 1991: 81–7

26. This view is contested by Diedrich in ibid., 152–3

27. Ibid., 132–3, 288–93

28. Mitter A., Wolle S. 1993: 101–2

29. Mitter A. 1991: 35

30. Kocka, J., Sabrow M. 1994: 50, 55

31. The details are to be found in Mitter A., Wolle S. 1993: 105, 126; Hagen M. 1992: 174–5; Diedrich T. 1994: 300; Richie A. 1988: 686

32. Wengst U. 1993: 280, 305, 321

33. Brant S. 1955: 160

34. Mitter A., Wolle S. 1993: 120–3, 136–7; Mitter A. 1991: 36–7

35. Diedrich T. 1991: 145–6

36. Rexin M. 1992: 94, 101; Larres K. 1994: 573

37. Cited in Steininger R. 1984: 130

38. Spittmann I. 1984: 204

39. Zubok V., Pleshkov C. 1996: 162–3

40. Hagen M. 1992: 188

41. Stulz-Herrnstadt N. 1990: 106, 109–10

42. Hagen M. 1992: 189

43. Müller-Enbergs H. 1991: 249; Loth W. 1994: 214

44. Gromyko A. 1989: 407

45. Zubok V., Pleshakov C. 1996: 161

46. Printed in Knoll V., Kölm L. 1993

47. Richter J. 1993: 671–2

48. Sudaplatov P., Sudaplatov A. 1994: 363–4

49. Wettig G. 1993: 676; Loth W. 1994: 200–1

50. Weber H. 1993: 138

CHAPTER FOUR

FROM REVISIONISM TO THE WALL

The resumption of the socialist project

After the suppression of the June Uprising, the SED did not immediately renounce the New Course as it was obliged to respect Soviet preference for a more conciliatory policy and it also needed to pacify the East German population. Accordingly, in July 1953, Grotewohl promised an improvement in living standards by shifting resources from heavy industry to the consumer goods industry and agriculture. In October, prices were reduced on a range of foodstuffs and semi-luxuries. However, like so many other little Stalinists in Eastern Europe, Ulbricht was opposed to reform. He had no intention of abandoning the SED's power monopoly and he was determined to restore order in the party through a major purge of the membership and the executive organs. By the end of 1954, 60 per cent of members of regional executives elected in 1952 and over 70 per cent of First and Second District Secretaries had been jettisoned.[1] The SED's Fourth Party Congress in February–March 1954 reaffirmed its commitment to Marxist-Leninist ideology; in the following year, Ulbricht, with reference to the New Course, asserted, 'It was never our intention to choose such a false course and we will never choose it.'

The reassertion of the party's socialist mission had major implications for the structure of the GDR economy.[2] By the end of the first five-year plan in 1955, state-owned enterprises in industry accounted for 87 per cent of gross industrial production and employed 2.2 million people. Although in light industry and foodstuffs only one-quarter of firms were state owned, they were responsible for two-thirds of employment and 70 per cent of production. Wholesale trade was virtually monopolised by the state. A different pattern prevailed in crafts, which remained basically under private ownership. In agriculture, a resumption by the SED in early 1954 of collectivisation boosted the number of LPGs; however, by the close of 1957, only about 25 per cent [79] of agriculturally useful land was worked by cooperative farms.

The pace of economic change had a radical impact on the social structure, notably in a marked decline in independents and a sharp rise in public sector employees.[3] Whereas in 1950 there were 4 million workers, 1.7 million white-collar employees, 1.1 million independents and 1 million family dependants, five years later the numbers were 6.5 million workers and white-collar employees (the two categories having been combined in the official statistics), 900,000 independents and 650,000 family dependants. By 1955, 68 per cent of all workers were in state employment, a clear indicator of the growing influence exercised by the state and party apparatus over the economy and of the decimation of the traditional property-owning middle class. The social revolution was well advanced. Despite new opportunities for social mobility, the continuing high level of emigration testified to a widespread opposition to the SED's comprehensive transformation of society. Emigration, though lower than in 1953, reached 184,198 in 1954 and 252,870 in 1955.

Destalinisation

The overcentralisation and the all-pervasive influence of the party and state bureaucracy came under fire from intellectuals tired of the overregulation of culture. A new philosophy journal, launched in 1953, the *Deutsche Zeitschrift für Philosophie*, encouraged a debate on the relationship between Marx and Hegel; in 1954, the journal published an article by Georg Lukács criticising the Stalinist concept of 'party-mindedness'. Political economists, too, sought to tackle the problem of overcentralisation by propagating ideas on price reform. But it was not until Khrushchev's denunciation at a secret session of the CPSU Party Congress in February 1956 of the personality cult and the terroristic methods of Stalin that a decisive impulse was given to a wide-ranging debate on reform.

Ulbricht rightly feared that Khrushchev's destalinisation campaign jeopardised his own political position and the fragile stability of the GDR. He had been closely associated with the late dictator and had lauded Stalin as 'one of the greatest living theoreticians of scientific socialism'. Ulbricht sought to limit the damage: no critique of the personality cult was permitted and only minor errors were admitted. The autocratic SED leader was unwilling to criticise Stalin beyond a begrudging admission that 'Stalin can no longer be

[80] ranked among the classics of Marxism'. Some concessions were made: 11,000 prisoners, including 600 former Social Democrats, were released by June 1956 and at the SED Party Conference in March the leadership dangled the bait of an increase in pensions and a reduction in the working week from 48 to 45 hours. The 1956–60 economic plan envisaged an improvement in labour productivity by at least 50 per cent and a rise in real wages by about 30 per cent. It was hoped that these targets would be achieved by further socialisation of the economy and by what the party hailed as a new industrial revolution based on modernisation, mechanisation and automation.

The blatant attempt by the SED to survive the shock of destalinisation by a modicum of self-criticism aroused widespread popular opposition, as is evidenced in Stasi reports on the continuing unpopularity of Ulbricht and widespread dissatisfaction with his muted reaction to the Soviet attack on the personality cult.[4] Another setback to the leadership was the poor performance of the economy, arousing fears that the poor supply situation might trigger off social unrest, as had happened in the Polish industrial city of Poznan in June. So serious was the situation by the autumn of 1956 that the SED was obliged to seek Moscow's assistance to relieve the shortages of foodstuffs and materials in the machine-building, chemical and light industries.[5]

Revisionism

Although the GDR was less affected by the tide of revisionism and popular unrest than Poland and Hungary, Ulbricht was unable to keep the revisionist genie in the socialist bottle. A lively debate ensued among artists and intellectuals in literature, history, economics and philosophy, and whereas worker dissatisfaction did not spark off another 17 June, new research has shown that workers were not so passive as was formerly believed. In the late summer and autumn of 1956, reports proliferated of strikes and spontaneous walkouts. The disturbances reached a peak in October. While Magdeburg was the centre of worker unrest, many other towns were affected, including Dresden, Wismar and Neubrandenburg. An official analysis of 44 strikes between April and early October concluded that disputes over wages and work norms were the main reason for the strikes. From about mid-October, not only did the strikes increase but also, under the impact of events in Poland and Hungary, the growing unrest at the universities acquired a political dimension.[6] However, despite predictions of another 17 June, the GDR working class was unwilling to risk another open confrontation with the SED regime and, unlike in Hungary, kept its distance from the dissent among the intellectuals.

Many university and college students were excited by Khrushchev's destalinisation campaign and by the revisionist ideas of GDR intellectuals. The political temperature in the universities was raised by the installation of Gomulka as First Secretary of the Polish United Workers Party on 19 October and by the appointment of Nagy as Hungarian Prime Minister soon afterwards. Both Gomulka and Nagy subscribed to more liberal policies than the arch-Stalinists in their parties. Gomulka favoured the decollectivisation of agriculture and a Polish path to socialism, whereas Nagy supported the restoration of a multi-party system. On 1 November, Nagy took a quantum leap when he proclaimed Hungary's neutrality. These developments in Hungary and Poland could be legitimised by reference to Khrushchev's reassertion of the concept of national paths to socialism. This was not, however, a path along which the SED could venture without drawing attention to the intractable problem of the division of Germany and to the party's subordination to Moscow.

An embryonic student opposition movement sprang up at the universities in Leipzig, Dresden, Halle, Rostock, Greifswald and East Berlin. Students, sometimes with the backing of their lecturers, demanded greater press and academic freedom, the founding of an independent student organisation, the dissolution of the FDJ, and free and open discussion without the threat of reprisals.[7] Both within the universities and the SED's own research institutions, historians, philosophers and social scientists attacked the dogmatism, the overcentralisation and other deficiencies of the socialist system, though not with the same degree of radical intensity as their Polish and Hungarian counterparts. Two economists, Fritz Behrens, the Director of the Central Statistical Office, and his senior assistant at the Institute for Economics and Sciences, Arne Benary, proposed a greater role for economic laws and the promotion of workers' initiatives and efficiency through economic levers such as prices, profit, taxation, wages and credit. Although the state was accorded a role in economic planning, they rejected the administrative method of planning and management. Behrens attacked as Prussian, not socialist, the view 'that the state can do everything and that every little concern, even the most private one, must be controlled and directed by the state'.[8]

Ernst Bloch, one of Germany's most eminent philosophers and a professor at the University of Leipzig, the historian Jürgen Kuczyinski, the scientist Robert Havemann and the philosopher Wolfgang Harich were among the many scholars who explored the possibility of a reformed socialism. Harich

[82]   and a loosely organised group of like-minded intellectuals, among them Walter Janka and Manfred Hertwig, were in the vanguard of the diffuse oppositional tendencies. Harich was a professor in philosophy at East Berlin's Humboldt University and editor-in-chief of the *Deutsche Zeitschrift für Philosophie*. Janka, the head of the *Aufbau* publishing house, had been imprisoned by the National Socialists and had commanded a battalion in the Spanish Civil War. Two other members of the intra-party opposition 'group', Heinz Zöger and Gustav Just, were editor-in-chief and deputy editor respectively of the weekly cultural paper *Sonntag*. Harich and his colleagues hoped that the thaw in the Soviet Union would enable them to promote a real debate on Stalinism – not simply on Stalin and his mistakes – which would lead to the creation of a democratic socialism.

Harich discussed his ideas not only with West German Social Democrats but also with the Soviet ambassador Georgi Pushkin and, on 7 November, at Ulbricht's command, with the SED leader himself. Pushkin advised Harich that his views were too theoretical to appeal to the masses and that he should support Ulbricht, the most 'competent' man in the German labour movement.[9] Despite this warning, Harich was persuaded by his colleagues to publish his basic theses in order to stimulate a general discussion. The programme, or 'Platform', which Harich drafted was a mixture of Social Democratic and Marxist-Leninist ideas. Conceived as a special German road to socialism, it advocated a series of reforms: a destalinised and democratised SED; the restoration of parliamentary democracy and freedom of thought; the dissolution of the Stasi and the introduction of the rule of law; the termination of the forced collectivisation of agriculture; and the introduction of workers' councils on the Yugoslav pattern. These reforms would, it was believed, provide the basis for a socialist, neutral, united Germany sealed by cooperation between the SPD and a reformed SED. Optimistically assuming that the SPD would win a majority in free all-German elections, Harich looked forward to the implementation of socialist policies such as the nationalisation of key industries and land reform.

Given the haste with which it was drawn up, it is not surprising that the 'Platform' contained many practical and theoretical loose ends. But before it could be refined and presented for discussion to a wider audience, Harich was arrested on 29 November and Janka soon afterwards. In March 1957, Harich and two colleagues, Bernhard Steinberger and Manfred Hartwig – and, three months later, Janka, Zöger and Just – were sentenced to imprisonment after two high-profile show trials. They were accused of membership of a treasonable group which aspired through counterrevolutionary methods to

liquidate the GDR. Harich was sentenced to ten years and Just to five years' [83]
imprisonment. This was the decisive blow in the campaign against intellectual revisionism in the GDR, an offensive which was propelled by the SED
leadership's fears of undesirable political shockwaves from Hungary and of
social unrest arising from the deteriorating economic situation. Ulbricht
branded revisionism as a form of Social Democracy or a 'Third Way' which
endangered the anti-fascist, socialist GDR. His counteroffensive was aided
by the failure of the East German intellectuals and workers to establish a common front and by the abstention of sections of the intelligentsia who did not
wish to jeopardise their social and professional privileges. Many other intellectuals, though not unsympathetic, remained loyal to the regime, preferring
the notion of building socialism in the GDR. The elimination of the Harich
'group' could not, however, be carried out until the Soviet leadership had
decided that liberalisation in Eastern Europe contained too many intrinsic
risks for Communist rule and had moved to crush the Hungarian Uprising in
early November 1956.

Harich's arrest was followed by a wave of arrests, denunciations and expulsions from the SED and the universities continuing into 1958. Among the
leading critical intellectuals, Behrens lost his position as head of the Statistical Office, Bloch was reduced to the status of emeritus professor and Kuczynski
went on an extended visit to China. The end of the intellectual thaw and a
harsher enforcement of the penal code produced a sharp increase in the number
of prisoners, from 22,861 in 1956 to 36,889 in 1958. The trials against the
revisionists were not terminated until December 1958, with the trial of Erich
Loest and four other writers.[10]

Schirdewan and the inner-party
opposition to Ulbricht

Ulbricht's position as party leader came under a renewed challenge from senior colleagues who favoured more internal party democracy, less centralisation and greater collective control over the General Secretary. Among the
proponents of destalinisation were: Karl Schirdewan, since July 1953 a
member of the Politbüro and Central Committee Secretary for Cadre Questions; Fred Oelssner, the Deputy Chairman of the Council of Ministers; Paul
Wandel, Central Committee Secretary for Culture; and Gerhard Ziller, the
Central Committee Secretary for the Economy. Schirdewan, born in 1907,

[84] had been a member of the KPD since 1925 and had been imprisoned during the Third Reich in the Sachsenhausen, Mauthausen and Flossenbürg concentration camps. Oelssner, three years older than Schirdewan, joined the KPD in 1920 and spent most of the war in the Soviet Union, where he was head of the German section of Moscow radio. Later, his political communication skills were deployed as editor of the SED's theoretical journal, *Einheit*; he entered the Politbüro in 1950.

Despite their sufferings at the hands of the Nazis, Ulbricht was always suspicious of cadres like Schirdewan and Selbmann who had not resided in the Soviet Union. Loosely associated with Schirdewan was Ernst Wollweber, who had succeeded the disgraced Zaisser as Minister of State Security in 1953. Wollweber, born in 1898, joined the KPD in 1919 and participated in the KPD's putschist actions during the Weimar Republic. A determined opponent of the National Socialists, he lived in Scandinavia for much of the Nazi era. As Minister of State Security, he soon came into conflict with Ulbricht over the General Secretary's attempt to strengthen party control over the ministry. Another source of conflict was the party's hard line against revisionists and students, a policy which Wollweber judged to be a tactical error. Wollweber, however, was not a liberal in Stasi clothing: he had no sympathy for revisionism and regarded Harich as a counterrevolutionary.[11]

The main planks of Schirdewan's reform programme included: an open debate on the problems arising from the authoritarian style of leadership in the party; the dismantling of democratic centralism; a relaxation of censorship; a slowing down of the collectivisation of agriculture and crafts; and striking a balance between heavy industry and the consumer goods industry. Unlike Harich, he did not put his ideas down in writing for fear of exposing himself to the charge of forming a faction, thereby presenting Ulbricht with an easy target to crush his internal critics.[12] Schirdewan claims in his memoirs, published after the downfall of the GDR, that he was personally encouraged by Khrushchev to initiate a political thaw and that top Soviet functionaries such as Semyonov and Tuil'panov expressed 'a certain moral support' for his ideas.[13] It is, however, highly unlikely that Krushchev ever regarded him as an East German Gomulka.

Schirdewan cherished the hope that a conciliatory and gradual approach to the construction of socialism would halt the flight to the FRG and ultimately enable the SED to emerge victorious in a reunified state.[14] It is not clear, however, how socialism was to be mixed with capitalism; perhaps Schirdewan hoped that better relations between the SED and the SPD and the development of a more attractive socialism in the GDR would provide the foundation for a socialist Germany. His form of socialism, though less doctrinaire than that espoused by Ulbricht and Polibüro members such as Matern and Neumann, was probably still too ideologically narrow to attract widespread support either in East or West Germany. Schirdewan reveals in his memoirs that he was willing to succeed Ulbricht but only after a critical discussion and a secret vote at a Party Congress.[15] Yet, like Herrnstadt several years earlier, Schirdewan lacked the determination and the adroitness to organise an effective opposition to Ulbricht. This is borne out by Wollweber's view, expressed in the manuscript which he drafted in 1964, that Ulbricht was the more skilful political operator of the two. The former Stasi chief favoured Schirdewan's appointment as Ulbricht's deputy, not his successor.[16]

When Moscow retreated from its liberalisation course after the troubles in Poland and Hungary, Ulbricht was able to seize the opportunity to undermine his critics' position during 1957 and then to remove them from office in 1958. Ulbricht was able to count on the support of Politbüro colleagues such as Matern and Neumann, the politically orthodox Kurt Hager and Erich Honecker, and the former Social Democrat Erich Mückenberger. The suicide of Ziller in December 1957, after he had been criticised by Ulbricht during a Politbüro meeting, was a cruel setback to a cause which had already been seriously weakened by the condemnnation of revisionism at the World Conference of Communist Parties in mid-November. At the decisive SED Central Committee Plenum in February 1958, Honecker moved on to the attack, branding Schirdewan, Oelssner and Wollweber as revisionists and accusing them, unjustly, of the deadly sin of forming a faction. Oelssner was removed from the Politbüro and became director of the Institute of Economics at the Academy of Sciences. Wollweber was forced to resign and Schirdewan was relegated to head of the State Archive in Potsdam. He had to surrender this post in 1965; however, he was rehabilitated by the PDS in 1990 and emerged after the *Wende* as a remarkably alert octogenarian.

Ulbricht's rout of his rivals secured his position as party leader so firmly that he did not face another serious challenge until the close of the 1960s, ironically from a group headed by Erich Honecker. Although outside events had favoured Ulbricht, his survival owed much to his own skills. His careful attention to detail and to cadre policy had enabled him to retain control over the party apparat. He had also kept his political nerve in steering a course between his revisionist critics and the fluctuations in the Soviet leadership's destalinisation policy. When President Pieck died in September 1960, Ulbricht, as Chairman of the recently created Council of State, became *de facto* head of state.

Overtaking West Germany?

As the undisputed ruler of the SED, Ulbricht felt able to set a bold agenda at the Fifth SED Party Congress in July 1958: the acceleration of economic growth; the attainment of world standards in certain areas of science and technology; and equalling and then overtaking the West German population's per capita consumption of all important foodstuffs and consumer goods within a few years. The achievement of the latter goal would, in Ulbricht's view, demonstrate the decisive victory of socialism in its competition with the capitalist order. A few weeks after the end of the congress, the SED fixed 1961 as the date by which the the GDR would overtake the FRG. These highly ambitious goals fitted in with the Soviet Union's strategy to overtake the USA in the most important branches of agriculture and industrial production. The ebullient Khrushchev ventured to predict that the Soviet Union and its socialist allies would soon be able to attain, more or less together, the higher phase of Communism.

The SED leaders appear to have been genuinely optimistic that the GDR could outstrip the FRG at a time when Soviet successes in military technology and space encouraged a belief in the global victory of Communism. Labour productivity, the Achilles heel of the GDR economy, was to be boosted by the concentration of scientific-technical work and R&D capacity in crucial industrial sectors and by the development of socialism in small business, crafts and agriculture. In an interview with *Neues Deutschland* in August 1959, Ulbricht asserted that the completion of the seven-year plan in 1965 would demonstrate the superiority of the GDR's socialist order. Chancellor Erhardt's attempts to convince West German workers of the SED's lack of realism were, according to Ulbricht, equivalent to Don Quixote tilting at the sails of the windmill. But this was precisely what the GDR was doing. The overtaking of the FRG in so short a time was unattainable when, as even the Politbüro realised, East German labour productivity lagged 25 to 30 per cent behind that of West Germany. Moreover, as Ulbricht informed Khrushchev in May 1958, the GDR was far inferior to West Germany in the vital raw materials needed for economic development and an improvement in living standards.[17] He could, if he had so wished, added modern technologies, materials and investments to the list of the GDR's disadvantages.

The GDR's transition from capitalism to socialism, as plotted by the Fifth Party Congress, encompassed not only structural changes in the economy but also the formation of a new, socialist consciousness and a higher development of culture. As the working class was, in Ulbricht's words, 'master' in the state and economy, it was enjoined to 'storm the heights of culture',[18] so overcoming the gap between art and life and the alienation between artists and people. This was the prelude to a conference on literature in the industrial town of Bitterfeld in April 1959 which launched the Bitterfeld Path. While the movement managed to stimulate considerable cultural activity among workers, the artistic quality did not match official expectations. The development of a new society and culture was to be underpinned by an appropriate code of ethics which raised collective over individual interests. The ten commandments of the new socialist morality unveiled by Ulbricht at the Fifth Party Congress were intended to fulfil this purpose. East Germans were exhorted to 'act in the spirit of mutual support and comradely cooperation', 'protect and increase the property of the people', 'always seek ways to improve thy performance, be thrifty and strengthen socialist labour discipline', 'bring up thy children in the spirit of peace and socialism to become citizens who are well educated, strong in character and physically healthy', and 'live a clean and decent life and respect thy family'.[19]

Of more significance than this mix of petty bourgeois and socialist values was the reorganisation of the entire education system. This was intended to equip young East Germans with the skills required for work in the socialist economy and to promote their development as socialist personalities.[20] In December 1959, new legislation paved the way for the establishment, by 1964, of the ten-year polytechnical secondary school. Polytechnical instruction was intended to give pupils an insight into the work environment and to enable them to cope with the new demands in science and technology. Seventy per cent of the curriculum was to be devoted to mathematics, engineering, the natural sciences and economics. Similar principles underpinned the discussions at the Third Higher Education Conference in February–March 1958 which established the basis of reforms in higher education. Science was to be closely linked to agriculture and industry and students would graduate as well-qualified specialists. Ideological indoctrination was not to be neglected, however: pupils and students were to become well versed in the canons of Marxism-Leninism. This aspiration was not readily reconciled with the need for professional expertise, a conflict which would become more acute after the advent of the New Economic System in 1963.

The reassertion by the Fifth SED Party Congress of the construction of socialism paved the way for a renewed acceleration of the collectivisation of handicrafts and agriculture. Between 1957 and 1960, the number of PGHs rose from 295 to almost 3,900 and the number of PGH members from 8,100 to 144,000. These cooperatives accounted for about 28 per cent of the total

[88] turnover in handicrafts.[21] The elimination of private ownership in the countryside was seen as removing a major impediment to the realisation of SED
goals: a higher level of production, an improvement in living standards, the
correction of the disparity between socialist development in industry and
agriculture, and a victory for the administrative-command economic order
over revisionist deviations concerning private agriculture.

A rapid increase in the number of LPGs was recorded in 1958; by the end
of the following year, the percentage of agriculturally useful land farmed by
cooperatives had risen to 45.1 per cent. Judging this as too slow a rate of
progress, the SED resolved to speed up the collectivisation process. By the
end of May 1960, 19,345 LPGs were working 83.9 per cent of agriculturally useful land. Within about three months, the 'socialist spring' had resulted
in the collectivisation of about 2.5 million hectares of land, or almost as much
as in the previous seven years.[22] According to the SED, collectivisation pro-
ceeded on a voluntary basis, with farmers being encouraged to participate by
the prospect of material rewards and by moral appeals to their role in strengthening the GDR peace state. The peasants were not so easily duped. Between
the beginning of 1957 and the end of 1960, 30,000 fled to the West. The
flight from the land gathered momentum in late 1960 and early 1961.
Opposition to SED policy also found expression in strikes, setting fire to the
harvest and neglecting livestock. The SED reacted harshly, particularly after
the building of the Berlin Wall. Labour camps, the death penalty and forced
evacuation from border regions were among the methods used to enforce
policy. With the approval of the Politbüro, the death sentence was imposed
on two rural workers, one for setting a barn on fire and the other for 28 acts
of arson.[23] Courts of justice were empowered to sentence recalcitrant farmers who sought to block collectivisation. Interrogations by the Stasi and
the People's Police forced many peasants to fall into line and special brigades
consisting of members of the Stasi, police and SED employed both physical
and psychological pressure.

The GDR's second existential crisis, 1960–61

The upheaval in the countryside demonstrated that the renewed attempt
to construct socialism as a viable and attractive alternative to the FRG
was drawing the GDR into another existential crisis. The crisis of 1960–61
was very much of the SED's own making: as in 1953, it misjudged the

population's willingness to absorb the shocks of the radical restructuring of society and it overestimated the socialist economy's potential for competing with the FRG. In addition, the international tension created by the Soviet Union's initiatives since 1958 to release the GDR from the Hallstein cage and to revise the status of the divided city of Berlin alarmed many East Germans and precipitated flight to the West.

Signs of an acute societal crisis mounted from early 1960 onwards with the onset of a deep economic depression. There were serious shortages of raw materials, foodstuffs and high-quality industrial products. A scarcity of foreign currency reserves disrupted trade with the West and the Soviet Union and necessitated cuts in vital investments. The GDR's growing economic problems increased the country's dependence on the Soviet Union and other creditors whose exports to the GDR were, to a great extent, paid for in short-term credits. Indebtedness to the West and the Soviet Union made it impossible for the GDR to cover its import requirements. Ulbricht, in a candid letter on 19 October 1960, informed Khrushchev of the deleterious effect which materials and raw materials shortages were having on the construction, motor vehicles and textile industries. By the beginning of 1961, Ulbricht had become even more pessimistic: the gap in labour productivity and living standards between the FRG and the GDR had widened and dissatisfaction was spreading among East German workers and members of the intelligentsia; by contrast, West Germany had recorded, in 1960, its highest rate of economic growth since 1945 and workers were enjoying large wage increases.[24]

Ulbricht painted a similarly gloomy picture at a meeting of the SED Politbüro on 6 June 1961. Advising his colleagues to discount doctored reports in the official media, he admitted serious shortages of consumer goods and foodstuffs, a high death rate among livestock and the failure to achieve plan targets.[25] Popular dissatisfaction with the shortages of foodstuffs, notably bread, butter and milk, was directly linked to the restructuring of agriculture. Residents in the Frankfurt/Oder *Bezirk* commented sarcastically that 'Adenauer can at least feed the population'.[26] The regime's difficulties were compounded by Bonn's decision in September 1960 to terminate the interzonal trade agreement of 1951 in protest against restrictions imposed on West Germans seeking entry into East Berlin. As GDR industry was highly dependent on West Germany for equipment, spare parts and materials such as high-grade steel, Bonn's action caused so much disruption that the SED implemented a series of measures aimed at freeing the GDR from undue interference by the FRG (*Störfreimachung*). This involved adjusting some areas of production to Soviet supplies, thereby making the GDR even more reliant on the Soviet Union for crucial imports. By tying the GDR more closely to Soviet

[90]   demands for investment goods, it impeded the modernisation of the East German economy. Khrushchev was sympathetic to SED requests for aid as he regarded the GDR as a crucial geopolitical and ideological ally; his patience snapped, however, when Ulbricht requested *Gastarbeiter* from the Soviet Union. He retorted, 'We won the war . . . Our workers will not clean your toilets'.[27]

Not the least of Ulbricht's problems was the surge in emigration to the West: 143,917 in 1959, 199,188 in 1960 and 155,402 by 12 August 1961.[28] As rumours spread that the border might be closed, panic set in, with 30,000 fleeing in April alone. The flow was increased, not stemmed, by Ulbricht's enigmatic statement at a press conference on 15 June that nobody had the intention of building a wall. According to East as well as West German analyses of emigration during these three years, the 18–24 age group and young workers were significantly overrepresented; these were groups which the GDR could ill afford to lose.[29] Flight was by no means confined to the young and the socially mobile; the high rate of exodus among SED members, pensioners and a high proportion of women all demonstrate that the GDR was in the midst of an acute crisis which was threatening its very existence. The immediate threat came not from a repeat of the 17 June Uprising, as the police and security forces were far more vigilant than in 1953, but from the draining away of the country's human potential, the blatant political bankruptcy of the regime and economic dislocation.

The reasons for the mass exodus were investigated by GDR agencies. A report prepared on 24 May 1961 by a unit of the Central Committee Department for Security Questions pinpointed a wide range of motives behind flight: deficiencies in the production and planning processes; a heartless bureaucracy; the SED's unrealistic policy aims; the desire of young people for travel; and the greater security offered by West Germany at a time of acute international tension. Other motives included personal and social problems such as marital difficulties, inadequate housing and a wish to join relatives in the West.[30] Western surveys, which arrived at similar findings, drew particular attention to the higher earnings and better career opportunities in the FRG and to political factors such as active opposition to the regime or a conflict of conscience in the crisis years of 1953 and 1961.

The second Berlin crisis, 1958–62

The SED's domestic problems were exacerbated by the second Berlin crisis of 1958–62. The crisis was triggered off in November 1958 by Khrushchev's famous ultimatum to the Western powers. Contending that the

Western Allies had forfeited the right to remain in Berlin because of violations of the Potsdam Agreement, he demanded that West Berlin become a free, demilitarised city, possibly under the auspices of the United Nations, and that access to the city would have to be negotiated with the GDR. If this demand were not accepted within six months, Khrushchev warned the West that the Soviet Union would implement the proposals by means of an agreement with the GDR. The Soviets raised the stakes in February 1959 by threatening to sign a separate peace treaty with the GDR unless a peace treaty was concluded between the two German states. On occasions, Khrushchev heightened tension by crude threats. In June 1959, he told the veteran American diplomat Averell Harimann, '[W]e are determined to liquidate your rights in Western Berlin . . . You can start a war if you like, but remember it will be you who are starting it, not we . . . West Germany knows that we could destroy it in ten minutes . . . If you start a war, we may die but the rockets will fly automatically'.[31]

The motives behind Khrushchev's gamble have been the subject of much debate. His challenge to the West was undoubtedly influenced by the boost to his confidence from his country's technological achievements, notably the Sputnik, and from a widespread – though erroneous – belief in the Soviet Union's superiority in missile capability over the USA. The time therefore seemed appropriate for a bold initiative to wrest concessions from the West by applying pressure on one of its exposed nerves, West Berlin, or, as Khrushchev put it, to make the West scream by squeezing on West Berlin, the 'testicles of the West'.[32] Not only was Khrushchev apparently hoping to neutralise West Berlin as a centre of subversion against Eastern Europe and as a magnet of consumerism and democracy for East Germans, but also to secure Western recognition of the GDR and, in time, to enhance the GDR's appeal to West Germans. Another major consideration was his desire to forestall NATO plans to deploy nuclear missiles in West Germany. These objectives were welcomed by the SED Politbüro. Although their optimum solution was the incorporation of West into East Berlin, the establishment of West Berlin with the status of a Free City would, it was hoped, close the main exit door to the West, remove a major destabilising factor and, through the full incorporation of the GDR into negotiations, lead to Western recognition of the GDR as a fully sovereign state. An increase in the GDR's room for manoeuvre in its relations with the Soviet Union was seen as another benefit.

The GDR's international position had improved in the mid-1950s when it had become more firmly integrated into the Soviet bloc. After the failure of the Foreign Ministers' Conference in 1954 to resolve the problem of German unification, Moscow entered into full diplomatic relations with East Berlin.

[92] Despite a treaty concluded in September 1955 which provided the GDR with sovereignty over its external and internal affairs, GDR sovereignty was circumscribed by the Soviet Union's retention of its rights as an occupying power. Other indicators of the enhancement of the GDR's status in the Soviet bloc were the GDR's involvement in the founding of the bloc's security system, the Warsaw Pact (in May 1955) and Khrushchev's announcement two months later, at a meeting in East Berlin, of Moscow's concept of two German states. German unification, Khrushchev assured his audience, would not take place to the detriment of the GDR's socialist achievements. Together with West Germany's entry into NATO and its regaining of sovereignty in 1955, this terminated immediate hopes of German unification; the GDR did not, however, formally abandon its commitment to unification as, for both internal and external reasons, it sought to pose as the true defender of the interests of the German people.

These undoubted improvements notwithstanding, the GDR's international status remained low. Only the Soviet bloc and a few Third World countries recognised the GDR diplomatically and West Germany refused to accept it as a sovereign state. The Hallstein Doctrine, which had been conceived in 1955 when West Germany had established diplomatic relations with the Soviet Union, was intended to underpin Bonn's claim to be the only legitimate voice of the German people. According to this doctrine, Bonn threatened to break off relations with any third country which, like Yugoslavia in 1957, accorded diplomatic recognition to the GDR. The Soviet Union, as one of the four occupying powers, was treated as an exception. Even in its relations with the Soviet Union, the GDR's position was a highly qualified one. While the Soviet Union withdrew, in late 1956, many of its political advisers on the State Planning Commission and other economic bodies, it exerted its influence through directives, informal structures, meetings of specialists and the transfer of many of the controlling functions of the Soviet High Commissioner to the Soviet embassy in East Berlin. The presence of the Soviet forces, too, represented another form of control but, as was so typical of the complex GDR–Soviet relationship, it also functioned as an essential prop for the East German Communist regime.

A sharp reminder of the GDR's reliance on Moscow occurred during the second Berlin crisis over the status of Berlin and the GDR's rights over the access routes to the city. Khrushchev refused to give unconditional support to the SED's wish for the GDR to swallow up West Berlin for, while the Soviet Union was anxious to enhance the GDR's diplomatic status, it was neither prepared to sacrifice entirely its rights as an occupying power nor its rights in Germany as a whole. The SED had to back down, too, over its unilateral efforts to restrict the entry of Western officials into East Berlin by insisting on the presentation of identification to GDR border guards. Another disappointment for Ulbricht was Khrushchev's failure to implement his ultimatum to the West, even though the Soviet leader did hold out hopes during 1959 and 1960 that a separate peace treaty would be concluded with the GDR. Faced by Western opposition to his policy, Khrushchev preferred a more flexible course than Ulbricht who, with one eye on the immense benefits to be reaped by the GDR, was more eager than the Soviets to press ahead quickly with the conclusion of a peace treaty and the transformation of West Berlin into a Free City.[33]

The Berlin question caught fire at the Kennedy–Khrushchev summit in Vienna in June 1961. During the heated exchanges, Khrushchev insisted that all of Berlin was on GDR territory and even threatened war if the USA refused to compromise on the issue. Kennedy, in his radio and TV address on 25 July, made it clear that the USA would not back down and that he was prepared to defend the freedom of and access to West Berlin, if necessary by nuclear weapons. The stress on West Berlin reflected the growing opinion in Washington that the USA could do little if the SED tightened controls in Berlin; it was also an indication that Washington was prepared to respect the Soviet sphere of interest.[34] With this formulation of the American stance on Berlin and with Khrushchev unwilling to precipitate a war, the immediate question was how to deal with the GDR's mounting internal crisis.

The Berlin Wall

One way out of the impasse might have been to abandon the hard-line construction of socialism in favour of a programme of domestic reform; however, such a course was not to the liking of committed Stalinists like Ulbricht and Honecker. Their solution was to close the exit door at its most sensitive spot, Berlin, despite the massive loss of prestige and the risk of popular unrest.[35] The SED leader finally received the green light to close the sectoral border in Berlin at a meeting of the First Secretaries of the Communist parties of the Warsaw Pact on 3 to 5 August 1961. Ulbricht, who had stressed the need for such a course of action at an earlier session in March, seems to have concluded, by mid-June at the latest, that the nettle had to be grasped. In early July, he requested the Soviet ambassador to the GDR to inform Moscow that

[94] the GDR was in danger of collapsing unless the borders were sealed. The Soviet leaders had many reservations. They were uncertain as to how the East and West German public would react. Khrushchev apparently continued to hope until the last moment that the problem of the GDR and Berlin could be resolved through diplomatic pressure. A barrier would torpedo this strategy and it would expose the political bankruptcy of socialism. On the other hand, as the Kremlin could not allow a key ally to disintegrate, Khrushchev let it be known in late July that he was not unsympathetic to Ulbricht's request for a barrier. However, it was probably not until the Warsaw Pact meeting in early August that Khrushchev finally agreed to the erection of a barbed wire fence. On 13 August 1961, with Honecker in charge of the operation, makeshift barbed wire fencing and wooden barriers severed the sectoral border in Berlin. The prefabricated concrete blocks soon followed.

Many East Germans found their leaders' actions a bitter pill to swallow. The fierceness of opposition to the Wall emerges from the remarks in the confidential reports on the popular mood compiled for the party leadership. 'There is no freedom or democracy if one cannot visit one's relations' and 'Tanks cannnot keep the peace' were typical comments.[36] Despite the widespread condemnation of the Wall, there was little organised group opposition, partly because of the regime's efficient security measures and the rapidity with which the border was sealed. The three Western powers largely restricted themselves to verbal disapproval. Although denouncing the violation of the four-power status of Berlin, they took no forcible counteraction for, as Kennedy informed his appointments secretary Kenneth O'Donnell, 'It's not a very nice solution . . . but a hell of lot better than a war'.[37] Nevertheless, the situation remained extremely tense and subject to occasional flashpoints, such as the dramatic face-off between American and Soviet tanks at the Checkpoint Charlie crossing point in the Friedrichstraße on 27 October. The immediate crisis over the status of Berlin did not finally abate until the end of the Cuban missile crisis ushered in a gradual improvement in Soviet–American relations.

References

1. Klein T. 1996: 43

2. Weber H. 1985: 260–1; Werkentin F. 1995: 92–3

3. Details in Weber H. 1985: 262–3

4. Mitter A., Wolle S. 1993: 208–10

5. Hoffmann D., Schmitt K.-H., Skyba P. 1993: 235, 261–3

6. Mitter A., Wolle S. 1993: 251–6

7. Weber H. 1985: 284; Meuschel S. 1992: 159; Mitter A., Wolle S. 1993: 260–1, 265

8. Cited in Steele J. 1977: 108

9. Just G. 1990: 110

10. Werkentin F. 1995: 376–9, 408

11. Ernst Wollweber 1990: 365, 375: von Flocken J., Scholz M. F. 1994: 180–2, 186–90

12. Meuschel S. 1992: 165; Schirdewan K. 1994: 81–2, 103–6, 130

13. Ibid., 122–3

14. Grieder P. 1996: 582–4

15. Schirdewan K. 1994: 107

16. Ernst Wollweber 1990: 374

17. Lemke M. 1995a: 53, 56

18. *Protokoll* 1959: 182

19. Translation in McCauley M. 1983: 88

20. Weber H. 1985: 307–8

21. Staritz D. 1996: 183–4

22. Werkentin F. 1995: 97–8; Weber H. 1985: 317

23. Werkentin F. 1995: 108–10

24. Lemke M. 1995a: 15, 63–4; Lemke M. 1995b: 153–4

25. Hoffmann D., Schmidt K.-L., Syba P. 1993: 389, 392

26. Mitter A., Wolle S. 1993: 349

27. Cited in Zubok V., Pleshakov C. 1996: 249

28. Wendt H. 1991: 390

29. Heidemeyer H. 1994: 49, 52

30. Hoffmann D., Schmidt K.-H., Skyba P. 1993: 385, 387–8

[96]   31. Cited in Gaddis J. L. 1997: 142

32. Ibid., 142

33. Lemke M. 1995a: 143, 151

34. Murphy D. E., Kondrashev S. A., Bailey G. 1997: 368

35. For the Soviet and GDR elites' views on a barrier see Lemke M. 1995a: 157–8, 163–6; Lemke M. 1997: 17; Murphy D. E., Kondrashev S. A., Bailey G. 1997: 361, 373; Zubok V., Pleshakov C. 1996: 251; Wettig G. 1997: 392–4

36. Mitter A., Wolle S. 1993: 351

37. Cited in Gelb N. 1986: 201

PART THREE

ULBRICHT AND THE STABILISATION OF THE GDR

CHAPTER FIVE

REBUILDING THE GDR

The world's ugliest frontier

The Berlin Wall, at first little more than a barbed wire fence and a series of barricades, eventually developed into an elaborate and sophisticated barricade 165.7 kilometres in length, including about 46 kilometres around East and West Berlin. It consisted of a concrete wall about 4 metres high, wire mesh fencing, 30 sentry towers, 22 bunkers, guard dog tracks, trip-wires, floodlights and anti-tank emplacements. The Wall claimed its first victim on 19 August 1961 when Rudolf Urban, a 47-year-old East Berliner, fell and died while attempting to escape by roping his way down from his apartment window to the street below, the Bernauer Straße in West Berlin. The most dramatic incident occurred on 17 August 1962 when Peter Fechter was shot while attempting to escape over the Wall near Checkpoint Charlie. Despite his pleas for help, he bled to death while hundreds of Berliners looked on from both sides of the Wall.

The total number of persons killed trying to escape across the divide in Berlin after 13 August 1961 is under constant revision as new tragedies are still being uncovered.[1] According to the records of one monitoring body, the *Arbeitsgemeinschaft 13. August*, at least 239 people were killed and 118 were injured by firearms at the Wall and a further 517 were killed elsewhere on the GDR's borders and along the Baltic coast after the construction of the rampart (see Table 5.1). These figures are perhaps on the high side as they include many cases which have yet to be verified.[2] Whatever the exact number, it does not lessen the culpability of the regime. Even as late as 1989, six people were drowned in the Baltic, three died on Czechoslovakia's western border and two on the Hungarian border. Ingenious methods were used to escape, whether through tunnels, in car boots, by means of forged passports or in air balloons. The penalties for failure were severe: in July 1962, three

Table 5.1:   Persons killed trying to escape across the East German borders

	Before 13/8/61 (1)	After 13/8/61 (1)	Total (1)	Total (2)
German-German border	100	271	371	290
Berlin border/Wall	16	239	255	96
Baltic	15	174	189	17
Bulgarian, Czechoslovak, Hungarian borders with GDR	3	41	44	26
Other methods of flight	0	7	7	–
GDR border guards	11	16	27	–
Soviet troops	1	5	6	–
Berlin ring road	–	–	–	90
Aircraft shot down	14	3	17	–
Total	160	753	916	519

(1) Figures given by the *Arbeitsgemeinschaft 13. August*
(2) Figures given by the *Zentrale Erfassungsstelle für Regierungs- und Vereinigungskriminalität*
Sources: Koop V. 1996: 352–3; Lapp P. J. 1998: 248

West Berliners and two East Berliners were sentenced by the Supreme Court to between five and fifteen years' imprisonment for trying to escape.

Although no explicit shoot-to-kill law has been discovered, there existed a series of instructions and regulations authorising border guards to use fire-arms if they could not otherwise prevent flight across the border. The guards were trained to obey these orders unconditionally. The declassified record of the National Defence Council meeting on 14 September 1962 reveals that escapees were vilified as enemies and, if necessary, were to be 'destroyed'. A further meeting, on 3 May 1974, reaffirmed that firearms must be deployed 'ruthlessly' to prevent escapes across the border.[3] One key document, the 1982 Revised Border Law, referred to the use of 'physical force' when other means proved inadequate to 'prevent serious consequences for the security and order of the border territory'.[4]

During the cold war, 'the world's ugliest frontier'[5] was instrumentalised as a political symbol. It fuelled Western charges that, by imprisoning its own citizens and denying them the basic right of the freedom to travel, the GDR was a totalitarian *Unrechtsstaat,* unworthy of joining the international community. The regime and its apologists struggled in vain to turn defeat into victory by concocting justifications for the Wall: a defence against a potential military attack on the GDR; a barrier against the economic war waged by the imperialists; and, by stabilising the situation on the border, a major force for peace and security in Europe. At each anniversary of the building of the Wall, the propaganda message was underlined by references to the 'anti-fascist Defence Wall' and to the GDR's 'Peace Wall'.

Necessary though the Wall was for the survival of the GDR and the SED regime, it was nevertheless both a symptom and a determinant of East German paranoia and ambivalence towards the state and party. The Wall symbolized and reinforced the regime's friend–foe image of a world in which the imperialists were the implacable foe of socialism. In this climate of fear and mistrust, functionaries strove to prevent both external and internal enemies from leading East German youth astray through the propagation of 'corrupt' materialistic values. This kind of mentality blocked open and critical discussion not only of sensitive issues such as '*die Mauer*' itself and the role of the individual in society but even of Western pop songs and fashion.

The Wall created numerous political, psychological and social divisions in East German society. Much envy and resentment centred on those cadres and intellectuals whose position and function entitled them to travel to the West in contrast to the vast majority of citizens who had to go through the laborious process of applying for permission either to leave the GDR or to visit their relatives in the West. Those without relatives or direct contacts felt aggrieved as they did not have the direct access to hard currency and goods enjoyed by East Germans with family members in the FRG. And the restrictions on travel to the Federal Republic not only stoked up frustration and anger but also helped to foster a distorted image of prosperity in West Germany through East Germans' selective use of the Western media.

Despite these many fundamental problems, the sealing of the Berlin escape hatch meant that the regime and population had to arrive at some form of arrangement. Indeed, there is good reason to regard 13 August 1961 as the real date on which the GDR was founded: the division of Germany into two republics was sealed for the foreseeable future, and the regime, once the initial danger of unrest had been overcome, was able to conduct its policy in the knowledge that it would not be undermined by any dramatic demographic haemorrhage. The East German populace, conscious that the FRG and its Western partners had once more failed to challenge the Soviet Union's

[102] reassertion of the Yalta division of Europe, and with little opportunity for leaving, came under greater pressure to adjust and conform, as well as to co-operate and collaborate, with the Ulbricht regime.

The GDR after the Wall: coercion and repression

The construction of the Wall was followed by a wave of repression to enforce the East German population into accepting the new political realities. Specific groups were targeted: farmers opposed to agricultural collectivisation; real or alleged idlers at work; recalcitrant young people; East Germans whose jobs required them to cross over the sectoral borders; people who tuned into the Western media; and whoever used abusive language against the regime. The SED press encouraged the use of physical force against regime critics. FDJ groups were let loose in a campaign against so-called NATO-stations; TV aerials tuned into Western stations were torn down from the roof tops or redirected towards GDR stations.

The 'law of the Communist jungle' was backed up by the ruthless application of the Criminal Code. The code covered a wide range of political offences, including flight from the republic, protests against the new Defence Law, strike action, the defamation of the GDR as a prison and encouraging other citizens to listen to Western programmes. New instruments of repression were created by a Council of Ministers decree on 24 August 1961. In addition to imposing prison sentences, the courts were empowered to place restrictions on an individual's place of residence and, at the request of local authorities, to authorise a period in a work camp in the interest of 'public order and safety'.

A sharp rise in the number of arrests and sentences was one of the consequences of the state's campaign of terror. An official survey of sentences for 'political offences' recorded an appreciable increase from 1,521 in the first half of 1961 to 7,200 in the second half of the year.[6] Those convicted of political offences, an elastic concept even in less turbulent times, were imprisoned in relatively old jails in Bautzen, Cottbus, Waldheim and Zwickau. Berlin-Hohenschönhausen and Bautzen II accommodated primarily political prisoners, whereas the other prisons had a mix of political offenders and criminals.

In 1964, a differentiation in sentencing policy came into effect. The length of a sentence was divided into three categories by the Council of State Decree on the Administration of Justice. Under category one, a sentence of three years or longer, and under the harshest of conditions in prison, could be imposed on serious offenders. Capital punishment was reserved for the most serious offences, a practice which was defended on the specious argument that it served the security of the state and the preservation of peace. Until 1968, when shooting was introduced, punishment was usually by beheading. Between 1949 and 1968, at least 194 executions took place, 69 for crimes against the state, mainly for sabotage or espionage. According to Gerhard Finn, about 260 death sentences were passed by GDR courts between the foundation of the GDR in 1949 and the abolition of capital punishment in 1987.[7]

The Ministry of State Security, which had its own detention centres and prisons, was integral to the system of repression. It grew rapidly during the Ulbricht years: full-time personnel almost trebled between 1957 and 1973, from 17,500 to about 52,700.[8] The number of unofficial collaborators grew quickly too, especially after the June 1953 Uprising. This army of spies created an atmosphere of suspicion which even extended to the Stasi itself, as informers frequently spied on each other. The Stasi's pivotal role in the GDR's political system, together with the many forms of repression such as the Berlin Wall, the politicisation of justice and a public sphere subject to party and state control, meant, as Fricke has observed, that while everday life in the GDR was not coterminous with political persecution, life was not conceivable without some form of political persecution.[9]

Rapprochement with the population

The wave of arbitrary and brutal repression began to ebb in the autumn of 1961 before its effective termination in mid-1962, partly because terroristic methods were inappropriate beyond the immediate suppression of opposition after the construction of the Wall. Even Erich Mielke recognised that the high rate of arrests could not be sustained.[10] A second reason for the shift in policy arose from the change in the political context after the launching of Khrushchev's second bout of destalinisation in October 1961. Taking his cue from the Soviet leader, Ulbricht denounced the personality cult of Stalin and the crimes committed by the Soviet dictator. The name Stalin disappeared from streets and squares. In East Berlin, the massive Stalin monument was removed and the Stalinallee was suddenly transformed into the Karl-Marx-Allee. The slogan which appeared in *Neues Deutschland* in November

[104] 1963 – 'The republic needs everyone, everyone needs the republic' – encapsulated the SED's new approach.

As part of the strategy to establish a *rapprochement* with the population, the SED implemented a limited and controlled political relaxation from above. The party leadership wooed the populace with promises of higher living standards, new job opportunities and the propagation of GDR-style socialism as a more humane system than capitalism. Indicative of its cultivation of specific groups in society were the Youth Communiqué (1963), the Youth Code (1964), the New Economic System (1963), the Law on the Integrated System of Education (1965) and the Family Code (1966). To these measures should be added the revision of the Criminal Code (1968), the amnesty of October 1964 on the occasion of the GDR's fifteenth anniversary, a modest cultural thaw and the promotion of mass and top-level sport.

The SED's vision of GDR society after the building of the Wall was revealed at the Sixth Party Congress in January 1963. It was summed up in the ungainly concept of 'the comprehensive construction of socialism', which, according to the new party programme, was now the party's key goal. The GDR, it was posited, could move on to the comprehensive stage of socialism now that, at least in the eyes of the leadership and its ideologues, the foundations of socialism had been established by the nationalisation of industry, the collectivisation of agriculture and the securing of the GDR's borders.

Reforming the command economy

While the construction of the Wall brought temporary relief to the hard-pressed regime, many East German leaders, notably Walter Ulbricht, realised that economic performance and living standards must be improved if a *modus vivendi* were to be established between populace and regime, leading, at some later date, to the resolution of the national question along lines acceptable to the SED. The GDR's economic development had, however, been hampered by fundamental problems in the promotion of industrial innovation and technological diffusion. The debate in the GDR was part of the general reappraisal in the Soviet Union and Eastern Europe of the need for changes to the administrative-command system. NES (New Economic System of Planning and Management) in the GDR, NEM (New Economic Mechanism) in Hungary and the most radical of the three reform projects, the Prague Spring in Czechoslovakia, were the outcome of this reassessment.

The debate was not simply about economic change; it took place within a broader context of the re-articulation of a socialist-type system, as attempted by Khrushchev in 1956 and 1961. Khrushchev favoured opening the windows to let in the air of change rather than the wholescale dismantling of the structures of socialism. In his typically erratic but bold way, Khrushchev was searching for a viable socialism which would be flexible enough to respond to the many different interests in an increasingly complex society and which would allow a limited participation by various specialist groups such as scientists and engineers. A major stumbling block to an understanding between party and different social groups was a fall in economic growth rates in the Soviet Union and its East European client states at the beginning of the 1960s. The fall highlighted the urgent need for a revision of the central planning mechanism and the strategy of economic expansion through the extensive use of resources. In the Soviet Union, a major discussion took place in late 1962 on the Kharkov economist Evsei Liberman's idea of utilising market-type levers to promote innovation and greater efficiency.

The defects of the old system

The three main defects in the central planning mechanism were overbureaucratisation, the enterprise bonus system and inflexible product prices. Central administrators were too fixated on the fulfilment of plan targets to worry too much about the quality of R&D and innovation which, from the perspective of many bureaucrats, disrupted the planning and manufacturing process. These problems were compounded by the tendency of enterprises to negotiate 'slack' plan targets and by the linkage of enterprise bonuses to 'gross production' as the main success indicator of an enterprise. This indicator was a disincentive to innovation as its measurement, for example, according to weight or price, encouraged the manufacture of heavy and expensive products respectively. Indeed, as a consequence of distorted prices, 'profit' was often more likely to be made out of the manufacture of out-of-date rather than of new products.

In order to overcome these deficiencies, Ulbricht announced, at the SED's Sixth Party Congress in January 1963, the leadership's intention to press ahead with important changes to the economic mechanism. This materialised in summer as the New Economic System of Planning and Management, the first serious attempt in the Soviet imperium at a revision of the existing system of central economic planning. Although not implemented in the Soviet Union, Liberman's ideas on more enterprise autonomy and a greater role for material

[106] incentives served as the green light for SED reformers, especially as they appeared to complement Khrushchev's renewed destalinisation campaign.

The GDR leadership probably failed to obtain the unqualified approval – as opposed to the tolerance – of the Soviets, partly because the Kremlin was uncertain as to the wisdom of pursuing the kind of reforms advocated by Liberman.[11] For their part, the SED reformers around Ulbricht were cool towards Khrushchev's unrealistic aspirations to construct Communism and catch up with the USA within one thousand days. Bitter experience had taught them that this kind of goal was an illusion.[12] The conclusion is that while Khrushchev appears not to have given NES his formal approval, the Kremlin was unwilling to block it, particularly as it focused on economic change rather than political reform. Instead, Moscow positioned itself at a distance from the GDR's cautious experiment, awaiting the outcome with a view to possible benefits for the Soviet Union's own economic system.

Ulbricht – the semi-enlightened despot

One major surprise is Ulbricht's role as the progenitor of NES. Justly regarded as one of Eastern Europe's most dogmatic Stalinist leaders, he had been instrumental in suppressing the revisionist ideas of Benary and Behrens a few years earlier, proposals which were congruent with the theoretical framework of NES. Ulbricht's advocacy of reform was the result of a hardheaded appraisal of the need for change in the administrative-command economic mechanism if the GDR were to have a long-term future as a developed industrial state in competition with the FRG and as a possible model for the whole of Germany. Although market elements were incorporated into the design of NES, Ulbricht had no intention of setting the GDR along a capitalist path. Instead, he was intent on devising a socialist alternative to West Germany's burgeoning social market economy, an alternative which, unlike that of the Prague reformers a few years later, shunned fundamental changes in politics and culture. Given his ultra-conservatism in intellectual and political matters, the Ulbricht of the 1960s is perhaps best termed a 'semi-enlightened despot', that is, an autocratic leader who, surprisingly, was open to new ideas on how to improve the economic system.

Flanking Ulbricht were the intellectual designers of NES: Eric Apel, Günter Mittag, the Deputy-Finance Minister, Walter Halbritter, Ulbricht's personal adviser, Dr Wolfgang Berger and Professor Claus Krömke, Mittag's assistant. Berger had been an assistant to Behrens at the Karl-Marx-University in Leipzig. To these should be added a group of young academics from the

Institutes for Social Sciences and Socialist Management and the universities   [107]
– among them Herbert Wolf, Otto Reinhold and Helmut Koziolek – as well
as staff in the state and party apparat. By far the most influential reformer was
Erich Apel. Born in 1917 and an engineer by profession, he had worked with
Wernher von Braun on rocket research at Peenemünde during the Second
World War and for the Soviet Union's rocket research programme between
1946 and 1952. His political ascent was rapid after his return to Germany: he
was appointed Minister of Heavy Machine Construction in 1955 and he entered the Politbüro as a candidate member six years later. Soon afterwards, in
January 1963, he was entrusted with the key post of Chairman of the State
Planning Commission. Apel, whose early career excluded him from the inner
circle of Communist veterans, was not heavily encumbered by ideological
baggage. He was self-confident, a hard taskmaster and, above all, a 'doer'.
His chief assistant, Günter Mittag, who was almost ten years younger, became a Central Committee candidate and Secretary of the Politbüro Economic
Commission in 1958; four years later, he succeeded Apel as Central Committee Secretary for the Economy and entered the Politbüro as a candidate member. He was a more skilful political operator than Apel, adroit at changing
tack with the prevailing political wind.

The ideas of the reformers were not to the liking of a group of more conservative SED politicians, notably Willi Stoph, Erich Honecker, Hermann
Axen, Hermann Matern, Werner Krolikowski and Ali Neumann. These conservatives favoured the traditional economic model and the extensive mode
of production and feared that NES would undermine party control. They were
also anxious that the GDR's close relationship with Moscow might be jeopardised by an economic experiment which not only contained market elements but also ran the risk of drawing the country into the orbit of the West.
Such concerns were shared by many cadres among the party's top bodies and
by the burgeoning bureaucracy.[13]

The new economic system:
a technocratic solution

NES saw the light of day when the principles of the project were issued by
the Council of Ministers in July 1963. It was not conceived as the final product ready for immediate implementation. Many of the changes, for example
those to industrial prices, were planned to take place in stages. Although the

[108]   term 'reform' is often applied to NES, it might perhaps best be described as a 'half-reform' in that no clean break was made with the old structures. The market elements were designed to enhance efficiency; they were not intended as the harbingers of a capitalist economy. In addition, Ulbricht, although countenancing a shift in decision-making from party bodies to the Council of State, did not envisage a fundamental revision of the existing power structures. In the final analysis, NES was an imaginative but technocratic attempt at a solution to the problems inherent in the economic mechanism.

The major goal of NES was to shift the emphasis of the work of central agencies like the State Planning Commission away from the minutiae of the planning process and towards the formulation of long-term goals. In line with this principle, the number of compulsory plan indicators to be fulfilled by the enterprises was drastically reduced and they were given more incentives and opportunities to carry out their own planning and management. The Associations of National Enterprises (VVBs) – intermediate-level administrative organs – formed an important link between central bodies and enterprises as regards planning and balancing tasks and they were made responsible for the development of their particular branch of industry. Crucial to the whole NES project was the system of economic levers; they offered enterprises incentives for greater initiatives while at the same time providing central planners with instruments for indirect steering of the economy. Costs, prices and wages were designated direct levers and the bonus and performance funds indirect levers. The high profile enjoyed by profit and bonuses underlined the importance attached by NES planners to material incentives. Profit, not gross production, was envisaged as the primary production indicator for assessing the performance of enterprises. Investments were to be financed, to a limited degree, from profits and bank credits.

But in order to make profit meaningful and to evaluate enterprise performance, the distortions in the old system had to be erased. This entailed, above all, a reform of industrial prices, a revaluation of fixed capital and a revision of the methods of calculating depreciation rates. An industrial price reform was implemented in three stages between 1964 and 1967, involving considerable price rises for raw materials, semi- and finished goods and a revaluation of stocks. These changes did not, however, produce a flexible system of price building responsive to rapid changes in the production profile. Moreover, as the prices of consumer goods were left unchanged and wages were linked to these prices, enterprises encountered problems in determining the relationship between labour and capital costs and the appropriateness of investments.[14]

Another feature of NES, one on which Ulbricht would place even greater emphasis in the later 1960s, was the attempt to integrate science into the production process. Ulbricht took his cue from the 1961 XXII CPSU Party Congress which had deployed the term 'scientific-technical revolution', hitherto ideologically suspect, and had upgraded science to the role of a productive force. Science was interpreted broadly to cover R&D, mathematics, cybernetics, engineering, the natural sciences and the political economy of socialism. From an early stage, it was Ulbricht's intention to concentrate R&D investments on such key economic branches as petrochemicals, optics, machine building and electronics.

Dilemmas of change

As NES unfolded, especially from mid-1965 onwards, leading party cadres were required to undergo intensive retraining; technical and professional skills had to be upgraded and ideological conviction was watered down as a criterion of career advancement. These requirements and the technical changes to the economic mechanism were not well received. Many party functionaries opposed the dilution of ideology and party control, and some enterprise managers disliked the emphasis on professional expertise. Technical difficulties in the design and implementation of the reform concept were legion. As retail prices continued to be fixed by the state and subsidies were not discontinued, the impact of the new industrial prices was limited. The failure to introduce price reform as part of a comprehensive package made it impossible to make profit the main performance indicator and produced distortions in enterprise performance and bonus payments.

The Soviet connection caused Apel and Ulbricht severe headaches. The toppling of Khrushchev reinforced the orthodox tendencies in political, cultural and economic matters in Moscow, as signified by Leonid Brezhnev's appointment as First Secretary of the CPSU in October 1964. At a secret meeting with Ulbricht, shortly before Khruschchev was deposed, Ulbricht failed to obtain Brezhnev's unreserved support for NES.[15] Brezhnev's coolness towards the economic experiment encouraged the more conservative forces in the GDR who were becoming increasingly disturbed by the political and ideological implications of NES as well as by the many intractable technical problems. During a Central Committee Plenum in Spring 1964, it was claimed that incentives and bonus payments to top researchers and management would lead to the undesirable phenomenon of 'socialist millionaires'.[16] This was the riposte of those who believed that the call for a differentiation in

[110] pay would undermine what many SED members believed to be a key ideological goal of the party, social equality.

Reds versus experts?

These clashes were symptomatic of the classic conflict between reds and experts. A leading West German authority on the GDR, Peter Christian Ludz, argued, on the basis of detailed empirical studies of the Central Committee and the Politbüro, that tensions and rivalries existed between a strategic elite of older, established functionaries and party leaders and the new institutionalised counter-elite of younger, more highly educated experts, technocrats and managers. The latter, according to Ludz, were less enslaved by narrow ideological doctrines, had not undergone the formative experiences of the older generation's involvement in the Communist movement in the 1920s and the struggle against fascism, and preferred to concentrate their energies on the concrete problems of society, especially its economic problems. Terror and the rigidities of Marxist-Leninist ideology were seen as dysfunctional for economic development. Ludz was correct in his depiction of conflicts between these two broad groups as they were inherent in the GDR's gradual transition to a less harsh but nevertheless monocratic system with strong elements of paternalism. Labels such as 'neo-Stalinism', 'administered society', 'post-totalitarianism' and 'consultative authoritarianism' have been pinned on Communist polities such as that of the GDR, from the later 1960s onwards, to take account of the changes implicit in the wider consultation with experts, the end of the purges, a limited toleration of criticism and the growing routinisation of ideology. Ludz was also correct to point out that the experts were institutionalised in that they regarded themselves as Marxists and that 'their pragmatic criticism of particular decisions of the Politbüro should not be misrepresented as a critique of the system or of its ideological foundations'.[17] Despite this important qualification, he nevertheless underestimated the overlap between the groupings. For example, leading reformers such as Halbritter and Apel belonged to the same generation as conservatives like Honecker, Stoph, Verner and Fröhlich; Ulbricht, the political oarsman of NES, came from an even earlier generation; and the politically ambitious Mittag was both a party *apparatchik* and a technical expert.

The ideological and political rifts and the disagreements over the technical design of NES came to a head in late 1965. At the same time, tense and difficult discussions with the Soviet Union about a five-year agreement on economic and scientific-technical cooperation were causing much anguish in GDR circles as it threatened to disadvantage the GDR and delay completion of the long-term economic plan. This was the culmination of long-standing problems between the two countries.[18] Brezhnev made a lightning visit to the GDR to lay down the law to his SED colleagues a few days before the agreement was signed in December.

The balancing of the five-year economic plan proved to be an impossible task for Apel. It became clear at a special Politbüro meeting in July that neither this nor the one-year plan for 1966 could be achieved at existing production levels.[19] Apel's critics exploited his embarrassment to launch an attack against Apel's personal position as well as the risks inherent in NES. The annual and five-year plans of the State Planning Commission once again came under fire at a special Politbüro meeting on 2 December, when the Finance Minister, Rumpf, accused Apel of relying too heavily on West Germany. With Ulbricht showing clear signs of losing confidence in his colleague's ability to deliver results, Stoph and Mittag joined in the barrage of criticism. Apel, depressed by these criticisms and worried by the threat of the disclosure of his earlier collaboration with von Braun, shot himself later in the day. His tragic death did not mark the end of NES but it did deprive the reform group of its most determined protagonist.

The new paternalism

Education

As part of the SED's search for an accord with the population and in order to adjust the education system to meet the requirements of NES, the education sector was restructured after a commission of enquiry in 1963 had revealed serious deficiencies in the natural sciences, mathematics and political education. In 1965, the third GDR education act, the Law on the Integrated Socialist Education System, was passed, which, with the exception of the changes introduced after the reform of higher education in 1967, put in place the structures which would survive virtually intact until the end of the Honecker era. The main features of the GDR's education system were a comprehensive pre-school provision of crèches and kindergartens, the obligatory ten-class polytechnic school, vocational training institutions, technical schools, universities and myriad opportunities for further training. In contrast to the egalitarian emphasis of the 1959 Education Act, which had made no reference to individual ability, the new law gave a boost to social differentiation by making allowance for the promotion of gifted individuals in special schools and classes, a development already in progress since 1963,

[112] notably in mathematics, the natural sciences and sport. The new law also made specific reference to the entry into higher education of the most able pupils.

The higher education reform of 1967 tightened research links between industry and universities, as for example between the city of Jena's Friedrich-Schiller-University and the Carl Zeiss optical firm. Such links would, it was envisaged, be conducive to the development of the scientific-technical revolution and to the GDR's position as one of the socialist world's leading industrial states. In addition to this objective, the education sector, including universities and colleges, was expected to make a vital contribution to the development of young people as all-round socialist personalities, thereby binding them politically and ideologically to the socialist system. This dual function exposed the education sector to the competing presssures of socio-economic modernisation and political-ideological conformity.

Several aspects of the GDR education system attracted favourable comment in Western publications. For example, it was noted with approval that whereas in 1951–52 only 16 per cent of pupils spent longer than eight years at school, this had risen to 72 per cent two decades later.[20] The vocational guidance system was highly developed and most school leavers were able to obtain an apprenticeship leading to a skilled-worker qualification. Opportunities via the further education and training route enabled workers without a full vocational training to complete their qualification for a job. Many women benefited from this provision. These positive developments should not, however, obscure some fundamental problems. By the 1970s, it had become apparent that a level of qualification had been reached which exceeded requirements in many parts of the economy. The hopes of educational planners that the scientific-technical revolution would lead to a more effective use of higher qualifications were not fulfilled. One sociological study in the early 1970s revealed that whereas about 70 per cent of production workers were classified as skilled, only about 55 per cent of the workforce needed to hold this level of qualification.[21] The resulting dequalification and job monotony led to job dissatisfaction, a high labour turnover and low motivation.

Youth policy

The conflict in the education system between conformity and individualisation bedevilled the SED's youth policy too. In keeping with the more moderate policy of the early 1960s, the Politbüro's self-critical and constructive Youth Communiqué on Youth Questions in 1963, followed by the Youth Code one year later, held out the promise of greater independence for young people. Ulbricht was scathing of the FDJ's unimaginative approach to young people's interests and problems and advocated a measured relaxation of the rigid controls imposed on young people by schools and the FDJ.[22] The youth movement tried, with mixed results, to promote a much livelier image, as symbolised by the FDJ First Secretary, Horst Schumann, dancing the hitherto forbidden twist. The highpoint of the new approach was the FDJ's festival, *Deutschlandtreffen*, at Whitsuntide 1964, when thousands of young East and West Germans gathered in a relaxed atmosphere in East Berlin; they danced down Unter den Linden, listened to jazz and rock music, and exchanged views on political and personal matters. The popular radio station DT64, which was named after this festival, catered for young East Germans' avid interest in Western pop music. However, the more flexible policy had inbuilt limitations: while Ulbricht spoke of enhancing independence, self-confidence and performance to make the GDR more attractive to young people, he was opposed to an erosion of the SED's power monopoly and to any appreciable slackening in the indoctrination of young people as socialist personalities.

The production of socialist personalities was one of the main tasks designated in the Family Code of 1966, a task which the family was enjoined to share with the FDJ, the school and other educational institutions. The SED, conscious of the family's primary socialisation function, was anxious to incorporate the family into the broader social and political network and to exploit it as a stabilising influence in society. Furthermore, the Code underscored the SED's mobilisation of female labour by exhorting men to help with the upbringing of children and the household chores. While the SED sought in these and many other ways to shape the family's structure and functions in accordance with its policy priorities, the Code did at least demonstrate that the party was not intent on destroying the family as an institution. Indeed, the Code recognised the family as the smallest cell in society, one where the intensity of the emotional ties between its members gave it a vital role in the upbringing of children. In the preamble to the Code, it was claimed that a new and lasting quality in family relations was feasible now that socialism had eliminated exploitation at work, fostered the equality of women and enhanced educational opportunities for all. Such ambitious goals and aspirations were not easily achieved.

Promoting sport

Women's employment and their disproportionate share of housework and childrearing restricted their participation in sport and recreational activities outside the home, thus undermining the SED's purported aim to make

[114]   physical culture and sport a mass activity. Ulbricht took a keen interest in
sport and, despite his rotund figure, was portrayed as a role model in the
GDR press. Sport was part of the school curriculum and participants in mass
sport festivals in the factories and residential areas numbered over nine million in 1963. The authorities hoped that active sport would enhance people's
well-being and boost their labour productivity.

Top-level sport was not neglected; it was promoted as a political lever to
break the diplomatic isolation of the GDR and to demonstrate the superiority of socialism over capitalism. At the 1964 Tokyo Olympics, the GDR's
sportsmen and sportswomen participated in the all-German team and obtained
the highly creditable total of 23 medals. In the following year, the International Olympic Committee agreed on a separate GDR representation at the
1968 Mexico Olympics. At these games, the GDR attained the unofficial third
place behind the USA and the Soviet Union, a notable achievement for its
'diplomats in tracksuits'. These advances owed much to the identification of
and concentration on those sports which were likely to reap a harvest of medals
and to the vast organisational network geared to these goals. The key figure
in the promotion of elite sport was Manfred Ewald, the President of the DTSB
between 1961 and 1988. Highly gifted children were selected early in their
school life for development at one of the GDR's elite sports schools (*Kinder-
und Jugendsportschulen*) and talented performers were concentrated in about
30 well-endowed sports clubs and in the sports associations of the armed
forces and the Stasi (*Vorwärts* and *Dynamo*). Four specialist sports schools were
founded in 1952; by September 1989, the number had risen to 25, with
10,052 pupils. The regime pumped resources into the schools, discipline was
strict and political indoctrination intensive.[23] The *Deutsche Hochschule für
Körperkultur und Sport* in Leipzig, founded in 1950, became famous for its
systematic training of thousands of top coaches and instructors. Powerful incentives were on offer to the elite: foreign travel, payments in Western currency,
bonuses and good career opportunities. Although performance-enhancing
drugs were taken before the 1968 Olympics, especially in power disciplines,
it was not until 1969 that a comprehensive doping programme was implemented. Drugs, notably anabolic steroids, were used to an unprecendented
degree as part of a central programme organised by top SED and state organs. The scientific centre of the programme was Leipzig's *Forschungsinstitut
für Körperkultur und Sport*, which was founded in 1969. The institute, in conjunction with sports club officials and trainers, the Jenapharm firm and partner institutions such as the Academy of Sciences, was responsible for the
systematic doping not only of thousands of leading athletes, such as the shot
putter Margitta Gummel and the sprinters Renate Neufeld, Marita Koch and

Marlies Göhr, but also of many talented children. Cases are well documented [115] of the systematic administering of minors with drugs, especially swimmers and athletes, without their parents' permission.[24]

Legal reform

The Family and Youth Codes were all part of the reassessment of the legal system's role in the SED's strategy to mobilise popular support. As part of this process of controlled internal détente, or of what Ludz described as 'an expanded system of institutionalised social controls',[25] the regime called a halt to the system of police and judicial terror of 1961–62 and implemented a series of legal and judicial reforms. In April 1963, the Council of State Decree on the Administration of Justice laid the foundation of a revision of the judicial system which accorded with the goal in the SED's 1963 Party Programme to improve socialist legal norms and to strengthen the rights of citizens. Furthermore, the programme boasted that as, for the first time in German history, guarantees were provided for freedom, equality and basic human rights, the GDR could rightly claim to be 'the German state based on the rule of law'. This highly dubious claim was underscored by the argument that the legal order in a socialist society was based on the unity of individual and societal interests and that the state and law were instruments of social progress. While the judicial reform of 1963 signally failed to remove the arbitrary and highly political nature of so many judicial decisions, this process, together with the codification of family and labour law, the Criminal Code of 1968 and new economic legislation, did at least introduce an element of predictability and regularity into the legal system. This should not, however, be exaggerated. The new Criminal Code still contained elements of repression intrinsic to a police state and it remained firmly linked to the political priorities of the SED leadership. The minimum sentence for certain political crimes was raised, in some cases even doubled. Among the most significant crimes were treason, espionage, acts of terror, sabotage and the formation of groups hostile to the state.[26] The recognition of the accused's right of defence was severely curtailed for political offenders as the preliminary proceedings remained in the hands of the Stasi.

A cultural thaw

A limited cultural thaw introduced in 1963 complemented the SED's relatively paternalistic approach to the family and youth as well as the greater autonomy granted to economic actors. The thaw saw the publication of

[116]   critical works by Christa Wolf, Erwin Strittmatter and other GDR writers as
well as the licensing of the works of Western authors such as Peter Weiss,
Carl Zuckmayer and Max Frisch. Wolf's novel *Der geteilte Himmel* (1963)
dealt with the personal anguish of a couple separated by the Wall, and Strittmatter's *Ole Biedenkop* (1963) and Neutsch's *Spur der Steine* (1964) explored
the conflicts with party policy of an idealistic farmer and construction worker
respectively. From the point of view of the regime, this kind of debate
on problems which were difficult to suppress acted as a useful safety valve,
particularly if, as the leadership hoped, contributions were delivered in a
spirit of solidarity with the socialist system. However, the cultural dogmatists in the upper reaches of the party, including Verner, Hager and
Honecker, were horrified at what they perceived to be the spread of Western
decadence and a decline in morality among GDR youth. A clampdown on
beat groups in Leipzig, ordered by Fröhlich's regional SED executive in
October 1965, triggered off a fierce clash between security forces and beat
music fans. The dogmatists were opposed to open debate about social and
political conflicts in socialist society, fearing that it would undermine the
foundations of the socialist system, and they condemned the decentralising
tendencies in the economy as a threat to the party's power. Ulbricht's position is not so easy to define as he had a foot in both camps and saw advantages in the encouragement of creative ideas in the economic and cultural
spheres. He did not, however, countenance truly independent thinking;
this had to be 'controlled' and set within the limits prescribed by the party's
strategists.[27]

Particular exception was taken to the acerbic poetry of Wolf Biermann
and the challenging critiques of Stefan Heym and Robert Havemann. Manfred
Bieler also came under fire for his comedy *ZAZA* (Central Office for the Preservation of Old Party Comrades). A biting satire on party functionaries in a
Stalinist system, it was condemned by Hager and Verner as hostile to party
and state. The Eleventh Central Committee Plenary in December 1965 was
the decisive point in the dogmatists' campaign. Honecker launched a vit-
riolic attack on those writers who were helping to spread the 'insidious immorality of imperialism' in the GDR. This kind of atmosphere, he argued,
encouraged a lack of respect for authority, criminal behaviour, sexual promiscuity, the broadcasting of beat music and poor discipline at work. Ulbricht
joined in the fray, accusing writers and artists of propagating anarchism and
nihilism and of fostering pornography and other undesirable American ways
of life. He directed much of his fire at the circle around Biermann, Havemann
and Heym which, in his opinion, was waging a political struggle against the

workers' and peasants' state.[28] The attack on literary nonconformists and other critical spirits was followed by a cultural frost, as exemplified by the acceptance of the politicians' criticisms by the executive of the Writers' Union in February 1966. At the time of the Prague Spring, GDR politicians would boast that they had nipped liberalisation tendencies in the bud at an early stage.

The economic system of socialism

Despite the cultural backlash and Apel's suicide, NES was still operating. It continued to command the support of the technical intelligentsia, many reform-minded economists and practitioners and, despite much political backtracking, of Ulbricht himself. At the Seventh Party Congress in April 1967, at which NES was re-christened the Economic System of Socialism (ESS), Ulbricht reemphasised the crucial role played by prices and profits in the economic mechanism. Work continued, too, on the improvement in the design of the project: a more dynamic method of price building was introduced to encourage the production of new and improved products, and during 1966 and 1967 many central indicators for production were lifted. Although technical improvements continued to be made over the next few years and enterprise autonomy in the foreign trade was enhanced, a significant modification occurred in 1968 when certain key 'structure-determining tasks' became an integral part of ESS.

These tasks were intended to ensure that key economic targets, such as the promotion of innovation and higher rates of economic growth and productivity, were not obstructed by conflicting enterprise objectives and plans. Ulbricht seems to have become impatient with the chequered progress of innovation and sought to accelerate progress in areas which would enable the GDR to attain world standards in science and technology. The main beneficiaries of the new state policy were electronics, instrument building, machine tools and sections of the motor vehicle industry. In addition, it was envisaged that cybernetics, system theory and computer science would improve the quality of planning, raise production and maintain the GDR's position as a leading industrial power. Other ways of promoting scientific-technical innovation included the establishment of closer organisational ties between researchers in the Academy of Sciences, the universities and industry. Efficiency and R&D were to be advanced by the acceleration, from 1968 onwards, of industrial

[118] concentration in combines. One serious flaw in the new strategy was the underestimation of the complexity of innovation and exaggerated expectations of the rapidity with which growth targets could be achieved.

Model GDR

The gradual stabilisation of the SED regime, a marked improvement in living standards and high expectations of the benefits of science and technology led an increasingly self-confident Ulbricht to devise a new ideological construct and to propagate the GDR as a model for other highly developed countries. To the annoyance of his fraternal colleagues in the Soviet bloc, Ulbricht assumed the role of the pedantic schoolmaster, lecturing them on the GDR's achievement in establishing socialism for the first time in a highly developed country divided by the imperialists. At the SED's Seventh Party Congress in April 1967, Ulbricht defined GDR socialism as 'the developed societal system of socialism' and as a relatively autonomous socio-economic formation in the transition from capitalism to communism. Later in the year, in his September address on the significance of *Das Kapital* for the GDR's system of socialism, Ulbricht boasted:

> *We have succeeded in one part of Germany, i.e., in the European country with the most fully developed state monopoly capitalism, in demonstrating the democratic road to socialism and the vitality of the socialist system in a developed socialist state.*[29]

The new definition of socialism reflected Ulbricht's obsession with esoteric systems theory. While the concept of the 'economic system of socialism' would later serve to differentiate the GDR from the Prague Spring's reform project, it also represented a departure from the official Soviet interpretation of socialism as a short-term transitional phase. At the Party Congress, Ulbricht deployed a second key concept, 'the socialist human community', to mark a new quality in relations between the social classes and strata. The reasoning behind this construct was that as socialism was developing along its own socio-economic base, no longer so deeply influenced by its capitalist past, the preconditions for class conflict were being eliminated and the social classes and strata were drawing closer together.

The socialist character of the GDR was stressed in the new constitution promulgated in 1968. Many of the fundamental changes which had occurred since the issue of the GDR's original constitution were incorporated into the new document. Political unity was regarded as having been erected on the basis of the social unity derived from the social ownership of the means of [119] production and the consequent harmonisation of public and personal interests. Article 1 left no doubt as to where power lay: 'The GDR is the political organisation of the urban and rural working people who are jointly implementing socialism under the leadership of the working class and its Marxist-Leninist party'. The socialist credentials of the GDR were underpinned by the reference in Article 1 to the GDR as the 'socialist state of the German nation'; in contrast, the 1949 Constitution had declared Germany to be an indivisible democratic republic. Before the close of the Ulbricht era, there were signs of an even sharper demarcation between the two German states, a precursor of Honecker's two nations theory. In 1970, partly as a reaction to Brandt's 'Report on the state of the nation', Ulbricht modified his concept of one German nation, referring to a 'socialist German national state' in the GDR and a 'capitalist NATO-state' in the FRG.[30] Despite the revelations in recent historical studies that Ulbricht was once more toying with the idea of a confederation between the GDR and the FRG, the SED documentation held in the federal archives indicates that Ulbricht remained firmly committed, as an immediate goal, to the development of a separate socialist GDR.[31]

A state that ought to be

In the later 1960s, a series of books by Western scholars, notably David Childs, Jean Edward Smith and Peter Christian Ludz, not only made the GDR a better-known land but also contributed to a partial revision of the negative image of the GDR as 'the state that ought not to be'. Ludz contended that at the end of the 1960s, 'An increasing number of citizens are becoming aware of their own state, which they view as being independent of the Federal Republic and which they accept, though not totally without criticism'.[32] In a short introductory text, which first appeared in West Germany in 1970, the head of the Second Television Service, Hanns Werner Schwarze, argued that with reunification ruled out in the foreseeable future, 'East Germans have no desire to be regarded as inhabitants of some second-class region, of some "Zone", but as normal citizens of a normal state which, by dint of its standard of living and its industrial achievements, can hold its head up with some considerable pride on the international scene'.[33]

Awareness of the GDR as a separate state was based to a great extent on the expansion of the economy and the substantial improvement in living standards

[120]   during the 1960s. By the end of the decade, East German workers could take considerable pride in the reconstruction of the economy and in turning the GDR into an economically viable state. Studies of coal and metal workers in the Leipzig region, for example, refer to the material and status benefits which they derived from the expansion of the basic materials industries in the 1950s and 1960s and which underpinned their accommodation with the regime.[34] Measured in terms of crude output, the GDR was often referred to as one of the ten leading industrial nations and many commentators spoke of a 'second German economic miracle'.[35] Reconstruction had meant diverting investments into the rapid development of the iron and steel, chemical, energy, electrical equipment, general machinery and light engineering industries. New towns emerged, such as Eisenhüttenstadt on the Polish border, industrial complexes expanded, such as Leuna II near Merseburg, and Rostock developed into a large port. After the economic stagnation of the early 1960s, economic growth accelerated in the second half of the decade.[36] Taking 1950 as the base year, that is as 100, produced national income rose from 310 in 1965 to 401 in 1970. The index of gross production in industry rose from 392 to 535. Growth was rapid in the chemical industry (423 to 613), metallurgy (433 to 587), building materials (427 to 571) and electrical engineering, electronics and instrument building (723 to 11,410). Rates of growth were less pronounced in agriculture, power and fuels, light industry, textiles and foodstuffs.

That consumer industries' growth rates lagged behind those in other sectors was a reflection of the priority afforded by the regime to investments in industry and the economic modernisation programme. However, for reasons of social stability it could not afford to neglect the aspirations of the consumer. Private consumption per household rose by about 24 per cent between 1965 and 1970, slightly above plan, and incomes were boosted appreciably by state contributions.[37] Between 1965 and 1971, the average net monthly income of workers and white-collar employees rose from 491 Marks to 619 Marks, and of PGH members from 628 Marks to 730 Marks. The improvement in living standards can be judged by the percentage increase, between 1960 and 1970, of households in possession of a television set (16.7 to 69.1), a refrigerator (6.1 to 56.4), a washing machine (6.2 to 53.6) and a car (3.2 to 15.6).[38] Certain goods were expensive relative to average incomes: in 1965, a television set cost 2,050 Marks and a washing machine 1,350 Marks. Even more vexing for the consumer were the frequent shortages of everyday items, ranging from toothbrushes and toilet paper to potatoes and matches. Other grievances concerned inconvenient opening hours of shops, the poor quality and the limited range of goods, and the politicians' aversion to young people's enthusiasm for Western pop music.

Before the collapse of the GDR, the relative paucity and the poor quality of empirical data made it difficult to delineate popular attitudes to the SED regime and to determine whether a specific GDR consciousness emerged at some point in the later 1960s. A pioneering work in this area was Gebhard Schweigler's assessment of the data assembled by West German public opinion institutes from interviews with West German visitors to the GDR. One of his sources, Infratest's 1969 poll, showed that, in the opinion of the West Germans, most East Germans favoured the diplomatic recognition of the GDR and that younger people were the group most likely to assert that the GDR was an independent state. On the basis of these data, journalistic accounts and the reports of individual experts on the GDR, Schweigler concluded that a consciousness of the GDR as a distinctive political entity was growing among many East Germans, but he ruled out an identification with the GDR as a separate nation.[39]

Schweigler's conclusions can now be assessed in the light of the declassified materials of the Leipzig Central Institute for Youth Research, the records of the Stasi and the mass organisations, and the findings of the Central Committee's Institute for Public Opinion Research. The latter body was founded in 1964 and closed down on Honecker's orders in 1979. Its function was to provide the Politbüro and other leading organs with information about East Germans' views on domestic and international issues. Other than the Leipzig materials, its numerous surveys, which were based on the principle of anonymity and carried out in the form of written questionnaires, provide the only comprehensive internal research on popular opinion which conform to certain basic social scientific criteria. Unfortunately, the representative nature of the surveys cannot easily be tested retrospectively and the relatively high proportion of those replying 'don't know' or 'no answer' suggest that they either did not hold a firm opinion and/or that they were reluctant to express their views on politically sensitive topics. In general terms, the materials record a higher level of acceptance of the GDR's social benefits than of economic performance or the opportunities for political participation. For example, about 90 per cent of those questioned in a 1967 survey in thirty enterprises in East Berlin and elsewhere were of the opinion that the GDR provided greater social security than the FRG.[40]

The results of another major survey appear in Table 5.2. They are derived from 3,445 responses from several enterprises, agricultural and artisan production cooperatives, private firms and extended secondary schools in the

Table 5.2:   East Germans' attitude to the level of development of socialist construction in the GDR, 1970

	Good (%)	Satisfactory (%)	Unsatisfactory (%)	No answer (%)
Social security	65.8	25.5	3.5	5.2
Education	77.2	11.2	1.0	10.6
Economic development	33.5	38.4	10.6	17.5
Science and technology	51.0	30.1	7.4	11.5
Socialist democracy	34.9	31.8	14.1	19.2
Cultural development	45.3	32.7	9.0	13.0
Free development of personality	34.4	29.3	19.9	16.4

Source: Niemann H. 1993: 43

Angermünde, Görlitz and Gera districts in the summer of 1970. Education and social security scored positive ratings above 65 per cent, thus underlining their importance to the stability of the system; in contrast, the free development of personality, socialist democracy and economic development attracted the least positive assessments. Although the latter percentage ratings are not particularly low, their position on the ladder should be interpreted as indicative of serious deficiencies.

The editor of a published edition of these internal public opinion surveys, Heinz Niemann, contends that the data support the argument that most East Germans regarded the GDR system as legitimate, at least between 1965 and 1978, before a wide gap opened up between the populace and the SED *nomenklatura* during the 1980s.[41] While it can be accepted that certain aspects of policy – guaranteed employment, general social security and educational opportunities – undoubtedly helped to bind East Germans to the paternalistic social welfare system and bolstered the stability of SED rule, the data do not point unequivocally to the conclusion that the GDR was a legitimate construct in the eyes of a majority of its citizens. First, there are the methodological problems of drawing this kind of conclusion from the materials of an institute which was firmly embedded in the SED-controlled system. Thus the high percentage of positive responses must be treated with caution as there was no guarantee that respondents would risk giving 'honest' answers. Another drawback is that the surveys give no indication of the double life typical of so many East Germans; they performed their public role as comrades but retreated into a semi-private sphere in which other standards and criteria applied. Furthermore, the division of Germany and the coercive and centralistic features of the system precluded the national and democratic preconditions of a legitimate polity. This does not rule out, however, the formation of a series of distinctive GDR identifications over several decades around a high expectation of the state as a provider of services, full employment, extensive vocational opportunities for women, relatively narrow income differentials and a high level of social security. This type of identity cluster, which was reinforced during the Honecker era, would prove to be a major psychological and cultural obstacle to the unification of Germany since 1990.

References

1. Lapp P. J. 1998: 248; Wolle S. 1998: 284

2. Koop V. 1996: 352–3; Lapp P. J. 1998: 248

3. Jochum D. 1996: 147, 153

4. Cited in McAdams A. J. 1996: 62

5. Shears D. 1970: 10

6. Werkentin F. 1995: 268

7. Fricke K. W. 1979: 522–7; Finn G. 1996: 52

8. Deutscher Bundestag VIII 1995: 14

9. Ibid., II/1 1995: 228

10. Werkentin F. 1995: 271

11. Kaiser M. 1997: 68–9

12. Roesler J. 1993a: 29

13. Pirker T., Lepsius R., Weinert R., Hertle H.-H. 1995: 39–40, 292–3

14. Leptin G., Melzer M. 1978: 30–1, 36–40

15. Kaiser M. 1997: 75; Przybylski P. 1992: 148–50

16. Wolf H. 1991: 26

17. Ludz P. C. 1970: 45

[124]   18. Kaiser M. 1997: 86–99

19. Kopstein J. 1994: 604

20. Weber H. 1985: 359

21. Dennis M. 1988: 170, 172

22. Kaiser M. 1997: 134–42

23. Kecht W. Ph 1999: 74–6

24. Berendonk B. 1992: 51–9, 107–30, 145–93; Deutscher Bundestag III/2 1995: 905–23

25. Ludz P. C. 1970: 13

26. Fricke K. W. 1979: 555

27. Bentzien H. 1995: 228

28. Jäger M. 1982: 115–18

29. Ulbricht W. 1968: 614

30. Ludz P. C. 1970: 233

31. Staadt J. 1996: 697

32. Ludz P. C. 1970: 30

33. Schwarze H. W. 1973: 102–3

34. Hofmann M., Rink D. 1993: 31–2

35. Childs D. 1969: 136–7

36. See Statistisches Amt der DDR 1990: 13, 21, 23

37. Bundesministerium für innerdeutsche Beziehungen 1974: 349

38. Neue Gesellschaft für Bildende Kunst 1996: 32–3

39. Schweigler G. 1975: 126–30

40. Niemann H. 1993: 133, 186, 206

41. Ibid., 47, 87, 113; Niemann H. 1995: 8

CHAPTER SIX

ULBRICHT'S TWILIGHT YEARS

Ulbricht's success in stabilising the GDR nurtured the growing personality cult of the SED's autocratic ruler and reinforced his reputation as one of the Soviet bloc's shrewdest leaders. Uncomplimentary remarks about Ulbricht ran the risk of swift retribution. A teacher was jailed for six months for having told his pupils at a vocational school that 'I am not omniscient like Walter Ulbricht'. The charge was defamation of the state.[1] Even poetry was used, as in the following extract by Johannes Becher, in praise of Chairman Ulbricht's ideological rectitude, his wealth of political experience and his familiarity with icons of the Communist movement.

> *He was present when the new Party was born.*
> *And knew Karl Liebknecht and Rosa*
> *He was there when we went to Lenin*
> *And he was with Thälman, too*
> *And when our old songs ring out*
> *Telling of the Party, he is at our side.*[2]

An unflattering description by a Western journalist provides a sharp contrast to such fulsome praise: 'Physically, Ulbricht was not much of a success. With his balding head, his wispy gray moustache and goatee, supposed to be a "Lenin-beard", his steel-rimmed glasses perched in school master fashion on a sharp nose and his comfortable paunch, he is a boon for cartoonists . . .'[3] Despite the best efforts of the SED propaganda machine, Ulbricht's position as head of party and state was becoming less secure by the end of the decade than the propagandists would have the outside world believe. It was being undermined by the ambition and scheming of his crown prince, Erich Honecker, by Brezhnev's impatience with Ulbricht's obstruction of progress on East–West détente and by the malfunctioning of the economic modernisation project.

Economic modernisation falters

One of the basic principles of NES, greater autonomy for economic agents, had been seriously eroded with the transition to the Economic System of Socialism and the prioritising of structure-determining tasks. Enterprises that benefited from the vast resources poured into these tasks were obliged to submit themselves to tighter planning controls. The proportion of investments absorbed by structural projects rose by 26 per cent in 1968 to 41 per cent in 1969,[4] leading to the neglect of other branches and sectors, such as the consumer industry, agriculture and the supply industries. The problems were exacerbated by unfavourable weather conditions in the winter of 1969–70 and by a growing though modest hard-currency indebtedness. The resulting popular discontent was picked up by local SED organs and the Institute for Public Opinion Research. Widespread dissatisfaction was reported with price increases, shortages of consumer goods, lower bonus payments, stoppages in production and the infringement of internal party democracy.[5]

Despite genuine progress in making enterprises more accountable and prices more flexible, many basic technical and attitudinal problems remained. Financial and physical planning was not harmonised, unprofitable firms could not be made bankrupt, the ownership concept was too imprecise, profit was not enforced as a binding budgetary restriction and economic criteria did not predominate. Had the SED elites wished to press on with ESS, various options were open to them. They might have reduced the structure-determining tasks, revised the price system further, provided greater clarity in the lines of authority between central planning bodies, the VVBs and the enterprises, granted more enterprise autonomy, and established a more effective linkage between work norms and earnings. The political will was too weak, however.

The doubts which Ulbricht's critics had long harboured about his pet project were strengthened by the economic problems at the end of the decade and by the political lessons which they drew from the Prague Spring. From the early summer of 1970, when Honecker set in motion a campaign against Ulbricht's policies, the Politbüro was the scene of many stormy arguments. Honecker gathered around him a powerful group of supporters. By late 1970, he could rely not only on Stoph, Axen, Matern and the other members of the Moscow-orientated orthodox wing but also on Günter Mittag. The Central Secretary for Economic Affairs, one of the main proponents of economic reform, had deserted Apel in 1965; in the autumn of 1970, his political instincts and opportunism led him to join the anti-Ulbricht campaign.

The decisive point was the Central Committee Plenum in December. In preparation for the meeting, Honecker formulated his criticisms in a paper entitled the 'Correction of Walter Ulbricht's Economic Policy'. He was rightly critical of the disproportions which had arisen from the structural policy, Ulbricht's unrealistic expectations of the benefits of electronic data processing, the neglect of infrastructure and the consumer, and the setting of unrealistic economic growth targets. Most party bureaucrats would also have concurred with his attack on Ulbricht's use of experts and specialist groups not directly under party control. Honecker's conclusion was that NES/ESS be abandoned rather than any further efforts be made to correct its flaws. Faced by such determined opposition, the ailing Ulbricht agreed to call a halt to further economic experimentation. However, the termination of ESS had to await Honecker's accession to power.[6]

Prague frost over Berlin

Ulbricht and the Prague Spring

Unlike the GDR's systems theorists, the Czechoslovak reformers targeted all the scared cows of Communism. What reformers such as Šik and Mylnár were seeking was neither a Western-style political democracy nor a capitalist system but some kind of hybrid, a socialism with a human face. Their concept of a democratic form of socialism encompassed greater political participation, a separation of society's institutions from party control, a respect for human rights and an extended role for the market and the enterprise. While the reformers envisaged that the party would be the pioneer of democratic socialism, its leading role soon came under threat from the upsurge in political pluralism.

Although the reformers of the Prague Spring stressed their socialist credentials and their loyalty to the Warsaw Pact, the ruling elites in Moscow and the East European capitals sensed that the reforms threatened not only the Czechoslovak Communists' hold on power but also the country's membership of the Soviet bloc. Furthermore, in the eyes of Ulbricht, Brezhnev, Kádár and the other leaders, the Czechslovak reform process posed a serious threat to their own rule as well as to the Communist power monopoly. Ulbricht did not welcome the Prague Spring as a boost to his own experiment but regarded it as a dangerous leap into democratisation. Ulbricht's fears were shared by senior SED figures such as Axen, Honecker and Matern. At a top-level

[128]   meeting in Dresden on 23 March 1968, the centrist Czechoslovak party leader, Alexander Dubcek, came under concerted attack from the Communist party leaders of the USSR, East Germany, Poland, Hungary and Bulgaria. The 'gang of five' insisted that developments in Czechoslovakia were a matter of common concern, not just an internal affair of the Czechs and Slovaks. Brezhnev and Ulbricht issued dire warnings against the activities of 'counterrevolutionaries' who, in their opinion, were using talk of 'democratisation' and 'liberalisation' as cover for a putsch. The common imperialist enemy, especially the West German imperialists, Ulbricht insisted, was not asleep but only too eager to take advantage of any opportunity to wage psychological war against socialism.[7]

The SED leaders' fears were quickened by the positive reception of the Prague reforms among broad sections of the GDR population.[8] Most East Germans, according to new findings from the SED and Stasi archives, were sympathetic to the Prague reforms, even though the majority were probably not in favour of their direct transfer to the GDR. The combination of socialism and democracy and the more liberal approach in Prague to pop music and fashion appealed to young East Germans in particular. Theatre students at the Humboldt University were encouraged to press for a more enlightened cultural policy and tolerance for prominent dissidents such as Wolfgang Biermann and Robert Havemann. However, the growing popular interest in the reform process did not translate into mass protests against SED policy before the Warsaw Pact invasion; indeed, many SED members supported the party line, a few even favouring military intervention.

The Warsaw Pact invasion – without the NVA

While a proposal by the Bulgarian leader, Zhivkov, to crush the reform movement by force was rejected at the Warsaw Pact meeting in mid-June, the radicalisation of the reform process finally persuaded conservatives in Czechoslovakia and elsewhere that the situation was running out of control. The decision to invade was finally taken by the CPSU Politbüro on 17 August and endorsed on the following day, in Moscow, by Kádár, Gomulka, Zhivkov and Ulbricht.[9] Although the historian Monika Kaiser, in her revisionist interpretation of Ulbricht's policies in the 1960s, argues that Ulbricht favoured a political rather than a military solution, she is obliged to concede that the SED leader had no sympathy for the liberalisation tendencies of the Prague Spring as they threatened the authority of the ruling Communist parties. Furthermore, preparations for an invasion had been made one month earlier and East German troops had been integrated into manoeuvres and put under Soviet command since the end of July. However, contrary to popular belief at the time, historians have been able to show that East German military units did not engage in military activities. Instead, NVA troops were assigned the task of sealing the GDR–Czechoslovak border and East German military advisers were despatched to Prague. Yet, while East German Panzers did not roll on 21 August, the SED leaders had no reservations against the use of force and were fully involved in the planning of the operation.[10] At a gathering of the SED Central Committee on 23 August, Ulbricht defended the crackdown on the grounds that it had preserved peace, secured the southern border of the GDR, averted the danger of a social-democratisation of a Communist party and prevented the contagion of counterrevolution and capitalism from spreading elsewhere in Eastern Europe.[11] This was a ringing endorsement of the so-called Brezhnev Doctrine of the limited sovereignty of Moscow's socialist allies.

Condemnation of the Warsaw Pact invasion of Czechoslovakia was by no means universal: many East German citizens were of the opinion that it had served the interest of peace and prevented a repeat of the 1956 Hungarian Uprising.[12] On the other hand, it defied belief that the Warsaw Pact troops had marched into Prague as invited guests; many older East Germans drew parallels with the Nazi occupation of 1938–39. Although research has revealed that popular protests were more widespread than was once supposed and that virtually all the large cities were affected, opposition occurred on a much smaller scale than in 1953. Few large-scale demonstrations took place, partly because of the intensive security measures to head off mass protests. Among the major outburts of public anger were demonstrations by 150 to 200 young people in the centre of Erfurt on 22 August and protests in Eisenach and Gotha. In East Berlin, several thousand people went to the Czechoslovak embassy in the Schönhauser Allee to express their sympathy for the Czechs and Slovaks. The protests against the military action covered a wide social spectrum, including not only intellectuals, pupils, students, soldiers and Church ministers but also, as records of disciplinary measures against SED members show, cooperative farmers and blue-collar workers in the industrial areas around Leipzig and Halle.

Harsh disciplinary measures were imposed on the protesters and the number of sentences imposed by the courts increased appreciably.[13] Hundreds of students were expelled from universities in East Berlin, Halle and Dresden, and the hunt for alleged counterrevolutionaries continued into the 1970s. Although Biermann and Havemann were accused of fomenting a hostile attitude to the

[130] socialist order, the authorities preferred to impose sanctions on the small fry rather than on the big fish. It was Havemann's teenage son, not Havemann himself, who received a prison sentence. But, as Mitter and Wolle have pointed out, the restoration of peace and order came at at a price: it inhibited that very creativity and willingness to take the risks which were necessary to Ulbricht's hopes of creating a more efficient and productive system.[14] And last but not least, with the crushing of the Prague Spring died the utopia of socialism which had inspired many young people.

The search for diplomatic recognition

Although the SED leaders could feel reasonably secure behind their concrete wall, they could not ignore their country's status as an international outcast. Diplomatic recognition of the country was restricted to its socialist neighbours in Eastern Europe and a handful of Third World states such as North Korea and the Democratic Republic of Vietnam. The enforcement of West Germany's Hallstein Doctrine threw the GDR into even greater dependence on its Soviet patron and its East European allies. Even in the socialist community, the GDR was by no means a welcome guest. Not only did some Eastern European leaders like Gomulka resent the GDR leadership's arrogant manner but the potential economic benefits from closer links with West Germany threatened to erode the principle of loyalty to a bloc ally. In an attempt to bolster its position, the GDR signed bilateral treaties of friendship with Poland, Czechoslovakia, Hungary and Bulgaria between March and September 1967 and actively pursued recognition by Third World countries. In 1969, it entered into diplomatic relations with Cambodia, Iraq, Sudan, South Yemen, Syria and Egypt. But whether the real logjam could be released, that is, the West's diplomatic embargo, would depend largely on Soviet–American relations and attitudes in the Federal Republic. The experiences of the Berlin and Cuban crises, which brought home the danger of a nuclear holocaust, eventually convinced the two superpowers of the need to establish a working relationship. Making the world safe did not rule out the development of new weapons systems, but it did include a tacit acceptance of the Soviet sphere of influence in Germany and Berlin.

Within this framework, Bonn sought to devise a more flexible policy toward Eastern Europe without surrendering the FRG's claims to speak for the German people and without boosting the SED regime. Of the utmost significance for the future of German–German relations was the famous speech delivered by one of Willy Brandt's advisers, Egon Bahr, at the Protestant Academy in Tutzing in June 1963. As impasse had been reached on the issue of unification, he reasoned that it was necessary to consider long-term solutions. In the broad context of an amelioration of East–West relations through security agreements and a substantial recognition of Europe's postwar borders, Bahr advocated a policy of 'change through *rapprochement*' (*Wandel durch Annäherung*). This was to encompass confidence-building measures with the GDR, such as the provision of credits and greater humanitarian contacts, in the hope that they would promote political liberalisation in the country and, in the distant future, culminate in a reunited Germany. Bahr's innovative ideas sharpened the debate on whether a more elastic policy and a willingness to compromise, rather than the isolation and non-recognition of the GDR, would alleviate the situation of the East Germans and pave the way to unity. Although the CDU chancellor of the Grand Coalition, Georg Kiesinger, explored the possibilities of an improvement in relations with the GDR, he was opposed to recognising it as a separate state, referring to it dismissively as a 'phenomenon'. However, with the creation of a new SPD-FDP government in 1969, many of the obstacles to the policy of 'change through *rapprochement*' could be swept aside, particularly as FDP politicians had been even more innovative than the SPD in their thinking on how to improve relations with the Soviet bloc.

Brandt's *Ostpolitik*

The coalition's new *Ostpolitik* was outlined by Willy Brandt in his inaugural address as chancellor in October 1969. Unlike his predecessors, Brandt was prepared to talk to the East European 'monkeys' as well as the Soviet 'organ grinder'.[15] He offered a comprehensive settlement with the Soviet Union, Poland and Czechoslovakia. With regard to the GDR, the chancellor dangled the bait of recognition of the GDR as a separate state but specifically ruled out treating the GDR as a separate nation. 'Even if two states in Germany exist', he averred, 'they are nonetheless not "foreign countries" for each other; their relations to each other can only be of a special kind'.[16] The notion of two German states in one German nation precluded full diplomatic recognition of the GDR under international law. Brandt, though proclaiming his government's commitment to unification on the basis of freedom and self-determination, faced a crucial dilemma: a closer relationship with the GDR, while promising benefits in terms of easing the physical and psychological costs of separation, keeping alive the idea of the cultural unity of Germany and perhaps promoting gradual unification, might, on the other hand, help to stabilise the SED regime and therefore cement the very division which the *Deutschlandpolitik* component of *Ostpolitik* was supposed to overcome.

Bonn's belated recognition of the GDR's existence was followed up by concrete proposals for talks on a treaty with the GDR. Politbüro records show that, despite the reservations of Honecker and other members, it was decided to test the West. Ulbricht personally welcomed the transition from a government led by the CDU to one under the SPD as a sign of 'political progress'.[17] The GDR's negotiating position was set out in the draft treaty presented to President Gustav Heinemann on 17 December 1969: the entry of the FRG and the GDR into the United Nations and other international organisations; recognition of the GDR as an independent sovereign state on an equal footing with the FRG, not on the basis of some 'special' relationship; and the acceptance of each other's borders. After much delay, two momentous meetings were held between the two heads of government, Brandt and Stoph, in Erfurt on 19 March and in Kassel on 21 May 1970. Although no diplomatic breakthrough occurred, the main point was that the meetings actually took place. The emotionally charged question of West Germany's relations with the GDR could not, however, be resolved as quickly as those with Moscow and Warsaw, and it was widely appreciated that German–German talks would not be productive until the USSR and the FRG had finalised the Moscow Treaty. Assuring the Soviets and Poles of their intention to treat existing state boundaries as inviolable, the FRG negotiated renunciation-of-force agreements with the USSR in August 1970 and with Poland in December. The Warsaw agreement with Poland confirmed West Germany's acceptance of the Oder-Western Neisse frontier, pending a final peace treaty.

The SED reaction to *Ostpolitik*

The melting of the diplomatic iceberg promised many benefits for the GDR but it was not without risk. East Berlin feared that its Eastern European partners might be tempted to enter into closer diplomatic relations with the FRG without insisting on the full recognition of the GDR as a separate, sovereign state. The SED's leaders were also concerned that the popularity of Bonn's new course among the East German population would undermine the GDR's socialist system. By no means the least of their worries was the reaction in the Kremlin. Would Moscow be tempted to reassess its German policy to the detriment of the GDR's desire for a separate peace treaty and of its aim to reduce the status of West Berlin to an independent political entity? And would not a four-power agreement on Berlin erode the GDR's claim to sovereignty over the access routes?

Despite the many pitfalls, Ulbricht was anxious to enter into talks with a more amenable negotiating partner than the CDU. Official negotiations could be expected to boost the GDR's efforts to gain international recognition and finally consign the Hallstein Doctrine to the diplomatic grave. Recognition by the other German state and the abandonment of Bonn's claims to speak for all Germans would, it was believed, finally bring the GDR in from the cold and enhance the legitimacy of the GDR in the eyes of its own population. Benefits were also anticipated from closer relations in the economic and technological field: the GDR's flagging economic experiment would receive an appreciable boost and the GDR would be better equipped to compete with the FRG both economically and politically. Ulbricht fully appreciated, on the other hand, that the GDR's political vulnerability and its limited resources would continue to make it highly dependent on Soviet economic and scientific assistance.[18]

Ulbricht gazed into his crystal ball: after a period of accelerated economic growth and closer relations between the two German states, the GDR system might become acceptable to both East and West Germans as a 'solution' to the national question on a socialist basis. Such a goal could only be achieved over a long period, perhaps ten years, during which time the allegedly superior GDR economic and political system would propel changes in West Germany's structures and strengthen anti-capitalist forces in the FRG. After the normalisation of relations between the two states, a period of gradual *rapprochement* would then be the prelude to the construction of a socialist Germany.[19] Although the scheme contained much wishful thinking, Ulbricht was not oblivious to the dangers. This is reflected in the materials prepared for Stoph's talks with Brandt in Kassel. The FRG, it was anticipated, was likely to back up its claim regarding the special nature of relations between the two German states by drawing attention to the reference in the GDR's 1968 Constitution to two states in the German nation. Stoph was advised to counter this with the argument that the unity of the nation had been destroyed by the USA and its West German allies and that two independent states now existed

[134]   on German soil. Only under socialism could the unity of the nation be restored.[20]

Ulbricht's desire for an agreement with Bonn was reflected in his initial willingness to compromise on the sovereignty question by conceding the exchange of missions rather than fully credited ambassadors. This surprising flexibility is at the heart of the thesis recently advanced by Kaiser, Stelkens and Grieder[21] that the Soviet Union was initially the main stumbling block to an East German agreement with the FRG as it was Moscow, not Ulbricht, which refused to make concessions on the issue of GDR sovereignty. Although the primary documents reveal an Ulbricht keener on *rapprochement* than hitherto suspected, the new records fail to clarify precisely why the Soviet Union abandoned its original insistence on prior recognition of the *de jure* sovereignty of the GDR, a move which triggered off a bitter dispute with Ulbricht who seems to have reversed his position on this issue.

Ulbricht's goal of a united Germany under socialism, in direct competition with the FRG, does not appear to have commanded the support of many of his Politbüro colleagues, although their criticism was couched in a guarded manner because of the authority enjoyed by Ulbricht in such a crucial policy area. The new research has shown that Honecker, Axen, Stoph and others were more worried than Ulbricht that closer relations with the FRG would undermine the GDR's social and political order; they preferred, at this juncture, to put deep red water between the two German states. In their defence, they could point to the enthusiastic popular reception accorded Brandt on the square in front of his hotel during his visit to Erfurt in May 1970. And they preferred to emphasise the GDR's separate identity rather than the features which it had in common with its West German sibling. Erich Mielke was particularly suspicious of the SPD's *Ostpolitik*, condemning it as a political-ideological device for undermining the GDR and for organising a counterrevolution by stealth. A higher level of revolutionary vigilance, he concluded, was needed against the West German foe.[22]

Tension between Moscow and East Berlin

Brezhnev was determined to retain control over his allies but in a more abrasive manner than was customary in American–West German relations. The Brezhnev Doctrine was still in full force. Details of East–West German talks had to be agreed in advance with the Kremlin. At the Warsaw Pact meeting in December 1969, Brezhnev, much to Ulbricht's annoyance, insisted that the Soviet Union's negotiations with the FRG over a renunciation-of-force agreement had priority over other states' contacts. The GDR, he stressed, was more likely to obtain its goals via the Soviet Union's negotiations with West Germany rather than through inter-German talks.[23] Although the Soviet Union concurred with the exploratory talks between Stoph and Brandt, the GDR had to take a backseat while Gromyko negotiated the Moscow Treaty with the West German delegation under Egon Bahr. Decisions were to be taken in Moscow, not East Berlin. Brezhnev did not hestitate to remind the SED leadership of political realities. In the course of two meetings with senior SED figures in July and August 1970,[24] he reminded them that the Soviet Union had acquired the GDR through the shedding of much blood and that Soviet troops were there to stay. Nor should they ever forget that 'The GDR cannot exist without the Soviet Union, its power and its strength. Without us there is no GDR'. Germany, he continued in the same blunt language, no longer exists: 'There is the socialist GDR and the imperialist FRG'. Brezhnev gave Honecker and Ulbricht the benefit of his opinion that Brandt was planning to undermine the GDR both economically and politically. Not only did the Soviet leader rule out any faint hope that the SPD intended to implement a socialist system in the FRG, but he warned that Brandt might be laying plans for the social democratisation of the GDR. Ulbricht, on the other hand, he accused of cherishing illusions about cooperation with the SPD; under no circumstances were the GDR and FRG to draw together.

Further disagreements between Ulbricht and Brezhnev centred on how the GDR might best secure its vital interests in negotiations with the West German government. Ulbricht now insisted on Bonn's recognition of GDR sovereignty as a precondition not only of the GDR's treaty with the FRG but also of the package of treaties being negotiated with Bonn by the Soviet Union, Czechoslovakia and Poland. The SED leader was also anxious to weaken the FRG's position in West Berlin and to tighten GDR control over access to the city. Brezhnev was sympathetic to Ulbricht's stance on the issue of sovereignty as he realised that West German acceptance of the GDR as a fully sovereign state would reduce the vulnerability of its strategically important East German ally. Accordingly, Gromyko, in his opening talks with Egon Bahr, insisted on *de jure* recognition of the GDR. The draft treaty sent by Ulbricht to the West German President Heinemann on 17 December 1969 was in line with this approach. The wide gap separating East and West Germany on these issues was in no way closed by the Brandt–Stoph summits in Erfurt and Kassel: whereas Stoph argued that West Berlin did not belong to the FRG and insisted on the recognition of GDR sovereignty, Brandt reaffirmed his views on the special nature of inner-German relations and the continuing 'reality of the German nation'. Ulbricht, in an assessment of the Erfurt meeting, informed Brezhnev on 1 April that Bonn's refusal to afford *de jure* recognition was tantamount to treating the GDR as a mere province or *Land* of the Federal Republic.[25]

From Ulbricht's perspective, the Soviet Union was playing a poor diplomatic hand: it had failed in the Moscow Treaty of August 1970 to make full recognition of the GDR a precondition of the normalisation of relations between the two German states, a position from which the Kremlin had been retreating since the early spring. Although the treaty did acknowledge the 'inviolability' of the postwar borders of the two German states, even this was a watering down of Gromyko's preference for the term 'irrevocability'. It had become clear that the Soviet Union's global interests dictated that the more narrow concerns of the GDR would not be allowed to jeopardise the détente package. In an attempt to assuage his East German allies, Brezhnev reassured them that the FRG's recognition of the existence of the GDR and its acceptance of the territorial status quo were acceptable concessions which would boost the country's international authority.[26]

There was further disappointment for Ulbricht over Berlin. At the CPSU Congress in March 1971, Brezhnev decoupled agreement on the status of Berlin from the question of the GDR's full sovereign rights. This had been predictable since August 1970 when the USSR had tacitly accepted Bonn's linkage of the Moscow Treaty to an agreement on Berlin which safeguarded the FRG's ties with West Berlin. For Ulbricht, the status of Berlin and the GDR claim to the exclusive right to control the access routes to West Berlin were intimately linked to the question of the GDR's sovereignty. West Berlin, in his opinion, should be treated as an autonomous political entity on 'GDR sufferance', not on the basis of the occupation statute. Yet, as Bonn had coupled an agreement on Berlin to the ratification of the Moscow and Warsaw treaties and to the calling of a European Conference on Security and Cooperation, Brezhnev was not prepared to allow Ulbricht's stubborn defence of GDR interests to obstruct progress.

Ulbricht's fall

During 1970, Ulbricht's position as undisputed leader of state and party came under serious threat for the first time since the later 1950s. Illness played a part in his failure to stem the tide of criticism both at home and abroad. Various witnesses testified to his lassitude at meetings, partly the result of age and heart problems. Ulbricht's critics, such as Honecker and Stoph, homed in on his policy of economic modernisation and experimentation. They were averse to the political risks and preferred the security of the traditional centralised economic mechanism. They were strengthened in this view by the recurrence of unrest in Poland and by the Prague Spring. The outbreak of strikes in Poland in December 1970 came at a sensitive moment in the internal struggle for power in East Berlin. Ulbricht fought hard, continuing to insist on the merits of a strategy which placed the emphasis on the diffusion of modern technologies as the key to the GDR's ability to overtake the FRG in certain areas.[27]

Crucially, Ulbricht's opponents had Brezhnev's support. Not only was there agreement with the Soviet leader on the political and ideological dangers of the GDR's economic experiment, but both parties feared that indebtedness to the FRG would boost Western influence in the internal affairs of the GDR. The question of the status of the GDR was a thorny subject. During the GDR delegation's uncomfortable meeting with Brezhnev in Moscow on 21 August, Ulbricht complained that the GDR was not Belorussia, not a Soviet state, and merited close cooperation as a 'genuine' German state.[28] Like his East German colleagues, Brezhnev found Ulbricht increasingly intolerable. The Soviet leader resented Ulbricht's schoolmasterly manner and he was greatly annoyed at Ulbricht's boast that he, not Brezhnev, had known Lenin personally. Another source of intense annoyance was Ulbricht's propagation of the GDR and NES as a model for other socialist states and of GDR-style socialism as a relatively autonomous socio-economic formation in the transition from capitalism to Communism. This conflicted with the Soviet Union's claim to political and ideological primacy and with Moscow's sharper differentiation between socialism and Communism. Brezhnev, so he informed Honecker in private, was particularly irritated by Ulbricht's talk of the GDR as developing the 'best model of socialism' and that 'everyone should learn from the GDR'.[29] While Brezhnev was sympathetic to the East German plotters' pressure from July 1970 onward to unseat Ulbricht, he nevertheless hesitated to depose a leader of Ulbricht's standing.[30] Brezhnev preferred a delay of two to three years, during which time party business was to be concentrated in Honecker's hands. Undeterred, Honecker organised a formal Politbüro request to Moscow for the veteran leader's ejection as First Secretary. Thirteen out of the twenty candidates and members of the Politbüro signed the letter of request, dated 21 January 1970.[31] The letter played on Soviet prejudices against Ulbricht: his deviation from the Soviet model of societal development, placing himself on a par with Marx and Lenin and a belief in his own infallibility. Under continued pressure from the Honecker group, Brezhnev finally

[138] succumbed and, during a private meeting with the East German leader in Moscow on 11 April, persuaded him to make way for Honecker.[32]

Ulbricht resigned at the Politbüro session on 27 April 1971, although the formalities were not enacted until the Central Committee meeting on 3 May. An attempt to sugar the pill by making him honorary chairman of the SED failed to assuage Ulbricht who, despite a heart attack on 14 June, tried in vain to use his position as Chairman of the Council of State to preserve the last vestige of his influence. At the final political battle at the Politbüro meeting on 26 October 1971, Ulbricht came under concerted fire from Honecker, Mittag, Krolikowksi and others. Accused by Mittag and Sindermann of behaviour unbecoming to a head of state, he was obliged to acknowledge the authority of the new First Secretary. Spied on by the Stasi and deserted by his former associates, Ulbricht rapidly became a non-person.[33] His political demise gave rise to the story that on a visit to Moscow he had asked Brezhnev where Khrushchev's grave was to be found. Irritated, Brezhnev retorted that he had never heard of the name Khrushchev. During a telephone conversation on the following day, Brezhnev informed Honecker that Ulbricht had been trying to find Khrushchev's grave to which Honecker replied, 'Did you say Ulbricht? Never heard of him!'[34]

Ulbricht died on 1 August 1973, alone in a guesthouse of the Central Committee. Although the veteran Communist leader was feared and respected, not loved, he had exhibited a surprising degree of openness to new concepts during the 1960s and had defended with great stubbornness what he perceived to be the GDR's fundamental interests against both the Soviet Union and West Germany. If anyone deserves the title of father of the GDR, it was Ulbricht. The country's future now lay with the next generation.

References

1. Stern C. 1965: 199

2. Ibid., 202

3. von Nesselrode F. 1963: 47

4. Kopstein J. 1994: 608

5. Naumann C., Trümpler E. 1990: 21–1, 26, 31–4

6. Przybylski P. 1992: 166–7; Przybylski P. 1991: 104–5, 280–1; Pirker T., Lepsius R., Weinert R., Hertle H.-H. 1995: 294–5; Kaiser M. 1997: 372–4

7. Prieß L., Kural V., Wilke M. 1996: 74–9; Wenzke R. 1995: 57–8

8. Ibid., 71; Mitter A., Wolle S. 1993: 433–4, 438

9. Prieß L., Kural V., Wilke M. 1996: 231, 236

10. Wenzke R. 1995: 99–105, 120–6, 135–59, 202–12

11. Prieß L., Kural V., Wilke M. 996: 258–61; Mitter A., Wolle S. 1993: 445–9

12. Ibid., 462–4; Wenzke R. 1995: 163–9, 196–7

13. Ibid., 163–8

14. Mitter A., Wolle S. 1993: 480

15. Pulzer P. 1995: 111

16. Cited in Nakath D. 1995: 8

17. Ibid., 8–9; Kaiser M. 1997: 328–9

18. Przybylski P. 1991: 194

19. Kaiser M. 1997: 335, 368; Staritz D. 1996: 268

20. Nakath D. 1995: 35

21. Stelkens J. 1997: 520–1; Kaiser M. 1997: 350–1; Grieder P. 1999: 177–82

22. Kaiser M. 1997: 347–8

23. Ibid., 343

24. The SED record of these meetings and the quotations in the paragraph are in
    Przybylski P. 1991: 280–1, 283, 287 and Przbylski P. 1992: 341–2.

25. Nakath D. 1995: 28

26. Przybylski P. 1991: 283

27. Staadt J. 1996: 693

28. Przybylski P. 1991: 296

29. Ibid., 284

30. Staadt J. 1996: 694

31. The letter is printed in Przybylski P. 1991: 297–30

32. Ibid., 113–14

33. Staadt J. 1996: 698–700; Przybylski P. 1992: 31–44; Kaiser M. 1997: 448–9

34. Wagner M. 1998: 42–3

PART FOUR

YEARS OF 'HONI', 1971–87

CHAPTER SEVEN

HONECKER'S SOCIAL CONTRACT

The new leader

The new First Secretary, the small and dapper Erich Honecker, was born in the market town of Neunkirchen in the Saarland. He followed in the political footsteps of his Communist father, joining the KPD in 1929 and becoming political director of the Saar branch of the Young Communist League two years later. The economic recession in Weimar Germany left a deep impression on Honecker. Not only did it convince him of the iniquities of the capitalist system but it also fostered feelings of solidarity with fellow members of the working class. A training year at Moscow's Communist Youth International School in the early 1930s created a deep emotional bond with the Soviet Union and reinforced his belief in Soviet-style socialism as the system of the future. After Hitler came to power, Honecker engaged in underground activities in Berlin, the Ruhr and the Saarland. Arrested in December 1935 on a charge of conspiracy for high treason, he was sentenced in 1937 to ten years' imprisonment in the Brandenburg-Görden jail. After the downfall of the Third Reich, he rapidly ascended the SED political ladder. He held the important post of FDJ Chairman between 1946 and 1958 and entered the Politbüro as a candidate member in 1950. Eight years later, he became a full member of the Politbüro as well as the Central Committee Secretary for Security.

Given his reputation as an ultra-dogmatist and his wooden style as a public speaker, most Western observers anticipated an unimaginative and drabber junior Ulbricht. Once in power, Honecker proved to be more relaxed and less bombastic than his predecessor. Like the veteran Saxon, Honecker was highly manipulative, devious and autocratic; he was, however, even more reluctant than Ulbricht to engage in critical debate with senior colleagues, often withholding key data and presenting them with a *fait accompli*. Too

[144]   critical an intellect, it might be argued, would disqualify a Communist from top office; what was needed in the Brezhnev era of streamlined centralisation was an *apparatchik* like Honecker who was experienced in the operation of the administrative-command system and fully committed to Marxist-Leninist doctrine. A political joke illustrates this. During a conversation with the West German Chancellor, Helmut Kohl, in 1987, Honecker expressed his curiosity as to the level of intelligence among members of Kohl's cabinet. As a test, Kohl posed the following question to his Foreign Minister, Hans-Dietrich Genscher: 'Who am I? I am not my brother but I am the son of my parents'. Without hesitation, Genscher gave the correct answer: 'It's me'. On his return to East Berlin, Honecker put the same question to his intelligence chief, Erich Mielke. Baffled, Mielke asked for more time. At the end of a week, during which he had mobilised the resources of his entire ministry, Mielke was still unable to come up with the answer. Honecker assured him that it was simple: 'Hans-Dietrich Genscher! . . . But don't ask me why'.[1]

Within the first two years of his accession, Honecker had tightened his hold on power by the temporary demotion of Stoph, a potential rival, to the post of Chairman of the State Council and by the promotion into the Politbüro of several close allies such as Joachim Herrmann, Konrad Naumann and Inge Lange, all former associates in the FDJ, and Erich Mielke. In terms of overall policy, Honecker was anxious to repair the damage done to GDR–Soviet relations under Ulbricht and to ensure that détente and the 1972 Basic Treaty with the Federal Republic did not harm the GDR's fragile social and political order. While Honecker was determined to maintain the SED's political primacy, he also sought to broaden the appeal of the regime by a cultural thaw and by an appreciable improvement in living standards. The development of an informal 'social contract' was indicative of this search for an accommodation with the East German population.

Cultural liberalisation

Honecker caused a minor sensation when he declared in December 1971 that 'If one proceeds from the social premise of socialism, there can be in my view no taboos in the realm of art and literature. This applies both to questions of content and style – in short, to the concept of artistic mastery'.[2] Ironically, this was the same Honecker who, in 1965, had spearheaded the attack on writers for allegedly inciting immorality and decadence. Further encouragement for writers and artists came in July 1972 when the Central Committee Secretary for Science and Culture, Kurt Hager, broadened socialist realism to encompass 'scope for a wealth of forms, varieties of presentation of style, and individual refinements'.[3] All this was part of a broader relaxation of controls. Jeans appeared in the shops, the playing of beat music was allowed, and long hair and short skirts lost much of their ideological edge. The highly popular film *Legende von Paul und Paula* (1973) received the go-ahead from Honecker shortly before its premiere despite the scene where Paul removed his FDJ uniform before making love to Paula on a flower-covered bed. Listening to Western programmes was no longer a taboo after Honecker bowed to the inevitable when, in May 1973, he kindly let it be known that anyone could switch on Western TV and radio according to their inclination. Although the SED retained its monopoly on the domestic mass media, the new approach was a belated acknowledgement that the GDR was unable to withdraw unilaterally from the battle of the air waves.

The cultural thaw released a backlog of work which had not been allowed to enter the public domain. They included Stefan Heym's critique of Stalinism under a biblical cover (*The King David Report*), Ulrich Plenzdorf's realistic depiction of GDR youth culture (*The New Sorrows of Young W*), and Brigitte Reimann's presentation of the clash between the idealism of a young woman architect and an inflexible bureaucracy (*Franziska Linkerhand*). Two other works by Heym, which had previously appeared only in the West, *Lasalle* and *Die Schmähschrift*, also received the publishing green light. Plenzdorf's work, which was performed on the stage before it appeared in book form, aroused great interest in both East and West Germany. It concerned a 17-year-old, Edgar Wibeau, who fled his family to leave a bohemian life in East Berlin. Jeans were his badge of independence:

> *Can you imagine a life without jeans? Jeans are the greatest pants in the world . . . It always killed me when I saw some twenty-five-year-old fogy with jeans on that he's forced up tight over his bloated thighs and then belted up tight at the waist. Jeans are supposed to be hip pants, I mean they'er pants that will slip down off your hips if you don't buy them small enough, and they stay up by friction. You naturally can't have fat hips and certainly not a fat ass, because otherwise they won't snap together. People over twenty-five are too dense to grasp that. That is if they're card-carrying Communists and beat their wives.*[4]

Why had Honecker given his seal of approval to an enlargement of the artists' creative space? Perhaps by allowing writers and artists to air their ideas on the development of society, he was hoping to exercise a more subtle form of control than he himself had practised in the past. This kind of approach

[146]   typified the precarious and fluid relationship between Communist regimes and critical intellectuals; it was part of a cycle of repression and relaxation of party control. Furthermore, Honecker probably expected to retain ultimate control of the cultural intelligentsia as it was so thoroughly infiltrated by the Stasi and as he was also aware that a belief in some form of socialism kept many writers loyal to the GDR.

There were, however, limits to the regime's tolerance, even in the years of the cultural thaw between 1971 and 1976. For example, Heym's book on the June 1953 Uprising only appeared in the West, and it was not until the beginning of the 1980s that Loest's *Es geht seinen Gang oder Mühen in unseren Ebenen* could be published in the GDR. Yet, despite the many restrictions and the ideological frost after Biermann's expatriation in 1976, GDR literature continued to be a vital and indispensable mechanism for the exploration of many social and political problems. Several important works in the 1980s probed some highly sensitive issues in an unusually frank manner: corruption in the SED (Volker Braun's *Hinze und Kunze*), the distortion of the historical record (Fühmann's *Märkische Forschungen*), environmental pollution (Monika Maron's *Flugasche*), superpower rivalry (Christa Wolf's *Cassandra*) and family, marital and gender conflicts.

The social contract

Like his Hungarian, Polish and other East European counterparts, Honecker was anxious to secure popular support and, hopefully, regime legitimacy by means of the socio-economic mode of legitimation based on the role of the party-state in providing social and economic benefits for its citizens. Legitimacy may be understood as 'the foundation of such governmental power as is exercised both with a consciousness on the government's part that it has the right to govern and with some recognition of the governed of that right'.[5] Anti-fascism and socialism had been deployed as modes of legitimation since the early years of the GDR and, though enjoying considerable resonance, had become increasingly ritualistic. For the SED regime, socio-economic performance offered another road to legitimacy, particularly in view of its difficulties in devising a new national identity and its refusal to contemplate the Western mode of legitimation described by the political scientist T. H. Rigby as the 'rational-legal' rule. Although rational-legal elements were applied to the administration of society, this was a far cry from the pluralistic concept whereby the state is not expected to dictate goals and tasks but, while engaged in substantial steering, primarily seeks to provide a stable framework within which the various units may pursue autonomous goals. In other words, although Honecker's SED made greater use of consensual elements, it was nevertheless unwilling to abandon its power monopoly.

The socio-economic mode of legitimation and the economic-political tradeoff on which it was based may be described as a tacit 'social contract' or 'social compact'. In return for widespread acknowledgement of its political primacy, the SED offered improvements in the supply of consumer goods and a guaranteed social minimum. The fundamental elements of the 'social contract' had been discernible in Ulbricht's last decade, but it remained for Honecker to assemble the components in a more cogent framework. The 'informal bargain' between regime and society was based on a high level of social welfare, improved housing and a comprehensive education and health care system. Other key aspects included full employment, stable prices, a less than tight correlation between earnings and performance, and steadily rising living standards.

The central features of the 'social contract' were enshrined in the 'Main Task' (*Hauptaufgabe*), announced by Honecker at the 1971 SED Party Congress. The SED committed itself to an improvement in the material and cultural standard of living of the people on the basis of a high tempo of development of socialist production, scientific-technical progress and the growth of labour productivity. Five years later, in the new SED programme, the notion of 'the unity of economic and social policy' was incorporated programmatically into the 'Main Task' in recognition of the close linkage between economic growth and social outcomes. Higher economic growth and greater efficiency were to secure the systematic improvement of working and living conditions. And then, as part of a virtuous circle, better welfare provision would help create a social environment appropriate to the release of new driving forces for further economic development. Although Honecker deliberately distanced himself from Ulbricht's rash talk of a breakthrough in the scientific-technical revolution and maintained a discreet silence on his predecessor's goal to overtake the FRG, the new strategy was beset by two major questions: how could the social programme be financed and would goulash Communism prove to be an acceptable alternative to the social market system of West Germany?

The subvention of the social programme was a question which troubled economic planners and financial experts throughout the entire Honecker period. The bill for the most heavily subsidised items – basic foodstuffs, rents

[148]   and public transport – rose from 16.9 million Marks in 1980 to 49.8 million Marks in 1988. For every 100 Marks spent on foodstuffs, the subsidy amounted to 85 Marks. For example, a kilo of rye cost about 0.50 Marks and whereas a kilo of salami cost 10.80 Marks in the shops, state support amounted to a further 13.99 Marks.[6] As early as 1972, the President of the State Bank, Grete Wittkowski, expressed serious reservations, believing that subsidies would exacerbate the country's hard currency debt.[7] Her view was shared by the head of the State Planning Commission, Gerhard Schürer. When, at a Politbüro meeting in 1972, Schürer questioned whether the GDR could finance the social programme, Honecker retorted that this was tantamount to sabotaging the decisions of the Party Congress. The problems could be solved, he assured Schürer, by the SED's mobilisation of the workers and by the stimulus given to work performance by higher earnings.[8] With a vivid recollection of the social deprivation of the 1930s, Honecker genuinely believed that the social security net was one of the outstanding achievements of the GDR system. His view of socialism, Schürer recalls, was simplistic: 'If people have a dry, warm apartment, cheap basic foodstuffs, a job, they will be productive and therefore socialism will flourish'.[9]

Goulash Communism

The first quinquennium of Honecker's rule has been referred to as 'Honi's best years' in the light of a considerable rise in East German living standards. The 1971 Party Congress, Honecker's first as party leader, introduced improvements in working hours and family loans. Further progress was made five years later. In May 1976, an increase in wages was announced for the one million workers whose gross monthly wage of 350 to 500 Marks placed them in the lowest paid category. The minimum wage was raised from 350 to 400 Marks. One year later, shiftworkers, a rapidly expanding group, received three additional holidays. Pensioners also benefited: from December 1976, the minimum monthly pension was increased from 200 to 250 Marks for those who had worked for up to fourteen years, and from 240 to 300 Marks for those with over forty-four years' service.[10] Despite these gains, the average pension was one-third below the average gross wage and expensive manufactured goods were out of the reach of many pensioners.

In terms of basic consumer goods, living standards during the 1970s and 1980s were by no means uncomfortable. Most households possessed a refrigerator and a television and by the early 1980s over 40 per cent of households owned a car. However, East German consumers experienced many frustrations. The quality of consumer goods tended to be inferior to those of West Germany and many semi-luxuries were in short supply. Microwaves, video recorders and tumble driers were simply not available. Long delays occurred in the delivery of even so modest a motor car as the GDR's own Trabant and its slightly superior version, the Wartburg. East Germans had to reckon with a wait of between twelve and seventeen years for the delivery of a new motor vehicle. The strange but logical outcome was that a secondhand car cost more than a new one. The hunt for a car, an apartment, building materials and a craftsman was, along with queues in shops, a constant theme of everyday life, a consequence of out-of-date technology and inefficient bureaucratic methods of distribution. The amount of time spent by households on shopping for groceries, about four hours per week, hardly changed throughout the Honecker era.[11]

Partly to fill the gaps in supplies, East German consumers were permitted to purchase high-quality clothing and leather goods, often of Western origin and at high prices, at the *Exquisit* shops and, since 1976, foodstuffs and drink at *Delikat* shops. Hard currency Intershops, which opened in 1962, the same year as the *Exquisit* outlets, and which stocked Western cosmetics, TV sets, clothing and other items for purchase by Western visitors, were made available to GDR citizens in 1974. The Intershops divided East Germans into Deutschmark 'haves' and 'have-nots', depending on whether or not they had relatives or other contacts in the West. Their very existence served to highlight the shortages in GDR society and the West's greater capacity to produce high-quality goods.

Family policy – '*Muttipolitik*'

The 1966 Family Code had deemed the family to be irreplaceable for the upbringing and socialisation of children and that socialism alone fostered a new equality in relations between spouses. The Code's notion of the ideal family was the nuclear unit centred around a married couple, a unit which allegedly found its fulfilment in the birth and raising of children. State support for the family was extensive. For example, in 1972 a package of social welfare measures improved maternity leave and eased working conditions for mothers in full-time employment. In addition, the state granted a birth allowance of 1,000 Marks per child and a marriage loan of 5,000 Marks. 1,000 Marks were then deducted for a first-born child and an additional 1,500 and 2,500 Marks for a second and third child respectively. Four years later, an even more generous set of measures was introduced. Women who

[150] gave birth to a second child were entitled to claim release from work for one year on pay equivalent to 65–90 per cent of their net earnings – the famous 'Baby Year' – and maternity leave was extended to six weeks before and twenty weeks after pregnancy. Further increases in child benefit allowances and loans for married couples followed in the later 1980s and the 'Baby Year' was extended to working women after the birth of their first baby.

East German women gave birth at a relatively early age, the majority between 20 and 25 years of age, and most returned to work after only a short break. 91 per cent of women of working age either had a job or were engaged in some form of training, one of the highest labour participation rates in the world. Women's desire to work and to combine a job with their family roles were such deeply engrained norms that they would survive the social and economic shocks of German unification. This was also true of their commitment to the right to an abortion. In March 1972, the *Volkskammer* agreed, despite the unprecented registration of fourteen votes against and eight abstentions by CDU representatives, to an abortion law, which gave women the right to decide on an abortion and made abortion available on demand within the first twelve weeks of pregnancy.

The provision of pre-school care expanded rapidly and special arrangements were made for shiftworkers' children. Between 1970 and 1980, the provision of kindergarten places per 1,000 children rose from 645 to 922 and that of crèche places from 291 to 612. The generous support for the family and working women reflected broader SED goals such as the legitimation of its rule, the mobilisation of women for work and the reproduction of the population. Not only had the mass emigration before the building of the Wall reduced the working population but the fall in the birth rate since 1965 threatened to exacerbate the labour shortage. By 1975, the birth rate had plunged to 10.5 per 1,000 inhabitants, one of the lowest birth rates in the world, and was expected to decline further. According to Arno Donda, the President of the State Central Administration for Statistics, the GDR's population would drop by 1.1 million between 1972 and the end of the millennium.[12] By 1989, the number of persons over 80 years of age was expected to increase from 402,000 to 506,000, thereby putting even greater pressure on medical and nursing care. The new social welfare measures referred to above did, however, help to stimulate an eventual rise in the birth rate from 1975 onwards as well as a modest and temporary baby boom in the late 1970s and early 1980s.

Many women opted to reduce the size of their families because of the strain of coping with their multiple roles as mother, partner, houseworker and employee. The task of taking children to the crèche or kindergarten in the early morning and then collecting them in the evening was often both arduous and hectic, and usually fell on mothers. The heavy burdens borne by women were alleviated, but not resolved, by the family policy measures of the 1970s and 1980s, partly because traditional patterns of labour within the family disadvantaged women as regards the amount of disposable free time and career opportunities. According to a 1972 time budget, women performed the housework without any assistance in 54 per cent and most of it in 34.5 per cent of households. A balanced division of labour was achieved in only 10.1 per cent. Childrearing exhibited a similar pattern.[13] In a political system dominated by older men, policy was imbued with strong paternalistic elements; in consequence, family policy tended to be *Muttipolitik*. Instead of introducing concrete measures to readdress fundamental disparities between men and women in the private sphere, the authorities tended to fall back on exhorting men to help their working partners.

The family as a niche

There are many indications of a widespread and increasing retreat by the family into a semi-private life. A high proportion of free time was linked closely to the family, performing jobs around the house and helping to raise children. In the GDR more disposable free time was spent with the family than in the FRG, attributable in part to the more limited range of leisure opportunities in the east and to the family's function as a retreat from the political pressures in the public domain. Watching Western TV programmes was the classic example of this retreat. Although the widespread consumption of the Western media meant, to the annoyance of the regime, that many East Germans only 'lived' part of the time in their own country, it nevertheless performed a stabilisation function by providing partial compensation for the dull fare in the GDR's own tightly controlled media and for the absence of freedom to travel.

Despite the amount of time spent by childern on pre-school care (on average about 35 hours per week in the kindergarten) and despite the considerable role played by the FDJ and the Thälmann Pioneers in the lives of young people, the family was by no means redundant as an agent of socialisation. Indeed, children and young people rated their parents highly as advisers and confidants in such matters as choosing a career and childrearing. And in broader terms, family members were even more crucial than work colleagues and friends in dealing with sensitive personal problems and in obtaining goods and services

[152] for everyday use.[14] All this was a far cry from the Family Code's ideal family
and indicates that East German society was by no means a pliable instrument
of the SED state. The regime had to trim its ideology and tolerate the partial
privatisation of family life, reassuring itself that this development posed no
threat to the pacification of society. Yet the family was by no means an autonomous niche in a socialist world. Its functions and structures were shaped
by the regime's economic and social policies and it was also penetrated by
agents of the Stasi. Close relatives are known to have kept watch on each
other, for example, the writer Hans Joachim Schädlich was spied on by his
own brother.

Although the predominant family type in the GDR was the nuclear family
and marriage was the preferred option of most East Germans, relationship
patterns underwent considerable change in the final two decades of the regime. Cohabitation, divorce, lone parenthood and illegitimacy rocketed.
Whereas in 1970 the proportion of children born out of wedlock was 13.3
per cent, by 1989 it had escalated to almost one-third of all live births, three
times higher than in the FRG. Lone parents, overwhelmingly women, who
were raising at least one child under seventeen years of age, numbered 358,000
at the time of the 1981 census. This was the last census to be conducted in the
GDR. As a result of the rising divorce rate and births out of wedlock, the
number of lone parents almost certainly increased during the remainder of
the decade. Lone mothers' financial outlook was by no means gloomy for,
despite having an income which was 20 per cent below the average per capita
income of two-parent households, they were economically self-sufficient, due
in no small part to the social welfare measures introduced in 1976. Although
lone parenthood was often the result of the desire to enjoy greater freedom
of decision-making and to terminate conflicts with a partner, many lone
mothers regarded their situation as a second-best and temporary alternative
to having a partner. Cohabitation, like lone parenthood, was regarded by East
Germans as a legitimate form of partnership but primarily as a short 'trial
marriage' rather than as a permanent alternative to marriage. It expanded
rapidly from the early 1970s onwards, involving 153,173 people or 10 per
cent of all unmarried persons in 1981. About 50 per cent of cohabitees had
children and the duration of a live-in relationship was, on average, one year
less than the 3.5 years in the FRG.

Despite East Germans' strong support for the notion of marriage, as
reflected in the frequency of first and second marriages, the GDR had one of
the highest divorce rates in the world. In the mid-1980s, it stood at 30 per

10,000 inhabitants. The average length of a marriage which ended in divorce was nine years, as opposed to twelve years in West Germany. Among the factors contributing to the frequency of divorce were the GDR's liberal divorce legislation, the relative economic independence of women, the multiple opportunities for social contact at work, and the emotional and practical difficulties in coping with the reality of married life. In general, women's expectations of marriage were higher than those of men. They tended to adopt a critical view of their relationship and were far more likely than their husbands to seek a dissolution of their marriage.

Traditional scruples against certain types of sexual behaviour crumbled from the 1970s onwards.[15] Not only did the normative barriers against pre-marital sex disappear but sexual relations commenced at an earlier age. By the beginning of the 1980s, the average age at which sexual intercourse commenced was 16.9 years; no significant difference existed between young men and women. GDR educationalists bowed to these developments, asserting that sexual fulfilment outside marriage and the family was characteristic of the 'all-round socialist personality'. Although more young people were opposed to extra-marital than to pre-marital promiscuity, a not insignificant number considered it to be acceptable. It would be no exaggeration to say that a revolution was occurring in sexual norms and behaviour – to which the regime had to adapt – even though the absence of Western-style pornography suggested a highly conservative society. As part of this development, some of the prejudices against homosexuality were eroded and a few gay partnerships were to be found in the large cities. The changing attitude to sexual relations can also be seen in the nature of prostitution.[16] Although prostitution was classed as a penal offence in the 1968 Penal Code, the police tended to turn a blind eye to professional prostitutes. Street prostitution existed only in the area around the Oranienburgerstraße in East Berlin and in the vicinity of the Interhotel Merkur in Leipzig. The Interhotels, such as the Metropol in East Berlin and the Bellvue in Dresden, were frequent haunts of female prostitutes, attracted by the prospect of Western customers. A rough estimate suggests that there were only 3,000 professional prostitutes in the country but considerably more if sexual services in return for gifts are included. The main motivation behind prostitution was the relatively high rate of payment and the hard currency which enabled the women to obtain goods and services which were in short supply in the GDR. It is typical of GDR society that the Stasi was heavily involved in this intimate sphere, using prostitutes as informers and threatening them with blackmail if they refused to collaborate.

Housing as a social problem

A principal reason for the decline in the birth rate was the poor condition of the GDR's housing stock. A housing census in 1971 revealed such an appalling picture of dilapidation that the SED launched a comprehensive housing construction programme two years later and thrust housing into the centre of the country's social policy. In order to achieve the regime's target of solving the housing question as a social problem by 1990, planners aimed at the construction or renovation of 3.3 to 3.5 million dwellings between 1971 and 1989. Substantial improvements occurred in the equipage of housing: between 1971 and 1981, dwellings with a bath/shower and inside toilet rose from 39 per cent to 68 per cent and from 36 per cent to 60 per cent respectively.[17] Considerable regional differences existed: East Berlin dwellings had the highest floor space per inhabitant and were above the republic average as regards equipage with a bath/shower and inside toilet.

In line with Honecker's social security (*Geborgenheit*) ideal, rents were pegged at an extremely low level. For example, the tenant of a new building in East Berlin paid only 1.00 to 1.25 Marks per square metre and in the other regions 0.80 to 0.90 Marks. The rents of older dwellings were not permitted to exceed 0.80 Marks. *In toto*, rents comprised no more than between 2.7 per cent and 4.0 per cent of the income of worker and employee households, depending on the size of household and on whether the occupants were employed or pensioners. With rents so low and covering only about one-quarter of the annual costs of the most urgent maintenance and modernisation requirements, a massive financial burden was imposed on the state budget. Charges for heating and electricity were also low: the monthly heating of apartments cost for the most part 0.40 Marks per square metre.

One striking development was the mushrooming of vast, new residential complexes, often situated on the outskirts of larger cities. Among the main complexes were Berlin-Marzahn (about 64,000 dwelling units), Berlin-Kaulsdorf-Hellersdorf (about 46,000), Berlin-Hohenschönhausen (about 47,000), Leipzig-Grünau (about 34,000) and Halle-Neustadt (about 33,000). Although the modern apartments in these areas enjoyed the advantages of better sanitation, fitted kitchens and central heating, the environment was dominated by the monotony of blocks of high-rise flats constructed according to a standard type. The lack of neighbourliness and social isolation were identified as key social problems. Yet there were other problems, which surfaced only after the fall of the GDR. An assessment carried out in 1990 revealed that 1.73 million new buildings had been constructed between 1971 and 1988, considerably lower than the official figure of 1.92 million.[18] 34 per cent of the GDR's housing stock stemmed from before 1919 and a further 19 per cent before 1945. So much frustration was caused by the inadequacy of services for minor repairs to apartments that many people turned to the black market for materials and for the services of plumbers and other craftsmen. Finally, despite the regime's crash construction programme, a shortage of housing was a fact of everyday life in the GDR. An astonishing 800,000 official applications for an apartment were still in the pipeline at the end of 1989.[19] To circumvent the local housing authorities, some East Germans occupied empty apartments; others placed advertisements in newspapers offering a new apartment in exchange for a larger and older one or, banking on the high divorce rate, two apartments for a more spacious unit.

An employment society

One of the SED's main arguments in favour of its own brand of socialism was that it had removed the scourge of unemployment and that, through public ownership and the economic restructuring of the 1970s, workers were free of exploitation and able to participate effectively in economic planning and management. The first claim was justified and underpinned the social contract. In September 1989, there were 8,547,349 employees, including apprentices; 48.9 per cent of the workforce was female. Industry was the largest sector, accounting for 37.2 per cent of the workforce, with trade and communications lagging a long way behind. Nominal working hours were relatively long; the weekly working time was 43.75 hours as against 41 hours in Hungary and 40 hours in Czechoslovakia. In 1989, 27.1 per cent of all women workers and white-collar employees were in part-time jobs. Part-time work declined by about 8 per cent between the early 1970s and the mid-1980s, and stabilised thereafter. While relatively high earners were to be found among senior and middle-range managers, independents, members of the intelligentsia and some employees in the state apparat, income disparities tended to be narrow. Considerable overlap and a significant levelling of incomes existed between various occupational and qualification groups such as master foremen and skilled workers. The levelling-down process was reinforced by the 'second wage packet' in the form of subsidies for consumer staples, rents, public transport and so forth. About 20 per cent of people's

[156] monetary income, it is estimated, was derived from state funds and 75 per cent from their work.

The workers' second home

The workplace has been dubbed the workers' 'second home' and the work collective a 'place of safe retreat and emotional warmth'. In a stable work collective, social relations were vital to the subjective well-being of the individual. Work colleagues acted as sources of information and as contacts for obtaining services which otherwise could only be obtained in exchange for Deutschmarks or by wasting time in queues. The enterprise provided a wide range of educational and social amenities, which also contributed to the creation of an environment in which the social harmony of the work collective often became the highest commandment; production and efficiency improvements were regarded as a threat. Thus, despite the many officially inspired labour rationalisation programmes, the application of new technologies, the expansion of multi-shiftwork and half-hearted efforts to relate wages more directly to work performance, the SED was far from implementing dynamic new work values and raising labour productivity to the levels of the advanced capitalist countries. This was intrinsic to the structure of the administrative-command economic mechanism and also reflected the regime's reluctance, for reasons of social peace, to tolerate underperformance. This is summed up in the old quip, 'We pretend to work and you pretend to pay us'. GDR sociologists discovered that not even R&D collectives were committed to 'management' values such as personal success and the absolute priority of work over leisure and the family.[20] These attitudinal and behavioural patterns suggest that the labour force, though lacking effective representation, had established an informal 'compact' with the regime.

This 'arrangement' can also be seen indirectly in the high rate of worker absenteeism and the excessive drinking during work hours. In February 1989, an analysis of six enterprises conducted by the State Secretariat for Labour and Wages drew attention to the increase in the amount of work time lost through absence without a valid reason. The statistics showed that this had grown from 3.9 hours per fully employed person in 1983 to 6.3 hours in 1988 in centrally managed industry and at an even faster rate in the regionally managed economy. About 80 per cent of absentees were away from work for up to about five times per annum. Of the remaining 20 per cent, the real hard core who rarely or never appeared at work, many had a criminal record,

pursued what the authorities regarded as an 'asocial life' or had psychological problems.[21]

Partial consent – partial abstention

Opinion surveys, both before and after 1990, indicate that East Germans were not unappreciative of the regime's social welfare policy, which, together with the absence of any real alternative to socialism, helps to explain why the SED was able to generate a partial consent for aspects of the system. This conclusion is drawn from the materials of the Institute for Public Opinion Research discussed in Chapter 5, the surveys conducted by the Leipzig Central Institute for Youth Research and opinion polls carried out during the final months of the GDR. The Leipzig materials indicate an appreciable level of support among young East Germans for basic tenets of official ideology and for the GDR as a socialist state throughout the 1970s until the mid-1980s, except for a slight fall in the late to early 1980s. Well over 50 per cent of apprentices and workers identified themselves strongly with the GDR in the mid-1970s and mid-1980s and were optimistic with regard to the future of socialism. In 1975, 46 per cent of apprentices and 61 per cent of students strongly identified with Marxism-Leninism.[22] A major survey conducted in 1976 by the Institute for Public Opinion Research followed the pattern of its earlier findings. Over three-quarters of the 4,777 respondents from 67 factories and institutions stated that basic material and social security was better in their country than in West.[23] Even if it is objected that such surveys were subject to various degrees of control, opinion polls carried out after the collapse of SED power, when respondents could express their opinions freely, found that support was still solid for basic components of the socialist welfare state. One pertinent example is the survey conducted in January 1990 by the Institute for Sociology and Social Policy. Of the 1,500 East Germans from various age and occupational groups, 58.4 per cent declared themselves to be 'very satisfied' or 'satisfied' with the social security system, 59.2 per cent with their work, 61.0 per cent with the system of child care and a surprisingly high 60.0 per cent with the housing situation.[24] On the basis of these and other materials, there is good reason to believe that the regime attracted the partial consent of broad sections of the population, especially in the early years of Honecker's rule when living standards and the GDR's international reputation underwent a marked improvement.

[158]   Too rosy a picture must be avoided, however. The surveys referred to above also show that East Germans were aware of their inferior living standards. By the time of the GDR's impending collapse, dissatisfaction was rife with wages and prices, the environment, the legal system, democracy and a standard of living which was lower than that of West Germany. And as discussed in Chapters 6 and 13, East Germans were by no means as docile as most historians once thought; protests and nonconformist behaviour were widespread and intellectual dissent remained a thorn in the side of the SED. However, before the late 1980s, the widespread grumbling did not threaten the SED with a crumbling of its rule. Most East Germans were too immersed in the realities of everyday life in their own country – raising children, queuing, searching for an apartment, hunting after spare parts, coping with political pressures, playing sport, going to discos, watching Western television programmes, meeting friends – to challenge the system. They had become adept at combining outward conformity with a life in the niches of a post-totalitarian society. Such an arrangement did not follow a uniform pattern but varied in diverse and complex ways which historians are now beginning to explore through studies of the family, the industrial workforce, the Protestant Churches, the 'unofficial cultural' scene in Prenzlauer Berg and so forth.[25] While these new insights, together with the notion of a niche society which Günter Gaus popularised in the 1980s, underline that the party dictatorship was far from exercising total control, equal care must be taken not to underestimate the extent to which the party's tentacles penetrated into the depths of society. Political decisions had determined the virtual elimination of private entrepreneurship, the emergence of new elites, the creation of new social differences and the comprehensive surveillance of the population down into the most intimate of niches, the family. The ruthlessly dominated society of the 1950s was now the comprehensively dominated society of the 1970s and 1980s.

References

1. Wagner M. 1998: 124, 127

2. Jäger M. 1994: 140

3. Cited in *Cultural Life* 1982: 73

4. Plenzdorf U. 1979: 13–14

5. Sternberger in Sills D. 1968: 244

6. Vortmann H. 1990: 38

7. Przybylski P. 1992: 49–51

8. Pirker T., Lepsius R., Weinert R., Hertle H.-H. 1995: 73–4

9. Ibid., 78

10. Winkler G. 1989: 195–7

11. Schneider G. 1996: 122

12. Przybylski P. 1992: 182–3

13. Wolle S. 1998: 176

14. Diewald M. 1995: 236–9

15. Dennis M. 1998: 44–5

16. Falck U. 1998: 14–20, 144–50, 201–2

17. Winkler G. 1990: 158

18. Buck H. F. 1996: 72

19. Wolle S. 1998: 186

20. Klinger F. 1985: 26–8

21. Krakat K. 1996: 146–7

22. Friedrich W. 1990: 27, 29–30

23. Niemann H. 1993: 6

24. Gensicke T. 1992: 1272; Winkler G. 1990: 8, 277

25. See Fulbrook M. 1995: 129–30, 141–5, 273–5, and the essays in Lüdtke A. 1998 and Lindenberger T. 1999

CHAPTER EIGHT

COMMANDING THE ECONOMY

Economic management

The return to the traditional mechanism

If the SED were to sustain the paternalistic social welfare system and the 'social contract', much would depend on the capacity of the economic system to deliver higher rates of economic growth and to improve labour productivity. Under Honecker, this was pursued by means of the traditional, centrally administered economic system. Ulbricht's economic experiment was not formally abandoned; it was eroded in effect by a series of new ordinances and measures and by the removal from their posts of some of its main proponents. The return to a more direct management of the economy entailed the abandonment of a more dynamic price system, an increase in enterprise plan indicators and a shift in enterprise decision-making powers to higher state bodies such as the Council of Ministers and the State Planning Commission. The linkage between enterprise profit and the salaries of managers and engineers was abolished in 1971–72. The centrally administered economy was seen as 'safer' than NES; it did not carry the intrinsic political risks to the ruling party's power monopoly nor the seeds of a market economy. It also accorded with the political inclinations of Brezhnev and the Kremlin's ruling conservatives.

One development which ran counter to the goal of higher living standards but which accorded with the ideological goal to construct 'real socialism' occurred in 1972 when several thousand partly nationalised and private enterprises and artisan cooperatives (PGHs) were transferred into state ownership. Employing about 585,000 people, they accounted for about 40 per cent of consumer goods production. A few private industrial enterprises

survived: in 1972, they employed a mere 0.1 per cent of industrial workers
and employees and produced the same proportion of goods.[1]

Economic tribulations

The growth targets in the economic plan for 1971–75 were relatively
unambitious and the results at the end of the planning period were not unsatisfactory: produced national income rose, according to the Central Administration for Statistics, by 13 per cent and labour productivity by 132 per cent.
Living standards improved considerably, too. Such positive results did not,
however, have a solid foundation. The economic system contained many
structural defects which manifested themselves when the period of social and
economic consolidation was disrupted by the explosion of world raw material and energy prices, especially those of crude oil, after the Yom-Kippur war
in October 1973. As a highly industrialised country with a limited supply
of raw materials, the GDR was immediately affected by these price changes,
but it was not until around 1975 that serious difficulties were experienced
when the Soviet Union revised the pricing system and increased prices for
raw materials traded within COMECON. A further shock followed when,
at the turn of 1979–80, OPEC suddenly doubled its prices. The USSR,
beset with its own economic and balance of payment problems, reduced its
oil supply deliveries to the GDR.

The GDR in debt

With the terms of trade so unfavourable, the GDR soon ran into heavy debt
with the majority of its trading partners.[2] Between 1975 and 1985, the
USSR alone accounted for between 29 per cent and 34 per cent of the GDR's
foreign trade. The Western industrial countries' share varied during this
period from 31 per cent to 36 per cent, including about 16 per cent with the
FRG. A high proportion of the GDR's capital goods were absorbed by its
socialist partners: for example, about 85 per cent of the GDR's machine-
building exports were delivered to these countries, mainly to the Soviet
Union. In return for such goods the GDR received from the USSR, on average, about 90 per cent of its total imports of crude oil, cotton wool, iron
ore and wood and 80 per cent of its rolled steel and sheet metal; hence the
importance of any disturbances in the prices of these materials.

[162]   In the first half of the 1970s, the GDR, like its East European neighbours Poland and Hungary, pursued a policy of importing Western technology, financed by means of credits from the West. The goal was to modernise the economy and promote the economic growth and productivity which would help it repay its debts via an export offensive in the second half of the decade. Although the GDR lagged behind the Hungarian and Polish pacesetters, it nevertheless imported a high level of consumer goods, all of which put immense pressure on its balance of payments. The GDR's net external debt with the West almost doubled between 1977 and 1981, reaching in the latter year $10.1 billion with the OECD countries, excluding the FRG, and a cumulative deficit in inner-German trade of DM 3.7 billion. The GDR's plight was exacerbated by debt rescheduling practices and a rapid increase in interest rates from 5.6 per cent in 1977 to 13.9 per cent in 1981.[3] Trade with the Soviets also went into the red, reaching a cumulative deficit of 2.3 billion transferable roubles in 1981. However, unlike those with the West, they could partly be financed on the basis of favourable Soviet credits.

A hard currency debt was not a new problem; it had been troubling the SED leadership since the mid-1970s. Schürer, the Chairman of the State Planning Commission, a Politbüro candidate since 1973 and a member of the special working group on the balance of payments, was an advocate of a policy shift. Unfortunately, he lacked the influence of political heavyweights such as Mittag; he was basically an administrator whose priority was to make the socialist system work more efficiently, not to reform it. Even when, in October 1979, Schürer presented the Politbüro with an alarming picture of the state of the economy, he failed to persuade his colleagues of the need for change. Data collected by the State Planning Commssion revealed that net investment in the producing sector as a proportion of national income utilised had fallen from an average of 11.4 per cent between 1966 and 1970 to 9.8 per cent in 1978, while that of the non-producing sector had been rising over a long period, especially investment in housing construction. Given the GDR's many other problems, such as the wastage of resources, further raw material price increases and too high a proportion of obsolescent equipment, the State Planning Commission concluded that high economic growth and the essential modernisation of fixed assets could not be achieved without heavier investment in the producing sector and in microelectronics. Unlike education and health, the housing programme was to be spared. Honecker was not convinced. He insisted that the education and health systems were integral to economic development, a position which was supported by Hager, Neumann, Inge Lange, Tisch and Sindermann. It was no coincidence that

only Neumann of this group was primarily concerned with economic policy.
The predictable outcome was a rejection of Schürer's plea for a revision of
investment policy.[4]

KoKo

One major reason for Honecker's stubbornness was his privileged access
to information on the high level of hard currency reserves accumulated by
the oddly named *Kommerzielle Koordinierung* organisation (Coordination of
Commerce – KoKo) and, secondly, from payments made by the Federal government and Western visitors to the GDR. KoKo, created in 1966 within the
Ministry for Foreign Trade, was allotted the task of earning hard currency
outside the normal economic planning system. In addition, it played an increasingly important role in the import of Western technologies, often by-
passing COCOM restrictions on technological transfer to the Soviel bloc.
Wolfgang Biermann, the influential general director of the Carl Zeiss Jena
combine, admitted after the *Wende* that his firm could not have developed
microelectronics without KoKo's assistance.[5] The head of the organisation, the ambitious and indefatigable wheeler-dealer Alexander Schalck-
Golodkowski, held high office in the Foreign Trade Ministry. KoKo and the
Stasi enjoyed close links: Schalck was appointed an officer on special service
in 1966, and the Stasi placed 19 of these officers and about 180 unofficial
collaborators in the organisation.[6] KoKo's gradual removal from the orbit of
the Foreign Trade Ministry was sealed by a Politbüro resolution of 1972,
which placed it under the direction of Mittag and, *de facto*, of Honecker, too.
Despite its links to the state apparat, KoKo's activities were so vital and
secretive that it was virtually independent of the State Planning Commission,
the Central Committee departments and even the Politbüro. It expanded
rapidly during the 1970s, proving to be a flexible and pragmatic instrument
for the party leadership at a time of severe economic difficulties.

Soviet oil

Soviet oil and raw material deliveries suddenly erupted as a problem. In
the summer of 1981, Brezhnev complained to Honecker that the Eastern
European socialist countries were benefiting at Soviet expense not only
from cheap Soviet deliveries but also from re-selling oil and oil products to
the capitalist countries.[7] Brezhnev's complaint was not unfounded. The
GDR had taken advantage of cheap Soviet oil and invested heavily in the

[164]   development of oil cracking capacity. The East Germans profited considerably from Soviet net price subsidies on 'soft' manufactured goods, and at least until 1982 the sharp difference between world market and intra-COMECON prices represented an implicit subsidy to the GDR. It was therefore a serious blow to the GDR when, in 1981, Moscow announced its intention to reduce oil deliveries to the GDR. It was particularly unwelcome as it came on top of the need to replace a sharp fall in Poland's hard coal deliveries in 1980–81 by imports from the West. Honecker protested to Brezhnev, by letter in September 1981, that the Soviet action would 'undermine the foundations of the German Democratic Republic'.[8] Further efforts by Honecker and Schürer to reverse the Soviet decision proved fruitless, despite Honecker's plea to Brezhnev not to risk destabilising the GDR for the sake of 2 million tonnes of oil. The GDR's response to the oil supply crisis was to expand the production of domestic lignite, a decision which had serious environmental repercussions as lignite has a high level of powerful sulphur pollutants. Power stations were restructured to enable them to use lignite instead of oil and the ancient carbo-chemical plants at Espenhain and Böhlen, both due for closure, had to continue functioning. Lignite extraction rose from about 256 million tonnes in 1980 to 312 million tonnes in 1985, thus reversing the trend towards oil since the mid-1960s.

The liquidity crisis

These and other measures could not, however, arrest the slide into a serious liquidity crisis in the second half of 1982. From the middle of the year, the GDR was unable to rely on acquiring new credits from Western bankers. The East German consumer was also affected: retail trade turnover was sluggish, and the supply of industrial consumer goods fell in 1982. Honecker and Mittag sought to escape from this impasse by obtaining credits from the FRG. Whereas the Federal government proved unreceptive to Honecker's feelers, Schalck utilised his Bavarian contacts, such as the former CSU party treasurer Josef März, to negotiate two massive credits from West German *Land* and private banks of 1 billion DM and 950 million DM in 1983 and 1984 respectively. The initiative for providing the GDR with the massive injection of credit lay primarily with a most unlikely source, the Bavarian Minister President, Franz Josef Strauß.[9] The negotiations took place under the strictest secrecy; only Honecker, Mittag and Schalck were involved on the GDR side. The Federal government in Bonn, under pressure from Strauß, eventually agreed to act as guarantor for the credits.

The GDR did not in fact use the credits but deposited them with the banks as credits. Their real significance lay in boosting the credibility of the GDR in the eyes of foreign banks; by the end of 1984, the credit markets were once more open to the GDR. Both the West German government and Strauß had been motivated, in part, by a desire to avert an acute political crisis in the GDR at a time when East–West relations had been destabilised by the troubles in Poland and by the threat of missile installations. And while there was no public acknowledgement of any linkage between the credits and humanitarian relief, there was an informal agreement that the SED would be more responsive to emigration applications and to dismantling the automatic killing devices on the inter-German border.

The GDR did not rely solely on West German credits to bale it out of its financial and economic crisis. It undertook a series of drastic cuts in domestic consumption of energy.[10] Crude oil and crude oil products were removed from the internal market and exported to the FRG and other Western countries in order to take advantage of high prices on the world markets. Within a period of thirty months after 1981, about 6 million tonnes of paraffin, diesel and carburettor fuel were released for export for hard currency. In order to increase the yield of the refineries in the oil-refining combines in Schwedt and Leuna, expensive modern processing plant for the deeper splitting of crude oil was purchased from the West and Japan. The mineral oil products derived from these processes constituted about one-third of the GDR's exports earnings in trade with the West and the FRG and helped to stave off insolvency in the early 1980s. One of the major drawbacks to this course was the draining of investments from vital sectors of the economy. For example, the streets of the GDR fell into increasing disrepair as the production of ashphalt, which is largely made from heavy crude oil, was drastically reduced. Nor did it help productivity that imports had to be squeezed as part of the savings campaign. Another problem was that a wide range of goods – eggs, furniture, bicycles and butter – had to be withdrawn from domestic consumption for sale abroad, usually for hard currency. The readjustment of the GDR's trade with the OECD countries, excepting the FRG, soon took effect: in 1982, at current prices, imports were cut back by 30 per cent, while exports rose by 9.1 per cent.

As a result of these measures – West German credits, the export drive, the reduction of imports from OECD countries other than the FRG – the GDR became creditworthy once more and, according to an internal report drafted in October 1989, was able to stabilise its hard currency debt at around VM

[166] 28 billion between 1980 and 1986.[11] This figure should, however, be treated with caution as it did not include the KoKo account. Unfortunately for SED economic planners, this relatively favourable development was soon undermined by a fall in the world market price of crude oil from the end of 1985, with obvious negative repercussions for the GDR's export strategy based on the sale of mineral oil and mineral oil products.

Combine formation

Despite the harsh economic and financial climate of the late 1970s and early 1980s, the SED leadership, rather than implementing a fundamental reform of the economic system, settled for efforts to improve the efficiency of industrial organisation and the planning system. In practice, these measures amounted to a further centralisation of the economy and additional impediments to modernisation. In 1979–80, the organisation of industry was overhauled. The three-tier structure of individual enterprises, VVBs and ministries was abolished. Combine formation, especially in industry and construction, was accelerated. Whereas only 45 combines existed in 1975, the number rose to 316 in all branches of the economy ten years later. The size of a combine varied from 20 to 40 enterprises and whereas the Robotron combine had a workforce of 70,000 spread over 19 enterprises, the tiny *Konsum-, Druck- und Papierverarbeitung* combine employed a mere 600 people in its six enterprises. Other large combines were *Mikroelektronik* with a labour force of 65,000 in 24 enterprises and Carl Zeiss Jena with 58,000 employees (1986 figure). The standard organisational type was a series of enterprises linked together by the parent enterprise and presided over by a general director.

Some combines, like Carl Zeiss Jena, disposed of vast resources in contrast to the smaller units. Leading combine general directors undoubtedly enjoyed greater authority than did the old VVB management and some used their party connections to further the interests of their combines against the wishes of the industrial ministers. There were, however, numerous restrictions on the autonomy of the directors. They remained subordinate to their minister and a decree issued in 1983 required general directors, as well as enterprise managers, to submit detailed reports to their superiors on their economic performance in such areas as R&D, investments and export profits.

The SED elites, above all Günter Mittag, had great expectations of combine formation. It fitted in well with the Marxist-Leninist conception of the economy and with the belief that large-scale concentration of labour in the production process guaranteed greater efficiency. Combine organisation was both a vertical and horizontal amalgamation of enterprises, with the emphasis on the latter. The combines were expected to achieve major benefits in economies of scale, an improvement in supplies and a more rapid diffusion of scientific and technological research as a result of the anticipated closer links between the combines and research institutes. A fundamental disadvantage of the concentration of so much economic potential in these large units soon emerged: their monopolistic position inhibited creativity and risk-taking, thereby compounding an intrinsic defect in central planning. The planning system comprised a highly complex system of balancing which determined the allocation of materials, equipment and consumer goods; over 4,540 individual balances existed in 1982. The central organs such as the Council of Ministers, the State Planning Commission and the ministries worked out balances affecting 76 per cent of production and over 87 per cent of exports and imports. Efficiency could not be guaranteed, however. Indeed, the sheer complexity of central planning and the inadequacy of data-processing techniques led to a proliferation of slack plans. The enterprises, which had a better insight into the economic microstructure, sought to withhold key data from the central planners and to negotiate a slack plan in which output targets were held down and inputs minimised. With fulfilment of the plan as the primary goal, there was no urgent need to rationalise on labour.

A scientific-technical revolution in the GDR?

The Honecker regime purported to embrace the scientific-technical revolution, an irony in that Honecker had been so critical of his predecessor's infatuation with new technologies and scientific management. Accelerated technological change was identified as the main reserve for economic growth and integrated into the 'Economic Strategy for the Eighties' unveiled at the 1981 Party Congress. The basis of SED economic strategy was, according to Honecker, to combine the 'advantages' of socialism still more effectively with the achievements of the scientific and technological revolution. Certain progressive or 'key technologies' were regarded as absolutely fundamental to the growth of labour productivity which in turn would determine the extent to which the GDR would be able to satisfy people's needs and hold its own internationally. The 'key technologies' included

[168] microelectronics, robotics, electronic data processing, bio-technology, flex-ible automated manufacturing systems and nuclear energy.

Given the dramatic shortening of the life-cycle of products, the flexibility and adaptability of key technologies and the potential for improvements in productivity, political leaders and economists reasoned that the GDR could not afford to ignore new developments in science and technology. Innovation was regarded as the *sine qua non* for a competitive economy and for creating the resources for financing social welfare and security goals. Microelectronics was to play a central role in the GDR's version of an economic modernisation strategy. The intensive production of microelectronics commenced in 1977–78, after earlier developments in the 1960s had been allowed to founder. But the new programme did not run smoothly. Microelectronics, which virtually acquired the status of a magic formula, came to absorb so large a proportion of total investments that the GDR's limited resources were overstretched and many so-called new technologies were not adequately incorporated into the production process.

A crude economic balance sheet for the performance of the GDR economy in the mid-1980s would have on the credit side the partial recovery from many of the earlier conjunctural problems. The country was once more cred-itworthy, the net hard currency debt had been reduced and some savings had been made in the consumption of raw materials and energy. Yet these were essentially 'one-off achievements' which had bought little more than breath-ing space. GDR planners had shown considerable skill in manipulating the levers of the traditional economic mechanism and the West German connec-tion, but the country's political leaders were reluctant, if not psychologically unable, to grasp the nettle of radical reform, to tackle the debt burden at its roots and to strike a balance between economic investment and social transfers.

References

1. Staritz D. 1996: 284–5

2. Haendke-Hoppe-Arndt M. 1996: 145

3. Ibid., 60–1; Staritz D. 1996: 307

4. Hertle H.-H. 1995: 323

5. Pirker T., Lepsius R., Weinert R., Hertle H.-H. 1995: 229

6. Hertle H.-H. 1995: 316

7. Ibid., 320–1

8. Cited in ibid., 321

9. Przybylski P. 1992: 66–8, 288–9; Potthoff H. 1995: 18–21

10. Hertle H.-H. 1995: 325–6; Haendke-Hoppe-Arndt M. 1996: 58; Wenzel S. 1996: 148

11. The document is printed in Haendke-Hoppe-Arndt M. 1996: 63. One VM or Valuta Mark was roughly equivalent to about one DM.

CHAPTER NINE

BETWEEN BONN AND MOSCOW

L ocated on the front line of the cold war, the GDR was peculiarly susceptible to external pressures. A myriad of economic, security, military, political and ideological ties still bound the GDR to its senior partner, the Soviet Union. And it was far more exposed than any of its East European allies to Western influences: West Berlin was implanted in the heart of the GDR; East Germans were accustomed to using West Germany as a yardstick against which they measured their own society's achievements; and West German financial and economic links had become a crucial variable in the regime's policy-making process. In consequence, the GDR's leaders were engaged in a delicate balancing act in coping with the countervailing pressures and interests arising from the triangular Moscow–Bonn–East Berlin relationship. Yet, when East German and Soviet interests clashed over fundamental issues such as the refusal of Bonn to recognise GDR sovereignty, the GDR had to bow to Soviet wishes. Even a leader of Ulbricht's standing had fallen from the political highwire for prioritising GDR interests over those of the Kremlin.

The GDR comes into the warmth

Ulbricht's downfall removed the major East German obstacle to the conclusion of a series of international accords: the Quadripartite Agreement on Berlin in September 1971; the transit accord between the FGR and GDR three months later; and the signing of the first general treaty between the two republics, the Treaty on the Bases of Relations (or Basic Treaty) in December 1972. The entry of both German republics into the United Nations followed in September 1973. Acceptance of the GDR snowballed: whereas 19

countries recognised the GDR between 1969 and 1972, 68 did so in the [171]
year following the signing of the Basic Treaty. Diplomatic relations were
established with the USA in April 1974. The détente process, of which the
German–German accords were an integral part, reached its climax in the
1975 Helsinki Accords ratified by the Conference on Security and Cooperation in Europe. Honecker, who as Chairman of the Council of State led the
GDR delegation to the conference, was seated between the West German
Chancellor, Helmut Schmidt, and the American President, Gerald Ford,
a potent symbol of the enhanced status of the GDR. The GDR, which
Honecker described at the conference as a 'socialist state in the heart of
Europe'[1] had, apparently, finally 'come in from the cold'.

Agreement with Bonn

Honecker and his colleagues could congratulate themselves on the final
breaching of Bonn's diplomatic *cordon sanitaire*. The Federal Republic was
committed by treaty to the 'inviolability of all states in Europe', a commitment which could be understood to include the GDR, and West Berlin had
been denied the status of a constituent part of the FRG. On the other hand, as
a sign of East Berlin's failure to gain full diplomatic recognition in the Basic
Treaty, permanent representatives, not fully accredited ambassadors, were
created. Furthermore, Bonn's view of the 'special' nature of relations was expressed by a reference in the preamble to the treaty to the two states' different
stance on the survival of a single German nation. Second, the GDR was
obliged to accept its failure to sever West Berlin from the FRG for, according
to the Berlin Agreement, ties between the two might 'be maintained and
developed'. In addition, the Soviet Union, not the GDR, acted as guarantor
of the free flow of German civilian traffic and goods between West Germany
and West Berlin.[2] The various agreements gave an enormous boost to
contacts across the German–German border. For example, in 1973, over
6 million visits were paid by West Germans and West Berliners to the GDR
in contrast to the 1.25 million only two years earlier. Telephone calls from
West to East soared from 1.8 million in 1971 to 11.3 million five years
later. In 1988, they reached a peak of 40 million.[3] Ordinary East Germans
welcomed the relaxation in relations with the FRG, with many desiring
even closer contacts.

Whereas Ulbricht had aspired to becoming 'king' in his socialist realm,
Honecker opted for the role of Brezhnev's 'baron'. The Saarlander was anxious to repair the damage to Soviet–GDR relations in Ulbricht's later years

[172] and, by drawing even closer to the Soviet Union, to protect the GDR from the negative consequences of the relaxation in relations with the Federal Republic. In October 1975, a Treaty of Friendship and Mutual Assistance was concluded between the Soviet Union and the GDR; this was intended to last for a period of 25 years. The interpretation of socialism as a relatively autonomous social formation, a claim which had so annoyed the Kremlin, was abandoned by Kurt Hager. In 1972, the SED distanced itself even further from the Ulbricht line by acknowledging that the GDR was still on the road to the creation of a 'developed socialist society', whereas the Soviet Union was at the stage where this kind of society was already functioning. Developed socialist society, whose characteristics were defined at length in the SED's 1976 Party Programme, was interpreted as a relatively long historical period.

Demarcation (*Abgrenzung*)

The regime was unwilling to pay the full price for recognition by the West as it feared that close contacts would destabilise the GDR. Accordingly, a policy of demarcation or delimitation (*Abgrenzung*) from West Germany was implemented. Certain groups, for example, party and state officials, as well as conscripts, were forbidden contact with foreign visitors. But by far the most striking aspect of *Abgrenzung* was the development of the socialist nation concept and the dilution of the GDR's 'Germanness'. The very term 'German' assumed negative connotations. The national hymn could not be sung as it referred to the 'united fatherland'. Leading bodies and organisations were renamed. The title of the German Gymnastics and Sports Association (DTSB) was changed to the DTSB of the GDR, thereby in effect referring twice to the term 'German', instead of once!

As the SED under Ulbricht had palpably failed to establish the GDR as a socialist Piedmont, it began to shift its position on the national question as a deliberate counter to the two-states-in-one-nation theory of Brandt's government. On 17 December 1970, only a few weeks after Brandt's report on the State of the Nation, Ulbricht referred, for the first time, to a new view on the national question. He argued that the bourgeois nation of 1871 to 1945 no longer existed, and that whereas the GDR had become a socialist German national state, out of which a socialist nation was beginning to emerge, the FRG embodied the remaining part of the former bourgeois nation.[4] But the thesis of the GDR as a separate socialist nation had to await Honecker's final blessing at the 1971 SED Party Congress. In 1974, the shift in policy found its way into the revised Constitution. The reference in the 1968 Constitution to the GDR as a socialist state of the German nation was removed; it was now defined as a socialist state of workers and peasants; furthermore, the commitment in the 1968 Constitution for the GDR to restore the nation on the basis of democracy and socialism was passed over in silence.

Leading historians and party ideologues were marshalled to devise the theoretical underpinnings for the new policy. In a joint article published in the SED's ideological journal, *Einheit*, Professors Alfred Kosing and Walter Schmidt, while not denying a role for ethnic components such as language, habits, customs and other traditions, argued that: 'The substance and character of the nation as a developmental form of society, a community of people united by national ties on a specific territory, are not determined primarily by certain ethnic, linguistic and socio-psychological factors, but rather by the economic bases of society, class relationships and historical actions of the classes at the time, and especially by the ruling class which leads the society and nation at any given time'.[5] The substance of 'the nation in the GDR' was, allegedly, 'determined by socialism, socialist conditions of production, the political power of the working class under the leadership of the Marxist-Leninist party, the authority of the Marxist-Leninist ideology, and finally the firm, irreversible integration in the community of socialist states and nations led by the Soviet Union'. Such traits, it was concluded, meant that the GDR stood 'in irreconcilable contradiction to the old capitalistic German nation existing up to the end of the Second World War as well as to the capitalistic German nation which continues to exist in the FRG'. Austria, which shared ties of language and certain ethnic traits, was held to demonstrate the validity of the thesis of the divergent path of nationhood.

The SED's new approach aroused much disquiet and opposition in the GDR. Not only was the concept of two nations rejected by the distinguished GDR writer Stephan Hermlin at the 1978 Writers' Congress but it bewildered ordinary East Germans. Had not the SED claimed for decades that the citizens of both states belonged to the German nation? Had not Ulbricht insisted that the restoration of the unity of the nation was an irrefutable law of history? Were they indeed still Germans? Honecker was unable to enlighten them. In December 1974, he left his subjects perplexed when he informed them that in filling out forms they should write: 'Citizenship – GDR; nationality – German'.

From the later 1970s onwards, the SED was obliged to modify its position, an indication that it had overreached itself. Although many East

[174] Germans had developed forms of identification with their state and society, the notion of a common German nationhood was certainly not extinct. Contemporary sociological data are not easily found to corroborate this assertion. However, a 1972 survey conducted by the Institute for Public Opinion Research among workers in industrial enterprises discovered that 51.6 per cent believed that the close ties between East and West Germans and the special nature of relations between the two states ought to preclude a strict demarcation. And whereas as many as 25.3 per cent rejected the existence of common ties and a special inner-German relationship, 16.5 per cent were opposed to any form of demarcation.[6]

While it did not abandon the socialist nation thesis, the SED once more mobilised historians and ideologues to undertake a wide-ranging revision of the GDR's historical heritage and to re-emphasise the 'Germanness' of the GDR. The more differentiated picture of the whole of German history included the unearthing of progressive traits among the absolutist rulers of Prussia and Saxony and the discovery of positive aspects in the work of Luther and Bismarck. Prussian absolutism, hitherto cloaked in negative colours, was judged to be Janus-faced in that not only did it benefit the Junkers and the forces of militarism but it also contributed to social progress by stimulating industrial and agricultural development. Frederick the Great was praised for his contribution to scholarship and for his policy of religious toleration. The Iron Chancellor, Otto von Bismarck, who had long been reviled for his anti-socialist laws and as being a key link in German history's 'chain of misery', was reassessed in Ernst Engelberg's important 1985 biography. Bismark's major achievement – the foundation of the Second Reich – was hailed as significant historical progress on the grounds that by ending Germany's territorial fragmentation it enhanced the further development of capitalism and thereby, according to Marxist-Lenist doctrine, paved the way towards the more progressive socialist stage. One obvious problem with this revised history was that it reminded GDR citizens of the ties that bound East and West Germans to a common history.

A German mini-détente

By the end of the 1970s, SED fears that closer relations with West Germany would seriously damage the GDR's social and political fabric had not been realised; on the contrary, the appreciable economic and financial benefits derived from the relationship had helped to stabilise SED rule. And from the [175] perspective of the West German coalition government under the SPD Chancellor Helmut Schmidt (1974–82), the increase in communications and personal contacts since the accords of the early 1970s had helped to make the division of Germany more bearable as well as sustaining West Germany's stance on the survival of the nation. This community of interest between East Berlin and Bonn was threatened by external developments. NATO's decision in December 1979 to deploy Pershing and Cruise missiles in Western Europe in response to the Soviet Union's installation of medium-range nuclear missiles in the western part of the Soviet Union was followed two weeks later by the Soviet invasion of Afghanistan. These events, together with the unrest in Poland and the emergence of Solidarity in the summer of 1980, terminated superpower détente. The election of the conservative Ronald Reagan as American president in January 1981, determined to halt the expansion of the 'empire of evil' in the East through a build-up of American military strength, confirmed the onset of a new ice age in East–West relations; this inevitably had major drawbacks for relations between Bonn and East Berlin. In a hard-hitting speech at Gera in October 1980, Honecker set out a list of preconditions for good neighbourly relations, ranging from West German recognition of GDR citizenship to the upgrading of the permanent representatives of the two states to the status of ambassadors. Honecker underscored his demands by a hike in the amount of currency Western visitors were obliged to change into GDR Marks. The result was a sharp fall in the number of visitors as West Germans were faced by an increase from DM 13 to DM 25 and West Berliners from DM 6.50 to DM 25.

The upheavals in Poland also threatened further disruption to German–German relations. When in August 1980 the Polish government conceded the right to strike and to form free trade unions, the SED Politbüro interpreted the move as a capitulation to the forces of counterrevolution and as a mortal threat to the leading role of the Communist party. Although in December 1980 preparations were made in the Soviet Union as well as in the GDR for a military intervention by the forces of the Warsaw Pact, an armed solution was ruled out by Soviet and East European leaders, for reasons which are still unclear.[7]

During the Polish crisis, Chancellor Schmidt undertook a highly symbolic visit to the GDR. His talks with Honecker in a hunting lodge at the Werberlinsee in December 1981 was a clear signal to the outside world of the determination of the two leaders to preserve their delicate mini-détente at a time when martial law was being imposed in Poland. Schmidt invited

[176] Honecker to pay a reciprocal visit to West Germany and both reiterated their support for the phrase, first used at Erfurt and Kassel in 1970, that war should never again go out from German soil, only peace; this reflected the wish of the two parties to curb the build-up of armaments. Honecker's West German policy, which had the backing of Mittag and Schalck-Golodkowski, caused the alarm bells to ring among Politbüro members such as Werner Krolikowski, Stoph, and Mielke. They feared that Schmidt and other West German politicians were seeking to drive an imperialist wedge between East Berlin and Moscow.[8] Mielke, in his usual blunt manner, informed Stoph in November 1980 that Honecker 'is taking us and the Soviet friends for a ride'.[9] At a time of growing Soviet weakness, they were, however, unable to offer a convincing alternative to the Western orientation of Honecker and Mittag and refrained from an open confrontation with the SED leader.

Continuity under Kohl

The change of government in Bonn after the collapse of Schmidt's social-liberal coalition in autumn 1982 did not lead to the widely predicted shift in West German policy towards the GDR and Eastern Europe. While the conservative-liberal coalition of Chancellor Helmut Kohl was more upbeat in the rhetoric of unification than the outgoing administration, in practice continuity was the essence of policy. In January 1983, Kohl personally assured Honecker that the invitation to visit the FRG was still open and that Bonn wished to continue cooperative relations with the GDR.[10] For his part, the General Secretary adroitly sought to reinforce the links by inviting Kohl, in October 1983, to join in a 'coalition of reason' with all those who wished to ward off a nuclear catastrophe. He concluded his letter with an appeal 'in the name of the German people' to pursue the goal of a Europe free of atomic weapons.[11] Inner-German relations could not, however, remain an island of détente. The West German government's commitment to the Atlantic Alliance resulted, despite its many reservations, in the vote taken by the Bundestag in November 1983 to proceed with the deployment of American medium-range missiles in the FRG in line with NATO's 1979 decision.

Feeling vindicated in its hard-line policy, Moscow responded with the installation of missiles in the GDR and Czechoslovakia. The German–German dialogue was, from the Soviet perspective, incompatible with the new cold war. Exception was taken to Honecker's plan to visit Bonn in September 1984 in response to yet another invitation from Kohl earlier in the year. Honecker and his colleagues were called to account at a tense meeting in the Kremlin on 17 August 1984. Faced by the determined opposition of the new CPSU General Secretary, Konstantin Chernenko, Gromyko and other leading Soviet politicians, including Gorbachev, they were obliged to back down.[12] As part of its face-saving exercise, the SED blamed the 'postponement' of the visit on offensive remarks made by the chairman of the CDU parliamentary group, Alfred Dregger. While the episode was a sharp reminder of the GDR's junior status, the collapse of the planned visit did not, however, put an end to East–West German discussions and agreements on border controls, transport, transit arrangements, credits and culture.

The melting of the German iceberg?

Despite Soviet protestations that the GDR was becoming too reliant on Western financial injections, West German economic and financial assistance was simply too attractive a proposition for Honecker and Mittag to close the diplomatic door. Not only was the Federal Republic the GDR's main trading partner in the West but also the quotas and tariffs of the European Community did not apply to trade between the two Germanies. A permanent interest-free credit swing allowed the GDR to delay payments of its trade deficit with West Germany until the annual settlement of balances. In the second half of the 1980s, trading links were boosted by the development of new forms of cooperation between East and West German firms and by the negotiations conducted by Mittag, Schalck-Golodkowski and Beil with leading West German managers such as Bertold Beitz.

As discussed earlier, the obligatory transfers derived by the GDR from its sovereign rights, which included road and other tolls, postal payments and visa charges, ranked among the main benefits of the West German connection.[13] Visa charges alone netted about DM 16 billion between 1968 and 1989. DM 4.5 billion were acquired from the compulsory currency charge of DM 1 to 1 GDR Mark on Western visitors to the GDR since the levy's inception in 1964. The standard charge from 1980 onwards was DM 25 (DM 15 for pensioners). Approximately DM 3.4 billion in cash or kind were acquired from Bonn to buy people free. This process was regularised in 1964 and negotiations on behalf of the GDR were conducted by the lawyer Dr Wolfgang Vogel. From then until 1989, almost 34,000 political prisoners were bought free by the West German government, over 2,000 children were reunited with their families and over 250,000 cases of family reunification took place.

[178]   In the early 1970s, buying a prisoner free normally cost DM 40,000, a figure which rose to over DM 95,847 from 1977 onwards; a family reunification amounted to about DM 4,500 during the 1980s.[14] These direct state transfers were supplemented by the 'welcome money' distributed by Bonn to East German visitors to the FRG, lump payments to cover the cost of sending presents privately to the GDR, and building materials and other goods received by the Protestant and Catholic Churches.

The grand total of transfers from West to East Germany from the 1950s to 1989 probably exceeded DM 91 billion, of which DM 21 billion went to the state. During the 1980s, an average sum of DM 810.5 million per annum reached the GDR's economic planning agencies from the Federal budget and from the minimum currency exchange transactions plus another DM 50 million to DM 100 million each year from smaller payments.[15] If sources such as visa fees, a proportion of the transfers to the Churches and some of the hard currency gains from orders through Genex and purchases in the Intershops are added, then the hard currency obtained from inter-German transfers during the 1970s and 1980s fluctuated between DM 1 billion and DM 2 billion annually. In terms of their nominal value to the GDR economy, such amounts do not seem to have been decisive if they are calculated as a proportion of national income. Provisional estimates of GDR national income based on 1985 prices suggest that it was DM 132.2 billion in 1970, DM 170.7 billion in 1980 and DM 177.5 billion in 1989. However, hard currency injections via transfer payments had the priceless advantage of being free of interest repayments and they were absolutely vital for the servicing of the GDR's hard currency debt. The drawback of the latter policy was that the transfers were dissipated in crisis management manoeuvres rather than being invested in the long-term modernisation of the GDR economy.

West German largesse had political strings attached. West German leaders, seeking to alleviate the human costs of division, applied pressure to increase the flow of émigrés, to improve postal and telephone communications, and to remove the minefields and automatic shooting devices on the border. Sometimes there was an observable linkage, as was the case betweeen the two large credits in the early 1980s and the granting of official permission for over 35,000 East Germans to emigrate to West Germany in 1984. All such negotiations were protracted and involved much hard bargaining, which did not always have a favourable outcome for Bonn. For example, the Schmidt government failed to obtain a reduction of the compulsory exchange payments by Western visitors when the swing facility was being renegotiated in 1980–81.

Growing together

Another element in Bonn's dual goal of alleviating the pain of separation and keeping open the question of unity was the acceleration in the 1980s of negotiations and agreements on a whole range of issues: cultural, sporting, academic and youth exchanges, cooperation in scientific and environmental projects and town twinning arrangements. A dramatic increase occurred in the number of East Germans under pensionable age who were allowed by the SED to pay visits to West Berlin and the FRG. Interpreting the term visits on 'urgent family matters' in a much more elastic manner, the GDR authorities permitted about 244,000 such visits in 1986, 1.2 million in 1987 and a slightly lower number in 1988. To these figures should be added the 3.8 million and 6.7 million visits by pensioners in 1987 and 1988 respectively. The flow in the other direction, that is, of West Germans and West Berliners to the GDR, was also high: for example, 5.92 million visits took place in 1986.

These visits and the many other links brought personal benefits to millions of East Germans and helped to keep alive the notion of a common German identity. Visits to the FRG and West Berlin also gave East Germans a personal insight into the contrast between living standards in their own society and those of the more affluent West, an experience which would contribute to the undermining of SED rule in 1989. Yet, until late 1989, unification was low on the agenda of the West; few West German politicians expected the GDR to disappear in the foreseeable future. Successive West German governments believed that their objectives could best be achieved by working through the ruling SED. The policy ran the risk of propping up the SED regime, thereby blocking rather than furthering the goal of a liberalisation of SED rule. The clampdown in January 1988 on demonstrators during the official annual commemoration in East Berlin of the murder of Luxemburg and Liebknecht was criticised by the Inner-German Minister, Dorothee Wilms, but Bonn refrained from interfering further for fear of triggering off an uncontrollable reaction in the GDR.[16] Despite much internal criticism and opposition from Moscow, Honecker appeared to be playing a skilful hand in his dealings with the FRG. West German credits and transfer payments helped to keep the GDR economy afloat, the relaxation of restrictions on visits to West Germany promised to take the head off the steam of the emigration movement in the GDR, and the pursuit of a 'coalition of reason' enhanced Honecker's international reputation as a negotiator between East and West.

[180]   SPD politicians, too, were active in exploring with their GDR counter-parts the possibility of an inter-German security system and confidence-enhancing measures such as an atomic-weapon-free corridor in Central Europe (1985–86) and a project for a structural non-offensive capability and the building of trust (1987–89). In August 1987, the SPD's Commission on Basic Values and the SED Central Committee's Academy of Sciences agreed a joint document entitled 'The Conflict of Ideologies and Common Security'. The document posited that both capitalism and socialism were not only capable of peace but also of development and reform. Although the paper was welcomed by those in the GDR who advocated a critical evaluation of the country's internal affairs, the document also left the SPD open to the serious charge that it had made too many concessions to the SED.[17]

Honecker in Bonn

The near-normalisation of inter-German relations culminated in Honecker's visit to the Federal Republic from 7 to 11 September 1987. Despite warmer relations between the two superpowers after Gorbachev's accession to power in March 1985, Honecker was kept waiting on amber. The new Soviet leader did not regard a visit by the SED leader as appropriate until the Bundestag election had taken place in January 1987 and until West German–Soviet relations had thawed out. Furthermore, he was anxious to be received in Bonn before his GDR counterpart. Once West German–Soviet relations began to improve after President Richard von Weizsäcker's visit to Moscow in July 1987, Honecker was able to proceed with the summit.[18]

The visit was marked by the formal signing of agreements on environmental protection and science and technology, but its real significance lay in the enormous boost it gave to the status of the GDR and to Honecker's reputation. Although the legal and political niceties of German–German relations required that the occasion be called a 'working visit', Honecker was nonetheless greeted with all the honours usually accorded to the head of a foreign state. The GDR flag was raised and the national hymn played. Honecker was received by von Weizsäcker and Chancellor Kohl in Bonn and by Franz Josef Strauß in Munich. While obliged, at the official reception in Bonn, to listen to Kohl's reiteration of his government's commitment to German unity through self-determination, Honecker proudly assured his Politbüro colleagues on 15 September that the visit was a clear demonstration of the independence and sovereignty of the GDR.[19] The Stasi's assessment of popular reaction was less positive. Its central assessment agency, ZAIG, reported that while 'progressive citizens' thought that the visit had underlined the GDR's sovereignty, young people's interpretation was that it signalled the obsolescence of the Berlin Wall and of the traditional negative image of West German imperialism.[20]

References

1. Bender P. 1995: 245

2. Ibid., 191

3. Ibid., 359–60

4. Schmidt W. 1996: 7–9

5. This and subsequent quotations in this paragraph are from McCardle A. W., Boenau A. B. 1984: 8–10

6. Niemann H. 1995: 112–18, 194, 199; Schmidt W. 1996: 11

7. Wilke M., Kubina M. 1993: 335–8; Schroeder K. 1998: 250–3

8. Nakath D., Stephan G.-R. 1995: 22–4, 49–50

9. Cited in Przybylski P. 1992: 60

10. Potthoff H. 1995: 118

11. Nakath D., Stephan G.-R. 1995: 144–6

12. Ash T. G. 1994: 169

13. Details in Volze in Deutscher Bundestag V/3 1995: 1767–94; also Ash T. G. 1944: 146, 153–5

14. Rehlinger L. A. 1991: 81

15. Volze in Deutscher Bundestag V/3 1995: 2791–3

16. Potthoff H. 1995: 34–5

17. Ash T. G. 1994: 325–6

18. Ibid., 170–1

19. Krenz's notes on Honecker's report in Nakath D., Stephan G.-R. 1995: 336–8

20. Ibid., 319–22, 338–42

PART FIVE

THE GDR ON THE EVE OF REVOLUTION

CHAPTER TEN

A SEMBLANCE OF STABILITY

At the time of Honecker's visit to Bonn, the GDR appeared to be a model of social and political stability and its position secure as a member of the international community of states. At home, the opposition groups, although becoming bolder, were still confined to the fringes of society and unable to mobilise extensive popular support; the mass of the population, entrenched in semi-private niches, remained outwardly conformist; and the SED leadership's hold on the decisive levers of power seemed to be as firm as ever. The party itself, unlike its ailing Polish counterpart, was still functioning as a cohesive and ostensibly efficient administrative force. Chapters 10–12 examine the structures of domination on the eve of the unexpected implosion of 'real existing socialism'. Particular attention will be paid to the political and administrative networks as well as the instruments of coercion, notably the Ministry of State Security. While these structures gave the GDR the semblance of stability, the extent to which this disguised an irreversible calcification of the political arteries would be crucial to the regime's very survival when the SED was required to respond to the general crisis of Communism in 1989.

Post-totalitarianism?

The system operated by Honecker's SED has been variously described as 'neo-Stalinist', 'late totalitarian' or 'post-totalitarian'. These concepts denote the less brutal and terroristic form of dictatorial rule which emerged gradually and uncertainly from the chrysalis of Khrushchev's destalinisation campaigns. Many of the basic features of the system prevailing in the Soviet bloc for much of the 1970s and 1980s have been well caught by the Czech dissident, playwright and later President, Vaclav Havel, in his book *The*

[186]   *Power of the Powerless*. He opted for the term post-totalitarianism not because he thought that the system had ceased to be totalitarian, but to highlight fundamental differences from classical dictatorships. Writing in 1978, Havel conjured up a system characterised by a 'far-reaching adaptability to living a lie'. Individuals were swept along by the automatic operation of a dehumanised power structure. Even the ruling figures, despite their immense power, were little more than 'blind executors of the system's own internal laws'.[1] He illustrated his thesis by the vignette of the greengrocer who declared his loyalty in public by following the party's instruction to display in his shop window the slogan 'Workers of the world unite'. The greengrocer is indifferent to the ideological content of the slogan but realises that to disobey would entail the loss of his job and problems for his family. But in accepting the given rules of the game 'he has himself become a player in the game, thus making it possible for the game to go on'.[2]

With the important exceptions of the opposition groups and the props of the regime, such as the *nomenklatura* cadres and the security forces, the mode of behaviour characteristic of most East Germans was not dissimilar to that of the greengrocer: a symbolic political participation in public and a withdrawal into the partially sealed-off area of family and friends where political pressures were not so oppressive as in the highly controlled sphere of parties and mass organisations. Many political rituals, such as attendance at the 1 May celebrations, made few demands on participants and non-attendance did not automatically incur the wrath of the athorities. However, the greater the desire for social advancement, the more difficult it was to resist political pressures.[3]

The most elaborate model of post-totalitarianism stems not from Havel, but from the political scientists Juan Linz and Alfred Stepan, both well known for their studies of regime transformations. Their approach has great taxonomic and analytic merit: it recognises that while the basic command structures remained intact, much had changed in the Communist world since the advent of Khrushchev. They identify four key dimensions – pluralism, ideology, leadership and mobilisation – in order to distinguish post-Stalinist regimes from totalitarian, authoritarian and democratic regimes. According to their model, authoritarian regimes such as Franco's Spain tolerate a limited political pluralism, do not impose a central and exclusive ideology and lack a political mass party. In post-totalitarianism, while a measure of institutional pluralism exists – encompassing the party, army, secret services, state-controlled economic units and mass organisations – this should not be confused with political pluralism which was virtually non-existent by virtue of the ruling party's formal monopoly of power. Turning to the differences between totalitarianism and post-totalitarianism, the latter is held to embody a varying degree of space for a second economy or a parallel society which is absent in a totalitarian regime. As for the belief system, a sense of mission and legitimation is derived from an elaborate and guiding ideology by leaders and groups in totalitarianism but, although still present in post-totalitarianism, the belief in utopia is much weaker and a shift occurs from ideology to pragmatic consensus. Havel's greengrocer encapsulates this shift. However, while technical competence becomes more significant, access to professional training is still controlled by political criteria and ideology often obstructs bureaucratic rationality. In keeping with overall developments, the top leaders in post-totalitarianism tend to be more bureaucratic and state-technocratic than charismatic and loosely constrained by socialist legal considerations. On the other hand, like their totalitarian predecessors, they are recruited exclusively from the official party. Finally, the extensive mobilisation of the population by an extensive array of societal organisations with an emphasis on activism gives way to a routine mobilisation of the population within mass organisations to achieve a minimum of conformity and compliance. Many cadres become mere careerists and boredom rather than enthusiasm characterises party membership. With regard to repression, post-totalitarian regimes do away with the worst aspects but maintain most mechanisms of control.[4]

One of the great merits of Linz and Stepan's model is their identification of three main sub-categories along a continuum of 'early', 'frozen' and mature' post-totalitarianism. The former is deemed to be the closest to its totalitarian predecessor with the important exception of some constraints on the leader. In the 'frozen' type, typified by Honecker's GDR, almost all the control mechanisms of the party-state remain in place despite a tolerance of some civil society critics and the state security apparatus may even expand in size. In extreme cases, as in the later Honecker era, the leadership exhibits geriatric tendencies. In the third sub-category, significant change has occurred in all dimensions of the regime: for example, it is less ideological and less repressive than the 'frozen' variant, except that the leading role of the official party remains sacrosanct, as in Hungary from 1982 to 1988. Even though in the mature variant leaders of the second culture might be imprisoned, they can nevertheless create enduring oppositional organisations in civil society.[5] Although Walter Laqueur is correct to point out that Linz's categories are no magic wand and that no pure, unalloyed systems exist,[6] they do at least provide historians and social scientists with a conceptual map for placing the GDR along a continuum from the period of high Stalinism in the 1940s and early 1950s to the repressive but more paternalistic system of the later Ulbricht and the Honecker eras. However, a modification of Linz and Stepan's sub-categories would seem to be desirable in view of the fact that society was

[188] by no means a puppet on SED strings. This has already been referred to in the discussion of the family and the employment society in Chapter 7 and will be further illustrated in the sections on the Churches, the unofficial political culture and the mass organisations.[7] Perhaps a 'half-frozen' post-totalitarian system might therefore be suggested as the most appropriate concept!

A thoroughly dominant force: the SED

The SED was not reticent in proclaiming its political dominance. In its 1976 statute, the SED defined itself as 'the highest form of societal-political organisation' and 'as the conscious and organised vanguard of the working class and the working people of the German Democratic Republic'. Two years earlier, Article 1 of the country's newly promulgated Constitution described the GDR as 'the political organisation of the working people in town and countryside under the leadership of the working class and its Marxist-Leninist party'. This leadership role was accepted unreservedly by the other four political parties. The SED justified its supremacy by claiming to represent the interests of the working class, the largest and allegedly the most progressive class, and by the assertion that Marxist-Leninist ideology provided the party with the keys to the correct scientific laws for determining and managing social progress.

This theoretical position was underpinned by a strict enforcement of the Leninist principle of democratic centralism on all party members and organs. The centralistic direction was paramount: all resolutions of the higher party bodies were binding on lower bodies and individual party members were subordinated to the party organisation. Democratic counterbalances such as the accountability of party organs to their electors had long been emasculated by rigorous disciplinary procedures, by the manipulation of elections and by a ban on inner-party factions and opposition groups. One Politbüro member, Günter Schabowski, recalls that his Politbüro colleagues would rather have committed sodomy than form factions.[8]

The party membership

The SED was both a cadre party and a mass organisation which penetrated deep into GDR society. By the end of the 1980s, the number of members and candidates had reached a record level of about 2.3 million. This represented over 17 per cent of the adult population and about 22 per cent of people in gainful employment. 57.5 per cent were classified as 'workers', thus bolstering the party's claim to be the representative of the working class. However, the term 'worker' was defined so elastically – it included full-time party functionaries and members of the armed forces if they had once been workers – as to render it meaningless as an indicator of social class or social status. It was essentially an ideological construct. Women were well represented in the party – increasing their share of the membership from 31.3 per cent in 1976 to 35.5 per cent in 1985 – and the proportion of younger members was slightly higher than in the 1960s. In keeping with the requirements of a more highly developed industrial society, an improvement in qualifications was also registered. By 1981, all secretaries of the regional and district party executives were graduates and one in three of ordinary members had completed a course at university or technical college.

Members had a statutory obligation to take an active part in political life. This involved regular attendance at party meetings and participation in party ideological training courses, thereby subjecting themselves to the disciplinary procedures of the party. Adherence to the party line was reinforced by 'confidential personal talks' with party functionaries. If members deviated from the party line or behaved in an 'inappropriate' manner, they could be censured or expelled from the party. The SED's inquisition, the Central Control Commission and its regional and district subsidiaries, kept watch over the 'unity and purity' of the party. Comprehensive membership reviews were carried out from time to time, and expulsions increased sharply during the 1980s.[9]

The SED territorial organisation

Below the central party organs, the SED was structured according to the territorial and production principle on three organisational tiers. The thicket of 59,103 basic organisations (1988) in factories, offices, cooperatives, institutions and residential areas constituted the bedrock of the party. Although the average membership of a basic organisation (*Grundorganisation* – GO) in the mid-1980s was about 26, many had several thousand members. The 4,673 larger GOs were subdivided into 96,694 party groups. On the next level of the hierarchy, the district (*Kreis*) party organisations were split into 242 territorial bodies in rural and urban districts and boroughs and 23 so-called functional groups located in major firms, the central state organs and the larger universities. The district party apparat was the crucial organ for the

[190] implementation of central party decisions into everyday life. Immediately below the central organs were the 15 regional (*Bezirk*) party organisations, plus two other bodies enjoying this status, the Wismut uranium mining area and the armed forces and border troops. All First Secretaries of the regional executives were either full or candidate members of the Central Committee and several, like Schabowski in East Berlin, sat on the Politbüro. The SED leadership and its apparat devoted considerable time and effort to questions of party organisation, not simply for reasons of efficiency but also because they were fundamental to the operation of the party's power monopoly.

One future task for historians will be to provide a fuller picture of the activities of the party organisations at the various levels and to evaluate their relationship with the centre. This will also include an assessment of the influence of regional party chiefs such as Hans Modrow in Dresden. The current state of knowledge suggests that the influence of GO executives and secretaries appears to have been largely restricted to the GO's own narrow area of operations. While this was particularly true of the residential party organisation (*Wohnparteiorganisation*), the small enterprises and LPGs, opportunities were greater in administrative bodies such as the district and regional councils. The SED party statute allowed for a certain degree of manoeuvre for lower party organs and executives in implementing the appropriate measures in their areas, albeit within the context of decisions already taken by higher bodies. This allotted space was, in part, a recognition of political and economic realities and a consequence of the sheer complexity of managing GDR society. Certain local initiatives had to be allowed for within the framework of competition for scarce resources and frequent setbacks in the implementation of the party's economic policy. However, the influence of lesser officials should not be exaggerated: the party leadership was still able to manipulate a vast array of control levers and the lower officials were constrained by the norms of party loyalty and discipline.

The central organs

Turning to the SED's central organs, the main body according to party statute was the Party Congress which since 1971 was held once every five years. 'Elected' representatives attended the Congress to hear and approve the lengthy and excruciatingly tedious reports of the Central Committee and other leading organs. Although the Congress was empowered by statute to elect the Central Committee and the Central Revision Commission and to determine the general policy of the party, the selection of delegates was in the hands of the Central Committee apparat. This turned the Congress into a supine body whose main purpose was the propagation of party policy to a wider public.

In accordance with the standard Marxist-Leninist model of party organisation, the SED Central Committee was in theory the highest authority of the party between congresses. It 'elected' the General Secretary, the Politbüro and the Central Committee Secretariat. A plenum was supposed to be held at least once every six months. Whereas the 1950s witnessed numerous conflicts over policy, the plenary sessions in subsequent decades increasingly concentrated on technical issues and under Honecker were reduced to empty rituals. The Central Committee elected in 1986 was a relatively large body of 165 full members and 57 candidates. Places were found for the most important functionaries in the party and state apparat. The 63 full-time party officials, including 17 departmental secretaries of the Central Committee, constituted the largest group. The State Security, Defence and Interior Ministries were also prominent. While this spread of functional groups gave the Central Committee the appearance of a representative party organ, it met too infrequently and members were too dependent on the party's higher bodies for it to exercise any appreciable influence on policy-making.

The two most influential SED organs were the Central Committee Secretariat and the Politbüro. Although these two bodies often dealt with the same problems and there was a considerable overlap of personnel, this usually enhanced rather than hindered coordination. There was, however, one major difference: whereas the Central Committee Secretariat tended to concentrate on the details of policy and administration, the Politbüro was more concerned with overall strategy. The Central Committee Secretariat met formally once per week, on a Wednesday, but *de facto* virtually every day.[10] According to party statute, the Secretariat was responsible for the direction of party work, above all for the implementation of party decisions, the appointment and supervision of party cadres and the control of the SED apparat. A relatively small body, the Secretariat consisted of the General Secretary, Honecker, and ten other secretaries, all of whom were members or candidates of the Politbüro. Each was responsible for at least one department, and some were also in charge of party institutes. Kurt Hager, for example, presided over the Departments for Sciences, Culture, Education and Health and was also head of the Central Committee Academy for Social Sciences and the Institute for Marxism-Leninism.

The Council of Gods

The Politbüro, often referred to as the 'Council of Gods', was authorised by party statute to discharge the political work of the Central Committee between that body's plenary sessions. The Politbüro dealt with important party matters in areas such as the economy, foreign policy, security, education, social policy, culture and cadre appointments. By virtue of the SED's leading role in society, it was also responsible for national policy. Under Ulbricht and Honecker the size of the Politbüro fluctuated between 14 and 27 candidates and members. The average age of the Politbüro elected after the 1986 Party Congress was 62.7 years. Elected formally by the Central Committee, the Politbüro was in reality self-recruiting by means of cooption. The General Secretary chaired the weekly Tuesday meeting, which usually lasted little more than two to three hours. Only two women, Inge Lange and Margarete Müller, sat on the Politbüro in the Honecker era. The former had been there since 1973 and Müller since 1963. As no woman ever became a full member, the presence of Lange and Müller appears to have been essentially a token gesture towards the official commitment to gender equality.

Various functional and territorial groups enjoyed a place on the Politbüro, although there was no apparent rule of proportionality. The central party apparat was by far the largest group. With six First Secretaries of regional party organisations in the later 1980s – including Schabowski from East Berlin and Werner Eberlein from Magdeburg – the regional apparat was also well to the fore. The armed forces and state security were 'represented' by the Minister of Defence, Heinz Keßler, and by the Minister of State Security, Erich Mielke. Keßler, born in 1920, and a founder member of the FDJ, joined the Politbüro in 1986 and was widely regarded as a loyal supporter of Honecker. The state apparat was served by, among others, the Chairman of the Council of Ministers, Willi Stoph, and numerous deputy chairmen such as Mittag and Horst Sindermann. The latter was also the President of the *Volkskammer*. However, these individuals did not necessarily see themselves as representing a particular sector or group, partly because many held a series of positions across the political spectrum. The accumulation of offices by individuals, notably Honecker, buttressed their influence and power; in institutional terms, it enabled the Politbüro to operate as the key political steering instrument. Several members of the Politbüro enjoyed more influence than others, a result of their appropriate administrative skills and experience, a keen political instinct and, above all, access to Honecker. Throughout the 1980s, an inner circle around the General Secretary consisted of Mielke, Mittag and Joachim Herrmann, who presided over their empires of security, the economy and propaganda respectively. The first two were cynical and ruthless autocrats who brooked no opposition inside their own sphere of interest. Dubbed the 'one-eyed economic king among the blind of the Politbüro', Mittag's economic management skills were indispensable to Honecker.[11]

Honecker: first among equals

After his accession, Honecker gradually developed from the 'first among equals' into the 'first above equals'.[12] A personality cult was orchestrated by the media. Full advantage was taken of photo opportunities: when Honecker attended the opening of the Leipzig Spring Trade Fair in 1987, the Berlin edition of *Neues Deutschland* carried 38 photographs of Honecker out of a grand total of 39. Although the cult of leadership is a traditional mechanism of system maintenance in dictatorships, Honecker was too uninspiring and awkward a speaker and too 'ordinary' a personality ever to exercise the personal appeal of the Nazi dictator or to indulge in the excesses of the full-blooded personality cult of Romania's 'supreme' leader Nicolae Ceausescu.

Possible alternatives to Honecker, like his erstwhile rival Stoph, usually preferred to keep his own counsel, while one irritating critic, Konrad Naumann, the First Secretary of the East Berlin region, was sacked from the Politbüro for an abusive attack on academics during a speech to the Academy of Social Sciences and for his criticism of Honecker's Western policy. His own personal indiscretions also counted against him; he was notorious for frequent bouts of heavy drinking and for 'whoring'.

Like Ulbricht, Honecker was the *apparatchik* par excellence. Well versed in the ways of the party apparat, he fully appreciated the first rule of a Communist system: retain control over the army of Central Committee bureaucrats. He took full advantage of his prerogative as General Secretary to intervene directly in the work of the Central Committee departments and to set the agenda of the higher bodies. His primacy was bolstered by his stabilisition of SED rule through his 'unity of economic and social policy' and by his relatively adroit negotiation of the perils of inter-German relations.[13] Honecker's anti-fascist past and his pioneering work in the early years of the FDJ also earned him the respect of his colleagues, including younger Politbüro members such as Egon Krenz.

Honecker kept a tight grip on the management of Polibüro business. Preparation for Politbüro and Central Committee Secretariat meetings required the submission of working papers and the processing of a vast amount of information before a decision was taken. These important draft documents had to obtain his seal of approval – 'Einverstanden E. H.' – before being forwarded to the full Politbüro, most of whose members were ill-equipped and reluctant to deal with matters which were not directly related to their own functional sphere.[14] Economic and financial issues, for example, were presented in such an esoteric language by economic planners that they were often incomprehensible to non-specialists.

According to former Politbüro members, open discussion was inhibited by the administrative *modus operandi*.[15] Dull routine was of the essence. The Politbüro usually reached agreement without a formal vote and on the basis of the position adopted in draft papers. Drafts were normally prepared so thoroughly that rejection was rare. Any changes required Honecker's prior approval. Another method favoured by Honecker was to resolve awkward issues on a person-to-person basis, thereby reducing the likelihood of controversy breaking out in meetings. Especially sensitive economic matters tended to be transferred for discussion to the so-called 'Small Circle' of Politbüro members who were responsible for economic affairs.[16]

Whereas the Politbüro was once a hermetically sealed body, since the end of SED rule most of its members have rushed to present their own version of events in a series of interviews and in memoirs of varying quality and criticality. Günter Mittag's argument that the absence of controversy was a result of members' lack of personal courage and of a reluctance to assume political responsibility is supported by Schabowski and Schürer who concede that nobody can fall back on the lame excuse that 'Erich Honecker was everything, we were nothing'.[17] Schabowski, who has provided the most revealing of all insider accounts, has likened the Politbüro to a disciplined body of troops who regarded the suppression of critical discussion as the positive outcome of solid preparation. And why rock the boat when, as other members have pointed out, the Politbüro was convinced that the GDR system was 'correct' and that the country was not destined for the 'cul-de-sac' of history.[18]

The privileges attached to membership of the Politbüro were a powerful incentive to remain loyal to Honecker. Most Politbüro members resided in the elite compound in Wandlitz, established in 1960 and set in a wooded area 30 kilometres north of Berlin. Each family had its own well-appointed house as well as access to a separate restaurant and to high-quality Western goods. Inside the closely guarded complex, members were cut off from society; most, except for keen hunters like Honecker and Mittag, tended to avoid each other's company, preferring to lead a separate family life. When Wandlitz's secrets became public knowledge in late 1989, East Germans were furious at [195] the disparity between their own modest standard of living and the privileged life led by the elites.

Despite the removal of Naumann and Herbert Häber from the Politbüro, the latter a sacrificial lamb to Soviet and internal criticism of Honecker's policy towards West Germany,[19] the Politbüro and the SED's other strategic elites rightly enjoyed a reputation as one of Eastern Europe's most cohesive and disciplined ruling groups, as well as one of the least transparent. The cohesiveness was partly based on the older functionaries' set of shared values and beliefs inherited from the political culture of the KPD. As was the case with so many other older Communists, the SED embodied the revolutionary ethos of its predecessor and commanded their unswerving loyalty. In the later 1980s, members of the old guard – notably Honecker, Mielke, Axen, Stoph and Hager – were well represented on the Politbüro and held many of the key positions in party and state. The majority of the veterans were born in the first decade of the century; in 1989, their average age was 76 years. As young men, most of them had been active in the Communist Youth Organisation of Germany and then in the KPD. During the Third Reich, many had engaged in resistance activities, suffered imprisonment and fought in the Spanish Civil War. Horst Sindermann had been imprisoned in the Sachsenhausen and Mauthausen camps and Hermann Axen experienced a similar fate in Buchenwald and Auschwitz. Members of Axen's Jewish family were murdered by the Nazis.[20] Other members of the elite had emigrated to the Soviet Union where they had managed to survive the Stalinist purges. After the end of the Second World War these older functionaries had been instrumental in the development of the Soviet system in East Germany and were determined to preserve the Communist hold over the GDR. They were also bound together by the conviction that the 'social achievements' of the GDR were socialism's answer to the kind of deprivation and misery inherent in the capitalism which they themselves had experienced in the 1930s. And until the arrival of Gorbachev, they looked to the Soviet Union as the model from which to learn. Honecker and Mielke both genuinely admired the Soviet Union as the 'motherland' of revolution and as the liberator of Germany from the scourge of fascism.

While the veterans remained true to the traditional core values of the Communist movement, the younger members of the power elite were well integrated into the ideological and political matrix of 'real existing socialism'. This generation encompassed those who, in 1989, were in their 50s to mid-60s. They had passed through the intensive political socialisation processes of the GDR and had successfully negotiated the rigorous recruitment and

[196] training procedures typical of their cohort. Representatives of this group – Krenz, Tisch, Mittag and Schabowski – were fully committed to the maintenance of the system and to the GDR as a separate and, in their own eyes, legitimate state. Yet, despite this belief in the justice of their cause and an outward self-confidence, even the toughest practitioners on the Politbüro must have been plagued by doubts over the loyalty of their subjects in what was an intrinsically insecure state. The Berlin Wall could not seal off the GDR from what its elites regarded as the pernicious influences of West German consumerism and political culture. The emigration movement and the trauma of the 1953 Uprising compounded their uncertainties and fears. This is observable in the most paranoiac of all SED leaders, Erich Mielke. At a meeting with his regional officers at the end of August 1989, at a time when the mass exodus was gathering momentum and embryonic citizens' movements were emerging, an anxious Mielke asked his colleagues whether a 17 June was about to break out.[21]

The party bureaucracy

The top SED leaders and the central organs were backed up by a vast bureaucratic apparatus which was indispensable for the operation of the SED administrative-command system of rule. About 2,000 key staff were spread over 45 departments (*Abteilungen*) (1986) and additional personnel were located in equivalent bodies such as *Neues Deutschland* and the party's theoretical journal *Einheit*; all were strictly subordinated to the General Secretary and the Central Committee Secretariat. Among the main departments were those for party organs, agitation, security questions, the allied parties, planning and finance. One of the major tasks of this elaborate machine was to prepare materials for the Politbüro, the Central Committee Secretariat and the Council of Ministers. It was also responsible for the supervision and control of the organs of state, the executives of the mass organisations and other central institutions. While the Politbüro and the Central Committee Secretariat had the final say on cadre policy, its implementation lay with the Central Committee Department for Party Organs, one of the most important of the departments concerned with internal party organisation.

During the 1980s, most departmental and section heads had been in office for between twenty and thirty years and, according to insider reports, were both dogmatic and inflexible.[22] However, while many implemented the [197] instructions of the Politbüro and Central Committee Secretariat in a routine manner, some were becoming disturbed at the burgeoning problems in society. Discussion of such problems was impeded by the hierarchical structure of the apparat and by the comforts afforded by the perks of office. For example, departmental heads and their deputies had their own restaurant and enjoyed privileged access to the Central Committee's holiday complexes.

The elite stratum of functionaries which helped the SED perform its leading role in society numbered between 300,000 an 400,000, that is, about 3 per cent of the adult population.[23] But this was just the tip of the political and administrative iceberg; one must also take into account those SED members who were lower functionaries in the party and the mass organisations as well as those who staffed the military and security apparat. According to Thomas Ammer's calculations, there were 691,000 SED members who occupied functions in the ruling party, 590,000 in the FDGB and 185,000 in the FDJ. In addition, many acted as propagandists in the Party Teaching Year, the FDJ Study Year and the FDGB Political Instruction; others served as deputies in the representative assemblies. Although these figures amount to 1.9 million, this is not the end of the crocodile's tail as one must also add the functionaries in the state system, the enterprise militia groups, the GST and other mass organisations. As many held more than one office, the actual number of those who belonged to the SED may have been about 1.2 million.

The *nomenklatura*

An examination of the *nomenklatura* cadres sheds further light on the operation of the system as well as on the composition of the political elite.[24] The *nomenklatura* system, an import from the Soviet Union, comprised those posts which the SED considered to be the key leadership positions in society. Over the years, the number of *nomenklatura* cadres rose from a modest 20,000 to between 300,000 and 400,000 in 1989. A secret list of positions was drawn up at each leadership level in the government, the economy, the mass organisations and the SED. The highest *nomenklatura* level, which was under the control of the Politbüro, covered 660 positions and 520 persons; 64 of the posts (44 persons) at this level constituted the core of the GDR's political elite. It included all members and candidates of the Politbüro, the Central

[198] Committee Secretaries, the Chairman of the Council of State, the Chairman of the National Defence Council, SED members of the Presidium of the Council of Ministers, and the First Secretaries of the SED regional executives. Appointment to positions at the level immediately below required the approval of the Central Committee Secretariat and, where appropriate, that of the Presidium of the Council of Ministers. Posts on this tier included the secretaries of state, deputy ministers and director generals of combines. A similar arrangement existed with regard to cadres in the economic apparat and the mass organisations; they were not only subsumed under the *nomenklatura* of their respective apparat but also under that of the party.

Given the pivotal role of the *nomenklatura* cadres, the regime took great care over selection procedures. The principal criteria for entry into the elite group of functionaries were political and ideological reliability, professional competence and an appropriate social background. The official preference for children from worker and peasant families was often watered down in practice as the intelligentsia were able to manipulate the system to their children's advantage. The rungs on the ladder into the upper echelons of the apparat were well defined: membership of the FDJ, the FDGB and other mass organisations; a college or university qualification; an honorary position in the SED; and further training for leadership cadres. Individuals occupying lower positions were also required to demonstrate their ability in a range of settings such as an enterprise, a state institution and a basic organisation of the SED. Above these lowly positions on the career ladder were the full-time functionaries in the large mass organisations, the SED party apparat at regional or district level, the security apparat and the diplomatic service. These functions corresponded to the lower and middle positions of the *nomenklatura* system and were known as the 'cadre reserve'. As in other systems, competence was not necessarily rewarded: promotion might depend on personal contacts and influence.

The loyalty of functionaries was also secured by preferential access to apartments, good-quality consumer items, holiday places, medical treatment, educational opportunities for their children and, to a certain extent, higher pay. If functionaries sought to withdraw from this state of dependency, they ran the risk of exclusion from the SED and the loss of their privileges. The tenacity of the centralised power structures and of the success of the SED leadership in controlling the *nomenklatura* cadres would be demonstrated in the autumn of 1989: most of them remained disciplined, still waiting for orders from above at a time when the system was beginning to disintegrate.

References

1. Havel V. 1989: 40, 54

2. Ibid., 45–6

3. Wolle S. 1998: 336

4. Linz J., Stepan A. 1996: 42–50

5. Ibid., 38–43, 47

6. Laqueur W. 1994: 84,, 87

7. See Chapters 11 and 13

8. Schabowski G. 1990: 25

9. Arnold O., Modrow H. 1994: 46

10. Ibid., 38

11. Przybylski P. 1992: 46–7

12. Hermann F.-J. 1996: 28

13. Schürer G. 1996: 132–3

14. Deutscher Bundestag II/1 1995: 485, 634; Pirker T., Lepsius R., Weinert R., Hertle H.-H. 1995: 128

15. See the remarks by Schürer in ibid., 28, and by Neumann in *Poltergeist* 1996: 49, 233

16. Przybylski P. 1992: 79, 81

17. Mittag G. 1991: 316: Deutscher Bundestag II/1 1995: 482

18. See the comments by Tisch in Pirker T., Lepsius R., Weinert R., Hertle H.-H. 1995: 123, and by Lorenz in Zimmermann M. 1994: 160

19. Nakath D., Stephan G.-R. 1999: 202–4

20. Axen H. 1996: 69

21. Mitter A., Wolle S. 1990: 125

22. Arnold O., Modrow H. 1994: 50–2

23. See Ammer in Deutscher Bundestag II/1 1995: 846–7

24. Ibid.; Schroeder K. 1998: 109–10; Uschner M. 1993: 98–9; Arnold O., Modrow H. 1994: 63

CHAPTER ELEVEN

THE SED'S LOYAL ALLIES: THE BLOC PARTIES AND THE MASS ORGANISATIONS

Although the SED was clearly the dominant political force, there were many other political players – the four minor or allied parties, numerous mass organisations and governmental organs at all territorial levels. All these groups were bound together in an elaborate interlocking mechanism of controls operated by the SED leadership to ensure the incorporation of millions of people into 'real existing socialism'. The fundamentals of the system of allied parties and mass organisations had been established at an early stage in the history of the GDR and, though modified from time to time, especially during the heyday of the New Economic System, were still intact in the late 1980s.

The basic function of the network of mass organisations and allied parties was to serve as transmission belts for the SED whose leadership role they accepted without reservation. This entailed transmitting SED policies to groups which did not come under direct SED control in order to propagate party goals, to mobilise members in the direction desired by the SED and to help produce 'all-round socialist personalities'. The mass organisations, in particular, enabled the SED to intervene in all areas of social, scientific, cultural, political and economic life, and to reach all age and social groups. In performing their basic transmission function, communication was primarily from top to bottom with only limited opportunity for feedback, thus severely restricting the autonomy required for large organisations such as the FDGB and the FDJ to act as effective interest groups. This helps to explain why oral history investigations both before and after unification have revealed that East Germans tend to liken the GDR's mass organisations to those of the Third Reich.[1] This interpretation of the mass organisations as relatively passive transmission belts of the SED represents a revision of the view, held by many Western social scientists before 1989, that the larger organisations, above all the FDGB, had enhanced their status under Honecker and that, like the minor parties, they had enjoyed appreciable consultative and representational influence.

Among other functions performed by the minor parties and mass organisations were the provision of information on people's opinions and attitudes, the maintenance of the illusion of a pluralistic political system for purposes of domestic and external legitimation and, as in the case of the FDGB, the CDU and LDPD, acting as a bridgehead to Western political parties and organisations. Furthermore, the mass organisations, above all the FDGB and the FDJ, served as training grounds for functionaries in the SED, the economy and the government.

The allied parties

The four allied parties – CDU, LDPD, DBD and NDPD – were little more than tame adjuncts to the SED. Even when the SED began to disintegrate in 1989, they were by no means enthusiastic at the prospect of independence. They were debarred from forming their own political organisations in the NVA, the enterprises and the universities; they were infiltrated by the Stasi; and much of their revenue came from SED sources. The SED Central Committee Department for Friendly Parties closely monitored developments in the four parties and Central Committee officials maintained regular contact with the chairs of the parties and intervened whenever they deemed it necessary.[2] The appointment of leading functionaries required SED approval and they remained in office only for as long as they enjoyed the trust of the ruling party. By the later 1980s, the allied parties' combined membership stood at 470,000, a considerable increase since the mid-1960s. Some members were attracted by the opportunity to escape the clutches of the SED, while others wished to involve themselves in social and political affairs even though access to a leading position was normally denied to them. The political space occupied by the allied parties was very narrow but their representatives did at least enjoy some opportunity to influence policy at the local and district level.

The mass organisations

All mass organisations recognised in their statute the leading role of the SED and their organisation was governed by the principle and practice of democratic centralism. As was the case with the allied parties, the SED manipulated a series of levers to ensure its control. For example, SED members

Table 11.1:   Membership of selected mass organisations

Confederation of Free German Trade Unions (FDGB)	9.5 million (1986)
Free German Youth (FDJ)	2.3 million (1989)
Democratic Women's Association of Germany (DFD)	1.5 million (1989)
Farmers' Mutual Aid Association	529,000 (1985)
Consumers' Cooperative Society	4.5 million (1985)
League of Culture of the GDR (KB)	263,874 (1985)
Society for German-Soviet Friendship (DSF)	6.4 million (1989)
Ernst Thälmann Pioneer Organisation	1.34 million (1985)
People's Solidarity	2.09 million (1985)
Chamber of Technology	275,236 (1985)
Association of Allotment Gardeners, Settlers and Breeders of Livestock	1.36 million (1985)
German Gymnastics and Sport Association (DTSB)	3.6 million (1986)
Society for Sport and Technology (GST)	600,000 (1982)

Sources: Dennis M. 1988: 105; Deutscher Bundestag II/2 1995: 1252–64.

formed the nucleus of the executives and the chairs and the secretaries of the most important mass organisations were simultaneously members of the corresponding SED executive. Several mass organisations were permitted representation in the *Volkskammer* and the territorial assemblies. The distribution of seats was determined in advance. Until the re-entry of the Farmers' Mutual Association into the *Volkskammer* in 1986 necessitated a minor redistribution, four mass organisations were allocated the following number of seats: FDGB 68, DFD 35, FDJ 40 and KB 22. Membership of one of these groups did not preclude membership of a political party: about 90 per cent of mass organisation deputies belonged to the SED. Indeed, multiple participation in mass organisations was common, especially the combination of membership of the FDGB, FDJ, DTSB and DSF, and the rate of mobilisation was extremely high (see Table 11.1).

The Confederation of Free German Trade Unions (FDGB)

The FDGB was the most important mass organisation in the GDR. All sixteen trade unions were affiliated to the FDGB, which was based on the territorial and production principle. Trade union branches were established in enterprises and institutions where there were at least ten FDGB members. Over 97 per cent of the labour force, with the exception of the cooperative farmers, troops and the self-employed, belonged to the organisation. It had over 2.5 million activists such as shop stewards, sports functionaries and labour safety officials. Not only did the FDGB have the highest number of full-time functionaries (16,250 in 1987) but also the largest annual budget. The top posts were monopolised by SED cadres. The FDGB chairman, Harry Tisch, his deputy, Johanna Töpfer, and all the chairs of the regional organisations belonged to the SED. The party's presence was also conspicuous further down the ladder: 98.2 per cent of the chairs of trade union executives in the combines and 47.5 per cent of the chairs of enterprise trade union executives were SED members.[3]

In addition to keeping a tight rein on cadre appointments and policy, SED control operated in other ways. The FDGB's enterprise bodies were obliged to commit themselves to the fulfilment of the economic objectives of the state plan. These targets were normally integrated into the framework of socialist competition, a system worked out by the FDGB's federal executive, the State Planning Commission and the various ministries. Material incentives and titles such as 'Collective of Socialist Labour' and 'Hero of Labour' were deployed as mechanisms for the attainment of economic targets and to secure workers' loyalty to the regime.

During the 1970s, the FDBG's functional role at the workplace was given a much needed boost. In 1972, a law of the Council of Ministers envisaged joint decisions and decrees between the FDGB and the Council in areas such as social welfare and income policy. This underlines the organisation's importance for the social contract. The FDGB's main activities lay in the administration of the social insurance programme, which included pensions, maternity allowances and cures. One of its crucial tasks was the provision of package holidays for members and their families. In 1983, it organised 1.8 million holidays in the GDR and 16,000 abroad. The FDGB and the enterprises owned more than 1,600 holiday complexes, which members were entitled to use at 28 per cent of the real cost.[4] Supply failed to meet demand, especially on the Baltic coast in summer. The distribution of places at such popular locations was often related to political criteria and work performance and aroused much criticism. The FDGB was also engaged in a broad range of political-ideological tasks as part of the inculcation of socialist norms among members. Honorary and full-time functionaries – in total, about 2 million in the 1980s – were trained in a network of educational centres, with the Fritz Heckert *FDGB-Hochschule* in Bernau at the apex. The college provided short courses as well as degree courses for the top full-time cadres. Over

[204] 3 million participants attended the Schools of Labour, the one-year political training courses which were obligatory for anyone hoping to obtain a post in the FDGB.[5]

Finally, the FDGB played a prominent role in industrial relations. The 1978 Labour Code defined the legal rights and obligations of the trade unions, the workforce and management. Workers, or rather their union representatives, were granted 'co-determination' rights in matters such as wages, bonuses, dismissals and contracts. Enterprise planning, especially the annual enterprise collective contract, was a central feature of trade union activity at plant level. This contract contained agreements between the manager and the trade union executive concerning the innovators' movement, wages, working conditions, social and educational measures, support for women employees, and the endorsement of extensive union rights over training, leisure pursuits, sickness pay and holiday places.

Given this wide range of rights and activities as well as the SED's wish to boost the role of the FDGB, the organisation seemed to have become an active junior partner of the SED. Such an interpretation exaggerates the real influence of the FDGB, partly for reasons discussed above relating to SED controls over the unions. It should also be borne in mind that workers' rights were severely curtailed by the absence of the right to strike in the 1961 and 1978 Labour Codes and by the integration of local economic planning within the broader framework of state planning. However, as outlined in Chapter 7, the GDR labour force was not a passive tool of the SED and a highly politicised management: labour turnover, absenteeism, downtime, the theft of materials from factories and shopping during working hours point to a labour force negotiating a certain degree of space under working conditions characteristic of the administrative-command economic mechanism.

The Free German Youth Movement (FDJ)

The FDJ, with 28,191 basic organisations (1983), was the country's second most important mass organisation. Open to all those between 14 and 25 years, it was one of the main mechanisms for integrating young East Germans into adult life along an officially prescribed route of school, vocational training, marriage, entry into the party and office-holding. About one-third of members held office in the FDJ, constituting a vital supply of potential cadres for the SED. In the early 1980s, virtually all pupils between 6 and 14 years of age belonged to the Thälmann Pioneers, and the FDJ's 2.3 million members comprised about 75 per cent of the 14–25 age group. Whereas the vast majority of young soldiers, apprentices and pupils in the eighth to twelfth grades at school belonged to the youth organisation, participation declined rapidly after an apprenticeship was completed. Only about one-third of the 18–25 age group remained in the FDJ.

The FDJ was defined in its 1976 statute as 'an active helper and reserve force' of the SED. As the only officially approved youth organisation, the FDJ was crucial to the integration of young people into the production process and, in conjunction with educational institutions, the family and other mass organisations, to the upbringing of young people as socialist personalities. This involved, according to official prescription, raising them to be faithful to the ideas of socialism, to acquire a high level of knowledge and vocational skills, to participate actively in official economic and social programmes, to commit themselves to the cause of peace and to join in the military training programmes. The latter included the Hans-Beimler contests, a form of military sports education for pupils in the eighth grade, which were jointly organised by the FDJ, the GST and the schools. Military education and training received an added impetus in the later 1970s and early 1980s as a result of the breakdown of détente between the superpowers.

The FDJ possessed a vast array of instruments for mobilising young people. Each year, holiday trips for hundreds of thousands of young people were arranged by the FDJ tourist agency, *Jugendtourist*, and free-time activities were organised as part of the 'Young Talents' movement and in the tens of thousands of youth clubs and discos. One FDJ goal was to ensure that every pupil spent some time in a holiday camp or carried out some activity during their holidays in a pupils' brigade. In 1983, about 1 million of the GDR's 2.2 million pupils attended a holiday camp and 110,000 pupils over the age of fourteen engaged in 'voluntary productive work' in a FDJ pupils' brigade in their home area. In these and other ways, the regime hoped to channel and control the free-time interests and activities of young people. Despite the initial opposition of cultural functionaries and the FDJ executive, the regime sought to accommodate young people's enthusiasm for rock music by conceding it a place in the youth clubs and discotheques of the FDJ and by introducing rock festivals.

Along with the Thälmann Pioneers, the FDJ was involved in controlling and disciplining rebellious pupils and students through denunciation and spying. Not only did it have a say in the allocation of university places and membership but also participation in the FDJ was an important criterion in the selection process. During the 1980s, the SED used the FDJ as a counter to the appeal of the unofficial peace and ecological groups among young people.

It sought to mobilise youngsters behind slogans such as 'Make Peace Against NATO Weapons' and 'Better Active than Radioactive'.

Although the FDJ occupied a central position in SED youth policy, severe limits existed on the extent to which the movement could influence young East Germans' everyday life. Time-budget surveys reveal that they spent relatively little time on political activities and GDR youth researchers, even before 1990, admitted that ritualism characterised many of the political meetings and demonstrations organised by the FDJ. The typical reaction of most GDR youth to the SED system, at least until the mid-1980s, was one of functional accommodation while trying to preserve an appropriately discreet ideological and moral distance from the regime. Their criticism tended to be levelled at everyday deficiencies and problems rather than of a fundamental systemic kind. Young people often turned to the free-time sphere as a relief from the pressures of public life. Surveys of free-time pursuits indicate that many young people preferred to spend their free time informally with friends, dancing and listening to music, especially of Western groups. A few turned to unofficial rock and punk groups, and some imitated Western skinheads and new romantics. The tendency to spend time in loose cliques and groups increased during the 1980s. Much of this type of leisure activity was orientated towards the Western media and influenced by Western consumer norms, a development which the FDJ was unable to control.[6]

Right-wing extremism

Another indicator of the failure of the SED to transform young people into 'all-round socialist personalities' was an upsurge in violence within sections of the skinhead movement, linked, especially since the mid-1980s, to right-wing extremist activities. One outrage occurred in October 1987 when about 30 skinheads, including several from West Berlin, attacked visitors at a rock concert held at the Zionskirche in East Berlin. Their attacks were accompanied by cries of 'Sieg Heil' and 'Jewish pigs'. One month after the Zionskirche incidents, a group of young, self-styled 'Faschos' terrorised pedestrians and attacked people in pubs in Oranienburg, the town where the former Sachsenhausen concentration camp is located. Among many other incidents were assaults on Africans in Halle in 1988 and the sealing off of the town of Eberswalde by the police in April 1989 to prevent the celebration of Hitler's birthday by radical right-wingers.[7]

Alarmed at the damage being done to the GDR's reputation as an anti-fascist state, the regime initiated legal proceedings against those involved in the Zionskirche incident and the Stasi launched a campaign of repression against right-wing radicals at the start of 1988. From then until the collapse of the SED regime, about 400 extreme right-wingers were imprisoned for violent acts; however, the regime was unable to suppress the phenomenon and numbers continued to increase until the autumn of 1989. Most of the groups tended to avoid open confrontation with the security forces and retreated into the privacy of their apartments. The criminal police identified about 1,500 young people who, in 1986, were predisposed towards extreme right-wing violence, and the Stasi and the Ministry of the Interior estimated that there may have been about 1,000 extreme-right activists organised in groups in 1988/89. East Berlin and Potsdam were the main centres. This was a minimum figure as it applied to skinheads only and not, for example, to sympathisers and Heavy Metals. Most of the activists were overwhelmingly male, with a disproportionately high number in their mid-to-late teens. Their educational and family background showed no deviation from the GDR norm.[8]

Although officials attempted to blame the West for the GDR's right-wing extremists, links between East and West German neo-fascists were tenuous. Internal investigations conducted by youth researchers and church represent-atives told a different story from the official version of contamination by the West.[9] They highlighted endogenous factors, in particular deficiencies in the education of young people and the yawning gap between the theory and prac-tice of socialism. A special working party of the Ministry of the Interior reached a similar conclusion. Lack of opportunities in socialist society, a racist atti-tude, an aggressive anti-Communism and problems of national identification were identified as the main reasons for the growing appeal of neo-fascism. Most right-wing extremists desired a re-united but authoritarian Germany and saw themselves as militant defenders of 'Germanness' against foreigners, homosexuals, punks and work-shirkers.

The German Gymnastics and Sports Association of the GDR (DTSB)

The DTSB was another mass organisation which exerted an influence on young people's development. Founded in 1957 as the successor to the Ger-man Sports Committee, it aspired to produce world-class athletes and, in conjunction with the FDGB, the FDJ, the Ministry of Education, the State Secretariat for Physical Culture and Sport and the GST, to make physical culture and sport a mass activity. The DTSB was the key body for the integ-ration of sport into the SED's central planning and command system and it had the task of producing for Politbüro approval plans for the development of sport. The significance attached to sport may be gauged by the fact that Egon Krenz, the Central Committee Secretary for Security Questions, was also co-responsible for sport and, in matters relating to finance and foreign policy, was empowered to issue instructions to the DTSB President. The Ministry of State Security, through its Main Department XX/3, was another control instrument: spies were planted in the West to obtain information about research and planning; groups of GDR athletes and administrators travelling abroad were accompanied by Stasi informers; and an elaborate network of informers was set up in sports clubs and research institutes to check on the political and ideological reliability of colleagues. Mielke, a sports fanatic, used his position as minister and head of the Dynamo Sports Association to influence referees and the transfer of players to help his favourite football club, BFC Dynamo, to an unbroken run of premier league (*Oberliga*) championships between 1979 and 1988.[10]

Sport was expected to demonstrate the superiority of the socialist system over capitalism, to enhance people's labour productivity and to develop key characteristics of the socialist personality such as discipline, honesty and willingness to defend the homeland. As late as 1987, the contribution of sport to the inter-systemic rivalry was underlined in a confidential document for GDR participants in the forthcoming Olympic Games in Calgary. They were reminded that their most important opponents were the representatives of rival social systems and that their achievements would contribute to the honour of their socialist fatherland.[11] To ensure their success, the doping practices of the Ulbricht era were consolidated, in 1974, into a comprehensive state plan for sport. The extensive use of drugs, together with the clear delineation of strategic goals and an elaborate organisation, enabled the GDR to become one of the world's top sports nations. Its athletes gained 25 medals (9 golds) at the 1968 Olympics and 102 medals (37 gold) in Seoul twenty years later.

Competitive bias was a striking feature of mass sports in the GDR. The 'Joint Sports Programme' of the DTSB, FDGB and FDJ encouraged not only active forms of relaxation such as swimming and walking but also the competitive spirit of participants. The insignia 'Ready to Work and Defend the Homeland' was the main element in the programme and was intended to underpin the regime's ideological goals. Over 4 million people were awarded one of the bronze, silver and gold medals in 1983. The children's and youth Spartakiads, organised by the DTSB, the FDJ, the Thälmann Pioneers and the Education Ministry, were staged each year in the schools, localities and districts and biannually, although in alternate years, at regional and national level. The movement stimulated a high level of performance and helped sports [209] functionaries to identify talented youngsters who could then be developed in the sports schools and training centres of the country's well-endowed and highly specialised sports clubs.

Despite the high participation rates, the SED failed to achieve its stated goal of 'Everyone in every place, several times a week sport'. Employed women and shift workers were relatively inactive and many East Germans deliberately abstained from the state-run sports organisations as they preferred to pursue sport individually or with relatives. The loss of the stimulus of obligatory sport after leaving school and college, the emergence of other free-time interests among young people and the poor quality of equipment, sports halls and open-air swimming pools were other impediments. According to a German Sports Federation survey published in 1992, only 11.3 per cent of sports fields, 10.6 per cent of sports halls and 8.6 per cent of outdoor swimming pools were in a satisfactory condition.[12]

The state system

Given that the GDR had not achieved 'true Communism', then some form of state machinery was deemed necesssary to carry out functions such as defence against internal and external threats, resource allocation and the settling of conflicts. The state apparatus, like the large mass organisations, was also essential for the incorporation of the millions of non-SED members into the existing political system and was a vital instrument in helping the party to administer a highly educated and diversified society. Moreover, throughout the state system cadres possessed the technical expertise and the access to information which were necessary for the shaping of policy by the SED's top bodies. The state (along with the mass organisations) and the SED were meant to complement each other: while the party's central organs determined policy guidelines and its apparat checked on the implementation of policy, the organs of state were essentially responsible for the administration of policy decisions. But the SED unquestionably enjoyed primacy over the state. Party members in the state organs were obliged to follow party instructions and the *nomenklatura* system enabled the SED to control the appointment of cadres to positions in the state apparat.

The *Volkskammer* was the supreme organ of state power with the right to elect the members of the Council of State, the Council of Ministers and the

[210] Chairman of the National Defence Council. Of these three major bodies, the Council of State's functions were largely ceremonial and the Council of Ministers' main responsibility lay in the planning and supervision of the economy in conjunction with the State Planning Commission. Despite its grand title, the Council of Ministers was the leading administrative economic organ of the GDR rather than a governmental decision-making body. Although the *Volkskammer* had fifteen standing committees with responsibility for areas such as education and citizens' petitions and its laws were supposed to be binding on everyone, in reality it was essentially an acclamatory and confirmatory body. Plenary sessions were infrequent, and usually lasted a mere one to two days. No discussion took place in the chamber on draft legislation and, with the exception of the vote on abortion in 1972, all bills were approved unanimously. Since 1971, the 500 deputies were elected for a term of five years and the five political parties and four mass organisations (five after the re-entry of the Farmers' Mutual Aid Association in 1986) were represented in the Chamber. The SED justified the absence of competitive elections by the fictitious claim that unity existed in a society free from exploitation. In practice, other than the obvious fact that elections provided a pseudo-legitimation for SED rule, the main purpose of elections was to propagate party policy and to lock people into the SED-dominated system. No effort was spared to ensure the highest possible turnout. Voters were encouraged to proceed to the polls together with members of their work collective or tenants' community. Once at the polling station, the vast majority opted to drop their ballot paper into the box rather than risk using a booth.

References

1. Deutscher Bundestag II/2 1995: 12401

2. Suckut S. 1994: 103

3. Deutscher Bundestag II/2 1995: 302–4

4. Ibid., 1269; Pirker T., Lepsius R., Weinert R., Hertle H.-H. 1995: 141

5. Deutscher Bundestag II/4 1995: 2668–9

6. Ibid., III/2: 1302

7. Ibid., III/1: 173–5; Waibel H. 1996: 58–67

8. Deutscher Bundestag III/1 1995: 175, 178, 184, 193–4; Golz H.-G. 1996: [211]
   210; Waibel H. 1996: 64–5

9. Golz H.-G. 1996: 214–7

10. Deutscher Bundestag III/1 1995: 664–7; ibid., III/2: 1340–2, 1350

11. Ibid., III/1: 648–9

12. Ibid., III/2: 1353

CHAPTER TWELVE

THE APPARATUS OF COERCION

The Ministry of State Security (MfS)

I f social security was one of the main planks of SED rule, then state security was another. Whereas the former was intended to control the population by means of a paternalistic social welfare system, the Stasi and other organs of coercion and political policing were to combat and root out 'negative' forces. The Stasi's final statute, issued in July 1969 as a top-secret document, defined its principal function as 'uncovering and forestalling the hostile plans and intentions of the aggressive imperialists and their helpers'. It was also entrusted with the protection of the sovereignty, 'the all-round political, military, economic and cultural strengthening of the German Democratic Republic' and 'the securing of the socialist achievements and the state border'.[1]

The mental world of the Stasi was characterised by a deep-seated paranoia, as exemplified by Mielke's conviction that everyone was a potential security risk. A recurrent theme in internal documents is the pressing need to thwart an omnipresent and hated enemy. In the 1985 edition of the *Dictionary of the State Security Service*, hatred is referred to as 'the emotional expression of Chekist feelings, one of the decisive foundations for the passionate and implacable fight against the enemy. Its strengthening and deepening through experience of the class struggle is the task and goal of a class-conscious training and upbringing'.[2] The enemy is defined in the text as persons who, either in groups or as individuals, hold political-ideological views which are intrinsically hostile to socialism and who seek to endanger or harm the socialist state and its social order. On the front line of the cold war, the GDR was seen to be under particular threat from imperialist secret services and underground agencies.

Officers and collaborators [213]

The number of MfS full-time staff rose inexorably throughout the history of the GDR: 1,100 in 1950, 19,130 in 1961, 43,311 in 1970 and 91,105 in 1989.[3] At the end of the 1980s, about half worked in East Berlin – 36,421 in the central organs and 11,426 in the Feliks Dzierzhinsky Guard Regiment – and most of the remaining 43,168 in the territorial organs. The carefully selected full-time officers constituted a highly qualified and politically reliable corps imbued with a strong sense of discipline and of their elite status. Women were underrepresented (about 15 per cent) and they were concentrated in secretarial positions, in postal control and the medical service.

The number of IMs (*Inoffizielle Mitarbeiter*), that is, unofficial collaborators or co-workers, also exploded, reaching 176,000 in the mid-1980s before falling slightly in 1988 and 1989.[4] This figure includes a large number – 33,000 – of IMKs (*Inoffizielle Mitarbeiter zur Sicherung der Konspiration und des Verbindungswesens*) who put their telephone, address or apartment at the disposal of the Stasi for clandestine meetings between controllers and IMs. The rapid expansion of the IM network is explained by the Honecker regime's determination to combat the negative effects of détente and by the emergence of an alternative political culture in the 1970s. The Stasi devoted enormous effort to the recruitment and training of its anonymous army of IMs. As the Stasi's 'eyes and ears', the agents were regarded as the 'main weapon in the struggle against the enemy', without whom the full-time officials could not achieve their goals. Not only were they deployed to combat subversion by an external enemy but also to protect socialist society against the disruption and harm caused by the 'hostile' actions of East German citizens.

Until 1968, unofficial collaborators were designated as GIs (*Geheime Informatoren*), that is, secret informers; thereafter, although IM was the generic term, the multiplicity of tasks performed by IMs required an ever more esoteric and bewildering differentiation. Some were classed as full-time IMs (*Hauptamtliche Inoffizielle Mitarbeiter* – HIMs) and others as societal collaborators for security (*Gesellschaftliche Mitarbeiter für Sicherheit* – GMIs). IMEs (*Inoffizielle Mitarbeiter für einen besonderen Einsatz*), of whom there were 7,213 in 1988, were recruited for work on special assignments and held important positions in the state apparat, the mass organisations, the economy and other spheres. They supplied information on the situation in their area of responsibility. Officers on special duties (*Offiziere im besonderen Einsatz* – OibEs) constituted a higher category of elite informers than the IMEs; there were 2,232 OibEs in 1989. FIMs (*Inoffizielle Mitarbeiter für Führung anderer Inoffizieller*

[214] *Mitarbeiter*), in addition to their own duties, recruited and ran other IMs. IMBs (*Inoffizielle Mitarbeiter zur unmittelbaren Bearbeitung im Verdacht der Feindtätigkeit stehender Personen*) were highly proactive agents: they infiltrated opposition groups and were involved in coordinated campaigns to damage their targets' careers and lives.

In 1988, those agents involved in political-operative work (*Inoffizielle Mitarbeiter zur politisch-operativen Durchdringung und Sicherung des Verant-wortungsbereiches* – IMSs) comprised the largest group, constituting 85.6 per cent of IMs; this figure excludes the IMKs.[5] IMSs were engaged in spying in all areas of public life, the economy, education, the Churches, sport and so forth. Their basic task was to provide information on people's attitudes towards the socialist system, especially those suspected of having contact with opposition groups. In the mid-1980s, there was an average of one IM per 120 inhabitants, ranging from 1 per 80 in the Cottbus *Bezirk* to 1 per 159 in the Halle *Bezirk*.[6] This extraordinarily high level of Stasi penetration of society may well be unprecedented in European history. There was a relatively high turnover of IMs: between 1985 and 1988 about 10 per cent per year stopped working for the Stasi but were in turn replaced by a similar proportion. In the course of the history of the GDR, at least 600,000 persons operated as Stasi agents; some authorities put the figure as high as between 1 and 2 million.[7]

A comparison between the Stasi of the Honecker era and Hitler's Gestapo shows that whereas the IMs were integrated into a highly developed and routinised administrative structure of reporting and denunciations, the Gestapo relied far more on the voluntary assistance of 'spite informers' than on its official agents. The Gestapo was a much smaller organisation, probably employing no more than 7,000 officers in 1937 out of a total population of 66 million. However, a similarity is observable if comparison is made with an earlier period of GDR history. Between 1953 and 1955, for example, a far higher proportion of arrests resulted from 'spontaneous denunciations' than from the ministry's own collaborators, whose number – 20,000 to 30,000 – was much lower than in the 1980s.[8]

Erich Mielke: the master of the silent empire

Erich Mielke was the undisputed boss of the sprawling Stasi empire. Born in 1907 to a Berlin working-class family, Mielke was a dedicated Communist. He joined the KPD in 1925 and, along with a colleague, Erich Ziemer, assassinated two police constables in 1931 during one of the many clashes between the KPD and the security forces in Berlin. He would be sentenced, in 1993, to six years' imprisonment for this action, only to be released on probation in 1995. Soon after the assassination, he fled abroad, trained at the Lenin School for cadres in Moscow in 1934–35, and then fought as a battalion commander in the Spanish Civil War between 1936 and 1939. He probably spent most of the war engaged in party work in the underground resistance in France.[9] After the downfall of the Third Reich, he was instrumental in the creation of a security force in the Soviet zone. He served as State Secretary in the MfS between 1950 and 1953 and, for a second spell, between 1955 and 1957 before his appointment as minister in the latter year. He owed his promotion not only to his Soviet connections and his operational skills but also to Ulbricht's desire for a loyal and politically reliable assistant after the upheavals under Zaisser and Wollweber.

A staunch Marxist-Leninist, Mielke was an untiring operator with a mania for information and secrecy. Extremely vain and addicted to wearing a white uniform with gold braid and medals, he basked in his status as a four-star army general. He was an opponent of détente with the West, fearing that it provided West German imperialism with an opportunity to liquidate the GDR's socialist system. Consequently, the inter-German accords of the early 1970s persuaded him of the need for even greater vigilance and a further expansion of the Stasi's activities.[10] Mielke ruled the MfS in a highly autocratic manner. Orders were issued to his subordinates in a curt manner, meetings, even with his top officers, were infrequent and he often terminated discussions abruptly with the phrase 'I am the minister'. Despite his overbearing attitude and the occasional humiliation at his hands, his close colleagues respected Mielke for his anti-fascist past and his dedication to the Stasi 'firm'.[11]

Mielke presided over his own personal secretariat as well as two central bodies, a *Kollegium* of Stasi generals and the Minister's Working Party with about 700 full-time staff. Although the *Kollegium* met several times per year and was formally empowered to take decisions on matters of fundamental importance, it was essentially an advisory body to the minister. Of the thirteen generals on the *Kollegium*, four were deputy ministers, including Colonel-General Rudi Mittig, a deputy minister since 1969 and a member of the SED's Central Committee. The military rank of Mielke and his deputies underlines the military ethos and structure which pervaded the entire ministry. All staff, no matter how lowly, held a military rank and the hierarchical system was buttressed by a strict disciplinary code and clear service rules.

The organisational structure

By 1989, the central organisation in East Berlin was spread across thirteen Main Departments (*Hauptabteilungen*), twenty Departments (*Abteilungen*), a Main Reconnaissance Administration (*Hauptverwaltung Aufklärung* – HVA), and numerous working groups, sectors and administrative units. An elaborate territorial structure encompassed 15 regional and 2,111 district organisations as well as several major industrial sites. Mittig, widely regarded as Mielke's number two, was in charge of several Main Departments, including XVIII (Economy), XIX (Transportation, Post and Communications) and XX. The latter was primarily concerned with the observation and control of the domestic population and its sections dealt with political underground activity, political-ideological diversion and the screening of the bloc parties, education and sport. Schwanitz's area of responsibility included Main Department III (Radio Interception and Screening) and Department XXVI (Monitoring of the Telephone System), while Großmann oversaw espionage against the FRG, NATO and the West. Neiber's domain covered five Main Departments, including those for the protection of the GDR's armed forces and border guards (I), passport control, the observation of foreign visitors and the Interhotels (VI), and anti-terror (XXII).

The administrative bodies under Mielke's personal command outnumbered those of his deputies. They included not only the Minister's Working Party but also the crucial Main Departments for Cadres and Training, Counter Espionage, Interrogation, and the Protection of Individuals and Property. Major-General Dr Willi Opitz, the rector of the MfS University for Juridical Affairs in Potsdam-Eiche, was directly answerable to Mielke. The university awarded its own degrees and ran professional training courses for the Stasi's full-time staff. The *Zentrale Auswertungs- und Informationsgruppe* (Central Evaluation and Information Group – ZAIG), the so-called 'brain' of the Stasi, evaluated data vital to the SED's control over society and it prepared reports on the mood of the population for the top party and state leadership. The ministry's Feliks Dzierzhinsky Guard Regiment was assigned to protect important buildings and individuals; it also served as an honour guard. At the time of its dissolution, the Stasi possessed a large arsenal, most of which belonged to the regiment, including 124,593 pistols, 76,592 light machine-guns, 3,611 rifles, 766 heavy machine-guns, 3,537 anti-tank weapons and 3,303 flare pistols.[12]

Stasi and party

The Stasi regarded itself as *the* vital instrument for asserting and safeguarding the power of the SED, as encapsulated in its self-image as the party's reliable shield and sharp sword. In 1977, Mielke, in one of his many authoritative statements in a similar vein, asserted that 'we carry out our entire activities under the well-established leadership of our Marxist-Leninist party and on the basis of its resolutions',[13] and that it was incumbent on all units of the ministry to realise the SED's leading role. The Stasi's second statute, issued in 1969, underlined this task: it defined the basis of the ministry's work as the SED programme and the decisions of the Politbüro, the Central Committee, the GDR Constitution and the National Defence Council.

The SED's military and security policy was in the hands of the Central Committee Secretary for Security Questions, a post occupied by Erich Honecker from 1958 to 1971 and for much of the 1980s by Egon Krenz. Although they exercised the ultimate political control over the security organs, their day-to-day influence over the MfS was by no means absolute. Their remit did not cover operational activities, many of which were clandestine, and Mielke's experience and political status enabled him to preserve a degree of autonomy for the ministry.[14] Determined not to play second fiddle to the younger Krenz, Mielke cultivated his personal links with the SED leader. Party control should not be underestimated, however. Krenz, like his predecessor Verner, relied on the Department for Security Questions in the Central Committee apparat to carry out the party's political control function. This was then implemented through the SED party organisation in the ministry, which had the status of a district organisation; at the end of the 1980s, its executive numbered 158 full-time staff. The party organisation in the Stasi's regional administration employed between six and thirteen full-time staff, and both the regional and district organisations were subordinated to the First Secretaries of the SED regional executives. In 1957, a service instruction required the heads of the Stasi at regional and local levels to draw up their work plans only after agreement with the respective SED First Secretaries.[15] Other examples of the interlocking of party and MfS are to be found in the area of cadre policy. The appointment of the minister and of Stasi officers with the rank of general required the approval of the Politbüro and all cadre decisions had to be agreed in advance between the Stasi's Main Department for Cadres and Training and the SED Department for Security Questions before they were submitted to Mielke.[16]

The Stasi files

The Stasi documents which survived the destruction and removal of so many files during the Modrow and de Maizière administrations in late 1989 and early 1990 would, if placed end-to-end, extend for 178 kilometres. The material includes files on individuals and groups compiled by IMs and their contact officers as well as documents relating to the administration of the ministry. The latter files comprise about one-third of all Stasi materials and include, for example, ministry guidelines (*Richtlinien*), service instructions, protocols of official meetings and planning documents.

Despite their great value as a historical source, the files and dossiers have to be treated with great care. One fundamental problem concerns the Marxist-Leninist ideology which underpinned the work and perceptions of the ministry. This often led to a crude division into friends and foes and a misreading, in the 1980s, of the attitude to socialism of the alternative peace and human rights groups. Moreover, as many files have been destroyed, false conclusions are sometimes drawn from the surviving evidence. For example, Reinhard Henkys, a West German expert on GDR Church affairs, was wrongly accused of being an IM on the basis of tapped telephone conversations which were mistakenly believed to be a record of his talks with Stasi officers. Another problem is the extent to which the files provide a reliable guide to an individual's motives and objectives. Many IMs now claim – sometimes with justification – that the record should not be taken literally as their cooperation was based on a desire to use, even manipulate, their controllers to achieve ends which were incompatible with those of the ministry and the SED.

Comprehensive surveillance

The declassified records of the Stasi testify to a remarkably comprehensive system of surveillance. The extant files contain approximately 6 million dossiers on individuals targeted by the ministry.[17] Some idea of the wide range of Stasi activities can be gleaned from the following catalogue of tasks performed by its full-time staff and IMs: surveillance of all border crossings, passport control and foreign visitors; vigilance over German and international terrorist groups, giving refuge to the Red Army Faction and liaison with the IRA, ETA and Palestinian groups; and monitoring Western radio broadcasts reaching the GDR. This list can be extended to include: vigilance over all military units in the GDR, including the Border Guards; investigation and interrogation of those suspected of 'crimes against the state and against public order'; counterdissidence work against all underground political activity; and 'ideological diversion' in state and societal organisations as well as in the autonomous basic groups. A few examples will serve to illustrate the extent of surveillance.[18] The control of letters and parcels was conducted in special rooms in selected post offices. In the Dresden administrative region 4,000 to 5,000 out of about 100,000 postal deliveries were investigated daily. Phone-tapping was widespread, with 1,000 phones being tapped per day in Leipzig alone. Even the smells of individuals were bottled to enable tracker dogs to pursue them. The thoroughness but also the banality of operational masures against suspects is well exemplified by the campaign against Katrin Eigenfeld of the Women for Peace group. Her files record which bus she caught in the morning, which articles she purchased in the shops and when she switched off the light at home in the evening.[19] It is the sheer volume of this kind of trivia which threatened to drown the MfS in a vast ocean of information.

Motives for collaboration

Collaboration with the Stasi can be explained, first, by a set of societal conditions: the regime's paranoia about internal and foreign enemies; the cloak of secrecy which protected agents from disclosure; a vast bureaucratic machine which reduced individuals to cogs in an impersonal assembly line of repression; and a psychological predisposition endemic in society – and not only in the GDR – to snoop on one's neighbours, friends and enemies. Second, although the motivation behind a particular individual's collaboration with the Stasi is often difficult to unravel, several primary motives – fear, a commitment to socialism, the sense of excitement derived from clandestine work, a feeling of self-empowerment, blackmail and personal gain – all help to explain why so many East Germans served as IMs. The MfS drew extensively, from the late 1960s onwards, on psychological research into human motivation, in particular on the research findings of its own University for Juridical Affairs in the Faculty for Psychology in the search for reliable informers.[20] Controlling officers were schooled in the art of creating a confidential and trusting relationship with their contacts. Falling in love with an IM was forbidden, however, and could have serious consequences for the officers.

[220]   Since the end of SED rule, some IMs connected with the Churches and the grass-roots groups have claimed that their dialogue with the Stasi emanated from a genuine wish to 'prevent the worst', that is, to protect individuals, to promote reform and to improve Church–state relations. While this blend of altruism and political calculation undoubtedly motivated some IMs, this was usually self-delusion. IMs who sought to instrumentalise the Stasi were engaged in an unequal relationship; they, not the Stasi, were the manipulated. There was also the attendant risk of entering into a labyrinth of double allegiances in which friend and foe, as well as the private and the political, became inextricably intertwined.

In enlisting new IMs, the Stasi was eager to recruit those who were well-disposed to GDR socialism or, in Stasi jargon, held 'Marxist-Leninist convictions' and had a 'scientifically-founded image of the enemy'.[21] 'True believers' were expected to be the most productive and committed agents. A 1967 internal investigation in the MfS Potsdam regional administration discovered that ideological-political factors played an important role for 60 per cent of IMs.[22] This was not an empty statement as several people who later became prominent dissidents were at one time involved in spying for these reasons. Robert Havemann worked for the KGB and the Stasi before becoming disillusioned with the SED system and the human rights activist Wolfgang Templin was an agent (IME 'Peter') in the early 1970s.

Also welcome were those who, like Monika Haeger, hoped that the Stasi could provide a sense of belonging. A participant in East Berlin's alternative political culture, she spied on the Women for Peace group and the Initiative for Peace and Human Rights. An orphan with a disturbed childhood, she sought emotional security and recognition. As she explained in an interview shortly after the collapse of the SED, '. . . the Stasi gave me roots. It seemingly gave me security . . . Day and night I could ring and my IM contact officer Detlef always had time for me'.[23] However, when she sought, in 1989, to terminate her connection with the ministry, the threats of her contact officer made her fear for her safety.[24]

The Stasi preyed on human frailties. Some IMs became involved with the Stasi in order to overcome problems at work or with the authorities. Fear of the disclosure of an adulterous relationship left many vulnerable to blackmail. The Stasi, in its internal documentation, avoided terms like 'blackmail', opting for euphemisms like 'atonement'. The bait of a university place or a much coveted job tempted many young East Germans into promising to serve the Stasi later in their career. Material rewards, services, foreign travel and a higher social status appealed to many others.[25] Given the shortages endemic in GDR society, many IMs were lured by the promise of a car, an apartment, a telephone or a holiday place. Remuneration was not necessarily a major incentive. IM candidates received a small basic sum of about 20 Marks per month; an additional amount was paid for the use of an apartment for clandestine meetings. This could be topped up by payments to IMs of 50, 100 or more Marks for good-quality work and information. Considerably higher sums of between 700 and 900 Marks were handed over to some of the collaborators in the GDR opposition.[26]

The collaboration of writers

Many intellectuals, whether natural scientists, historians, artists or writers, collaborated with the powerholders. To illustrate the nature of cooperation and collaboration, the relationship between creative writers and the Stasi will be examined, a sorry chapter which has been researched with exemplary thoroughness by the GDR writer Joachim Walther. The SED regarded many of the country's writers as Trojan horses of 'counterrevolution', fearing that the enemies of the GDR might persuade them that socialism could be made 'more humane' by open criticism and by the establishment of an internal opposition. The Hungarian Uprising and the Prague Spring were cited as examples of how 'hostile-negative forces' targeted writers and artists to foster revisionism and counterrevolution. In the eyes of the Stasi, cultural questions were also political questions, as exemplified by Mielke's contention in 1966 that 'If Heym and all such men of letters and artists gained power, then the GDR would soon be eaten up'.[27] Given this kind of crude mentality, it is not surprising that Heym, Christa Wolf and other critical writers were treated as actual or potential enemies despite their professions of loyalty to socialism and to the GDR.

Control of cultural life was the responsibility of HA XX's Department 7 for Culture and the Mass Media. Its basic task was to influence literary output and to suppress negative influences among the cultural intelligentsia by means of IMs, censorship and spying. Division 4 (*Referat*) of this department dealt with writers. Walther has uncovered about 1,500 IMs who were active in the literary and cultural sphere in the Honecker era. In 1987, as many as twelve out of nineteen members of the Presidium of the Writers' Union were former or current IMs. Already widespread, surveillance was intensified in the mid-1970s under the impact of détente and the Biermann affair. Systematic

[222] subversion, which was mainly carried out by the IMs, aimed to fragment, cripple and isolate 'enemies' of the state. The Stasi exploited human emotions and weaknesses such as jealousy, excessive drinking, extra-marital affairs and financial problems. Targets, referred to as 'objects', might suffer house arrest, a ban on the publication of their work and expulsion from the Writers' Union.

The carefully organised and 'integrated operational clandestine campaign' (*Operativer Vorgang* – OV) was the most elaborate form of surveillance. Victims had to cope for many years with surveillance and discrimination and often suffered from a persecution mania and other symptoms which damaged their health. Among the many instances of this type of campaign were OV 'Lyrik' against Reiner Kunze, OV 'Ecke' against Gabriele Eckart and various operations against Erich Loest. Reiner Kunze came into conflict with the SED over his positive attitude to the Prague Spring and over his publications, notably *Die wunderbaren Jahre*. The latter, a collection of short stories and poems concerning the everyday problems of young East Germans, confirmed the Stasi in its view of Kunze as an enemy of the GDR. The book was published in the West, but not in the GDR. The publication of excerpts from Kunze's Stasi files in 1990 reveal that his phone had been tapped, his mail intercepted, his foreign contacts investigated, his movements observed by his neighbours and his wife's professional reputation undermined. One of the Stasi agents deployed against Kunze was Ibrahim Böhme – IM 'Bonkarz' – who would emerge in 1989 as chair of the reconstituted SPD.[28]

Why so many writers and functionaries worked for the secret service can be explained by reference to the complex of motives identified earlier. The GDR's most famous writer, Christa Wolf (IM 'Margarete'), collaborated for a brief period, from 1959 to 1962, out of a somewhat naive ideological conviction and with little apparent benefit to the Stasi. Her thin IM file contrasts markedly with the voluminous files which the Stasi later kept on her and her husband Gerhard for over three decades as part of the ministry's operation '*Doppelzüngler*'.[29] Meetings with her controllers were infrequent and involved little more than supplying them with information on the literary scene and the *Mitteldeutscher* publishing house. There is not the slightest suggestion that she was implicated in any denigration or harassment of her fellow writers.[30] What does jar, however, is the belated recovery of her memory of her Stasi past after initial denials. This fits uneasily with her earlier emphasis on the role of memory and was a severe blow not only to Wolf's own reputation but also to GDR writers' 'somewhat uncritical faith in their moral impeachability'.[31]

Sascha Anderson, one of the most notorious Stasi agents, belonged to a comparatively new category of IMs whose various tasks were to paralyse, influence the aims or subvert a particular group. Böhme and Wolfgang Schnur (IM 'Torsten') are other well-known cases. Anderson, a gifted poet, was groomed by the Stasi for his future role. In the early 1980s, he established contact with East Berlin's alternative sub-culture and by about 1984 had become one of the most influential figures among the writers and artists in the Prenzlauer Berg area. Anderson's chief goal was the de-politicisation of this artistic community. His main activities included spying on the initiators of the Berlin Appeal, controlling the contacts of GDR artists with members of the FRG's permanent representation in East Berlin and informing against people like Rüdiger Rosenthal. The latter was imprisoned for collecting signatures against the new Defence Law. In 1986, Anderson moved to West Berlin where he spied on the city's colony of former GDR artists and opposition figures such as Roland Jahn and Jürgen Fuchs. Cynical and gifted, Anderson's first and second identity merged until he internalised the role which he was supposed to be playing, unable to separate fantasy from reality.[32]

Foreign intelligence

The MfS targeted foreign countries, above all the Federal Republic, in order to protect the security of the GDR and the socialist community of states, to collect information about enemy organisations and methods, to implement offensive measures against enemy centres and to boost the economic and military strength of the GDR.[33] In this respect, the Stasi bore a striking resemblance to other countries' intelligence and secret services. During the cold war, the intelligence services of both West and East experienced an exponential growth, generated a paper mountain, vied with each other in the use of advanced technology to spy on foes, snooped on their own citizens, and were adept at avoiding constitutional and legal controls.

Thanks in part to the publicity skills of Markus Wolf, who headed the GDR's foreign intelligence service between 1952 and 1986, the Main Department Reconnaissance (*Hauptverwaltung Aufklärung* – HVA) has been semi-heroicised as a remarkably efficient and professional espionage service allegedly untainted by the excesses of its domestic counter-intelligence counterpart. The latter claim is a fabrication as the two wings of the MfS cooperated closely in operational activities. Descended from Spanish Jews, Wolf was the son of Friedrich Wolf, a Communist free thinker and writer. In contrast to the coarse Mielke, Wolf was an urbane and extroverted individual who

[224] emerged in the dying days of the SED as an advocate of reformed socialism. The fact that John le Carré, in *The Spy That Came In From the Cold*, allegedly modelled his spy master, Karla, on Wolf before his identity had been uncovered adds to the mystique surrounding East Germany's own spy master. Wolf owed his appointment as head of East German foreign intelligence in 1952 not only to his skills in intelligence work but also to his dedication to the Communist cause and to his unswerving loyalty to the Soviet Union. Emigrating to the Soviet Union in 1934 at the age of ten, he later became a Soviet citizen and adopted the Russian name 'Misha'.

HVA had its origins in the Institute for Economic Research, which was set up in 1951 as a cover for the foreign intelligence service. Restructured as the *Hauptabteilung* XV and incorporated into the MfS in late 1953, it received its final name in 1956. The full-time staff was relatively small, numbering only 4,126 officers and technical personnel (1989), spread across fifteen operational departments and a department responsible for communications and supplies. Separate departments dealt with the FRG, North America, Western Europe, NATO and the European Community. HVA was able to recruit at least 20,000 West German citizens as its 'spies on the invisible front' and to infiltrate thousands of East Germans into the FRG. A network of spies, contact persons, wireless operators and many others enabled the MfS to penetrate and influence the 'nerve centres' of West German society – its political parties, government, military and security organs, the media and the economy.[34] One of its outstanding successes was the planting of a top spy, Günter Guillaume, as personal assistant to Chancellor Willy Brandt. The Stasi was located at the very heart of the FRG's security services. A leading official in the Federal Office for the Protection of the Constitution, Klaus Kuron, spied for Wolf's department for about eight years and Gabriele Gast, a top official in the Federal Intelligence Service since 1973, was HVA's prize mole. She was recruited by a well-tried method, the use of Stasi officers as 'Romeos' to recruit female secretaries and officials in government and NATO offices. Sometimes, this led to a marriage of convenience, or what the Stasi termed an 'operational fictional marriage'. The academic world did not escape Wolf's clutches; Dietrich Staritz, a leading West German expert on the GDR, worked for many years as an IM.

HVA's record was by no means unblemished. Despite a far more extensive surveillance than that achieved by West German security agencies, it failed to undermine the loyalty of the overwhelming majority of West German citizens to the Federal Republic. It also lost several officers, notably Werner Stiller, a First Lieutenant in its science and technology sector. Punishment was

severe for those HVA staff who were uncovered. In 1981, Dr Werner Teske
was arrested and executed on a charge of spying for the FRG. Mielke's judge-
ment on officers such as Teske and Stiller was typically brutal. At an internal
meeting in February 1982, he declared, 'We are not immune against scoun-
drels in our ranks. If I knew about this now he would not be alive tomorrow!
Over and done with fast! Because I'm a humanist, that's why I take such a
view. All the nonsense about not execution and not the death penalty – all
nonsense, comrades. Execution, if necessary without a court verdict'.[35]

Other agents of coercion and control

The activities of the MfS were underpinned by a vast network of armed
forces and other security organs. It is estimated that about 750,000 East Germans, whether full-time or voluntary, served in the military, paramilitary and
security forces of the GDR. These ranged from the 209,000 voluntary members of the combat groups of the working class, which were geared to resist
the incursions of counterrevolutionary and subversive elements, to the
highly organised and disciplined People's Army. With about 10 per cent of
the working population involved in this system, a heavy burden was imposed
on the state budget and the economy. The Ministry of Defence was the main
drain on resources, followed by the Ministries of State Security and the Interior. As a percentage of the country's produced national income, the net
expenditure on defence and security rose from 9 per cent in 1970 to about 11
per cent in the 1980s.[36] Central direction of the security and defence sectors
lay in the hands of the National Defence Council (NVR). Established in 1960
as the successor to the Security Committee of the SED, it was a small body
monopolised by SED Politbüro and Central Committee members. Ulbricht
served as chairman until his downfall in 1971, when he was succeeded by
Honecker. The latter had full control over the NVR and was the *de facto*
commander-in-chief of the country's armed forces. According to its statute
and the Defence Law of 1978, the NVR was responsible for defining and
implementing the measures required for the defence of the country. Among
these measures was the infamous Revised Border Law of 1982 regulating the
border troops' use of firearms to prevent East Germans from escaping across
the border. That Honecker was in full agreement with such measures can be
seen from a protocol of a meeting of the NVR in May 1974. During a discussion on the situation on the border, Honecker endorsed the 'unhampered'

[226] use of firearms to prevent escapes and urged that troops be commended for doing so.[37]

The border troops

In the 1980s, the total strength of the border troops was about 50,000. The key personnel were deployed on the GDR's Western border with the FRG (about 30,000) and in Berlin (about 8,000). After the construction of the Berlin Wall, the border troops were formed from the German border police and placed under the command of the Ministry of National Defence. From 1973–74 onwards, the border troops, no longer formally a part of the NVA, enjoyed an enhanced role in the integrated system of border control, which included the Ministry of State Security and the other security organs as well as local SED and state authorities. While the units were responsible for the military protection of the GDR from any external threat, their main activity was to prevent escapes from the republic. Flight became increasingly difficult with the development of the border into a fortified barrier of sentry towers, anti-vehicle trenches and column tracks. Only one in fifteen attempts to escape the GDR succeeded.[38] Although there was no explicit shoot-to-kill order, a series of instructions and binding instructions authorised the border troops to use firearms if they could not otherwise prevent flight across the border. As part of an intensive training programme, guards were commanded to obey these instructions unconditionally; disobedience could lead to a prison sentence of up to five years. Decorations, bonuses and additional holidays were awarded to those guards who prevented flight by killing fellow citizens.

The National People's Army (NVA)

Although the NVA was not founded until 1956, when the GDR joined the Warsaw Pact, the People's Police in Barracks had operated as its precursor. Compulsory military service was delayed until 1962 as the regime did not have the courage to introduce such a controversial measure before the erection of the Berlin Wall. It was, however, possible from 1964 onwards for East Germans to serve in a construction unit instead of doing normal military service, although they were obliged to wear their own uniform with a spade emblem on the epaulette. About 12,000 to 15,000 opted for this alternative as against the 2.5 million who served in the NVA until the fall of the GDR in 1990. In addition to the construction soldiers, several hundred young people, most of them Jehovah's Witnesses, refused each year to perform any form of service, despite the high risk, at least until 1986, of a prison sentence.

In the later 1980s, the numerical strength of the NVA stood at 179,000, of which 123,000 troops were in the army. The SED exercised a tight control over its armed forces. A political organ was located within the NVA down to regimental level. Virtually all officers and over one-third of warrant officers and NCOs belonged to the party and were thus subject to party discipline which, together with a careful selection of personnel, intensive professional training, political indoctrination and a ban on Western contacts, resulted in a loyal and cohesive regular force. The Main Political Administration (PHV) was the highest political organ in the NVA. Its 6,000 officers were responsible for the implementation of party directives, cooperation with the PHV of the Soviet Union, and the political and ideological training of troops.

Military traditions and rituals, many of them derived from earlier periods in German history, were fostered as part of the indoctrination of troops and of the political legitimisation of the NVA. Ideological training reflected the general militarisation of life in GDR society. Until the onset of superpower détente in the later 1980s and the evolution of a new military doctrine in the Warsaw Pact, troops were taught to hate the class enemy and to believe in the inherent aggression of imperialism. The general system of socialist defence education for young people, which was conducted by the FDJ, the GST and other public bodies, was reinforced in 1978 by the introduction of compulsory defence studies for pupils in the ninth and tenth classes at school and three years later for those in the eleventh class at the extended secondary school. Even the kindergartens were enmeshed in the system: young children aged four and five years were taught to value the role of the armed forces in the defence of the country and were encouraged to develop friendly contacts with troops. The close collaboration between educational bodies and the military and defence organs, the pervasiveness of the military principles of obedience and discipline among so many party and large mass organisations, and the high level of control and conformity achieved by incorporating large sections of the population in these structures underpinned what has been termed the 'militarised socialism' of the GDR.[39]

In the field of military doctrine, the NVA basically followed the Soviet lead and developed few original ideas of its own. By the end of the 1960s, however, the NVA had emerged as a professional army with a significant role

[228] in the first operational echelon of the Warsaw Pact's forces. Its growing status as a junior partner was reinforced in subsequent decades by the modernisation of its weapon systems and equipment and by its provision of military advice, training and equipment to several Near Eastern and African countries.

The Soviet forces

The Soviet forces in the GDR, known as the Group of Soviet Forces in Germany, represented the largest concentration of Soviet military power outside the Soviet Union, totalling about 400,000 men in the mid-1980s.[40] Widely regarded as the ultimate guarantee of SED power, they had rescued Ulbricht in 1953 and Soviet troops had intervened to suppress challenges to Communist rule in Hungary in 1956 and Czechoslovakia in 1968. Until Gorbachev's abandonment of the Brezhnev Doctrine, it was assumed that the Soviet Union would be prepared to deploy a measure of force to prop up so vital an ally as the GDR. The crucial role occupied by the GDR in Soviet strategic thinking was reflected in the fact that the NVA was the only East European military establishment directly under the Warsaw Pact Supreme Command in peacetime and that the commander-in-chief of the Soviet Forces in Germany could in theory declare a state of emergency in the GDR.

Political justice

In the later Honecker era, the judicial system was still strictly subordinated to the policy and goals of the SED. Many East Germans languished in prison convicted of criminal offences when in reality their 'offence' was political. In the 1950s in particular, the Politbüro intervened in trials of special political significance. It is estimated that at least 170 death sentences were passed for political offences throughout the GDR's history. Although the GDR, bowing to international pressure, resorted to reprieves and clemency after 1975, it did not abolish capital punishment until 1987, applying it against members of the Stasi and the armed forces who were convicted of spying. Executions were carried out in secret and the death certificates were falsified. The last execution, in 1981, was that of the former Stasi officer Dr Walter Teske. Although the Honecker Politbüro no longer interfered directly in specific trials, it maintained a general control over justice and legislation. Operational supervision was in the hands of the Central Committee Department for State and Legal Questions.

The Politbüro could rely on an obedient judiciary. All public prosecutors and 96 per cent of judges in regional courts were SED members, and lawyers accorded the maintenance of SED rule priority over the interests of their clients. Many lawyers and judges cooperated closely with the Ministry of State Security, often merely endorsing the recommendations of MfS investigators. The Stasi's prisons and interrogation centres functioned independently of the State Prosecutor, to whom in theory they were responsible. Main Department IX was empowered by the GDR code of criminal procedure to carry out investigations, in particular of offences which could be designated as 'hostile to the state'.[41]

The high level of party-politicisation of justice is revealed in the 200,000 to 250,000 East Germans who, according to recent estimates, were imprisoned for political reasons between 1949 and 1989.[42] Although the numbers of 'political offenders' dropped under Honecker, the records of the Ministries of the Interior and State Security indicate that as many as 55,000 persons were sentenced in the final eleven years of the Honecker regime. The main type of political offence, attempted flight from or an application to leave the republic, was normally dealt with under one of the many elastic categories in the criminal code, such as riotous behaviour, subversive activities and undermining public order by 'asocial' activity. Members of the alternative political culture were caught in this net.

Conditions for all categories of prisoners showed some improvement during the 1970s and 1980s in comparison to the immediate postwar period. For example, the provision of medical supplies increased and the use of physical torture and isolation cells declined. Nevertheless, conditions remained harsh for political prisoners, especially for those in Stasi detention centres like Berlin-Hohenschönhausen. The prisons in Cottbus, Torgau and Bautzen were particularly notorious. Prisoners were expected to fulfil high work norms despite working on obsolete equipment and machinery, hygiene was poor and food had a low vitamin content. Prisons were overcrowded: in the mid-1980s, the number of prisoners was between 180 and 200 per 100,000 inhabitants, a far higher proportion than in the FRG. Informers frequently occupied the same cells as political prisoners. In the case of a failed attempt at flight from the republic, entire families might be victimised. Threats to send children to a state-run home were often used to extract a confession. Interviews with 360 former political prisoners, conducted after unification, reveal that many were still suffering from psychological disturbances and long-term physical injury. The illnesses can be linked to the unacceptable hygiene conditions and the labour system in prison and to maltreatment by guards and other inmates. 60 per cent had been subjected to threats and blackmail and 80 per cent had been forced to endure solitary confinement.[43]

Dealing with the crimes committed by the SED state has proved to be one of the most controversial and intractable problems of post-unification Germany. The Unification Treaty of 1990 provided the legal basis for placing politicians as well as the border guards and their officers on trial. GDR law was held to apply to crimes committed before unification and FRG law thereafter. With the exception of the first border guard trial in 1991, in which the judge applied the principle of a higher morality over codified law, other trials have been based on *nulla poena sine lege*, that is, an act is only punishable if it is an offence against existing law. This means that GDR officials and soldiers have been called to answer for offences which the GDR criminal code itself recognised as manslaughter and bodily harm. Sentence has been passed on three members of the SED Politbüro and six of the GDR's military leadership. In September 1993, Heinz Keßler, the former Minister of Defence, his Chief-of-Staff, Fritz Strelitz, and the Suhl party secretary, Hans Albrecht, all members of the National Defence Council, were found guilty for their part in the border deaths. It was held that they had ignored, for political reasons, the recognition in GDR law of the primacy of protecting human life over state interests. Keßler was sentenced to seven and a half years. Proceedings against Honecker and Stoph on the charge of collective manslaugher were suspended in January 1993 and November 1992 respectively on grounds of the poor health of the defendants. Proceedings were initiated against a further seven members of the Politbüro in January 1995 for not having attempted to prevent the shootings on the German–German border. In August 1997, Krenz was sentenced to six and a half-years' and Schabowski and Kleiber to three years' imprisonment. All were bailed pending appeal.[44] The trials have been variously criticised as an exercise in 'victor's justice' and, on the other hand, because of the cumbersome legal niceties, for failing to hand out adequate punishment to the GDR's erstwhile rulers.

References

1. In Deutscher Bundestag VIII 1995: 120, 124

2. Suckut S. 1996: 168

3. Süß W. 1997b: 230

4. Müller-Enbergs H. 1996: 59

5. Vollnhals C. 1994: 508

6. Ibid., 510

7. Müller-Enbergs H. 1996: 7, 59; Childs D., Popplewell R. 1996: 86

8. Müller-Enbergs H. 1996: 94

9. Schwan H. 1997: 54–75

10. Müller-Enbergs H. 1996: 52–4

11. See the interview with Mittig in Riecker A., Schwarz A., Schneider D. 1990: 177

12. Fricke K. W. 1991: 37, 190; Childs D., Popplewell R. 1996: 72

13. Cited in Fricke K. W. 1991: 12

14. See the interview with Herger in Riecker A., Schwarz A., Schneider D. 1990: 119, 121

15. Süß W. 1997b: 224–6

16. Ibid., 220–1; Vollnhals C. 1994: 499

17. Schroeder K. 1998: 444

18. Childs D., Popplewell R. 1996: 91; Fricke K. W. 1991: 48

19. Deutscher Bundestag VIII 1995: 83

20. Müller-Enbergs H. 1995: 103–7; Behnke K .1995: 12–26

21. Cited in Müller-Enbergs H. 1996: 347

22. Müller-Enbergs H. 1995: 120–1

23. Cited in ibid., 111–12

24. Deutscher Bundestag VIII 1995: 69–72

25. Müller-Enbergs H. 1995: 113, 119–20

26. Deutscher Bundestag VIII 1995: 521–2

27. Cited in Walther J. 1996: 51

28. *Deckname 'Lyrik'* 1990: 24, 30–1, 39–42, 50–1, 66–9, 73–8, 113–20

29. Walther J. 1996: 21

30. Vinke H. 1993: 9–17, 111–40

[232]   31. Wallace I. 1994: 114, 122–3

32. Walther J. 1996: 641–2

33. Fricke K. W. 1997: 8

34. Knabe H. 1997: 9

35. Fricke K. W. 1992: 158

36. Diedrich T., Ehlert H., Wenzke R. 1998: 1, 21–4

37. Filmer W., Schwan H. 1991: 393

38. Lapp P. J. 1998: 236

39. Diedrich T., Ehlert H., Wenzke R. 1998: 35

40. Artl K. 1998: 616

41. Schroeder K. 1998: 423, 426

42. Werkentin F. 1997: 143

43. Müller K.-D. 1997: 122–4

44. *Der Tagesspiegel*, 31 October 1998: 9

CHAPTER THIRTEEN

OPPOSITION AND DISSENT

Forms of opposition

Marxist-Leninist ideology dictated that 'No objective political or social basis exists for the existence of an opposition in socialist states, for the working class – in alliance with the working people – is the class which not only exercises power but is also the main productive force in society'.[1] SED dogma and the elaborate state security system notwithstanding, opposition proved endemic to GDR society. In particular, the highly ambitious experiment in constructing a socialist system in the Stalinist mode provoked widespread resistance and opposition in the early years of the republic. Despite the carrot of the social contract, Honecker, too, was confronted by several major types of opposition ranging from various shades of intellectual dissent to the highly variegated alternative political culture of the small, autonomous peace, ecology and human rights groups. However, not until the end of the 1980s would it be possible to speak of the emergence of a conscious political opposition from among some of these basic groups in the sense that it began to take on a rudimentary organisational form with alternative ideological and political concepts to those espoused by the SED, in particular the notion of a civil society.

In addition to these forms of opposition and dissent, nonconformist behaviour proliferated, above all in the niches of society. An impressive attempt to categorise oppositional behaviour in the GDR has been undertaken by Ilko-Sascha Kowalczuk. Clearly influenced by studies of *Resistenz* in the Third Reich, his typology embraces four basic forms between which considerable overlap exists: societal refusal (*gesellschaftliche Verweigerung*), social protest, political dissent, for example of reform socialists such as Havemann and Bahro, and mass protest.[2] The latter, although relatively rare, occurred in its most spectacular form in June 1953 but also on a minor scale during the clashes

[234] between young people and the security forces in October 1977 on the Alexanderplatz in East Berlin. Societal refusal, which Kowalczuk regards as the form of action practised by most East Germans, even if only temporarily and usually alone or in small groups, was highly diverse: the avoidance of SED-speak such as the 'anti-fascist wall'; not joining political parties and mass organisations; and tuning into the Western media. The list also extends to non-participation in official demonstrations; rowdy behaviour; telling political jokes; mocking party functionaries in private; listening to 'subversive' music; not casting a vote; joining the *Junge Gemeinde*; and daubing swastikas on walls. Social protest, of which strikes, shop-floor disputes and other work conflicts were the most common examples, was not so widespread as societal refusal. Absenteeism may also be added to this repertoire.

The broadening of what constitutes opposition and resistance under a dictatorship and the uncovering of non-conformist behaviour – or *Resistenz* – raise the question, also posed by historians of the Third Reich, as to whether it is justified to speak not of a 'resistance without the people' but rather of a 'resistance of the entire people'. The latter interpretation is too broad and inflates the degree of opposition. Although research by Mitter and Wolle, notably in their book *Untergang auf Raten*, has unearthed widespread popular opposition and non-conformist behaviour throughout the history of the GDR, it would be an exaggeration to assert that the East German population from the later 1960s onwards was a seething mass of unrest and civil disobedience. Only a tiny minority entered into conscious actions against the SED; the majority stood aside and came to some form of arrangement with the regime. Furthermore, most East Germans who engaged in societal refusal and social protest probably rarely did so with wide-ranging political goals in mind; their actions were essentially related to material interests and aspirations, individual values and local circumstances. It was often spontaneous, rarely organised and its manifestations were usually contained by the regime, at least on the surface, without undue difficulty. There is, of course, the sometimes intractable problem of identifying the motivation behind specific forms of such behaviour. Take, for example, work absenteeism and production slowdowns; they might be the result of political discontent but, equally, they might be predicated on sickness and an enterprise's out-of-date production methods. In a thoroughly dominated society, they might, however, be interpreted as a rejection of the regime and criminalised by the authorities. The great advantage of the *Resistenz* concept is that it highlights the complexity of individual attitudes and responses to the regime and its policies. East Germans, on balance, should not simply be divided into rulers and ruled; the lines of conformity and nonconformity stamped a crisscross pattern on most [235] individuals. While the view taken here is that opposition is an appropriate umbrella term for behavioural forms such as societal refusal, protest, intellectual dissent and resistance, the classification will need further refining, especially as research continues to shed new light on such activities.

Intellectual dissent

Robert Havemann

Honecker inherited from Ulbricht several well-known intellectual dissidents – Heym, Havemann and Biermann – and acquired another notable one, Bahro, as well as the so-called Federation of Democratic Communists of Germany in the late 1970s. Robert Havemann (1912–82) joined the KPD in 1932 and during the Third Reich was incarcerated in the same prison as Erich Honecker. In 1950, he moved to the GDR after he was ejected from his academic posts in West Berlin on account of his Communist ideals. He spied for the Soviet Union between 1946 and 1952 and for several years worked as a Stasi agent, reporting on West German scientists and on developments at the Humboldt University. As he became increasingly critical of the Stalinist system, his work for the Stasi became less productive and the connection was terminated in 1963.[3] In the following year, he was expelled from the SED and from his post of Professor of Physical Chemistry at the Humboldt University after a series of critical public lectures on dialectical and historical materialism.

Although Havemann was unable to publish in the GDR and was placed under strict house arrest between 1976 and 1979, he managed to smuggle his writings out to the West. He focused on how the advantages derived from the abolition of private property and the elimination of capital could be turned into a true socialism by the introduction of greater liberty. Socialist democracy, Havemann envisioned, could be realised by freedom of speech and association, the founding of independent opposition parties, competitive elections to the *Volkskammer* and the abolition of censorship.[4] Whereas he had been dismayed by the Warsaw Pact invasion of Czechoslovakia, he saw reason for hope in the spread of Eurocommunist ideas and in the development of the alternative political culture in the GDR in the later 1970s and 1980s. His criticism of consumerism in capitalist and socialist societies corresponded with concerns among many autonomous groups over the degradation of the environment and the negative effects of scientific-technical progress.

The Biermann affair

Wolfgang Biermann, the son of a Communist, Jewish father who had been murdered in Auschwitz, moved to the GDR from Hamburg in 1953. Committed to the GDR and to a human socialism, he flayed the excrescences of the SED's bureaucratic 'real existing socialism' in his acidic political poems and songs, as in the following extract from 'Don't keep waiting for the good times' by Wolf Biermann:

> *I hear a lot of people saying*
> *'Socialism — well, all right*
> *But what they're pulling on us here*
> *It isn't worth a light!'*
> *I see a lot of people clenching*
> *buried fists in mackintoshes*
> *Dog-ends hang cold from their lips*
> *And in their hearts are ashes*

Although a virtual *Berufsverbot* was imposed on Biermann in 1965, he did appear from time to time at the press club during the Leipzig Trade Fair and in the East Berlin artists' club *Möwe*. Eager to be rid of so critical and popular a figure, the Stasi hatched plans to deport him to the West. The opportunity finally arived in 1976. After permitting him to undertake a concert tour of West Germany at the invitation of *IG Metall*, the Politbüro decided, on 16 November, to forbid him to return to the GDR. It was alleged that his performance in Cologne's Sports Hall was hostile to the socialist state.

The Politbüro's arbitrary action immediately elicited an open letter of protest to *Neues Deutschland* from twelve well-known authors and one sculptor, among them Stephan Hermlin, Christa Wolf, Volker Braun, Heiner Müller, Franz Fühmann and Stefan Heym. Within a few days, over 100 hundred writers and artists had joined the chorus of protest. The majority did not regard themselves as an opposition group; they were registering their objection to the expatriation rather than their rejection of the regime. The SED had not anticipated such widespread protests from the cultural intelligentsia, as was apparent from Honecker's confidential admission to Swiss diplomats that the expatriation had been a mistake.[5]

The elimination of Biermann proved to be part of a broader campaign against sections of the cultural intelligentsia. While the SED did not, as some writers feared, have recourse to widespread expatriation of its critics, it deployed a well-calibrated policy. Prominent authors such as Jurek Becker and

Günter Kunert were expelled from the SED and Christa Wolf, Volker Braun and Ulrich Plenzdorf were ejected from their positions on the East Berlin section of the Writers' Union. Several lesser-known figures were arrested and numerous writers and artists, among them Sarah Kirsch, Kunert, Loest and Becker, left for West Germany, either permanently or on long-term visas. In addition, criminal proceedings were initiated against East German citizens who openly sympathised with Biermann.

A second wave of repression occurred in 1979. Two writers, Heym and Rolf Schneider, had aroused the wrath of the cultural and party functionaries for the publication in the West of their novels *Collin* and *November*. Schneider took as the theme of *November* the Biermann affair and Heym attacked corruption among the GDR's cultural and political elites. In June, Heym, Schneider and seven other authors were thrown out of the Writer's Union, precipitating a series of letters calling for the rescinding of the decision. The authorities' response was to increase the pressure on the writers. In August 1979, paragraph 219 of the Criminal Code was revised to allow for a sentence of five years for the unauthorised transmission of material which was supposedly 'harmful' to the GDR. Failure to submit a manuscript to the Copyright Office could also lead to the same penalty. The 'Lex Heym', as it was soon called, was denounced by Heym in a sharp attack delivered on West German television; ironically, it was not applied against Heym for publishing in the West after 1980.

The regime's harsh treatment of Biermann and its other critics was motivated above all by the fear that their critique of the SED's brand of socialism might flow into the broader channel of human rights issues. Their fears were not without foundation. Justifying their actions on the basis of the 1975 Helsinki agreement on human rights, 79 would-be émigrés signed a petition drafted in July 1976 by the Risa doctor Karl-Heinz Nitschke, demanding the full implementation of human rights. In the following month, the Protestant pastor Oskar Brüsewitz committed suicide in Zeitz by setting himself alight as a form of protest against the SED's policy towards the Church. Another cause of concern for the regime was that some of the main principles of West European Eurocommunism, notably greater political pluralism and an extension of civil rights, were attracting the sympathy of leading GDR dissidents like Havemann. Although the CPSU and the SED staged a conference in East Berlin in June 1978 for all Communist parties, ostensibly as a bridge-building exercise between Eurocommunists and Marxist-Leninists, in truth both the Soviet and GDR leaders were determined to halt the spread of Eurocommunism as it appeared to pose a threat to their power monopoly.

Bahro's alternative

Rudolph Bahro (1935–97), a former philosophy student at the Humboldt University, was moved by the crushing of the Prague Spring, and by his own experience working as a labour expert in an East Berlin enterprise, to analyse the defects of the socialist system in his book *The Alternative in Eastern Europe*, which was published in the West but not in the GDR. Soon after excerpts appeared in the West German weekly *Der Spiegel* in August 1977, Bahro was arrested and eventually sentenced, in 1978, to eight years' imprisonment on the trumped-up charge of betraying state secrets. He was released the following year as part of a general amnesty. Bahro attacked 'real existing socialism' as a system in which the whole of society stood property-less against the state machine and in which the masses were pitted in an irreconcilable conflict with the dictatorship of the Politbüro. His solution was for the elimination of the existing routinised division of labour and the chanelling of the resultant release of emancipatory drives by a League of Communists in place of the ruling party.[6] Although the League was to be open to all social forces, the elitist nature of the League left Bahro open to the charge that he was pursuing a democratic goal along a non-democratic path.

Democratic Communists of Germany

Bahro's call for a League of Communists appeared to have been answered when, in late 1977, a Federation of Democratic Communists of Germany drafted a Manifesto which was published in *Der Spiegel* in January 1978. The Federation was a loose and small group of disaffected middle- and high-level functionaries. The inspiration behind the document was Hermann von Berg, formerly a departmental head of international relations in the Council of Ministers' Press Office. Although it was a highly eclectic mixture of democratic, pluralistic and Communist ideas, the Manifesto was potentially an explosive political cocktail. The Federation's basic goal was the establishment of a democratic Communist order in Germany. Fiercely critical of the imposition of the 'reactionary' and 'parasitical' Soviet system, the Manifesto demanded the abolition of the dictatorship of the Politbüro and Central Secretariat clique. In addition, it advocated the introduction of an independent parliament and judiciary, and the implementation of freedom of assembly, the press, association and religion. In foreign policy, the Federation broke the national taboo: not only did it urge the departure of all foreign troops from Germany and the withdrawal of the two German states from their respective military pacts but it also aspired to a reunited Germany in which Social Democrats, socialists and democratic Communists would prevail over conservative forces. The GDR's close relationship with the Soviet Union was condemned as a threat to peace and détente in Europe because of the Soviets' military build-up and the militarisation of life in the Soviet bloc.[7]

Although the intellectual opposition around Havemann and other dissidents attracted considerable interest in the West during the 1970s, its influence was relatively weak. A clandestine group like the Federation of German Communists was not in a position to attract much popular support and Bahro's *Alternative*, while arousing animated debate in many small circles, assumed political significance primarily as a source of ideas for the citizens' movements. The limited appeal of the dissidents can be attributed in part to the crushing of internal party opposition centred around Herrnstadt, Zaisser and Schirdewan during the 1950s. The security apparat was also sufficiently alert and powerful to restrict Havemann's room for political manoeuvre and to force Bahro and von Berg to leave the GDR. Bearing in mind the fate of the Prague Spring and the party leadership's firm grip on cadre policy, reform from above looked ever more unlikely. The political sclerosis which would be fatal to the SED at the close of the 1980s was thus already well advanced a decade earlier.

Emigration to the West

The westward exodus was the most visible expression of the SED's legitimacy deficit. Between 1950 and 1961, about 2.6 million left for the West, while only 400,000 West Germans opted for the GDR. Even the Berlin Wall failed to deter East Germans from trying to escape. From the building of the Wall to the end of 1988, 616,000 left for the West, of whom 235,000 (38 per cent) fled without the permission of the authorities.[8] The GDR's entry into the United Nations and its signing of the 1975 Helsinki Conference on Security and Cooperation acted as a powerful spur to apply for official permission to leave the GDR. The Nitschke initiative was a crucial development as it encouraged others to set up self-help groups. Collective exit applications were made on various occasions during the 1980s, for example, in Jena and Leipzig in 1983. Some applicants resorted to demonstrative actions: staging silent marches of protest in town centres and occupying Western embassies, like the 607 East Germans who did so in 1984. The arbitrary nature of the

[240]   whole process of applying to emigrate or travel to the West underpinned popular perceptions of being held under the tutelage of an insensitive bureaucracy.

The SED was confronted by a mass movement which it was increasingly unable to control. Official records show a sharp increase in the number of applicants, from almost two applicants per 1,000 inhabitants under pensionable age in 1980 to over twelve during the second half of 1989.[9] A central coordinating group was set up to tackle the problem and MfS agents were assigned to dissuade people from leaving. Many applicants had to pay a heavy price: interrogation, charges of treasonable activity, imprisonment, job discrimination and rejection by friends. In a vain attempt to defuse the enormous political pressure building up behind the number of exit aplications, the regime allowed over 21,000 of its citizens to leave in the first three months of 1984. By the end of the year, about 35,000 had been given official permission to leave; a further 6,000 had fled the country.[10]

Exit, it is sometimes argued, does not strictly belong to resistance and opposition on the grounds that in abandoning the opportunity to change the system, émigrés were weakening oppositional potential. A second argument is that only a tiny minority of émigrés, such as Jürgen Fuchs and Roland Jahn, attempted to assist opposition inside the GDR from their West German outpost.[11] These objections notwithstanding, emigration ought to be classified as a form of opposition for a number of reasons: it can be regarded as a protest vote against SED socialism; the emigration movement constituted a permanent source of discontent which kept the issue of human rights on the political agenda; and, lastly, it undermined the party's aspirations to create affective as well as functional support for the GDR. By opting for West Germany, the émigrés were directly challenging not only the SED's depiction of the FRG as a danger to peace but also refuting the party's conception of two separate German nations.

The alternative political culture

Numerous small, autonomous groups attained a relatively high political profile from the later 1970s onwards. Many emerged from existing circles and they recruited heavily among the so-called GDR generation, that is, the 25- to 40-year-olds who had grown up in the shadow the Wall. Members of this generation had been influenced by emancipatory tendencies in the West since the mid-1960s and by the democratic socialism of the Prague Spring. The autonomous groups constituted an 'alternative political culture', that is, the articulation outside official channels of a series of peace, ecological, human rights, gay and Second–Third World issues. Because of the severe restrictions imposed by the SED, autonomous activities in the public sphere were largely confined to the protected space afforded by the Protestant Churches, the only major public institution with a significant measure of control over its own affairs. The autonomous groups tended to have a cultural rather than a power-political orientation, to be reactive rather than proactive and to favour grass-roots democracy over parliamentary forms.[12] The thrust of their activities and programmes was for a reform of the existing system, not its overthrow. They wanted a democratic socialism which respected civil liberties but, with the exception of individuals such as the Naumburg theologian Edelbert Richter, little attempt was made to develop a theoretical framework.

The German question as taboo

The opposition groups were circumspect with respect to one of the main taboos, the German question, which, according to Ulrike Poppe, an active participant in the opposition during the 1980s, was underestimated, possibly even suppressed, by the opposition groups. The majority belonged to a generation which had no direct personal experience of the other part of Germany. Although they resented the restrictions on their freedom, the division of Germany into two states was by no means perceived in negative terms. A Europe without frontiers had a greater attraction. Not that the national question was entirely ignored. In the Berlin Appeal of 1982, Eppelmann and Havemann regarded the overcoming of the division of Germany as a prerequisite to the safeguarding of peace in Europe, and several discussion circles, for example, the Naumburg peace circle around Edelbert Richter, thematised the German question. However, many regarded it as counterproductive to discuss such an unlikely occurrence as unification while Europe remained divided.[13]

Limited appeal of the basic groups

The groups were small in number and isolated from society. Their limited appeal may be attributed in part to their relatively underdeveloped institutional and communication networks. This remained a serious problem

[242] despite the boost to networking in the 1980s by the formation of the Church from Below, the ecological network *Arche* and the environmental libraries in Berlin, Leipzig and elsewhere. *Frieden-konkret*, which emerged from the annual Peace Workshops, developed into the most important communication network among the basic groups. Another reason for the low level of popular support was the unwillingness of most citizens to involve themselves in such highly politicised issues as civil rights because of the risks to themselves, family members and their careers. Coercion, too, played its part: the regime subjected its 'unpalatable' dissidents to regular surveillance, occasional detainment and expulsion, sometimes forcibly, to the West. In January 1988, in the aftermath of the intervention of some 100 activists in the SED's traditional rally commemorating the death of Luxemburg and Liebknecht, many were arrested and deported to the West, among them Stefan Krawczyk, Vera Wollenberger, Ralf Hirsch, Bärbel Bohley and Wolfgang Templin.

The Stasi and the groups

MfS penetration of the groups was extremely thorough: for example, Ibrahim Böhme and Wolfgang Schnur, two of the leading figures in the citizens' movements which helped to sweep away the SED in 1989–90, were unveiled, in 1990, as long-standing Stasi informers. One tragic case was the revelation after the East German revolution that Vera Wollenberger's husband Knud (codename 'Donald'), the son of a distinguished Jewish academic, had been spying on her, reporting not only on her activities in the independent peace and ecological movement but also on the details of their private life. Ironically, other Stasi agents, not knowing that IM 'Donald' was one of them, were describing him to their superiors as a 'negative, hostile element'. MfS agents sought to undermine the effectiveness of the groups by, for example, inciting divisive internal discussions and conflicts and by encouraging radical activities in order to provoke counteraction by the state authorities. Many groups collapsed because members suspected that the Stasi was 'amongst them'.

The peace issue

Central to the alternative political culture in the GDR was the isssue of peace. Since 1978, when the introduction of compulsory theoretical and practical pre-military training in schools for pupils aged fourteen to sixteen triggered off widespread protest on the part of the clergy and parents, the autonomous peace groups became more outspoken and peace initiatives attracted considerable popular interest, above all among the younger generation. The rapid growth in these initiatives can be attributed not only to GDR-specific preconditions such as the growing militarisation of life at school and in the mass organisations such as the FDJ and the GST, but also to the advent of a new ice age in East–West relations and to the NATO–Soviet confrontation over the deployment of nuclear missiles.

Perhaps the most famous event was the annual Dresden Peace Forum, especially that of February 1982 which was attended by between 4,000 and 5,000 people, despite the attempts by the SED and state authorities to suppress news of the meeting and hinder travel to Dresden. Considerable pressure was exerted by Hans Modrow and Klaus Gysi on the Saxon regional Church to ensure that the activities were contained within the framework of the Church.[14] Despite protests from Church leaders such as Bishops Gottfried Forck and Werner Krusche, the state authorities forcibly suppressed the wearing of the 'Swords into Ploughshares' emblem which had mushroomed in popularity after the 1982 Forum. Other notable activities included the Peace Weeks and the Peace Workshops which attracted thousands of young people. The former, organised each November, included discussions, seminars, music and poetry. These events were not confined to peace groups: the Peace Workshop held at East Berlin's Church of the Redeemer in July 1983 was also attended by women's, gay and ecology groups. The East Berlin pastor Rainer Eppelmann organised highly popular blues masses at his church. Many attempts were made by the authorities to stop them. Eppelmann was accused of an anti-socialist attitude and it was alleged that the events led to unruly and drunken behaviour in the vicinity of the church. Although some Church leaders, such as Schönherr, were not against restraining Eppelmann, they were unwilling to impose a ban on the blues masses for fear of being criticised as servants of the state.[15]

Conscription was another controversial issue. Conscripts were entitled by law to serve in a construction unit instead of performing formal military service, the only instance of its kind in Eastern Europe. In 1981, a group in Dresden proposed a more radical solution: a community peace service as a truly civilian alternative to military service. This envisaged employment in homes for children, old people and the physically handicapped, auxiliary service in hospitals and community care. The SED rejected the proposal outright, the Politbüro candidate Werner Walde countering that the GDR was in itself a community peace service. The idea of a community peace service was part of an attempt to thematise political conditions in the GDR and to indicate how

[244] conflicts could be overcome through various mechanisms, including peace education and the responsibility of the individual for peace. The authors of the 'Berlin Appeal' of January 1982, Havemann and Eppelmann, developed the theme of the internal preconditions of peace. They proposed a great debate on peace in an atmosphere of tolerance, the renunciation of the production and sale of military toys and the replacement of defence studies in school by lessons about problems of peace.[16] The Appeal, which attracted 2,000 signatures within three months, was probably the most significant document to emerge from the alternative political culture before 1989. It also touched on an even more sensitive political issue: it called for the withdrawal of all 'occupation troops' from the GDR and the FRG and the signing of a peace treaty between the victors of the Second World War and the two German states. The former allies, it was proposed, should then agree on guarantees of non-intervention in the internal affairs of the two German states.

Small women's peace groups emerged in several cities, notably the Women for Peace group in East Berlin, under the protective cover of the autonomous peace movement and the Protestant Churches. Their main themes concerned peace and peace education, the campaign against atomic war and disarmament. The decisive impetus to the women's peace movement occurred in March 1982 when a new Military Service Law was passed, providing for the conscription of women aged 18–50 in the event of an emergency. In a letter of protest to Honecker in October 1982, signed by 150 women, it was contended that military service for women was not an expression of their equality but in contradiction to their being female, and it called for a public discussion of issues such as disarmament and ways of avoiding a nuclear catastrophe.

East German Greens

Ecology groups, which were frequently linked to the Protestant Churches, became increasingly active from the late 1970s, spreading information about the high level of environmental degradation in the GDR. Among their main activities were bicycle demonstrations against the noise and pollution caused by cars, exhibitions, the distribution of literature with ecological themes and protests against the use of nuclear power. There existed about 80 to 90 ecological groups in the GDR towards the end of the 1980s, located above all in the larger cities with environmental problems, such as Halle, Dresden, Leipzig and Berlin.[17] An important stimulus to debates on the environment was provided by the dissemination of information obtained from Western sources and by the activities of prominent ecological centres such as the

Church Research Centre run by Hans-Peter Gensirchen in Wittenberg and
the Church and Society Committee under the chairmanship of Dr Heino
Falcke. In September 1986, an environmental library was established in the
basement of the parish house of the Zionskirche in East Berlin. Its in-house
journal, *Umweltblätter*, with a circulation of about 2,000 copies per month,
covered not only environmental problems but also human rights, women's,
Third World and peace issues. The Stasi kept a close watch on the library; in
November 1987, it arrested several leading members and seized the printing
press.[18]

Human rights and the IFM

The activities of the autonomous groups, together with popular discontent
over restrictions on travel, were all aspects of a common theme: the denial
of human rights. From about the mid-1980s, the issue of human and civil
rights came to occupy a more prominent place within the alternative political
culture and to attain a dynamic quality lacked by the single issue movements.
The accession to power of Gorbachev and efforts in Hungary and Poland
to establish the roots of a civil society encouraged human rights activists in
the GDR. A key role was played by the Initiative for Peace and Human
Rights (IFM). Formed in late 1985 and its foundation announced in early
1986, it numbered no more than 30 participants before the autumn of
1989.[19] Several of its leading figures – it did not have a formal membership –
such as Martin Böttger and Bärbel Bohley would later play an influential
role in the founding of New Forum. The IFM cultivated contacts with dissidents and opposition groups elsewhere in the Soviet bloc, for example, Char-
ter 77, and it deliberately pursued its activities beyond the confines of the
Church.

One of the IFM's first moves was to despatch an appeal to the GDR government, jointly drawn up with Eppelmann, calling for a democratic system
of voting, the right to freedom of assembly, demonstration and association,
the creation of a civilian peace service and the right of GDR citizens to travel.
Over 100 East Germans signed the appeal. In June 1986, the IFM produced
the first issue of its journal *Grenzfall* in which it publicised the views and
activities of opposition groups inside and outside the GDR. It is not surprising
that the IFM was targeted by the Stasi. About 50 per cent of IFM members
were MfS unofficial collaborators who sought to provoke unrest and dissen-
sion within the group. Various members suffered arrest and expulsion from
the GDR.

[246]   By the late 1980s, the activities of the IFM and the other autonomous groups ensured that hardly a Church synod took place without a debate on the democratisation of political life. Characteristic of the debate were the 'Twenty Theses for Social Renewal' submitted by the Wittenberg pastor Friedrich Schorlemmer to the Church meeting in Halle in June 1988. Reformers like Schorlemmer envisaged renewal through secret elections, the division of powers between the executive, judiciary and legislature, freedom of association and travel, and greater independence for the political parties in the SED-controlled Democratic Bloc. The replacement of the practice of internal *Abgrenzung* by a climate in society conducive to dialogue and tolerance was the target of the group's 'Rejection of the Principle and Practice of Delimitation'.

The Protestant Churches between compliance and opposition

The Protestant Churches provided the essential shelter for the autonomous groups, partly because they had managed to preserve some organisational autonomy after the fierce Church–state struggle abated in the later Ulbricht era. Ulbricht's statement to the People's Chamber in 1960 that 'Christianity and the humanist goals of socialism are not irreconcilable' heralded a change in SED strategy: the Churches were to be gradually coopted or incorporated into the socialist order. The regime was unhappy, however, with the Protestant Churches' links with their West German partners. Not until 1969 did the GDR branch finally withdraw from the all-German umbrella organisation, the Protestant Church of Germany, and establish its own separate League of Protestant Churches in the GDR. This separation was not complete as about one-third of the East German GDR Churches' total budget was derived from West German subsidies.

The Protestant Churches' membership continued to fall during the Honecker years as a result of the long-term forces of secularisation and urbanisation. By 1989, membership had dropped to 5.1 million or about 30 per cent of the population as against 80.4 per cent in 1950. Attendance at church service was confined to a much smaller number: about 1.8 million.[20] The Roman Catholic Church, though more successful in resisting secularisation, also suffered a decline in numbers, from 11 per cent of the total population in 1950 to about half that figure in 1989. A tightly knit community of believers, it played a less active role in GDR political life than its Protestant counterpart. By their very presence, both the Protestant and Roman Catholic Churches constituted a challenge to the SED's ideological primacy; the Protestants' *Junge Gemeinden* in particular aroused the ire of the party and the FDJ. As well as spreading the Christian gospel, the Protestant Churches also cared for the aged, the physically and mentally handicapped, and social outcasts in their many homes and hospitals.

The 'concordat'

Honecker's meeting in March 1978 with the executive of the League of Protestant Churches and its chairman Bishop Albrecht Schönherr bore witness to the development of a more harmonious relationship. Schönherr himself had made a significant personal contribution to laying the groundwork for the compromise. His famous statement in 1971 was a clear indication of the Churches' new attitude: 'We do not want to be a Church against or alongside but we wish to be a Church within socialism'. There was, however, no clear consensus as to whether this entailed closer cooperation or whether it might be construed as a critical form of opposition to the party dictatorship.[21] As part of his side of the bargain, Honecker reaffirmed, at the 1978 meeting, the permission, first conceded in 1976, for the construction of church buildings in new towns and new suburbs; he granted the League a modest amount of TV time and additional access to the state radio; and he accepted the import of Church literature from the West. These and other concessions were not enshrined in a formal agreement, but they did represent the party's acknowledgement of a role for the Churches within socialism.

The 1978 accord should be primarily understood as the outcome of a greater readiness on both sides since the early 1970s to establish a working relationship. From the standpoint of the SED leaders, Church policy was yet one more aspect of their general policy to integrate diverse social and political groups into the socialist system. Furthermore, the Churches, due to their links with the West, were regarded as a useful ally in the party's efforts to influence Western political leaders and peace movements. The Churches were supportive in other respects: they opposed NATO's military build-up in the 1980s and, to the annoyance of Bonn, advocated recognition of GDR citizenship in 1985. However, the SED was still not satisfied: it was determined to bind conservative elements in the Churches ever more closely to the SED and, according to a circular from Mielke to Stasi officers on 19 April 1978, to subvert, divide and paralyse 'hostile-negative' persons and groups in the Church.[22] This lends

[248] weight to Clemens Vollnhals's argument that while the SED's methods might have changed over forty years, its long-term goal remained constant even in periods of relative political liberalisation: that is, it wished to eliminate the Churches as an association with a high level of internal autonomy.[23] The Churches were regarded as an alien body in real existing socialism. In 1983, one of the top-ranking Stasi officers, Mielke's deputy, Rudi Mittig, stated that 'Religion is and remains a type of bourgeois ideology and is incompatible with Marxism-Leninism. At this particular time, such an assessment cannot be the subject of public discussion but it must always determine the political as well as the basic political-operative conception'.[24]

The Churches and the autonomous groups

Within Church circles numerous conflicts and disagreements erupted over relations with the regime and over the position of the autonomous groups in the Church. With regard to the former, a basic divide existed between those ministers and leaders who, like Bishop Schönherr, preferred to avoid confrontation and others, notably Bishop Gottfried Forck, who were prepared to take greater risks, for example, in aiding the basic groups. In general terms, the Church hierarchy sought to embrace the autonomous groups but without jeopardising the fragile compact with the state. It had no intention of becoming a centre of an overt political opposition against state and party. This balancing act left Church leaders open to charges of expediency from the more impatient peace and human rights activists. Tension within the Churches also arose over to what extent the groups, which contained many Church members, should be incorporated more firmly into the organisational framework of the religious community. Attempts to bind such groups firmly to the Church were resented, not without reason, as a form of control and discipline.[25] Not until the late 1980s would the groups and members of the congregation leave the confines of the Church and begin to enter the public domain.

Inevitably, the Stasi made deep inroads.[26] Although unofficial agents were planted in the Church at all levels, the Stasi concentrated its efforts on the leading bodies. High-ranking officials such as the East Berlin Superintendent Günter Krusche and Bishop Horst Gienke in Greifswald served as informers. The personal secretary of Bishop Schönherr, Anita Steinmetzger, worked for many years as an IM, supplying the MfS with highly confidential documents on Church policy. As the Church was only able to train a few of its own jurists and therefore had to appoint ones trained in state institutions, the Stasi

was able to place lawyers as IMs in important positions in the Churches. At
some Church synods as many as 25 out of 100 synod members and assistants
might be operating as IMs. Many top officials, who were not officially agents
of the state security service, engaged in highly secretive conversations with
party and state bodies such as the State Secretariat for Church Questions, and
were frequently indiscreet in disclosing information on Church policy and
individual members. The agency with major responsibility for the Churches
was the relatively small Department 4 of Main Department XX, which
employed 223 IMs in 1987.[27] The ministry's goal was to depoliticise and
neutralise the Churches and to use its agents to influence policy and appointments. Critical individuals and groups were to be contained and, where necessary, silenced by the repressive methods employed in other spheres of society.
Bishops and prelates were caught up in this net: campaigns were organised to
isolate and discredit them and their private life was subjected to close scrutiny.

As elsewhere in society, the Stasi recruited agents by taking advantage of
personal weaknesses and needs such as the desire for personal security, material goods, career advancement and a university place for their children. IM
controllers were adept at encouraging IMs to believe that they were contributing to a relaxation in the regime's methods of control. Most Church IMs do
not seem to have believed that working for the Stasi was tantamount to changing sides; indeed, many who betrayed friends convinced themselves that they
were working in the best interests of the Church. Neubert refers to this as a
kind of dual loyalty which is not readily classified into distinctive categories
such as collaboration and refusal, resistance and accommodation.

Manfred Stolpe's involvement with the MfS encapsulates the dilemmas of
dualism and the problems facing historians when seeking to reconstruct the
motivation of IMs. A Church jurist, Stolpe was the top lay official of the Protestant Churches and since 1990 has been the SPD Minister President of the
Land Brandenburg. Although registered by the Stasi as an unofficial collab-
orator (IM 'Sekretär') in 1970, Stolpe denies that he worked as an agent. While
there is no evidence that Stolpe entered into a contractual relationship, he
undoubtedly worked closely and in conspiratorial conditions with Stasi and
party officials for almost twenty years. This kind of relationship was not untypical of Church IMs.[28] Praised before the *Wende* as a skilled intermediary
between East and West and as a protector of dissidents against the state, his
files reveal him to have been a highly compliant Stasi contact. Rather than
acting as the man of the Church in the state, he stands accused of being the
man of the state in the Church. He informed his Stasi and party contacts on
the political views of Church leaders and he warned them of the danger of an

[250]   alliance between the alternative political culture and Christians with 'negative' political attitudes. He was also exceptionally indiscreet in his views on pastor Rainer Eppelmann and discussed ways and means of reining him in. Not surprisingly, some former dissidents have turned vehemently against their former 'protector'.

In his defence, Stolpe has argued that he had been working in the best interests of the Church and had helped thousands of would-be émigrés.[29] Given that the GDR appeared to be a permanent feature, the pragmatist in Stolpe probably persuaded him that the Church's interests and its internal autonomy could be safeguarded and advanced through dialogue with the party and state authorities while, hopefully, ameliorating some of the regime's negative features. In a justification of this position after the collapse of Communism, he claimed that the GDR 'was a dictatorship, but one which wore velvet gloves, and despite everything, it was possible to do a great deal'.[30]

For many, this kind of defence is unacceptable. In 1992, Joachim Gauck, a former pastor from Rostock and subsequently head of the office responsible for the Stasi files, opined, 'The argument that the church or the opposition could only be effective because there were good "diplomats" at work overlooks the danger that the "diplomats" would set the norms for activities within the church, and that it was then child's play for the state to limit those activities. It also overlooks the fact that in church discussions of individuals and issues, the "diplomats" had often internalised the ideas and behaviour of SED comrades'.[31]

In retrospect, it is clear that the Stasi enjoyed considerable success in shaping Church policy and curtailing critical potential. But the Churches were not a pliant and defenceless object. The plurality of opinions and organisations, as well as the dedication of individuals and groups, ensured that critical voices were not silenced and policy was not a mere reflection of the ruling party's priorities. And it was in no small part thanks to the protection of the Churches that the basic groups, though infiltrated by the Stasi, constituted a countervoice to the SED in areas such as human rights and peace.

References

1. *Kleines politisches Wörterbuch* 1978: 652

2. Kowalczuk I.-S. 1995: 95–103

3. Vollnhals C. 1998: 12–13

4. Jäckel H. 1980: 202; Neubert E. 1997: 220–3

5. Kleinschmid H. 1996: 914–15

6. Bahro R. 1978: 11, 244, 367

7. Geppert D. 1996: 123–4, 147–8, 163, 167–9

8. Wendt H. 1991: 387–90; Eisenfeld B. 1995: 192–3

9. Ibid., 203

10. Ibid., 214

11. Poppe U., Eckert R., Kowalczuk I.-S. 1995: 19

12. Knabe H. 1990: 23

13. Meckel M., Gutzeit M. 1994: 69

14. Besier G. 1995: 484–7

15. Ibid., 320–1, 473–6

16. Sandford J. 1983: 95–6

17. Kühnel W., Sallmon-Metzner C. 1991: 176

18. Ibid., 174–6

19. Templin W., Weißhuhn R. 1991: 150–1

20. Wolle S. 1998: 247

21. Wagner H. 1993: 112; Goeckel R. F. 1994: 88

22. Wagner H. 1993: 111

23. Vollnhals C. 1996: 80

24. Cited in ibid., 80

25. Deutscher Bundestag VI/1 1995: 212–13

26. See in particular Neubert E. 1993

27. Mählert U. 1998a: 142

28. Reuth R. G. 1992: 33–4, 42–3

29. Ibid., 51

30. Cited in Sa'adah A. 1998: 191

31. Cited in ibid., 206

PART SIX

EAST GERMANY'S UNEXPECTED REVOLUTION, 1989–90

CHAPTER FOURTEEN

EAST GERMANY IMPLODES

The unexpected revolution

In retrospect, the collapse of SED power in the autumn of 1989 and the reunification of Germany in October 1990 appear to have an inexorable logic, a result of the structural defects with which the GDR emerged from the Soviet test-tube in the immediate postwar years. This is overly deterministic and risks turning historical hindsight into assertions of inevitability. As late as 1989, it was by no means apparent that the Soviet world-system – and with it the GDR – was doomed to rapid disintegration and extinction. The new year started in routine manner: in January, Erich Honecker let it be known that the Berlin Wall would remain in place for another fifty to a hundred years. His perception was shared by most contemporaries. Indeed, the only person to predict that the Wall would fall in the autumn was a woman who ran naked through Halle in the spring of 1989; people thought she was mad. The Soviet ambassador in Bonn, Yuli Kvitsinsky, has admitted in retrospect that even in the latter half of 1989 virtually no top Soviet leader envisaged that a supposedly prosperous GDR would vanish from the map of Europe within a matter of months.[1] Many Western politicians and commentators had little or no expectation of dramatic change. In September 1988, ex-chancellor Willy Brandt asserted that West Germany's search for unification was equivalent to living a lie. Popular sentiment bolstered this view; only a bare majority of West Germans felt that unification should continue to be one of Bonn's policy goals.

Labels such as 'implosion', '*Wende*' (the political 'turning point' of 1989) and 'revolution' have been attached to developments in the GDR during its final year. Revolution, perhaps the most appropriate concept, is usually preceded by an adjective defining crucial aspects of the process. Among the ones most frequently used are 'peaceful', 'civic', 'Protestant', 'social' and

[256]   'rectifying'. The political philosopher Jürgen Habermas, in defining the latter term, captures what many regard as the essence of the revolution: East Germans sought 'to make up for all the things that have divided the Western half of Germany from the Eastern for forty years – its politically happier, and economically more successful, development'.[2] Drawing on the criteria developed by scholars such as Charles Tilly to define modern revolutions, it can be argued that the GDR experienced a revolution, not simply a system collapse. A transfer of power to a new ruling coalition occurred; the process had an overwhelming urgency; there was concerted action from below; and the sweeping institutional, economic, legal and personnel changes consequent on unification marked the end of the old Communist order. Furthermore, although non-violence predominated and proved to be a surprisingly effective weapon against the SED regime, acts of violence were committed by the security forces against demonstrators and members of opposition groups.

The varying characterisations of the revolution denote, in part, the different stages of the process, with the fall of the Berlin Wall in November 1989 as one watershed and the *Volkskammer* election of March 1990 as another. Thus Helmut Walser Smith refers to a revolution for socialism in the first phase until the Wall came down and, thereafter, to a swift transition to a national revolution.[3] Using a similar framework, Konrad Jarausch identifies these two stages as civic and national, and adds a 'social revolution' stage to cover the social and economic transformation of the GDR after the introduction of economic and monetary union on 1 July 1990.[4] What we have, however, is not a revolution in separate stages but a disjointed process which moved from an early phase with a civic and reformed socialist emphasis, with national undertones, to one in which the national option, on the basis of the West German model, became predominant after the fall of the Wall. The culmination of the process was the incorporation of the GDR as the five new *Länder* into the Federal Republic on 3 October 1990.

No single explanation can be identified which provides *the* key to the demise of the GDR; instead, it must be sought in a combination of explanations and theories. Several broad types of explanation can be identified. They range from the emergence of an embryonic civil society and the SED's political legitimacy deficit through to the immobilism of the GDR's political structure and global developments. The remainder of this chapter will examine Gorbachev's vain attempts at reforming the Communist order and the flaws in the SED system before turning, in the final chapters, to the collapse of SED rule and German unification.

The structural flaws of communism [257]

The precipitous fall of the GDR was related inextricably to the Soviet Union's retreat from its Eastern European empire and to the general crisis of the Communist administrative-command system. The guiding principle of this type of system was that the elaborate steering instruments of the central party-state apparatus would ensure the efficient management and allocation of resources for the fulfilment of critical societal goals. Despite its serious deficiencies, throughout the 1950s and even into the 1960s many Western commentators gave the Soviet-type system the benefit of the doubt. The Soviet Union was able to keep in step with the USA in such fields as nuclear energy and to score a spectacular technological success with Sputnik. However, the defects of the system became critical with the advent of the scientific-technical revolution when developments in microelectronics demanded greater flexibility, higher rates of innovation and a greater adaptive capacity. With bureaucratic criteria such as plan fulfilment enjoying precedence over economic considerations and the political elites averse to unrestricted contact with the capitalist world, the result was difficulties with innovation and a technological gap with the leading Western industrial nations and Japan. But as reform of the economic mechanism was an integral element in the ruling Marxist-Leninist party's societal strategy, fundamental reform could only be realised in tandem with the political system, a step which threatened the jealously guarded power monopoly of party leaders and functionaries. Such a challenge was taken up by the new Soviet leader, Mikhail Gorbachev.

Gorbachev: *perestroika* and *glasnost*

Gorbachev's accession to the post of General Secretary of the CPSU in March 1985 was the signal for the long-delayed programme of reform. His 'new thinking', which commenced as a modest attempt at industrial reorganisation by means of economic 'acceleration', soon developed into a programme for economic reconstruction (*perestroika*) underpinned by the necessary openness (*glasnost*) and an enhancement of political democratisation. In order to achieve his domestic goals, Gorbachev and his allies pursued détente with the West as a means of reducing the cost of the arms race, redirecting resources to the ailing Soviet economy, enabling the Soviet

[258] Union and its East European allies to participate more effectively in the international division of labour and improving the chances of obtaining Western economic aid. Yet the notion of a forced retreat from the old system is only part of the explanation. Gorbachev and like-minded colleagues drew heavily on the conciliatory and integrationist alternatives to Stalinism which had been evolving in think-tanks such as the Institute of World Socialism in Moscow and, in the regions, the Novosibirski Institute.

The SED leadership's rejection of Gorbachev's reforms

The top SED leaders were not unduly disturbed by Gorbachev's initial reassessment of the Soviet Union's policies. Indeed, the Soviet Union's interest in the GDR's combine organisation as a possible model for the Soviet Union was welcomed by GDR planners and Gorbachev's desire for better relations with the West appeared to vindicate Honecker's earlier efforts at amelioration. Yet leaders like Honecker, appointed in the Brezhnev era, soon began to resemble political dinosaurs. Gorbachev's relative youth contrasted so sharply with the venerable SED leader that a contemporary Soviet joke must have had an uncomfortable ring: 'Is Gorbachev supported in the Kremlin? No, he can walk unaided'.

Unease over the early stages of *perestroika* and *glasnost* developed into outright hostility when it became apparent in the autumn of 1986, and particularly after the CPSU Central Committee plena in January and June 1987, that Gorbachev was enagaged in a massive overhaul of the Soviet Union's economic and political structures. Another worrying development in the eyes of the SED leaders was Moscow's radical reassessment of its relations with the socialist community. The belief had been crystallising in Moscow since early 1987 that each socialist country must devise a solution to its own problems and that it would not be obliged to imitate the Soviet Union. On the other hand, it was equally clear that Gorbachev preferred the Eastern European countries to follow the Soviet Union along the path of *perestroika*. His highly ambitious goal was to devise a socialist 'Third Way' between capitalism and neo-Stalinism, an experiment which was to be initiated by a reformed Communist party and its outcome viable and legitimate polities throughout the region. Reformed democratic socialist states in Eastern Europe would, it was hoped, establish a cooperative relationship with the Soviet Union.

The rethinking of the Soviet Union's relations with its client states led to the erosion and then the momentous abandonment of the Brezhnev Doctrine. This was made clear by Gorbachev in his address to the Council of

Europe in July 1989 when he asserted the 'right of all countries to unimpeded independence and equal rights'.[5] It remained an open question, however, as to whether the Soviet leadership would regard the GDR as an exception to what the Soviet government spokesman Genadii Gerasimov referred to as the Sinatra doctrine of 'I had it my way'. Greater leeway also meant that the East European communist regimes would not be able to rely on the Soviet Union for life support and would thus become more dependent on their own resources for regime legitimation and survival. At a meeting of the Warsaw Pact Defence Ministers in July 1988 in Moscow, Gorbachev made it clear to his audience, which included the GDR Defence Minister, Heinz Keßler, that the time had come to put an end to military intervention in fraternal countries.[6]

The SED gerontocrats were highly alarmed at what they regarded as a radical, ill-considered and dangerous departure from the fundamentals of the traditional Communist system, and they were determined to prevent the spread of the reform virus to the GDR. The new Soviet attitude had already released ever more radical reform impulses in Eastern Europe, above all in Poland and Hungary. Widespread market reforms, the partial denationalisation and privatisation of industry, and greater political pluralism emerged as the platform of many reformers in the region. At first, the SED leaders sought to discredit the Soviet reforms by belittling them. The first public expression of this tactic was Kurt Hager's April 1987 interview with the West German weekly magazine *Stern*. Hager, who had been the Central Committee Secretary in charge of ideology for over 30 years, likened *perestroika* to mere redecoration and asked sarcastically why anyone should wish to decorate his house simply because his neighbour did so.

Honecker, Hager and Axen, and other SED leaders, were alarmed at the Soviet critique of the 'distortions' and 'deformations' of the Stalinist era as it threatened to destroy their carefully constructed ideological legitimation of the traditional socialist system. From January 1987 onwards, on the instructions of Honecker and Joachim Herrmann, several issues of Soviet journals were denied to GDR citizens and Soviet films such as *Die Reue* (Repentance) which dealt with the 'blank spots' in Soviet and Communist history were refused exhibition in the GDR. The October 1988 German issue of *Sputnik*, which contained sharp criticism of the KPD's failure to cooperate with the SPD against Hitler, led to the imposition of an immediate ban on this monthly digest of the Soviet press. This was underlined by Honecker's protest to the Soviet ambassador to the GDR that the history of the Soviet Union was being reduced to a chain of errors.[7] Even Gorbachev was targeted. The SED

[260] leadership sought to prevent the circulation of his ideas by ordering the censor to cut key passages from his speeches and by conducting an indirect attack on *perestroika* by citing criticisms from Gorbachev's internal opponents and from hostile commentaries emanating from Beijing.

Further alarms for the SED:
Hungary and Poland opt for reform

At the December 1988 Central Committee Plenum, Otto Reinhold, the Rector of the Central Committee's Academy of Social Sciences poured cold water on the political pluralism which was being introduced into several socialist countries and thereby eroding the Communist power monopoly. The GDR, he insisted, would not reduce the role of the party to a mere debating club; nor would it pursue the transition to a so-called 'market socialism'. From the narrow viewpoint of the SED leadership, post-totalitarian Eastern Europe was lurching from one crisis to another. In June 1989, the Polish Communists suffered a massive defeat at the hands of Solidarity in the elections to the Senate, and on 24 August Tadeusz Mozowiecki became the first non-Communist head of government in Eastern Europe. In Hungary, reform Communists such as Imre Pozsgay and Reszo Nyers pushed aside conservatives in the party and agreed in September 1989 to hold multi-party elections in the following year. In October, they embarked on the bold course of renouncing Marxism in favour of democratic socialism.

The alleged success of the GDR economy was crucial to the SED's Canute-like efforts to hold back the tide of reform. According to Honecker, the GDR was reaping rewards in the form of higher labour productivity and greater social security from the economic intensification programme launched in 1971. Each country, so his argument ran, had to take heed of its own specific conditions and its own level of development, a position which was ostensibly legitimised by Gorbachev's acceptance of the diversity of development. The imposition of a uniform socialist model, it was now averred by SED spokespersons, was incompatible with the diversity of social, ethnic and economic developments in the socialist world and would be harmful to the greater efficiency of the more advanced GDR economy. After four decades of 'learning from the Soviet Union', the SED had discovered the merits of socialism in the colours of the GDR. However, it was the Soviet Union of Gorbachev, not of Brezhnev, from which Honecker no longer wished to learn.

Moscow rethinks its German policy

At the same time as the SED was propagating the virtues of its version of the traditional model, influential figures among the Soviet political and economic elites were initiating a debate on the future of the administrative-command system of socialism. Oleg Bogomolov, the Director of the Institute of the Economy of World Socialism, contended that the crisis had its roots in the original sin of imposing the flawed Stalinist model on Eastern Europe. Vyacheslav Dashichev, one of Bogomolov's colleagues, correctly diagnosed that the GDR, too, was caught up in the general crisis afflicting the Communist system. The GDR's relatively high living standard, he argued, was sustained to a considerable extent by West German transfer payments and by the imports of relatively cheap raw materials from the Soviet Union. He attributed the GDR's poor economic performance to the obsolete administrative-command system; by contrast, West German prosperity derived from its federal political system, its market economy and its full incorporation into the international division of labour. As a way out of the impasse, he advocated the gradual drawing together of the two German states, culminating in a confederation or unification.[8] Dashichev's ideas, which were transmitted in the form of a memorandum to the Soviet leadership in April 1989, were predicated on a growing conviction that Eastern Europe had become too heavy a political, economic, military and psychological burden on the Soviet Union. While reformers such as Schevardnaze and Chernayiev in the political circle around Gorbachev were more conservative in their views on German unification, they were determined to avoid a repetition of 1953, 1956 and 1968. The use of force would mean the termination of their aspirations for internal reform and a new international order. In August 1989, in line with this approach, Gorbachev instructed the Soviet forces not to intervene in the GDR's internal affairs and to remain in barracks. Moscow consciously adhered to this policy during the crucial period of demonstrations and protests in late September and early October 1989.[9]

The notion of a 'common European home stretching from the Atlantic to the Urals', part of Gorbachev's wooing of Western Europe, inevitably led to a rethinking of the bases of Moscow's German policy and the division of Germany. By the autumn of 1986, fears were quickening in East Berlin that this reconceptualisation, in conjunction with West German assistance for the economic modernisation of the Soviet economy, might jeopardise the very existence of the GDR. In spring 1990, a bitter Honecker contended that, as

[262]   early as 1987, he had been informed by the GDR ambassador in Moscow that some Soviet thinkers were looking at how to end the division of Germany.[10] Indeed, Soviet commentators and experts on Germany were dropping hints of a fundamental reassessment. In early 1987, Portugalev, a member of the Central Committee Department for Foreign Affairs, stated that 'the people of the GDR are still German and belong to the same nation' as the citizens of the FRG,[11] a clear departure from the SED thesis of a separate socialist nation. However, *Realpolitik* persuaded him of the need to respect the existence of two German states with different social systems.[12]

Although Soviet thinking on the German question was clearly in a state of flux, Gorbachev and his close advisers appear to have regarded German unification as an undesirable outcome and were against treating the GDR as a mere pawn on a larger chess board. This was underlined in June 1989 when Gorbachev informed both Kohl and Honecker that the Soviet Union would not abandon the GDR.[13] What the Soviet leaders had in mind was a form of *perestroika* for the GDR: political liberalisation and economic reform would, it was hoped, enhance regime legitimacy and stabilise the division of Germany. In the Kremlin's view, the SED possessed the organisational potential and the cadres, at least on the middle and lower levels, to overcome the country's problems and carry out a reform programme.

Determined not to do it Gorby's 'katastroika' way, Honecker sought desperately for allies among Gorbachev's critics in Moscow and tried to erect a mini-entente with Romania and Czechoslovakia as a conservative bulwark against reform. Was this a fatal error? According to the Soviet Foreign Minister, Eduard Shevardnaze, a reformed system of socialism might have saved the GDR.[14] There was potential support for reform among covert Gorbachev supporters on the Central Committee and some economic planners in the State Planning Commission were not opposed to the introduction of market elements. However, the attitude of the top leadership was reflected in Otto Reinhold's famous statement in August 1989: 'What right to exist would a capitalist GDR have alongside a capitalist Federal Republic? In other words, what justification would there be for two German states once ideology no longer separated them?'[15] A balanced conclusion would seem to be that while reform might have slowed down the speed of the GDR's economic collapse and eased the pain of transition to a new economic and social system, the attraction of the FRG was so powerful and the symptoms of decay so advanced that reforms would in all probability have failed to halt the disintegration of the SED and some form of merger between the two states.

The economic malaise

Although the SED leadership boasted that the GDR had an efficient economy which, based on the 'advantages of socialism', delivered economic growth and a high standard of living, the lifting of the curtain on the true state of the economy revealed that the country had been living not only on borrowed time but also on borrowed money. Labour productivity was much lower than in the FRG; far too high a proportion of the capital stock was obsolescent; heavy investment in new technologies was not paying dividends; far too much R&D activity was concentrated on imitation rather than innovation; and the ecological situation bordered on the catastrophic in many parts of the country. The lack of competitiveness of GDR products expressed itself in an escalating hard currency debt, which was so heavy a burden that it threatened the solvency of the republic and demanded a fundamental reassessment of the traditional economic mechanism and a drastic reduction in state subsidies. The main symptoms of the economic crisis are outlined below.

The SED economic modernisation strategy relied heavily on the development of new key technologies such as microelectronics and robotics. The decision to accelerate the development of microelectronics was taken in January 1986 at a meeting of top economic planners and officials. Despite the injection of credits from KoKo for the import of special components and equipment, most of which were under embargo, the microelectronics programme overstretched the GDR's resources. Planned investments in the microelectronics industry alone accounted for 15 billion Marks in the 1986– 90 five year plan period, mainly for developments in the Carl Zeiss Jena, *Mikroelektronik* Erfurt and Robotron Dresden combines.[16] The new technologies proved to be a false investment as they were not fully integrated into the production process. Not surprisingly, the GDR was unable to close the technological gap with the leading Western and Japanese firms. Klaus Krakat, a Western expert on GDR science and technology, has placed the gap with the West at between five and ten years.[17]

The reasons for the technological gap and the mediocre standard of many GDR products and services and for the slow diffusion of basic research are to be found in a combination of: the isolation of so many GDR researchers from the international research community; the obstacles to innovation arising from the existence of large, highly bureaucratised combines; a planning system which encouraged conformity rather than creativity; the conservatism of the

[264] heads of scientific and university departments; and too high a proportion of obsolescent scientific equipment. Furthermore, a distorted investment strategy and underinvestment in key areas resulted in far too high a proportion of obsolescent capital stock.[18] In 1989, 27 per cent of industrial plant was less than five years old, 23 per cent six to ten years, 29 per cent eleven to twenty years and 21 per cent over twenty years. The level of electrification on the East German railway system and the road network was badly neglected and 72 per cent of telephone technology was more than 30 years old. Given an obsolescent capital stock and the lack of effective material stimuli to labour motivation, it is not surprising that labour productivity was perhaps two-thirds lower than that of the FRG, with the manufacturing sector lagging even further behind. There could be no doubt that the GDR was a clear loser in what Lenin had once identified as the crucial arena in the struggle between capitalism and socialism.

Foreign trade

Newly released data shed light on the declining international competitiveness of GDR products.[19] GDR planners calculated that between 1980 and 1988 the outlay required by GDR firms to earn one DM in trade with the West had risen from 2.40 GDR Marks to 4.40 GDR Marks. In 1989, the highest costs of earning foreign currency (GDR Marks per DM) were incurred in chemicals (4.11), electronics (4.82) and food, drinks and tobacco (4.09), and the lowest in energy (2.08) and metallurgy (3.22). Combines and enterprises were protected by the allocation of subsidies for costs in excess of the secret shadow exchange rate used by planners. Only one enterprise outside the energy sector, the famous Meissen porcelain works, had costs less than zero.

The internal plight of so much of GDR industry was responsible for the spiralling hard currency debt. After a period of stability between 1982 and the end of 1985, indebtedness grew appreciably from 1986 onwards. Not only did this greatly trouble SED economic and political leaders but it also caused much friction between East Berlin and Moscow. The debt mountain imposed, it was feared, an excessively heavy burden on the GDR and was drawing the country into an undesirably close relationship with the FRG. Following in Brezhnev's footsteps, Gorbachev personally warned Honecker against being tied to Bonn's purse strings.[20]

The ultra-conservative members of the Politbüro's pro-Soviet wing, that is, Stoph, Krolikowski, Neumann and Mielke, continued to snipe at the Honecker–Mittag line. But they were a sorry crew. Not only did they lack the courage to express their concerns openly but also the Soviet Union, whether under an Andropov or a Gorbachev, was in no position to bail out the GDR economically and was having to cut back on supplies to its client states. For example, in December 1987, the Soviet Union, hit by the fall in the world market price for crude oil since 1985–86, gave notice of a further reduction in oil supplies when the existing agreement ran out in 1990.[21] Further difficulties were caused by the Soviet Union's determination to raise COMECON foreign trade prices to world market price levels from 1991 onwards. The GDR was extremely concerned as over 70 per cent of its imports from the Soviet Union consisted of raw materials. The State Planning Commission regarded such imports as a matter of life and death for the GDR. Another disadvantage of a stronger orientation towards the Soviet Union and the GDR's Eastern European neighbours was that the structure of economic relations in COMECON and the traditional economic mechanism had palpably failed to provide powerful innovation stimuli. This was a serious handicap to the GDR as about 60 per cent of its foreign trade in the late 1980s was conducted with the socialist countries, including about one-third with the Soviet Union.

On the other hand, closer links with the West did not constitute an easy option. As so many Eastern European states had discovered to their cost in the 1970s, trade with the West, which included the import of investment goods, was based on the raising of credits whose repayment depended on the ability of the recipient to boost exports. But as GDR products tended to be less sophisticated than those of the West and as it also had to face fierce competition from South Korea, Singapore and other Asian rivals, the GDR had to pump ever more resources into maintaining exports with the West, a state of affairs which simply could not continue. After the collapse of the GDR, top state planning officials such as Schürer and Siegfried Wenzel have claimed that, from the mid-1980s, they were coming to the conclusion that the GDR's only chance lay in closer cooperation with West Germany and that this might have to extend to a confederation.[22] Even Mittag asserted, in interviews as well as in his published memoirs, that by the end of 1987 he saw no alternative to unification.[23] Whether or not Mittag was at that time a genuine convert to reunification – and there is no documentary evidence before 1990 to substantiate his claim – it is undeniable that economic failure was beginning to undermine confidence, however belatedly, in the country's survival among some members of the strategic elite.

Abortive plans to reduce the debt

A confidential memorandum prepared for Mittag in September 1989 revealed a dire situation. The memorandum was drafted by Schürer, Schalck-Golodkowski and other members of the special working party concerned with the balance of payments. The hard currency debt, they predicted, would soar from 41.5 billion Valuta Marks to at least 52.6 billion Valuta Marks gross between 1989 and 1995. Given the GDR's heavy dependence on West German, Japanese and other foreign creditors, intervention by the International Monetary Fund in a debt-rescheduling process was regarded as highly probable. Believing that the solvency of the republic was the decisive prerequisite for political stability and economic development, they advocated cuts in consumption and a new export drive to the non-socialist area based on manufactures.[24] Despite this alarming forecast, the Honecker Politbüro was incapable of a change of direction; only after Egon Krenz replaced Honecker on 18 October could a reappraisal commence.

In a second memorandum drawn up one month later for Krenz, the experts' tone was even more gloomy: the estimated hard currency debt in 1990 was revised upwards to about 57 billion Valuta Marks gross. Rejecting a drastic reduction in consumption by 25 per cent to 30 per cent for fear it would destabilise the GDR, they put forward alternative proposals: the strengthening of the role of productive accumulation, especially in the export-orientated sphere of industry; the rigorous implementation of the 'socialist' performance principle; and the dismantling of unproductive jobs in the SED, the economy and the security forces.[25] In addition to the existing requirement for DM 8 billion to DM 10 billion credits, the GDR had no option but to go cap in hand to Bonn for additional credits in order to achieve solvency in 1991. While they ruled out German unification or a confederation as the price of West German assistance, they appreciated that the political price would be higher than for the 1983 and 1984 loans. The opening of the Berlin Wall was therefore proposed as bait or, as the memorandum put it, the creation of conditions which would make the existing border 'superfluous'. Although the Politbüro discussed the report on 31 October and agreed to terminate the unity of economic and social policy as well as the microelectronics progamme, no reference was made to the Wall.[26]

Armed with the information provided by his experts, Krenz, at his meeting with Gorbachev on 1 November 1989, acquainted the Soviet leader with the GDR's economic plight. With the Soviet Union also plagued by its own problems, Gorbachev, though deeply disturbed, was unable to offer any assistance to a key strategic and economic partner.[27] This was yet another step in Moscow's retreat from empire. Eight days later, the Berlin Wall was opened without any financial or economic *quid pro quo* from Bonn.

Krenz, however, had been fed inaccurate data.[28] Subsequent investigations by the State Planning Commission and the Finance Ministry unearthed additional hard currency reserves and the production, at the end of April 1990, of a new, and probably the most reliable, estimate of the GDR's net hard currency debt at 27.3 billion Valuta Marks ($14.8 billion). As the country's debt had increased in the first four months of 1990, the net debt at the end of 1989 probably stood at between $13 billion and $14 billion. The main reason for the lower figure was the omission of KoKo's total assets in the earlier statement.

The reassessment of the GDR's hard currency debt highlights the hollowness of the SED's claim to be running an efficient system of economic planning and management. The State Planning Commission, the Politbüro and central economic bodies were not fully conversant with such a vital area as the balance of payments. Mittag had deliberately kept them all in the dark as he wished to tap KoKo's assets personally in order to prevent a repeat of the traumatic liquidity crisis of 1981–82. The revised data also suggest that the GDR did not stand on the verge of bankruptcy in 1989, and, in all probability, neither in 1990 nor in 1991. However, it should not be concluded that the GDR's economic and hard currency situation was less than chronic. Far too many firms were inefficient and operating at a loss and the high proportion of short-term credits endangered fiscal and economic stability. Moreover, the size of the secret reserve meant that opportunities had been lost for earning additional interest and for the acquisition of sophisticated investment goods from the West. Thus, while the GDR's economic and hard currency problems were not sufficient in themselves to account for the collapse of SED rule in 1989, they were, nevertheless, so serious as to throw the GDR into greater dependence on Bonn and to undermine both mass and elite belief in the capacity of real existing socialism to withstand the challenge of capitalism.

The ecological nightmare

Another symptom of the GDR's economic plight was the ecological nightmare, notably in the industrial regions of Leipzig and Halle, the upper valley of the Elbe in the Görlitz area, the district around the Schwedt

[268] petro-chemical combine, the Erfurt-Arnstadt area and the eastern Erzge-birge. The situation deteriorated rapidly during the 1980s because of the decision to increase the production of lignite, which contains a high level of sulphur pollutants, and to process it in obsolescent plant. Dust emissions were particularly critical in the vicinity of old power stations, briquette factories, chemical enterprises and cement factories in the Leipzig, Cottbus and Halle regions. Towns such as Bitterfeld were so badly polluted that if the criteria devised by the United Nations had been applied, they would have been declared unfit for inhabitation. Respiratory problems were 20 per cent higher in the southern industrial regions than in the north of the country. According to some estimates, life expectancy would have risen by four years if the emissions of sulphur dioxide, dust and ashes had been halved in the most heavily polluted areas. Air pollution in the GDR was the highest in Europe on account of the emissions of sulphur dioxide and dust. Sulphur dioxide emissions per inhabitant were about six times greater than in the FRG.

With 21 per cent of the GDR's citizens exposed to excessive levels of pollution, with damage to the forests widespread (in 1988, 54.3 per cent of forests suffered some damage) and with water supplies heavily polluted, it made a mockery of SED claims that only socialism provided the key to the solution of environmental problems. Environmental degradation undoubtedly contributed to the mass emigration and the explosion of popular unrest on the streets of Leipzig, Halle, East Berlin, Dresden, Erfurt and elsewhere in the autumn of 1989. Leipzig's emergence as 'the city of heroes' is explicable partly in terms of a deterioration in living and working conditions. Leipzig ranked among the most environmentally damaged areas in the GDR. Over 80 per cent of all forests in the *Bezirk* were damaged and 91 per cent of the city's inhabitants were exposed to excessive levels of sulphur dioxide, dust, carbon monoxide and heavy metals.[29]

The melting of the ideological glue

Under these circumstances, could the East German population still be expected to believe in the ultimate victory of socialism? Was unification with West Germany becoming more attractive? To what extent were new values undermining the old ideological system? It is easier to pose than answer these questions as so little representative research had been conducted on popular opinion. However, several high-level research bodies, notably the

Institute for Sociology and Social Policy of the Academy of Sciences, the [269]
Academy of Social Sciences of the SED Central Committee and the Central
Institute for Youth Research in Leipzig, managed to produce a realistic insight into the views of employed people in the 1980s. An investigation conducted by the Institute for Sociology and Social Policy in late 1988 and early
1989 found that workers were becoming increasingly pessimistic about the
likelihood of improvement in three key areas: the environment, the supply of
consumer goods and the standard of living. On the other hand, high levels of
satisfaction were recorded, as in previous surveys, with the so-called achievements of the GDR such as social security, the equality of women and child
care facilities,[30] a reminder that the GDR still had 'reserves' of support. What
the research also established was the existence of a generation gap: younger
East Germans were much more committed than their elders to individualistic
values and far less to the collective norms of the past.

The declassified findings of the Leipzig youth research team demonstrate
unequivocally a precipitous and terminal decline between 1985 and 1989 in
young people's support for the system after a period of relatively broad consent for much of the 1970s.[31] Their mass defection can be measured by the
collapse in support for the basic tenets of official socialist culture such as a
belief in the eventual victory of socialism over capitalism. Marxism-Leninism
was dismissed as too abstract and of little practical value. Students, partly for
career reasons and partly as a result of intensive political socialisation pressures, tended to be more conformist, more outwardly loyal to the goals of the
regime. The decline in their commitment set in later than was the case with
young workers and apprentices (see Table 14.1). There are, however, a number
of serious problems inherent in the data. It is possible that most respondents,
despite guarantees of anonymity, were reluctant, at least until the system started
to crumble, to opt for such highly negative responses as 'hardly' or 'not at all'
as these might have been interpreted as a form of dissidence. During the 1970s,
respondents may have preferred to opt for the neutral response of 'with reservations', thereby exercising a form of self-censorship and leading to an underestimation of dissatisfaction with the state socialist system. It is, nonetheless,
incontrovertible that by the time the SED regime had reached its crucial survival test in the autumn of 1989 younger people had lost their respect for the
authority of the party and the FDJ. Their admiration for Gorbachev's reforms
only served to magnify the deficiencies of the world to which Honecker and
his colleagues still clung.

The Leipzig data reveal many other symptoms of disaffection and disillusionment: a widespread rejection of the thesis that socialism enjoyed a higher

Table 14.1: Young people's attitudes towards the GDR, 1975–89

	Identification with the GDR*		
	Strong (%)	With reservations (%)	Hardly/Not at all (%)
Apprentices			
1975	57	38	9
1985	51	43	6
1988 (May)	28	61	11
1988 (October)	18	54	28
Young Workers			
1975	53	42	5
1985	57	39	4
1988 (October)	19	58	23
Students			
1975	66	32	2
1985	70	28	2
1988 (May)	52	45	3
1989 (February)	34	51	15

* Until 1979, the respondents were asked whether they were proud to be citizens of the socialist state and from 1983 whether they felt closely attached to the GDR.
Source: Friedrich W. 1990: 27, 29, 30

level of productivity than capitalism and the greater trust in the West German media as sources of information. Furthermore, unlike the regime, young people were increasingly of the opinion that the division of Germany was an open question.[32] In a series of confidential memoranda which he drafted before the *Wende*[33] the head of the Central Institute for Youth Research, Walter Friedrich, addressed what he regarded as the cardinal issue: the onset of a cultural revolution which, in his opinion, was more problematic than the country's economic malaise. What he interpreted from his institute's research was a growing self-awareness on the part of young people and a desire to shape their own lives free of party and FDJ control. This individualisation was reflected in a greater involvement in informal cliques, unofficial peace and environmental groups and the pursuit of more diversified leisure activities beyond the reach of the FDJ. It also found expression in changing attitudes towards marriage and the family, which resulted in the growing popularity of cohabitation, spiralling divorce rates and a liberalisation of sexual behaviour. These value changes, which also mirrored the spread of postmaterialism in Western society since the later 1960s, were undoubtedly instrumental in eroding the foundations of the old order; however, it should also be stressed [271] that they co-existed with widely held traditional views on the role of the paternalistic state and on the gender-based division of labour in the family.

References

1. Elbe F., Kiessler R. 1996: 69

2. Habermas J. 1990: 4

3. Smith H. W. 1991: 237–8

4. Jarausch K. H. 1994: 70–2, 132–4, 194–6

5. Cited in Görtemaker M. 1994: 50

6. Hertle H.-H. 1996b: 230

7. Kotschemassow W. 1994: 72–3

8. See Dashichev's April 1988 memorandum in *Der Spiegel*, 5 February 1990, pp. 148, 152

9. Interviews with Gorbachev, Modrow, Portugalev and Dashichev in Kuhn E. 1993: 44, 50–2, and with Falin in Kuhn E. 1992: 29

10. Andert R., Herzberg W. 1991: 21

11. Cited in Gedmin J. 1992: 45

12. Portugalev in Kuhn E. 1993: 23

13. Falin V. 1995: 487; Dashichev in Kuhn E. 1993: 42

14. Brown J. F. 1991: 58

15. Cited in ibid., 125

16. Wolf H. 1991: 50

17. Krakat K. 1990: 5–6, 25–7, 40–1, 58

18. Details in Kusch G., Montag R., Specht G., Wetzker K. 1991: 31–2, 56–7, 61–2

19. Details in Akerlof G. A., Rose A., Vellen J., Hessenius H. 1991

20. Küchenmeister D. 1993: 89–90

21. Hertle H.-H. 1995: 331

[272]   22. Pirker T., Lepsius R., Weinert R., Hertle H.-H. 1995: 112, 119

23. Mittag G. 1991: 297

24. *die tageszeitung,* 19 March 1990, p. 4

25. Hertle H.-H. 1992: 1024

26. 'Das reale Bild war eben katastrophal!' 1991: 1037; Roesler J. 1993b: 571

27. Hertle H.-H. 1992: 1027

28. Details in Volze A. 1996: 701–13

29. Hofmann M., Rink D. 1990: 116–19

30. Gensicke T. 1992: 1270, 1282

31. Friedrich W. 1990: 33–7

32. Förster P., Roski G. 1990: 51

33. Stephan G.-R. 1994: especially 39, 44–6

CHAPTER FIFTEEN

THE UNLAMENTED END OF THE GDR

V alue dissonance between party and young people, Moscow's reappraisal of its foreign policy goals, political liberalisation in Hungary,
Poland and the Soviet Union, and the chronic state of the economy were all
eroding the SED monolith without, however, threatening it with immediate
collapse. Then, in the autumn of 1989 a combination of the pressures generated by mass flight from the republic, the formation of civil rights' groups
and ever bolder public demonstrations finally brought about the demise of
the *ancien régime.*

Mass exit

Emigration had long been the most visible indicator of the rejection of the
GDR by sections of the population. The regime's carefully calibrated policy
of an increase in short-term visits to the West and the granting, in January
1989, of a quasi-legal right to emigrate was not without some success but it
became redundant once Hungary began to dismantle the Iron Curtain. The
trickle of East Germans fleeing to the West after the barbed wire separating
Hungary and Austria was cut on 2 May 1989 turned into a torrent when, on
10 September, the liberalising Hungarian government, to the fury of the
SED, suspended its bilateral agreement with the GDR. By the time the Wall
came down, over a quarter of a million East Germans had left their country
either illegally or with official permission. Of those leaving between January
and October, 101,947 fell into the latter category and 65,257 into the
former. Even the opening of the Wall did not stem the flow: by the end of the
year, 343,854 had departed for the West. The number of East Germans who
opted for the FRG between 1950 and the end of 1989 was an astronomical
4.86 million; in contrast, only 471,000 had moved in the other direction. If

Table 15.1:   Motives for leaving the GDR, 1984 and 1989

	1984 (%)	1989 (%)
Lack of freedom to express one's own opinion	71	74
Political pressure	66	65
To be able to shape one's own life	–	72
Limited opportunities for travel to other countries	56	74
Supply situation	46	74
Lack of/or unpromising prospects	45	56
Relatives in FRG (reuniting family)	36	28
Making a fresh start	28	–
Unfavourable career opportunities	21	26

Sources: Köhler A., Ronge V. 1984: 1282; Hilmer R., Köhler A. 1989: 1385

account is taken of the 129,000 in 1949 and the 238,000 in the first six months of 1990, then emigration amounted to a grand total of 5.2 million.[1]

The motives behind the mass exodus of 1989 were, according to West German sources, similar to those in 1984, with political considerations still narrowly outweighing material factors in a complex set of motives (see Table 15.1). As regards the social profile of the émigrés,[2] younger cohorts were significantly overrepresented. Over three-quarters were younger and one-fifth older than 40 years of age; the GDR average in the latter population category was 60 per cent. The émigrés were highly motivated, career-orientated and keen to integrate themselves into West German society. Many possessed skills and qualifications in areas such as medicine and health which were in demand in the West. Most were well qualified, with 90 per cent having completed an apprenticeship or some form of training. While these émigrés enjoyed an adequate standard of living according to criteria such as the possession of consumer durables, the vast majority anticipated an appreciable improvement by moving to the FRG. In addition, the erosion of the economic base during the 1980s was making it more difficult for the regime to sustain the social contract based on the unity of economic and social policy.

Not only did the mass defections touch a sore spot – the GDR's competition with its sibling for the support of the German population – but they also catalysed opposition within the GDR, whether as popular demonstrations on the streets of Leipzig, Dresden and East Berlin or as organised opposition movements such as New Forum and Democracy Now. In Leipzig, citizens recalled that the exodus had encouraged them to try to change the system by taking part in demonstrations and other forms of political protest.[3] This conjunction of exit and voice, at least while both movements were serving to undermine the regime and while the issue of reunification was not being articulated in public, has been likened to 'a joint gravedigging act'.[4]

The catalyst function of the émigrés entitles them, in the opinion of some observers, to be recognised as the 'first children of the revolution' and 'the actual motors of all societal change in the GDR'. While this kind of argument runs the danger of underestimating the contribution of both the citizens' movements and the demonstrators to the undermining of SED rule, it does, nevertheless, highlight the crucial importance of what New Forum's Jens Reich called 'the emotional frenzy which gripped the country',[5] encouraging people like Reich himself to come out into the open. No less significantly, in 'voting with their feet' for West German consumerism and political pluralism, the emigrants were swelling the political current which would not only sweep away the citizens' movements' idea of a 'Third Way' but would also generate powerful pressure against the border barricades. Seen from this perspective, the desire of so many East Germans for a personal form of unification, albeit on the territory of the FRG, not merely in 1989 but throughout the history of the GDR, was a major, though obviously not the sole, factor in the crumbling of the Wall.

The protests take to the streets

Demonstrations in the towns and cities throughout the GDR were another manifestation of opposition to the regime. Public protests had taken place in East Berlin, Leipzig and Dresden in the late 1980s but they had been sporadic and often split between those who demanded the right to leave the country and others who aspired to reform the GDR from within. Demonstrations escalated after the pressures generated by the emigration wave and by changes in the socialist bloc began to weaken the security forces' iron grip. Leipzig emerged as the major centre of protest. An alternative political culture had developed there in the 1980s, coordinated by Church representatives such as pastor Christian Führer of the St Nikolai Church and by the *Arbeitskreis Gerechtigkeit*. The latter, founded in 1987, cooperated with one of

[276] the small exit groups, the *Arbeitsgemeinschaft Staatsbürgerschaftsrecht*. Joint activities centred on the weekly Peace Prayers which had been held in St Nikolai Church most Monday evenings since 1982; from March 1989 onwards, the service was followed almost every week by a small public rally.[6]

The number of demonstrators in the city rose from 5,000 on 25 September to 20,000 on 2 October, and then to 70,000 on the fateful night of 9 October. These numbers, though probably an underestimate, do at least provide an indication of the relative size of the demonstrations. The demonstration virus soon spread to other towns and cities, among them Plauen, Jena, Potsdam, Magdeburg, Halle and Karl-Marx-Stadt. The security forces were responsible for much gratuitous violence, especially on 4 and 5 October against East Germans seeking to climb on board the trains from Prague while they were passing through Dresden, and then later against demonstrators during the GDR's fortieth anniversary celebrations in East Berlin and Leipzig on 7 and 8 October. At this moment of crisis for the old regime, Gorbachev, while reluctantly attending the GDR anniversary, gave it a significant push when he expressed his impatience with Honecker's obduracy in his famous phrase, 'Whoever comes too late is punished by life itself'. And with rumours abounding of his refusal to authorise Soviet troops to assist in the work of repression, the SED appeared to be losing the ultimate guarantee of its power – the Soviet forces stationed in the GDR.

Leipzig: 9 October

A turning point in the course of the 'gentle revolution' occurred in Leipzig on 9 October when a GDR version of the Tiananmen Square massacre was narrowly avoided. Two days prior to the demonstration, the Defence Minister, Heinz Keßler, had issued an order for the NVA to be made fully combat ready and for a paratrooper regiment to be moved near to the city for deployment.[7] Mielke, too, hatched plans for crushing the demonstration, including the use of special Stasi forces and the workers' militia. On the day of the demonstration, Mielke ordered that 'Members [of security forces] who regularly carry arms are to have their weapons on them at all times according to the given requirements'.[8] By the evening, security forces with live ammunition were waiting in readiness in the narrow side streets; hospitals had been warned to prepare beds for the wounded.

After the revolution, one police officer claimed that an order to shoot had been issued. Although an explicit order to this effect has yet to be discovered, there was a real danger of a bloody outcome until the head of the police force

in Leipzig, Gerhard Straßenberg, ordered that only self-defence measures be [277]
implemented. There is some speculation that Honecker lay behind this
move, not because of any scruples but in order to prevent his opponents from
blaming him for the outbreak of civil war.[9] The peaceful outcome cannot,
however, be attributed simply to the machinations of the Politbüro; it must
also be sought in the self-discipline of the crowd and the appeal for non-
violence made in the churches and by six local luminaries, including Kurt
Masur, the director of Leipzig's famous *Gewandhaus* orchestra. Although the
danger of a violent suppression of the protests did not disappear immediately,
9 October was a decisive turning point as it exposed the political bankruptcy
of the SED hardliners. Despite the vast machinery at the disposal of the SED,
which would have been sufficient to crush the demonstrations, 1989 was not
1953, nor even 1968: the Soviet forces were confined to barracks and the
ideological and political structures of a socialist world were beginning to
disintegrate. With force no longer a realistic option, the hardliners would
soon be removed from power.

And with the threat of reprisals subsiding rapidly, the GDR equivalent
of 'Havel's compliant shopkeeper' could take down the party signs in his
shopwindow. The demonstrators openly articulated their political demands
on a sea of banners and in pithy and often humorous chants: 'The street is the
tribune of the people' and 'We are staying here'. Although further studies
will no doubt delineate the diversity of regional patterns of protest, the central goal of the rapidly evolving political culture of the streets was initially
the renewal of GDR society on the basis of traditional liberal values: freedom of speech, travel, assembly and association. The rallying cry 'We are the
people' must not be dismissed as an empty slogan; it reflected a pride in at last
becoming the subjects rather than the objects of history. One expression of
this feeling was the 'Appeal For Our Country' drafted by artists and writers
such as Stefan Heym and Christa Wolf on 28 November. This posed the stark
alternative of rebuilding the GDR as a society based either on principles of
solidarity and socialism or the selling out of its moral and material values and
a complete takeover by the FRG. Although the Appeal failed to attract much
popular support and the cry 'We are the people' was soon superseded by 'We
are one people', an East German identity based on common experiences and
a feeling of resentment against 'colonisation' by West Germany's elites would
surface when the early euphoria of unification had subsided.

The many demonstrations before the breaching of the Berlin Wall were
not organised by any specific individuals or groups but tended to be spontaneous gatherings to express popular dissatisfaction with the regime. The large

[278]   squares in Leipzig and other towns provided convenient meeting places where protesters could expect to meet like-minded people at a given time. One of the Leipzig 'six', the cabaret artist Bernd Lutz-Lange recalled, 'There was no head of the revolution. The head was the Nikolai Kirche and the body the center of the city. There was only one leadership: Monday, 5 P.M., the Nikolai Kirche'.[10] It should be mentioned, however, that the citizens' groups and small political parties provided a sense of identification as well as a rallying point for protest: for example, New Forum's application for official recognition helped to mobilise many thousands of demonstrators in Leipzig and elsewhere who were protesting for basic democratic rights.

East Berlin: 4 November

The demonstrations reached their climax shortly before the opening of the Berlin Wall. On 6 November, an estimated 500,000 braved pouring rain in Leipzig to demand a new travel law and an end to the SED's leading role in society. Two days earlier, an even larger number had gathered on the vast Alexanderplatz in East Berlin for a demonstration coordinated by the artists' federations. The Stasi and the SED were only able to organise a damage limitation exercise, a clear sign of the growing weakness of the old regime. In the heady atmosphere, it appeared that the people and the cultural intelligentsia had at long last come together to renew the GDR. Stefan Heym rejoiced that people had recovered the power of speech and could now proceed with the construction of socialism. Leading SED figures like Markus Wolf and Günter Schabowski, who sought to use the occasion to voice their own ideas on reform, had to retreat in the face of a cacophony of derisive whistles. Unfortunately for idealists such as Heym and Jens Reich, who were calling for dialogue rather than propounding concrete programmes to rebuild society, East Germans were pouring across the open Czech border into West Germany.

The citizens' movements and a civil society

A crucial form of opposition to the SED emerged from the chrysalis of the alternative political culture in the shape of small citizens' movements and proto-political parties. Although still on the periphery of society during the 1980s, several developments occurred which enabled the autonomous

groups to play an active role in the revolutionary events of 1989. Enormous [279]
encouragement was afforded by Gorbachev's policy of *glasnost* and democratisation in the Soviet Union and the groups were increasingly shifting from
individual issues towards the umbrella themes of human rights and political
reform in the GDR. However, despite these important developments, not
only was the opposition divided between the would-be emigrants and the
'voice' dissidents but the autonomous groups and critical Church circles were
numerically weak. In June 1989, a Stasi report indicated that there were
about 150 opposition groups associated with the Evangelical Churches and
an additional 10 groups, such as the Church from Below, which performed a
coordinating function. The Stasi reckoned with about 2,500 activists in
these groups, 60 of whom were described as the hard core 'fanatical' enemies
of socialism. This is probably too low a figure. Other calculations suggest
that the number of activists may have been between 10,000 and 15,000, and
the total number of groups around 320.[11]

The citizens' groups take shape

Between July and September, New Forum and other citizens' movements
and initiatives were established in a first wave of activity followed by a second wave between October and January 1990 with the foundation of the
Green Party and the Independent Women's Association. The new groups
would later claim to have been the revolutionaries of the first hour. After an
exploratory meeting in June, the initiative group Democratic Awakening
(DA) was launched on 21–22 August, principally by Church workers engaged in human rights and peace activities, notably Rainer Eppelmann and
the Wittenberg pastor Friedrich Schorlemmer. On 30 October, it constituted
itself officially as a political party. In line with its left–liberal and ecological
orientation, it advocated a socialist order on a democratic basis with a plurality of ownership forms. In its founding appeal of 12 September, it warned
that 'Socialism must rediscover its intended, democratic form if it is not to be
lost to history. It cannot afford to fail; this endangered species, called human-
ity, needs other options to save human coexistence than the example set by
Western consumer societies . . .'[12]

Other groups also helped to melt the political ice. An initiative group was
established on 24 July by Ibrahim Böhme, pastors Meckel, Gutzeit and Noack
and others, with the aim of re-establishing a Social Democratic Party in the
GDR. Despite the efforts of the Stasi, the founding of the SDP (retitled SPD
in January 1990) took place in the ministry house of the village of Schwante

[280] on 7 October. A third group, Democracy Now (*Demokratie Jetzt* – DJ), which had its roots in the circle 'Rejection of the Practice and Principle of Delimitation', took shape in August. On 12 September, it issued the draft of the 'Appeal for Intervening in our own Affairs', signed by, among others, Hans Fischbeck, Ulrike Poppe, the Church historian and lawyer Wolfgang Ullman and the film director Konrad Weiß. The early activists were recruited mainly from intellectuals, scientists, artists and pastors.[13]

But it was New Forum which emerged as the most significant group among the new political formations. On 9 September, about 30 representatives of different groups from all parts of the GDR, including Bärbel Bohley, Katja Havemann, Jens Reich, Sebastian Pflugbeil, Rolf Heinrich and Reinhard Schult, signed the manifesto 'Awakening '89 NEW FORUM'. Lamenting the breakdown in communication between the state and society, it called, in plain and simple language, for the establishment of a broad political platform which would enable people to take part in a widespread discussion on reform and give them an alternative to emigration. Although it declared its willingness to work within the framework of the Constitution, it was unsuccessful when it applied on 19 September for official recognition as an association in accordance with Article 29 of the Constitution. A receptive chord was struck among many East Germans by this bold act as well as by the manifesto's deliberate avoidance of the term 'socialism' and by the absence of precise programmatic details. By the beginning of October, 10,000 people, at considerable personal risk, had signed the manifesto. New Forum commanded much greater support than did the other opposition groups: whereas its manifesto attracted about 200,000 signatories within two months, the membership of DA and the SDP lay between 10,000 and 15,000; Democracy Now, never exceeded 4,000 supporters.[14]

A Protestant revolution?

Some authors are persuaded that the overthrow of the SED regime was a 'Protestant revolution'. According to the political commentator Gerhard Rein, the revolution commenced in September 1987 when the document 'Rejection of the Practice and Principle of Delimitation' was submitted to the Church synod in Görlitz.[15] In support of this interpretation one can point to: the active involvement of pastors in the citizens' movements; the Churches' vital role in protecting the alternative groups during the 1980s; the moral authority commanded by the Churches in the summer of 1989; and the embedding of the revolutionary events in a Protestant culture dedicated to

human rights and non-violence. The election of so many Church represent- [281]
atives to the *Volkskammer* in March 1990 and the entry of five pastors into de
Maizière's cabinet were the culmination of this process. While the significance of the Churches' contribution cannot be denied, it is nevertheless
misleading to designate the momentous events in 1989 and 1990 as a Protestant revolution. Such an interpretation underplays the contribution of the
émigrés and other actors. Surveys of participants in the Leipzig demonstrations reveal that Church members participated only slightly more frequently
than non-members in general protests and that no difference existed as
regards participation in demonstrations.[16] Furthermore, revelations about
leading Church officials' cooperation with the Stasi have produced a more
critical assessment of the Churches' role in society than was current during
and immediately after the revolution.

Democratic socialism in a sovereign GDR

As the new movements began to take shape, they sought to define a common
set of principles. On 2 October, representatives issued a short Joint Declara-
tion calling for the democratic restructuring of state and society and for free
and secret elections under the auspices of the United Nations. The Joint De-
claration embodied the basic goal of the new opposition movements and
groups before the opening of the Wall: the establishment of a democratic
sovereign GDR encompassing the separation of SED and state, political
pluralism, freedom of association and assembly, freedom of travel, an independent judiciary, the removal of censorship and the introduction of an
ecologically responsible policy. All of these ideas had developed during the
1980s within the niches of the alternative political culture and, in late 1989,
constituted an effective lever for mobilising popular resistance to the SED
regime. There were, however, important differences between the groups.
The most left-orientated group, the United Left, advocated a special status
for Berlin, public ownership of the main means of production and worker
codetermination and self-management. The SDP, on the other hand, turned
its back on traditional Marxism: it favoured an ecologically orientated social
market economy with democratic controls over economic activity, codetermination in the enterprises and different forms of ownership. In general, its
economic programme was much closer to the West German model than that
of the other groups.

But was the 'new' GDR to be attired in the colours of a reformed socialism? Most of the groups were circumspect as it was generally recognised that

the term 'socialism' had been contaminated by its semantic association with the SED version, 'real existing socialism'. However, West Germany was not widely regarded as a desirable alternative and socialism found favour among those who, like Konrad Weiß of Democracy Now, feared that the GDR might be reduced to a mere *Land* of the Federal Republic. Edelbert Richter, one of DA's co-founders, averred that 'not only the word socialism but also certain social principles of socialism possess for us, as before, a good ring'.[17]

This stubborn adherence to a socialist future, though as yet ill-defined, is perhaps not altogether surprising as the democratic discussion within the alternative political culture had been conditioned by socialist traditions as a reaction by many intellectuals and dissidents against the perceived close association of the nation and capitalism with Nazism.[18] 'Why', as one dissident, Ludwig Mehlhorn of Democracy Now, asked, 'abolish what you wanted to reform?' And he concluded, 'Therefore, we were continuously under pressure to hold on to "socialism" as the only legitimacy of this state, in clear distinction to the Federal Republic of Germany'.[19] A second factor was that, while the SED remained the most influential political force in the country and the Stasi had not been tamed, it was a sound tactic to retain socialism as the political compass for change. In an interview on 26 October, Sebastian Pflugbeil criticised as unrealistic the demands for the abolition of the SED's leading role and advocated pushing through reforms jointly with the SED. This standpoint was unacceptable to some New Forum activists: Böttger in Karl-Marx-Stadt and Tschiche in Magdeburg aspired to the destruction of the SED's power monopoly, a reflection of the more radical mood which seems to have distinguished the provinces from the capital.[20] Only after the SED's decay became palpable from late November onwards and Chancellor Kohl began to take a more active part in the GDR's internal developments was it no longer imperative to remain within the framework of socialism.

Sooner than could have been anticipated, the embryonic political parties and citizens' movements had to face several difficult questions: would the informal alliance between the masses, the citizens' movements and the cultural intelligentsia in the struggle against the SED and the Stasi endure once the *ancien régime* went into its unexpectedly rapid terminal decline and would democratic socialism within an independent GDR have much appeal for the East German populace? The answer to these questions was almost certainly 'no' even before the Wall was opened for, despite the courage of New Forum and the other movements, their idealistic notions of grass-roots democracy and many aspects of their economic and ecological policies lacked a popular resonance. Moreover, the continuing demographic haemorrhage testified to the powerful appeal of the West German system. The citizens' movements, like their direct predecessors in the alternative political culture of the 1980s, did not represent a majority of GDR citizens; they saw themselves, above all, as mediating the active political participation of increasingly 'mature' citizens in the creation of a civil society. And it should be recalled that while New Forum and the other groups were one of the crystallisation points for the masses, these groups, in Detlef Pollack's opinion, did not lead the masses, but it was rather the masses who had set the groups in motion and pushed them temporarily to the head of the popular movement.[21]

A conspiracy theory: the Stasi as engineer of revolution

The uncovering during the revolution of Wolfgang Schnur of Democratic Awakening and Böhme of the SDP as unofficial collaborators and later revelations of the involvement with the Stasi of prominent individuals such as Manfred Stolpe (IM 'Sekretär') and Lothar de Mazière (allegedly IM 'Czerny') have given rise to a conspiracy theory of the revolution. According to this interpretation, the activities of the citizens' movements in the early stage of the revolution were largely steered by the Stasi and its numerous agents as part of a broader scheme to remove Honecker, whose intransigence was regarded as endangering the SED power monopoly. There is also irrefutable evidence that after the failure of the security forces in the summer to quell the protests and movements by the selective use of arrests and imprisonment, the Stasi deployed its informers as *agents pacificeteurs* rather than as *agents provocateurs*. A report issued by the head of the Stasi's Dresden regional administration reveals that between 80 and 100 unofficial collaborators had been planted in the citizens' movements.[22] The new approach was outlined by Mielke at a meeting with his top officers on 21 October. Agents were to be planted so that the Stasi could shape the policies and activities of the new movements and groups.

Although the Stasi was undoubtedly successful in infiltrating the citizens' movements, the conspiracy theory exaggerates the organisation's ability to influence the powerful forces generated by the mass exodus, the citizens' movements and the demonstrators. Rather than steering developments, the Stasi tended to be reactive and its leaders' plans were often confused and uncertain. Moreoever, even such indefatigable researchers as Mitter and Wolle have been unable to find a single shred of evidence to support one of the central planks of the conspiracy theory, that is, a plan to build up an opposition in order to overthrow Honecker and the other SED hardliners.[23]

The disintegration of the SED

Grass-roots unrest

The SED could not remain immune from the crisis in society despite Honecker's contention in October that socialism would continue to 'glow in the colours of the GDR'. Grass-roots unrest and dissatisfaction in the SED with the party leadership was apparent as early as 1986 but not until late 1987 and 1988 did the mood worsen appreciably. District and regional party reports and Stasi analyses of popular opinion in those years refer to SED members' frustration with the lack of inner-party democracy, the inadequate supply of consumer goods, restrictions on travel to the West and the artificiality of reports in the media. Furthermore, the Honecker team's antipathy towards the Soviet reform process 'from above' contrasted with the positive attitude of many rank-and-file members. Outrage erupted at the banning of the German language version of the Soviet magazine *Sputnik* in October 1988 and of several critical Soviet films. These actions demonstrated, so people believed, the leadership's lack of trust in their political maturity. Yet, despite the widespread sympathy in the party for Gorbachev and the growing dissatisfaction with the party leadership, the SED membership, even at this late stage, had not entirely abandoned hope in Honecker. The overwhelming majority remained disciplined comrades for whom the socialist system was not without merit and job security.[24]

In 1989, unrest among party members was spurred on by the blatant manipulation of the local elections in May, the partial opening of the Hungarian–Austrian border and the leadership's sympathy for the Chinese Communists' bloody suppression of the student movement in Beijing. Modrow in June, Schabowski in July and Krenz in September all went on solidarity visits to China. The visits were a none too subtle warning to the GDR's own dissidents. But it was not until much later in the year, when the initiative had been seized by others, that the party base at last began to fall apart. Many members took part in the demonstrations in Leipzig and others were in the crowds calling out 'Gorbi, Gorbi' in East Berlin on 7 October. On the other hand, the rank-and-file hesitated to take open, direct action against the leadership: not until 8 November did the party base stage its first mass demonstration when over 50,000 members gathered in front of the Central Committee building to protest against the half-hearted reforms of Egon Krenz. Soon afterwards, the party began to haemorrhage members with 907,480 quitting between November 1989 and January 1990.

The Politbüro, with an average age of 67 years, exhibited 'the powerlessness of the powerful' in the face of the burgeoning societal crisis. The absence of the 77-year-old Honecker through a serious gallbladder illness for about six weeks between mid-August and 25 September deprived the SED of its chief pilot. Mittag, who served as acting head for much of this time, continued the march towards the last ditch. On his return, Honecker only succeeded in exacerbating matters. He attempted in vain to shift responsibility for the GDR's domestic crisis on to the policy of the West German government. His total failure to appreciate the concern of his 'subjects' is illustrated by the infamous statement which he instructed *Neues Deutschland* to publish on 2 October that 'no tears should be shed' for East German refugees who 'have all trampled upon our moral values and have separated themselves from our society'.[25] Instead of reform and dialogue, Honecker came increasingly to favour a hardline policy towards the demonstrators and civil rights groups. On 22 September, in a letter to the First Secretaries of the SED regional organisations, he demanded that measures be taken to isolate the organisers of 'counterrevolutionary activity'.[26] Plans had been prepared for somewhile by the SED and the Stasi for the arrest of about 3,000 and the internment of perhaps 11,000 opponents of the regime in the event of an emergency. Camps had already been earmarked for this purpose in East Berlin and elsewhere. 1,500 were to be interned in the Erfurt *Bezirk* alone.[27]

The eerie silence of the Politbüro on the country's escalating problems and Honecker's obduracy finally persuaded some of its members that action was imperative. It was no longer a question of disagreement over policy details; the stakes were now much higher. Honecker's removal was essential if the SED were to cling on to its leadership role and the political crisis overcome. A bitter Honecker would later claim that his overthrow was the result of an elaborate international plot dating back to the mid-1980s. He conveniently forgot that he had conspired with Brezhnev against Ulbricht. Contending that the real wire-pullers had remained in the background, he poured scorn on the so-called lesser lights who boasted of their deeds. He was particularly contemptuous of one of the latter, Egon Krenz, who, in his opinion, had led the people of the GDR into the abyss.[28]

Honecker's removal was the outcome of an alliance of convenience forged between Krenz and Willi Stoph and other members of the SED's 'Moscow' wing. According to Ivan Kusmin, the head of the KGB information department in East Berlin from 1984 to 1991, the Stoph group had put out tentative

[286] feelers to the Kremlin on various occasions since 1984 regarding the dismissal of Honecker. Their feeble manoeuvres failed to elicit any response from Gorbachev, who could hardly have warmed to the notion of cooperation with such pronounced traditionalists against a leader of Honecker's authority.[29] It was not until Krenz, widely regarded as Honecker's crown prince, decided to break with Honecker that a palace coup could be staged. Krenz held a series of key positions on the Central Committee Secretariat, being responsible for security, youth and legal issues. At 51 years of age, his relative youth made him a more appealing candidate for the post of General Secretary than the taciturn 75-year-old Stoph. However, although Krenz was becoming increasingly dismayed by his Politbüro colleagues' intransigence, his own pusillanimity and respect for Honecker held him back from an open challenge to his patron. Günter Schabowski, who had run out of patience with the old guard, played an important part in persuading Krenz to overcome his doubts. Born in 1929, the energetic and forceful Schabowski had succeeded the disgraced Naumann as First Secretary of the SED Berlin regional administration in 1985 after having served for six years as editor-in-chief of *Neues Deutschland*. Entering the Politbüro as a candidate in 1981, he became a full member three years later. After the fall of the SED, two of his publications, *Der Absturz* and *Das Politbüro*, would provide by far the most critical assessment of the political system to emanate from the former council of gods.

At the Politbüro meeting on 10 October, Krenz and Schabowski managed to persuade a highly reluctant Honecker to authorise a Politbüro statement on the crisis in society. This statement, which appeared in *Neues Deutschland* two days later, was the first public admission that the mass flight was partly home-grown and not, as hitherto contended, the work of external foes. In proposing an open discussion of the country's problems, the statement struck a different chord to the same paper's reference only ten days earlier not to shed tears after the émigrés. A resentful Honecker procrastinated and sought to outmanoeuvre Krenz, thereby signing his political death warrant. After preparing the ground with other sympathisers on the Politbüro, Krenz and Stoph moved into action. Gorbachev, when informed by Harry Tisch of the plan, replied that the appointment of a new leader was an internal matter for the GDR. Although he probably preferred a reform figure such as Hans Modrow, his stance was in keeping with his principle of non-interference and reflected the sea change in relations between Moscow and the East European states. With Gorbachev acquiescing, the *frondeurs* seized the initiative at the decisive Politbüro meeting on the morning of 17 October. Stoph proposed that Honecker be relieved of all his posts. Surprised by this turn of events, Honecker responded with a vigorous defence of his record and warned that changes in personnel would, as in Hungary, fatally wound the cause of socialism and expose the GDR to blackmail. With Mittag also joining in the fray, Honecker was forced to accept his fate. Ironically, but in true Communist fashion, he preserved a united front by voting with his colleagues to recommend to the Central Committee his removal from office. On the following day, Honecker, citing health reasons, resigned before the Central Committee and proposed Krenz as his successor.[30]

It is difficult to shed many tears for Honecker. He had organised the building of the Berlin Wall and had presided, with Erich Mielke, over a vast machinery of repression. His obdurate rejection of Gorbachev's reform course and his hostility to the citizens' movements and the émigrés destroyed the improvement in his image derived from his cautious liberalisation at home in the early 1970s and his labours to preserve détente in the 1980s. Had he retired after his visit to the Federal Republic in 1987, then history's verdict might have been more generous and he would at least have been spared the ignominy of his final year in power and of his flight to Moscow in 1991. He was extradited from Moscow and brought to trial in Berlin, charged with collective responsibility for the death of thirteen East Germans on the border. After the collapse of his trial in 1993 on account of his ill-health, he obtained exile in Chile where he died of cancer in May 1994. In his Canute-like efforts to keep reform at bay, the tough and resilient Honecker was at least being faithful to his Communist creed and striving to preserve what he genuinely regarded as the 'better Germany' and the SED's role as the avant-garde of the working class. This heritage and its protective barrier had, however, become an anachronism.

The Krenz interregnum

The toppling of Honecker was part of the putchists' scheme to preserve the political primacy of the SED, as evidenced by Krenz's appointment not only as General Secretary but also, on 24 October, as Chairman of the Council of State and of the Defence Council. All three offices had been held by Honecker. New faces were brought into the Politbüro and members of the old guard, such as Hager and Mielke, discarded. Honecker, Mittag, Tisch and other notables were ejected from the party and Stoph and his government resigned on 7 November. Six days later, the unassuming 61-year-old

[288] Hans Modrow, who was known to have reformist credentials, was confirmed by the *Volkskammer* as the new Chairman of the Council of Ministers. Despite these changes, Krenz too often appeared to be reacting to events and too inclined to half measures to convince people that he was an East German Gorbachev. He was too tainted by his SED past and memories were still fresh of his assurances of support for the hard-line Chinese leadership. Even the SED's abandonment of its leadership role as enshrined in Article 1 of the Constitutution failed to help his cause. One popular joke summed up his predicament: 'What is the difference between Krenz and Honecker? Krenz's gall bladder is still working'. With the SED grass-roots also in rebellion, Krenz was obliged to surrender his position as General Secretary on 3 December. Even the event for which he is best remembered, the opening of the Berlin Wall, was a confused and desperate last throw of the political dice.

A new travel law – and a slight miscalculation

With the mass exodus gathering momentum, popular dissatisfaction escalated sharply at the news of the continuation of restrictions on the freedom of travel in the draft of a travel law issued on 6 November. The SED leaders, also under pressure from the Czechoslovak government to prevent the GDR's crisis from destabilising its neighbours, returned to the drawing board. A special working party was commissioned by the Politbüro on 7 November to devise a temporary solution until a new travel law could be finalised. Two days later, after hasty deliberations, the working party recommended that, as long as East German citizens possessed a passport or a visa, no restrictions should be imposed on applications for permanent emigration and private visits. Permanent emigration was to be allowed at any border crossing between the GDR, the FRG and West Berlin – but in an orderly manner. An announcement to this effect was to be made in the morning of 10 November. Although Politbüro and the Council of Ministers' approval soon followed, confusion was rife at a time when membership of the two bodies was being reshuffled in a kind of political 'musical chairs'.[31] That the reconstituted SED leadership was not working to a pre-determined plan but responding to overwhelming internal and external pressures is clear from Schabowski's press conference at 18.00 hours that evening. As the newly appointed Central Committee Secretary for the Media, Schabowski was entrusted with announcing the new travel regulations. It soon became apparent under questioning that he was not familiar with the details. He had only received them from Krenz shortly before the conference and he had not been

present when the document had come before the Politbüro earlier in the day.
What Schabowski did confirm was that applications for private visits would
be expedited with speed and that permanent emigration could take place via
checkpoints in Berlin and between the FRG and the GDR with 'immediate
effect'.[32] He had, however, overlooked the reference in paragraph three of
the document that the new dispensations should not be introduced until the
following day!

Did this mean that the Berlin Wall was about to be lifted? Immediately
after the end of the conference, a flustered Schabowski acknowledged in
response to a correspondent's query that 'It is possible to go through the
border' and, as to whether this amounted to freedom of travel, 'Yes. Of course.
It is no question of tourism. It is a permission of leaving the GDR'.[33] With
uncertainty prevailing, press and TV correspondents drew their own conclusion and announced that East Germans would be able to pass through the
Wall without restrictions on the following day.

The Wall opens

By 20.30 hours several hundred East Berliners had gathered at the
Bornholmerstraße checkpoint to test the new measures and soon began to
shout 'Open the gate'. Under growing pressure and without clear guidelines
from their superiors, the checkpoint guards sought to defuse the situation by
allowing a few East Germans to cross at about 22.00 hours. But with the
crowd growing too large to be held back, the guards finally opened the barriers 30 minutes later. Similar pressure at Checkpoint Charlie, Heinrich-
Heine-Straße and elsewhere led to the opening of all checkpoints by
midnight. Thousands flocked through into West Berlin and joyous celebrations began on the Kurfürstendamm and the city's other streets. At the
Brandenburg Gate young people climbed and danced on top of the Wall.
Over the next three days, about 3 million East Germans rushed to visit West
Germany and West Berlin. Even if Krenz had not wished to open the Wall,
the GDR's protective shell was so brittle by early November and the popular
pressure so intense that the final lifting of the Iron Curtain could not have
been long delayed.

Although discussions had taken place between Moscow and East Berlin
on the opening of crossing points in the south of the GDR for permanent
émigrés and Schevardnaze favoured a more liberal system, the new travel
regulations had not been agreed in advance. The Soviet embassy in East Berlin was extremely annoyed by the SED leadership's failure to disclose the full

[290]   details and was shocked by the completely unexpected opening of the Wall.[34] With Gorbachev ruling out the use of Soviet troops, the only realistic alternative was to make the best out of a bad job. Later in the day, both Schevardnaze and Gerasimov hailed the new travel arrangements as a sovereign and positive action of the GDR leadership. Gorbachev wished Krenz well in his pursuit of reform and urged the governments of France, the USA, the UK and West Germany not to destabilise the GDR. Moscow's relatively calm reaction was in keeping with the principle of non-intervention and its approach to events in Poland and Hungary earlier in the year. Gorbachev, it appears, was hopeful that Krenz and Modrow would be able to stabilise the country by means of the kind of moderate democratic and economic reforms which he himself favoured.[35]

But as events unfolded, neither Krenz nor Gorbachev could halt the disintegration of the SED. The gamble to relax travel restrictions and the opening of the Wall compounded rather than relieved the regime's problems and were a fatal blow to Krenz's muddled plans to win over the populace. Even before he resigned as General Secretary, the legitimacy crisis of the old regime was so deep that unification was rising rapidly towards the top of the political agenda. As for the Berlin Wall, not only was it condemned to redundancy as a political barrier by the restoration of transport links between the two parts of Berlin but its concrete fabric was chipped away by the hammers and chisels of individuals seeking souvenirs before wholescale demolition commenced after Lothar de Maizière assumed power in March 1990.

The end of the SED monolith

The carefully constructed SED political monolith was also crumbling. The old keepers of the seals of power – Honecker, Mielke, Stoph, Kleiber and Werner Krolikowksi – were charged by the Prosecutor-General, on 8 December, with misuse of office and corruption. The *Volkskammer* was finding its voice. In a defining moment at its 13 November session, Mielke was unveiled as a latter-day Wizard of Oz. In a rambling valedictory speech, Mielke aroused both derision and anger by his failure to express regret and by his pathetic protestation 'But I love you all'. The Democratic Bloc began to unravel; all the leaders of the bloc parties, with the exception of Gerlach, were ejected from office. The first of the bloc parties to stir was the CDU: a new chairman, the seemingly untainted Lothar de Maizière, was elected on

10 November, and on 4 December it announced that it was leaving the Bloc.
The LDPD withdrew soon afterwards.

The SED, desperate to halt the outflow of members from the party, regrouped under a triumvirate of reform figures – Modrow, Dresden's Lord Mayor Wolfgang Berghofer, and Gregor Gysi, the quick-witted East Berlin lawyer and son of a former minister. On 9 December, Gysi was elected party chairman at the SED's Extraordinary Party Congress. The post of General Secretary was abolished. Traditional Marxist-Leninist bodies such as the Politbüro and Central Committee were replaced by a Presidium and a party executive respectively. Although the Congress declared that the people were no longer under subjugation and committed the party to democratic socialism, it failed to make a clean break with the past. This can be seen in the decision on 11 December to rename the party the 'Socialist Unity Party of Germany-Party of Democratic Socialism' (SED-PDS), partly because a final dissolution might have deprived the party of the SED's enormous assets, and partly because many delegates were still wedded to the traditions and norms of the old system. However, faced with a continuing membership loss and with the need to refurbish its image for the *Volkskammer* election in March 1990, the party dropped the SED prefix and adopted the title of Party of Democratic Socialism (PDS) at its Congress in February. It defined its aim as the creation of a humanistic, democratic socialism and declared its vehement opposition to any annexation of the GDR by the FRG.

Modrow seeks to stem the tide

In the meantime, the Modrow government, composed of a majority of SED members, was labouring hard to prevent the absorption of the GDR by its powerful West German neighbour. In his governmental statement of 17 November 1989, Modrow promised free elections, a state based on the rule of law and an accountable judiciary. His economic reform package included an increase in the autonomy of economic entities and a scaling down, though not abandonment, of central planning and an acceptance of the market as an organic element of the planned socialist economy. Modrow's personal qualities of modesty and hardwork earned him much respect and as the SED went into free fall, the Council of Ministers became the main policy-making body. However, Modrow's position was undermined by the weakness of the SED, by economic dislocation and by the continuing population exodus. In January 1990 alone, 73,729 people left for West Germany. Modrow was also the victim of his own hesitancy in cutting the umbilical cord with state planning and controlled prices. And his evasiveness in the dismantling of the state security system brought him into conflict with the opposition groups. Although the Ministry of State Security was renamed the Office for National Security, many opposition group members rightly feared that the new body was essentially a reduced version of the old agency. This eventually led to the famous storming of the Stasi headquarters in the Normannenstraße on 15 January and the uncovering of the Stasi's secrets.

The Round Table

The opposition groups, though suspicious of Modrow, were, like the Minister President, anxious to preserve the GDR as an independent state on the basis of some form of reformed socialism. But not only did the civil rights movements lack the organisation and personnel but, rooted in the philosophy of the social-ethical groups, they also lacked the will and confidence to assume the responsibility of government. The Central Round Table eventually emerged as a forum for the new civil rights groups to develop their own ideas on reform and to explore ways of overcoming the crisis in society in conjunction with representatives of the old order. Lothar Probst describes its goal as 'not to seek political power but to participate in exercising it'.[36] The Central Round Table, on which Church representatives acted as moderators, met for the first time on 7 December in East Berlin and concluded its work on 12 March 1990. A balance was struck on the composition of the Round Table between the new opposition forces and those from the SED-dominated Democratic Bloc. The SED-PDS, the four 'bloc' parties, the FDGB and the Farmers' Mutual Aid Association represented the rapidly changing old order, while New Forum, the SDP, Democratic Awakening, the Initiative for Peace and Human Rights and several other small groups constituted the new order. The Central Round Table, as well as the Round Tables at local, district and regional level, debated the restoration of the GDR in accordance with the civil rights groups' notions of basic democracy and social justice.

But the Round Table was more than a debating chamber. In mid-January, Modrow, anxious to prevent the country from becoming ungovernable, invited members of the Round Table to join the government and to participate in the legislative process. On 5 February, eight members of the opposition, including Rainer Eppelmann (DA) and Gerd Poppe (IFM), entered the 'government of national responsibility' under Modrow, albeit with the main posts remaining in SED-PDS hands. The opposition's involvement in government and the enhancement of the Round Table's legislative function signified the

transformation of the Round Table from a control and supervisory body into   [293]
one with direct steering powers.

The unification bandwagon

After the opening of the Wall and with the SED disintegrating, unification
calls surfaced on the streets of Leipzig during the Monday evening demonstration and rapidly gathered momentum. Surveys of Leipzig demonstrations
between 4 December 1989 and 12 February 1990 illustrate this trend: those
strongly in support of unification rose from 39 per cent to 72 per cent and
those firmly against fell from 12 per cent to 2 per cent.[37] And whereas in early
November only a few placards had proclaimed unification on Leipzig's
central square, Karl-Marx-Platz, by early December the number of black-
red-gold flags on display indicated that unification already enjoyed a slim
majority.

The shift away from the civil rights groups' notions of a 'Third Way' not
only in Leipzig but throughout the GDR was determined, above all, by the
realisation that the West German model might be within reach, by a reluctance to embrace risky and untried experiments in basic democracy and by a
rejection of a politically and economically bankrupt state socialism. The un-
imaginable could be imagined. With the GDR's economic difficulties mounting
and with revelations accumulating daily in the media about the ecological
catastrophe, the corruption of leading cadres and the Stasi's vast system of
repression, the social market economy and federal system of the FRG grew
ever more attractive. Much would depend on the reaction of the West German chancellor.

Helmut Kohl: chancellor of unity

Even when SED rule began to show signs of erosion, Bonn moved cauti-
ously, anxious to avoid exacerbating the situation. In his letter to the General
Secretary in early August 1989, Kohl reassured Honecker that he wanted
relations to continue in a rational and sensible manner.[38] Kohl and his Foreign Minister, Genscher, were anxious not to precipitate a crisis which might
endanger the stability of Europe, antagonise the Soviet Union and reverse
the reform process in Eastern Europe and the GDR. Although Kohl began
to shift his position on the feasibility of reunification under the impact of the

dramatic developments in the GDR in late summer, it was not until the fall of the Berlin Wall that he translated his emotional and political commitment to unification into positive action. He was encouraged to do so by cries of 'Wir sind ein Volk' which were beginning to echo on the streets of Leipzig and by the Kremlin's reassessment of its German policy. On 21 November, in a discusion which astonished Horst Teltschik, Kohl's chief adviser on for-eign and security policy, Nikolai Portugalev informed the West German unofficially that the Soviet Union might be prepared to give the 'green light' in the medium term to a German confederation.[39] In pursuing unification, the support of the American government would be crucial: President Bush and Secretary of State James Baker had already made it known in late October that they were prepared to accept unification. And on 21 November, Baker reiterated Washington's commitment to German reunification, stating that the difficult question was only when and how.

Kohl's ten points

Kohl also needed to respond to the new SED leadership's efforts to thwart unification. The SED's strategy was outlined in Minister President Modrow's proposal for a cooperative coexistence between the two German states on all issues and cemented by a treaty community. Kohl and his closest advisers, although Genscher was deliberately excluded, countered with a plan for gradual unification. In his address to the Bundestag on 28 November, Kohl held out the prospect of large-scale aid to the GDR when fundamental polit-ical and economic reform was made irreversible and he unveiled a ten-point programme with a federation as its goal. After the holding of free elections, 'confederative structures' would be established with the GDR as the basis for the gradual transition to a federal system for the whole of Germany. In order to placate foreign concerns, Kohl sought to embed unification in an all-European process and structure.

While Kohl's plan was a bold move to ensure that West Germany had a major say in the rapidly changing course of developments in Germany, the chancellor and his advisers were still expecting unification to be a relatively long process of between five and ten years. However, the failure of Krenz and Modrow to stabilise the GDR, Gorbachev's growing weakness at home and the collapse of Communist regimes throughout Eastern and Central Europe dramatically shortened the time span. Kohl's meeting with Modrow in Dres-den on 19 December was a defining moment. While both the East and West German representatives committed themselves to a treaty community and the

West Germans promised comprehensive aid to the GDR, the euphoric recep- [295]
tion given to Kohl's improvised speech by tens of thousands of East Germans
at an evening rally at the ruin of Dresden's *Frauenkirche* may have finally persuaded him to revise his ideas on confederation. Kohl's emotional references
to the German nation were reciprocated by the crowd's chants for reunification.[40] After the West German delegation left Dresden on 20 December,
Bonn's policy shifted to rapid unification.

Modrow, Gorbachev and a united fatherland

Modrow, unable to halt the unification tide, attempted to slow it down by
launching his initiative 'For Germany, United Fatherland'. Announcing the
plan on 1 February after discussions in Moscow with Gorbachev, Modrow
proposed that the two states' powers of sovereignty be gradually transferred
to a confederation after a period of economic and political cooperation. Both
were to remain militarily neutral during this process.[41] By this time, the
Soviets had become reconciled to the inevitability of German unification,
although they remained determined to strike a hard bargain on issues such
as nuclear weapons and the stationing of NATO forces on GDR territory.
Soviet acceptance of German unification had already been signalled by
Gorbachev on the eve of his meeting with Modrow when he informed the
media that no one doubts in principle the unification of the Germans.[42]
Gorbachev had not, however, originally wished to abandon the GDR; he
had only become reconciled to unification with the chronic weakening of his
own domestic position and with the realisation that the Soviet Union lacked
the FRG's capacity to resuscitate the GDR. It was West Germany which had
become central to the Kremlin's hopes for the modernisation of the Soviet
economy, a role which the GDR had once been expected to play. Gorbachev's reluctant acceptance of unification was also an unintended, but
inherent, consequence of his notion of a common European home. The
GDR's allotted place, however, was to be that of a reformed socialist state
rather than an enfeebled part of an enlarged Federal Republic. And in the
final analysis, unification was a resolution to one of the fundamental problems which, as Gorbachev admitted to Modrow, had bedevilled the GDR
throughout its history, that is, the magnetic appeal of an alternative German
state.[43]

Moscow's reappraisal was confirmed a few days later when Gorbachev
and Kohl and their two key advisers, Chernayiev and Teltschik, met at the

Kremlin on 10 February. The West Germans talked up the chaotic situation prevailing in the GDR and the need for rapid unification. Gorbachev assured Kohl that he was willing to accept the prospect of German unification and that the Germans were entitled to decide for themselves if they wished to unite and under what kind of government.[44] Yet another momentous decision had already been taken by Kohl. On 7 February, Kohl's cabinet agreed to offer speedy economic and monetary union to the GDR, thereby overturning the government's existing plan to place a currency union at the end of a gradual process of economic reform and restructuring in the GDR. The proposal required the Bundesbank to take responsibility for the GDR's monetary policy and thus a loss of GDR sovereignty in a crucial policy area. This decision to 'jump start' economic recovery flew in the face of the advice of the Bundesbank and of most economists. Perhaps recalling Gorbachev's warning to Honecker in October 1989 that 'He who comes too late is punished by life itself', Kohl pressed ahead in order to take advantage of the window of opportunity offered by Gorbachev's agreement 'in principle' to unification and by American preference for a rapid solution. The chancellor, in addition to the electoral benefts to be accrued by the CDU from unification, was anxious to arrest the mass exodus which was disrupting the GDR and putting a great strain on West German resources for housing and the social security system. Consequently, Kohl and his advisers put forward a more far-reaching plan: the incorporation of the GDR into the existing Federal Republic through Article 23 of West Germany's Basic Law, not via Article 146, as preferred by the SPD. The latter was the slower route as it provided for the election of delegates to a national assembly which would decide on a new constitution for the unified state.

GDR political groups and parties had to adjust to the popular mood and to West German intervention in the internal affairs of their country. From December onwards, the SDP grew closer to its West German counterpart, committed itself in mid-January to a united, federal Germany, and defected from its electoral pact with the other new opposition groups. The German Social Union (DSU), a new political party founded in January 1990 with its base in Saxony and Thuringia and a fierce opponent of socialism, advocated rapid union. Democratic Awakening shifted from a socialist agenda to unification and a market economy. And, after an agonising series of debates, New Forum bowed to the inevitable and gave its approval to unification, albeit in the slow lane. New Forum feared that too rapid a process would lead to high unemployment, prosperity for a minority and the legalisation of neo-fascist organisations. It wanted the democratisation of the GDR, the stabilisation and reform of the GDR economy, restrictions on the market mechanism and firm social security guarantees before the completion of unification.

[297]

By the time of the pivotal *Volkskammer* election on 18 March – the date had been brought forward from May – the question was no longer whether German unification might occur but how quickly and with what kind of safeguards. The most determined advocates of rapid economic and monetary union, and of unification on the basis of the West German model, were the parties constituting the Alliance for Germany which Kohl had cobbled together as an election vehicle on 5 February. The three parties were the DA, the DSU and the former East German bloc party, the CDU, under its newly elected chairman, Lothar de Maizière. Two days later, three civil rights groups – New Forum, the Initiative for Peace and Human Rights and Democracy Now – joined together in Alliance '90 (*Bündnis '90*); they would fight the election on a platform of a gradual drawing together of the two states underpinned by guarantees of the right to work, of the equality of the sexes and of a social minimum standard for everyone. The SPD, while more committed to unification than Alliance '90, also favoured a relatively slower pace.

East Germany votes for the West

Confounding predictions of an SPD victory, the conservative coalition scored an astonishing 47.79 per cent of the vote, including 40.59 per cent for the CDU. Its sweeping victory was a strong endorsement by the electorate of Kohl's programme and a legitimation of the fast track to unification. The SPD obtained 21.76 per cent, Alliance '90 a bitterly disappointing 2.9 per cent and the PDS 16.32 per cent. In terms of seats, this resulted in 192 for the Alliance for Germany, 88 for the SPD, 66 for the PDS and 12 for Alliance '90. The poor performance of the civil rights groups was partly a result of their inferior resources and poor organisation. However, in addition, their commitment to basic democratic principles and the absence of a broad social base with firm roots in the working class left them ill-equipped to fight a conventional election. Most voters were more interested in catching up materially with West Germany than with notions of a 'Third Way' or the slow lane to this goal. The vision held out by Chancellor Kohl during his election appearances in the GDR of blooming landscapes in the East within five years and the rapid acquisition of the Deutschmark reassured Eastern voters and helped the CDU and its allies to garner the working class vote. Ironically, the PDS, the successor to the self-styled party of the working class and peasants, was far more successful among leading functionaries (20.2 per cent) and the

[298]   intelligentsia (31 per cent) than among workers (11.0 per cent). The Alliance for Germany gained the majority of votes across all social groups, with the exception of the intelligentsia, and as much as 55 per cent of the working-class vote. The CDU and its smaller partners were particularly successful in the industrial south where social and environmental problems had fed the emigration movement. The PDS fared badly there, suffering from the southern workers' hour of revenge; on the other hand, it performed well in East Berlin and some of the leading regional cities.[45]

The internal and external modalities of unification

Armed with a popular mandate, the new government, a grand coalition of CDU, DA, DSU, SPD and Liberals, headed by the Minister President, Lothar de Maizière, pushed ahead with the conclusion of economic and monetary union. Unification remained highly popular: in May, 83 per cent of West Germans and 89 per cent of East Germans were in favour according to an opinion poll conducted by the West German institute *Forschungsgruppe Wahlen*.[46] The GDR negotiators had little scope for bargaining; they were the supplicants, not equal partners. In the First State Treaty on Monetary, Economic and Social Union, which came into operation on 1 July 1990, the GDR accepted the principles and institutions of the social market economy of the FRG and the Deutschmark became the sole legal currency in East Germany. Although certain safeguards were built into the treaty to protect the GDR from the sudden impact of monetary union, the consequences for the far less competitive East German economy confirmed the dire warnings of the PDS, Alliance '90 and the Deutsche Bundesbank.

The State Treaty was seen as an essential step towards eventual unification but before this could be completed the external modalities had to be finalised in the 2+4 talks between the two German states and the four 'occupying' powers. Although the Soviet Union was at first opposed to a united Germany's membership of NATO, it had to be content with a reduction in the size of German forces to 370,000 and with guarantees that non-German troops would not be stationed in the former GDR until the phased departure of Soviet troops was completed in 1994. Other arrangements included the four powers' abrogation of their rights and responsibilities in Berlin and for Germany and Poland to confirm their borders by treaty.

Finally, a second treaty, the Unification Treaty, was signed on 31 August 1990 after often difficult negotiations. This treaty, mainly drafted by the West German government, dealt with the legal aspects of unification, such as the

Constitution, property rights, abortion, access to the Stasi files and the applica-
tion of administrative and penal law to the five new *Länder* in the GDR.
The old *Bezirk* system was abolished and replaced by the newly constituted
Länder of Saxony, Saxony-Anhalt, Brandenburg, Mecklenburg-Western
Pomerania and Thuringia on the basis of a law passed by the *Volkskammer* on
22 July. On 3 October, these five *Länder*, together with the eastern part of
Berlin, were incorporated into the FRG.

References

1. Wendt H. 1991: 387, 393

2. Deutscher Bundestag VII/1 1995: 324–8, 449

3. Opp K.-D., Voß P., Gern C. 1995: 193–4

4. Hirschmann A. O. 1991: 186

5. Reich J. 1990: 71

6. Dietrich in Deutscher Bundestag VII/1 1995: 607–10, 645

7. Schell M., Kalinka W. 1991: 312–13

8. Cited in Opp K.-D., Voß P., Gern C. 1995: 179

9. Schell M., Kalinka W. 1991: 314–17

10. Cited in Opp K.-D., Voß P., Gern C. 1995: 23–4

11. Deutscher Bundestag VII/1 1995: 690–1; Pollack D. 1990: 1217

12. Jarausch K. H., Gransow V. 1994: 48

13. Rein G. 1989: 59–61

14. Schulz M. 1991: 14; Rein G. 1989: 13–14; Wielgohs J., Schulz M. 1990: 18

15. Rein G. 1990: 17; Neubert E. 1991: 21, 24

16. Opp K.-D., Voß P., Gern C. 1995: 135–6

17. Cited in Wielgohs J., Schulz M. 1990: 18–19

18. Joppke C. 1995: 185–212

19. Philipsen D. 1993: 88

20. Deutscher Bundestag VII/1 1995: 731–2

[300]   21. Interview with Pollack in Opp K.-D., Voß P., Gern C. 1995: 12

22. Mitter A., Wolle S. 1993: 533; Süß W. 1997a: 256–8, 263–5

23. Mitter A., Wolle S. 1993: 531

24. Bortfeldt H. 1991: 20–9, 34; see also the Stasi reports in Stephan G.-R. 1994: 35–8, 53–7

25. Hertle H.-H. 1996b: 74

26. Dornheim A. 1995: 68–9

27. Knabe H. 1993: 23–4, 33–4; Schroeder K. 1998: 462

28. Andert R., Herzberg W. 1991: 19–22

29. Kusmin I. 1995: 286–90

30. Hertle H.-H. 1996a: 130–2; Hertle H.-H. 1996b: 86–7

31. Sarotte M. E. 1993: 277

32. Hertle H.-H. 1996b: 145–6

33. Ibid., 148

34. Ibid., 233–7; Maximytschew I. F., Hertle H.-H. 1994: 1146–7; Kotchemassow W. 1994: 185–7

35. Hertle H.-H. 1996b: 241–2, 245; Maximytschew I. F., Hertle H.-H. 1994: 1154

36. Probst L. 1996: 170

37. Förster P., Roski G. 1990: 164

38. Potthoff H. 1995: 38

39. Teltschik H. 1991: 44

40. Zelikow P., Rice C. 1995: 232; also Kohl's statement in Kuhn E. 1993: 89–90

41. Zelikow P., Rice C. 1995: 163–4; Görtemaker M. 1994: 130

42. Nakath D., Stephan G.-R. 1996: 233

43. Ibid., 290

44. Zelikow P., Rice C. 1995: 188; Görtemaker M. 1994: 136–7

45. Glaeßner G.-J. 1992: 87–8

46. Korte K.-R. 1994: 101

CHAPTER SIXTEEN

THE NATIONAL QUESTION RESOLVED?

U nification was not simply the outcome of East Germans' positive response to Chancellor Kohl's offer of the Deutschmark and of popular fury at revelations of corruption, the ecological blight, surveillance by the Stasi and the economic malaise. Division had been eroded in a multitude of ways long before 1989. The millions of East German visitors to the West and the tens of thousands who fled the country in the 1980s had lowered the Berlin Wall by several metaphorical blocks. Family and other personal contacts preserved a sense of national community. The Leipzig Central Institute for Youth Research data collected between 1969 and 1988 show that about three-quarters of young East Germans wrote to and received visits from West German relatives and friends. From the mid-1960s, the proportion of young East Germans who listened to the Western electronic media grew from year to year. Although musical and entertainment programmes were the main attraction, political information came to play an increasingly important role and greater trust was invested in the West than in the East German media. The selective consumption of Western programmes served, in the opinion of the youth researchers, to highlight the advantages of life in the West such as a higher living standard and personal liberties, which, in the long term, prepared the ground for unification.[1]

Yet, once unification euphoria had subsided, it became clear that constitutional and institutional unification was easier to achieve than social, economic and cultural unity. Kohl's prediction, in March 1990, that the GDR would become a flourishing region within five years wildly overestimated the recovery powers of the GDR economy and the efficacy of market instruments to transform the socialist economic system. Despite the many advantages of unification, for example, higher wages and pensions, a wider range of commodities and political pluralism, the five new *Länder* have had to pass through a 'vale of tears'. The conversion of wages and salaries at a rate of one

[302] Deutschmark to one East German Mark exposed the grave deficiencies of the GDR economy in a merciless manner and set off one of the sharpest economic depressions in European history. Within two months of economic and monetary union, industrial commodity production had dropped by almost 43 per cent and by the spring of 1992, the number of gainfully employed people in the new *Länder* had fallen from 9.9 million to 6.25 million. In the early 1990s, real unemployment hovered around 30 per cent. Social status and traditional skills were devalued. Furthermore, the flood of West Germans into the upper and middle levels of political and economic decision-making bodies led to charges of the colonisation of the ex-GDR by the 'Wessis' (westerners), despite vast public financial transfers from west to east of DM 1.7 billion gross between 1991 and 1998 to prop up east German consumption, wages and social services.

With capitalist realities tarnishing the image of the 'golden West', many east Germans have come to regard themselves as second-class citizens in the new Berlin Republic and look back with a mixture of nostalgia and appreciation to the social security, full employment, child care provision and the lower level of crime in the former GDR. The physical wall may have been removed but a wall in the mind remains. 'Ossis' (easterners) are more likely than 'Wessis' to attach a higher value to an interventionist role for the state and to believe that socialism is good in theory. East German women remain highly committed to the traditional GDR norm of combining family tasks with full-time employment. What has come to be called *Ostidentität* (east German indentity) can also be traced in easterners' self-identification as 'East Germans'. An investigation in the spring of 1995 found that whereas 71 per cent of easterners regarded themselves as 'East Germans' and 57 per cent as 'Germans', only 46 per cent of westerners looked upon themselves as 'West Germans' and 66 per cent as 'Germans'.[2]

The socialist PDS has profited electorally from this divergence as well as from its ability to articulate eastern grievances, gaining 21.6 per cent of the vote in the eastern *Länder* in the 1998 Bundestag election. Its success is a sharp reminder of the inbuilt limitations of unification based overwhelmingly on the transfer of the constitutional and political structures of the old Federal Republic. Although these structures undoubtedly represented a welcome departure from the repressive traditions of the GDR and the acceptance of democratic values and norms is widespread in the new *Länder*, easterners' frustration has been especially severe because their initially high idealistic notions of democracy have been undermined by the confrontation with the complexities and realities of the political order. In the early years of unification, public opinion surveys recorded appreciably lower rates of satisfaction in the east than in the west with the operation of the democratic system;[3] and many east Germans continue to object to their incomplete inclusion in the system and remain critical of their limited influence on political decision-making.[4] The preservation and use of the Stasi files is but one of the many issues which illustrate the problems inherent in the establishment of a common identity. The files have been used to prosecute GDR leaders, exclude eastern officials from public service and to discredit prominent intellectuals such as Christa Wolf. However, when, in March 2000, Stasi files based on bugged telephone conversations of CDU leaders suggested that ex-Chancellor Kohl was more deeply implicated in irregular party funding than he had previously admitted, he and other officials thundered against information acquired in an illegal manner by the agents of a criminal regime. This animated former GDR civil rights activists such as Ulrike Poppe to protest against what they saw as yet a further example of the unjustifiable discrimination between eastern and western politicians.[5]

If *Ostidentität* is partly grounded in the negative socio-economic and psychological impact of unification and disillusionment with the political system, it is also shaped by strong support for such aspects of the *ancien régime* as social security, full employment and low income disparities. However, matters have to be kept in perspective. Only a minority of east Germans would welcome the return of the old GDR – 10 per cent according to a survey conducted in 1997 by the Berlin-Brandenburg Social Scientific Research Centre[6] – for they are aware of the many benefits of unification. No political movement exists to reverse unification; the issue concerns how best to integrate the two former republics into a balanced polity and society and to achieve self-sustaining economic growth in the east. Yet the erosion of eastern dissatisfaction concerns not only improvements in the areas of social welfare and economic performance; changes in attitude are required, including competing perceptions of GDR history.

If before 1989 the GDR provoked numerous lively political and historiographical disputes, controversy has gathered momentum since its demise. It is partly a debate over the punishment of perpetrators and compensation for victims, but it also concerns what Konrad Jarausch refers to as the struggle for dominance in political discourse and for the control over memory.[7] East German resentment at what is sometimes perceived to be an unjustifiable conflation of the GDR with the Stasi and western colonisation of memory of the GDR is reflected in the 97 per cent of easterners who agreed with the statement in a 1995 survey that 'only those who lived there can have a say

[304] about life in the GDR'.[8] The struggle is not restricted to an east–west German dimension but it also cuts across 'Ossis' and 'Wessis' (see Introduction).

The GDR and the Third Reich – similar but not the same

One of the most contentious historical debates concerns the supposed generic similarity between the Third Reich and the GDR. An advocate of the latter view is Horst Möller, the director of the Institute for Contemporary History in Munich. While recognising that comparison does not imply equation, he insists that the structural similarities are so pronounced that the GDR as well as the Third Reich should be classed as totalitarian dictatorships.[9] While this kind of thesis runs a two-fold danger – of trivialising the Third Reich and of demonising the GDR – there is no doubt that the two regimes constituted links in the illiberal tradition in German and European political culture. In the case of the GDR, the latter tradition was reinforced by the Stalinist structures imposed by the Soviet hegemon. Among the many similarities between the two German dictatorships were: a rejection of the basic value system of Western liberalism; the power monopoly enjoyed by a single party or, more pertinently, of a monocratic ruling elite; the repression of opponents and dissidents; the mass organisations' function as transmission belts; a tight control over the mass media and an elaborate system of propaganda; a comprehensive system of surveillance and security; and a restructuring of societal norms and values in accordance with an elaborate and exclusive ideology. Although the SED regime used force against its own population in 1953 and was prepared to do so against the Prague Spring and Solidarity, Möller is surely stretching credibility too far, however, when he contends that the GDR would have readily followed the Soviet Union in launching a global war.[10]

Turning to the many differences,[11] the regimes had contrasting origins and structures. The Third Reich was more 'home-grown' than the GDR, whose birth owed much to the victory of the Red Army and superpower rivalry. But the GDR's German roots must not be overlooked. It arose from the disastrous failures of Germany's conservative and fascist elites and it was shaped by the traditions of the Communist movement and by the actions of Stalin's many willing East German collaborators. There is, however, one overwhelming difference which makes the Third Reich 'singular'. The GDR did not pursue the physical annihilation of Europe's Jews, murder countless gypsies and homosexuals, enslave 'lesser races' and conduct a comprehensive programme of euthanasia against the allegedly mentally and physically retarded. While the thousands who died in the Soviet camps in East Germany and the hundreds who were killed trying to flee across the border must never be forgotten, the moral turpitude is of a lower order than that of the Third Reich. This observation should not be interpreted as a condonement of the crimes and injustices committed in the GDR. It should also be stressed that whereas the Third Reich intensified terror and repression, especially during the war, the GDR turned increasingly towards sophisticated methods of 'structural violence'. This contrast is captured by Heiner Geißler's differentiation between the mountain of corpses and files left behind by the Third Reich and the GDR respectively. An explanation for this fundamental difference can be sought in the absence of extreme nationalism and social Darwinism in the GDR, its antifascist credentials, the humanistic residue of Marxism and the German labour movement, and the radically different international context. The GDR, as a small country with limited resources and sensitive to West German influences and highly penetrated by its Soviet patron, enjoyed far less room for manoeuvre than the Third Reich.

Other basic differences concern the organisation of the political system and the social structure. From around the later 1960s, and especially under Honecker, the East German system lost most of its earlier dynamic in contrast to the Third Reich which was characterised by an increasingly destructive momentum and by widespread administrative confusion involving struggles for power and influence between powerful satraps. Whereas the NSDAP declined in influence, the SED apparat imposed a highly bureaucratised form of rule which enabled it, with the exception of the early 1950s and the NES period, to keep a tight rein on subordinate bodies and to avoid the dualism of party and state characteristic of the Third Reich. The radical restructuring of East German society entailed a more rapid turnover of elites than occurred in Nazi Germany. Members of the working class experienced rapid upward mobility in the earlier decades; on the other hand, access to elite positions was closed to blue-collar workers in the Third Reich. Public ownership became the norm in the GDR, unlike in the Third Reich, where private owners in agriculture, banking and industry managed to survive. Many profited from and indeed helped to shape Nazi economic and foreign policies. The PDS likes to stress what it perceives to be perhaps the fundamental difference between the two systems, that is, the GDR's paternalistic social policy and the Third Reich's 'systematic deprivation of rights in the social and labour sphere'.[12] This contrast is overstated. During the Third Reich, unemployment was overcome, real wages rose gradually and, in general, the rulers provided sufficient social incentives and activities in the Hitler Youth and the Strength through Joy movement to pacify and attract the support of a wide range of social groups.

One final point of comparison concerns the political legitimacy of the two states. According to the PDS, a general acceptance of, and identification with, the GDR was established on the basis of its anti-fascism, its social welfare system, its commitment to peace and its socialist credentials. While PDS representatives acknowledge that serious existential crises arose, as in 1953, the party claims that a clear majority of East Germans accepted the GDR from the close of the 1950s until the early 1980s before a loss of trust set in.[13] The PDS portrayal is not without some merit from the later 1960s to the early 1980s, even though it surely exaggerates overall support for the system and underplays the level and intensity of oppression. It also underscores the argument underlying this book that the history of the GDR is not simply one of decline in stages but one of fluctuating fortunes and that most East Germans conformed, at least outwardly. However, for reasons outlined in Chapter 7, this should not be confused with an overall intrinsic regime legitimacy. And, as far as can be ascertained from studies of popular opinion in Hitler's Germany, the GDR was denied the same level of popular acceptance as the Third Reich. One crucial reason relates to the national question. Unlike the GDR, the Third Reich was able to use the national card to mobilise support and to underpin it with spectacular military successes. Furthermore, Hitler's charismatic form of leadership was a more effective instrument for generating mass support and for regime legitimation than the stiff bureaucratic style and the personality cult of the lacklustre Ulbricht and Honecker. The very fact that the Third Reich had to be overthrown by the military forces of the grand coalition and that the GDR imploded internally at the same time as the Soviet Union was retreating from empire is also relevant in this context.

Where does this lead in terms of a classification of the GDR? One can agree with the PDS that the 'dictatorship' concept is imprecise and that 'state socialism' was different in the GDR from those versions prevailing in Poland, North Korea and Albania.[14] Likewise, one can accept that the differences between the Third Reich and the GDR were so fundamental that subsuming them under a uniform conceptual label may give rise to misunderstanding and a manipulation of the political discourse. But this should not lead to the abandonment of paradigms and overarching concepts. Even the PDS uses labels for the GDR such as 'state socialist dictatorship' and 'dictatorship of the SED leadership'. What is required is a paradigm – or perhaps paradigms – which does justice to social and political realities, while recognising the intrinsic difficulty of devising one which embodies all aspects of, and changes in, social, economic and political life, especially if the diachronic method is [307] being used for comparative historiography.

In summary, it has been argued in this book that the Stalinist paradigm has much to commend it for the late 1940s and early 1950s before it evolved via the chequered course of destalinisation into the post-totalitarianism of the later Ulbricht and the Honecker eras. Modifying Linz's categories, 'half-frozen' post-totalitarianism would seem to encapsulate the years 1963 to 1987 before the final meltdown occurred. However, two qualifications are necessary. The term 'half-frozen' should not be allowed to obscure a degree of adaptability on the part of the regime. Both Ulbricht and Honecker strove, at various times, to implement flexible instruments of control. NES and the 'unity of economic and social policy' are two such examples. The concept of *Fürsorgediktatur* captures the thrust of the SED's social welfare policy.[15] Second, in recognition of the fact that the Communist saddle never fitted the East German cow, 'post-totalitarianism' must encompass the diversity of life under Communism and the varying degree of space for leading one's own life. A decade after the fall of the Berlin Wall, it now remains to be seen whether capitalism can now lead eastern Germany to the meadow of plenty promised by Helmut Kohl.

References

1. A selection of the data can be found in Deutscher Bundestag 1995 V/2: especially pp. 1220–78

2. Zelle C. 1997: 12, 15, 23

3. Statistisches Bundesamt 1992: 645

4. Priller E. 1999: 336–9

5. *Neues Deutschland*, 31 March 2000, p. 1

6. Winkler G. 1997: 35

7. Jarausch K. H. 1997: 37

8. 'Stolz aufs eigene Leben', *Der Spiegel*, 3 July 1995, p. 49

9. Möller H. 1994: 127–8

10. Deutscher Bundestag X 1995: 609

[308]   11. See Kocka J. 1995: 95–101; Heydemann G., Beckmann C. 1997: 20–40

12. Deutscher Bundestag I 1995: 711

13. Ibid., 714–15

14. Ibid., 709

15. Jarausch K. H. 1997: 44

.

BIBLIOGRAPHY

Akerlof G. A., Rose A., Vellen J., Hessenius H. 1991, 'East Germany in from the Cold: The Economic Aftermath of Currency Union', *Brookings Papers on Economic Activity*, no. 1: 1–105

Andert R., Herzberg W. 1991, *Der Sturz. Erich Honecker im Kreuzverhör*. Aufbau-Verlag, Berlin and Weimar

Arendt H. 1966, *The Origins of Totalitarianism* (3rd edn). George Allen and Unwin, London

Arnold O., Modrow H. 1994, 'Das Große Haus. Struktur und Funktionsweise des Zentralkomitees der SED', in Modrow H. (ed.), *Das Große Haus. Insider berichten aus dem ZK der SED.* edition ost, Berlin

Artl K. 1998, 'Sowjetische (russische) Truppen in Deutschland (1945–1994)', in Diedrich T., Ehlert H., Wenzke R. (eds), *Im Dienst der Partei. Handbuch der bewaffneten Organe der DDR*. Ch. Links Verlag, Berlin, pp. 593–632

Ash T. G. 1993, *In Germany's Name. Germany and the Divided Continent*. Vintage, London

Axen H. 1996, *Ich war ein Diener der Partei. Autobiographische Gespräche mit Harald Neubert*. edition ost, Berlin

Badstübner R., Loth W. (eds) 1994, *Wilhelm Pieck – Aufzeichnungen zur Deutschlandpolitik 1945–1953*. Akademie Verlag, Berlin

Bahro R. 1978, *The Alternative in Eastern Europe* (trans. D. Fernbach). New Left Books, London

Behnke K. 1995, 'Lernziel: Zersetzung. Die "Operative Psychologie", in Behnke K., Fuchs J. (eds), *Zersetzung der Seele. Psychologie und Psychiatrie im Dienst der Stasi*. Rotbuch Verlag, Hamburg, pp. 12–43

Bender P. 1995, *Die 'Neue Ostpolitik' und ihre Folgen. Vom Mauerbau bis zur Vereinigung* (3rd edn). Deutscher Taschenbuch Verlag, Munich

Bentzien H. 1995, *Meine Sekretäre und ich*. Verlag Neues Leben, Berlin

Berendonk B. 1992, *Doping. Von der Forschung zum Betrug*. Rowohlt Taschenbuch Verlag, Reinbek bei Hamburg

Besier G. 1995, *Der SED-Staat und die Kirchen 1969–1990. Die Vision vom 'Dritten Weg'*. Propyläen Verlag, Frankfurt/Main

[310] Biermann W. 1977, *Wolf Biermann: Poems and Ballads*, translated by S. Gooch, Pluto Press, London: p. 29

Bordjugow G. 1998, 'Das ZK der KPdSU(B), die Sowjetische Militäradministration in Deutschland und die SED (1945–1951)', in Weber H., Mählert U. (eds), *Terror. Stalinistische Parteisäuberungen 1936–1953*. Schöningh, Paderborn and Munich, pp. 283–349

Bortfeldt H. 1991, *Von der SED zur PDS. Wandlung zur Demokratie?* Bouvier Verlag, Berlin

Bracher K. D. 1995, *Turning Points in Modern Times* (trans. T. Dunlap). Harvard Univesity Press, Cambridge, Massachusetts, and London

Brandt H. 1970, *The Search for a Third Way* (trans. S. Attanasio). Doubleday, New York

Brant S. 1955, *The East German Uprising 17th June 1953*. Thames and Hudson, London

Brown J. F. 1991, *Surge to Freedom. The End of Communist Rule in Eastern Europe*. Adamantine Press, Twickenham

Buck H. F. 1996, 'Wohnversorgung, Stadtgestaltung und Stadtverfall', in Kuhrt E., Buck H. F., Holzweißig G. (eds), *Am Ende des realen Sozialismus (2). Die wirtschaftliche und ökologische Situation in der DDR in den 80er Jahren*. Leske + Budrich, Opladen, pp. 67–109

Bundesministerium für innerdeutsche Beziehungen (ed.) 1974, *Materialien zum Bericht zur Lage der Nation*. Elsnerdruck, Berlin

Childs D. 1969, *East Germany*. Ernest Benn, London

Childs D., Popplewell R. 1996, *The Stasi. The East German Intelligence and Security Service*. Macmillan, Basingstoke and London

Connell B. 1957, *Watcher on the Rhine. A Report on the New Germany*. Weidenfeld and Nicolson, London

Creuzberger S. 1996, *Die sowjetische Besatzungsmacht und das politische System der SBZ*. Böhlau Verlag, Weimar, Cologne and Vienna

Cultural Life in the GDR. Review and Current Trends 1982, Panorama, Berlin (East)

'Das reale Bild war eben katastrophal!' Gespräch mit Gerhard Schürer 1991, *Deutschland Archiv* **25** (10): 1031–39

Deckname 'Lyrik'. Eine Dokumentation von Reiner Kunze 1990. Fischer Taschenbuch Verlag, Frankfurt/Main

Dennis M. 1988, *German Democratic Republic. Politics, Economics and Society*. Pinter, London and New York

Dennis M. 1993, *Social and Economic Modernization in Eastern Germany from Honecker to Kohl*. Pinter, London

Dennis M. 1998, 'Family Policy and Function in the German Democratic Republic', in Kolinsky E. (ed.), *Social Transformation and the Family in Post-Communist Germany*. Macmillan, Basingstoke and London, pp. 37–56

Deutscher Bundestag (ed.) 1995, *Enquete-Kommission 'Aufarbeitung von Geschichte und Folgen der SED-Diktatur in Deutschland'*, 9 vols in 18 parts. Nomos Verlag, Baden-Baden, and Suhrkamp Verlag, Frankfurt/Main

Diedrich T. 1991, *Der 17. Juni 1953 in der DDR. Bewaffnete Gewalt gegen das Volk*. Dietz [311]
Verlag, Berlin

Diedrich T., Ehlert H., Wenzke R. 1998, 'Die bewaffneten Organe der DDR im System von Partei, Staat und Landesverteidigung. Ein Überblick', in Diedrich T., Ehlert H., Wenzke R. (eds), *Im Dienste der Partei. Handbuch der bewaffneten Organe der DDR*. Ch. Links Verlag, Berlin, pp. 1–67

Diewald M. 1995, ' "Kollektiv", "Vitamin B" oder "Nische"? Persönliche Netzwerke in der DDR', in Huinink J., Meyer K. U., Diewald M., Solga H., Sørensen A., Trappe H. (eds), *Kollektiv und Eigensinn. Lebensverläufe in der DDR und danach*. Akademie Verlag, Berlin, pp. 223–60

Djilas M. 1962, *Conversations with Stalin* (trans. M. B. Petrovich). Rupert Hart-Davis, London

Dornheim A. 1995, *Politischer Umbruch in Erfurt 1989/90*. Böhlau Verlag, Weimar, Cologne and Vienna

Eisenfeld B. 1995, 'Die Ausreisebewegung – eine Erscheinungsform widerständigen Verhaltens', in Poppe U., Eckert R., Kowalczuk I.-S. (eds), *Zwischen Selbstbehauptung und Anpassung in der DDR*. Ch. Links Verlag, Berlin, pp. 192–223

Elbe F., Kiessler R. 1996, *A Round Table With Sharp Corners. The Diplomatic Path to German Unity*. Nomos Verlagsgesellschaft, Baden-Baden

Erler P. 1995, 'Das sowjetische Speziallager Nr. 3 in Hohenschönhausen (Mai 1945–Oktober 1946)', *Horch und Guck*, **4** (1): 37–44

Erler P., Laude H., Wilke M. (eds) 1994, *'Nach Hitler kommen wir'. Dokumente zur Programmatik der Moskauer KPD-Führung 1944/45 für Nachkriegsdeutschland*. Akademie Verlag, Berlin

Ernst Wollweber 1990, 'Aus Erinnerungen. Ein Porträt Walter Ulbrichts', *Beiträge zur Geschichte der Arbeiterbewegung*, **32** (3): 350–78

Falck U. 1998, *VEB Bordell. Geschichte der Prostitution in der DDR*. Ch. Links Verlag, Berlin

Falin V. 1995, *Politische Erinnerungen*. Droemersche Verlagsanstalt, Munich

Filitov A. M. 1995, 'Die Sowjetische Deutschlandplanung zwischen Parteiräson, Staatsinteresse und taktischem Kalkül', in Volkmann H.-E. (ed.), *Ende des Dritten Reiches – Ende des Zweiten Weltkriegs*. Piper, Munich and Zurich, pp. 117–39

Filmer W., Schwan H. 1991, *Opfer der Mauer. Die geheimen Protokolle des Todes*. C. Bertelsmann, Munich

Finn G. 1958, *Die politischen Häftlinge in der Sowjetzone 1945–1958*. Kampfgruppe gegen Unmenschlichkeit, Berlin-Nikolassee

Finn G. 1996, *Mauern – Gitter – Stacheldraht*. Westkreuz, Berlin

Finn G. 1998, 'Zwei Singularitäten', *Der Stacheldraht*, no. 5: 5–6

von Flocken J., Scholz M. F. 1994, *Ernst Wollweber. Saboteur – Minister – Unperson*. Aufbau-Verlag, Berlin

Förster P., Roski G. 1990, *DDR zwischen Wende und Wahl. Meinungsforscher analysieren den Umbruch*. LinksDruck Verlag, Berlin

[312]   Fricke K. W. 1979, *Politik und Justiz in der DDR. Zur Geschichte der politischen Verfolgung 1945–1968. Bericht und Dokumentation.* Verlag Wissenschaft und Politik, Cologne

Fricke K. W. 1991, *MfS intern. Macht, Strukturen, Auflösung der DDR-Staatssicherheit. Analyse und Dokumentation.* Verlag Wissenschaft und Politik, Cologne

Fricke K. W. 1992, 'The State Security Apparatus of the Former GDR and its Legacy', *Aussenpolitik. German Foreign Affairs Review*, **41** (4): 153–63

Fricke K. W. 1997, 'Ordinäre Abwehr – elitäre Aufklärung? Zur Rolle der Hauptverwaltung A im Ministerium für Staatssicherheit', *Aus Politik und Zeitgeschichte*, 5 December, no. 50: 1–16

Friedrich C. J., Brzezinski Z. K. 1956, *Totalitarian Dictatorship and Autocracy.* Praeger, New York, Washington and London

Friedrich U. W. 1994, 'Bürokratischer Totalitarismus – Zur Typologie des SED-Regimes', *German Studies Review*, **17** (Special Issue): 1–21

Friedrich W. 1990, 'Mentalitätswandlungen der Jugend in der DDR', *Aus Politik und Zeitgeschichte*, 13 April, no. 16–17: 25–37

Fulbrook M. 1995, *Anatomy of a Dictatorship. Inside the GDR 1949–1989.* Oxford University Press, Oxford

Gaddis J. L. 1997, *We Now Know. Rethinking Cold War History.* Oxford University Press, Oxford

Gedmin J. 1992, *The Hidden Hand. Gorbachev and the Collapse of East Germany.* AEI Press, Washington

Gelb N. 1986, *The Berlin Wall.* Michael Joseph, London

Gensicke T. 1992, 'Mentalitätswandel und Revolution. Wie sich die DDR-Bürger von ihrem System abwandten', *Deutschland Archiv*, **25** (12): 1266–83

Geppert D. 1996, *Störmanöver. Das 'Manifest der Opposition' und die Schließung des Ost-Berliner 'Spiegel'-Büros im Januar 1978.* Ch. Links Verlag, Berlin

Glaeßner G.-J. 1992, *The Unification Process in Germany. From Dictatorship to Democracy.* Pinter, London

Gniffke E. W. 1966, *Jahre mit Ulbricht.* Verlag Wissenschaft und Politik, Cologne

Goelkel R. F. 1994, 'The GDR Legacy and the German Protestant Church', *German Politics and Society*, no. 31: 84–108

Golz H.-G. 1995, '"Kopien und Nachaffer": Rechtsextreme Gewalt im letzten Jahrzehnt der DDR', in Helwig G. (ed.), *Rückblicke auf die DDR.* Verlag Wissenschaft und Politik, Cologne, pp. 208–19

Görtemaker M. 1994, *Unifying Germany 1989–1990.* Macmillan, Basingstoke and London

Grieder P. 1996, 'Eine unabhängige britische Sicht auf die Konflikte im SED-Politbüro 1956–1958', in Klein T., Otto W., Grieder P., *Visionen. Repression und Opposition in der SED (1949–1989).* Frankfurter Oder Editionen, Frankfurt/Oder, pp. 562–619

Grieder P. 1999, *The East German leadership 1946–1973.* Manchester University Press, Manchester and New York

Gromyko A. 1989, *Memories* (trans. H. Schuman). Arrow Books, London [313]

Gruneberg A. 1997, 'Antitotalitarianism Versus Antifascism – Two Legacies of the Past in Germany', *German Politics and Society*, **13** (2): 76–90

Habermas J. 1990, 'What Does Socialism Mean Today? The Rectifying Revolution and the Need for New Thinking', *New Left Review*, no. 183: 3–21

Hacker J. 1992, *Deutsche Irrtümer. Schönfärberei und Helfershelfer der SED-Diktatur im Westen*. Ullstein, Berlin and Frankfurt/Main

Haendke-Hoppe-Arndt M. 1996, 'Außenwirtschaft und innerdeutscher Handel', in Kuhrt E., Buck H. F., Holzweißig G. (eds), *Am Ende des realen Sozialismus (2). Die wirtschaftliche und ökologische Situation der DDR*. Leske + Budrich, Opladen, pp. 55–66

Hagen M. 1992, *DDR – Juni '53. Die erste Volkserhebung im Stalinismus*. Franz Steiner, Stuttgart

Havel V. 1989, *Living in Truth* (trans. A. G. Brain). Faber and Faber, London and Boston

Heidemeyer H. 1994, *Flucht und Zuwanderung aus der SBZ/DDR 1945/1949–1961. Die Flüchtlingspolitik der Bundesrepublik Deutschland bis zum Bau der Mauer*. Droste Verlag, Düsseldorf

Heitzer H. 1981, *GDR: An Historical Outline*. Dietz Verlag, Berlin (East)

Herf J. 1997, *Divided Memory. The Nazi Past in the Two Germanys*. Harvard University Press, Cambridge, Massachusetts, and London

Herrmann F.-J. 1996, *Der Sekretär des Generalsekretärs. Honeckers persönlicher Mitarbeiter über seinen Chef. Ein Gespräch mit Brigitte Zimmermann und Reiner Oschmann*. edition ost, Berlin

Hertle H.-H. 1992, 'Staatsbankrott. Der ökonomische Untergang des SED-Staats', *Deutschland Archiv*, **25** (10): 1019–30

Hertle H.-H. 1995, 'Die Diskussion der ökonomischen Krisen in der Führungsspitze der SED', in Pirker T., Lepsius M. R., Weinert R., Hertle H.-H. (eds), *Der Plan als Befehl und Fiktion. Wirtschaftsführung in der DDR*. Westdeutscher Verlag, Opladen, pp. 309–45

Hertle H.-H. 1996a, *Der Fall der Mauer. Die unbeabsichtigte Selbstauflösung des SED-Staates*. Westdeutscher Verlag, Opladen

Hertle H.-H. 1996b, *Chronik des Mauerfalls. Die dramatischen Ereignisse um den 9. November 1989*. Ch. Links Verlag, Berlin

Heydemann G., Beckmann C. 1997, 'Zwei Diktaturen in Deutschland', *Deutschland Archiv*, **30** (1): 12–40

Hilmer R., Köhler A. 1989, 'Die DDR läuft die Zukunft davon. Die Übersiedler-/Flüchtlingswelle im Sommer 1989', *Deutschland Archiv*, **22** (12): 1383–93

Hirschmann A. O. 1991, 'Exit, Voice and the Fate of the German Democratic Republic. An Essay in Conceptual History', *World Politics*, **45** (2): 173–202

Hoffmann D., Schmidt K.-H., Skyba P., (eds) 1993, *Die DDR vor dem Mauerbau. Dokumente zur Geschichte des anderen deutschen Staates 1949–1961*. Piper, Munich and Zurich

[314]   Hofmann M., Rink D. 1990, 'Der Leipziger Aufbruch 1989. Zur Genesis einer Heldenstadt', in Graebner W.-J., Heinze C., Pollack D. (eds), *Leipzig in Oktober. Kirchen und alternative Gruppen im Umbruch der DDR. Analysen zur Wende.* Wichern-Verlag, Berlin, pp. 114–22

Hofmann M., Rink D. 1993, 'Die Auflösung der ostdeutschen Arbeitermilieus', *Aus Politik und Zeitgeschichte*, 15 July, no. 26–7: 29–36

Hurwitz H. 1997, *Die Stalinisierung der SED. Zum Verlust von Freiräumen und sozialdemokratischer Identität in den Vorständen 1946–1949.* Westdeutscher Verlag, Opladen

Jäckel H. (ed.) 1980, *Ein Marxist in der DDR: Für Robert Havemann.* R. Piper, Munich and Zürich

Jäger M. 1982, *Kultur und Politik in der DDR. Ein historischer Abriß.* Verlag Wissenschaft und Politik, Cologne

Jäger M. 1994, *Kultur und Politik in der DDR 1949–1990.* Verlag Wissenschaft und Politik, Cologne

Jarausch K. H. 1994, *The Rush to German Unity.* Oxford University Press, New York and Oxford

Jarausch K. H. 1997, 'The German Democratic Republic as History in United Germany: Reflections on Public Debate and Academic Controversy', *German Politics and Society*, **15** (2): 33–48

Jarausch K. H., Gransow V. 1994, *Uniting Germany. Documents and Debates 1944–1993.* Berghahn Books, Providence and Oxford

Jesse E. 1994, 'War die DDR totalitär?' *Aus Politik und Zeitgeschichte*, 7 October, no. 40: 12–23

Jessen R. 1994, 'Professoren im Sozialismus. Aspekte des Strukturwandels der Hochschullehrschaft in der Ulbricht-Ära', in Kaelble H., Kocka J., Zwahr H. (eds), *Sozialgeschichte der DDR.* Klett-Cotta, Stuttgart, pp. 217–53

Jochum D. 1996, *'Das Politbüro auf der Anklagebank'.* Magnus Verlag, Berlin

Joppke C. 1995, *East German Dissidents and the Revolution of 1989. Social Movements in a Leninist Regime.* Macmillan, Basingstoke and London

Just G. 1990, *Zeuge in eigener Sache. Die fünfziger Jahre in der DDR.* Literaturverlag, Frankfurt/Main

Kaiser M. 1997, *Machtwechsel von Ulbricht zu Honecker: Funktionsmechanismen der SED-Diktatur in Konfliktsituationen 1962 bis 1972.* Akademie Verlag, Berlin

Karlsch R. 1993, *Allein bezahlt? Die Reparationsleistungen der SBZ/DDR 1945–53.* Ch. Links Verlag, Berlin

Keiderling G. (ed.) 1993, *'Gruppe Ulbricht' in Berlin April bis Juni 1945. Von den Vorbereitungen im Sommer 1944 bis zur Wiedergründung der KPD im Juni 1945. Eine Dokumentation.* Berlin Verlag Arno Spitz, Berlin

Kilian A. 1993, 'Die "Mühlberg-Akten" im Zusammenhang mit dem System der Speziallager des NKWD der UdSSR', *Deutschland Archiv*, **26** (10): 1138–58

Kilian A. 1997, 'Stalins Prophylaxe. Maßnahmen der sowjetischen Sicherheitsorgane im besetzen Deutschland', *Deutschland Archiv*, **30** (4): 531–64

Klein T. 1996, 'Parteisäuberungen und Widerstand in der SED', in Klein T., Otto [315]
W., Grieder P., *Visionen. Repression und Opposition in der SED (1949–1989)*. Frankfurter Oder Editionen, Frankfurt/Oder, pp. 9–135

Kleines politisches Wörterbuch. 1978 (3rd edn). Dietz Verlag, Berlin (East)

Kleinschmid H. 1996, 'Vor 20 Jahren: Ausbürgerung von Wolfgang Biermann', *Deutschland Archiv*, **29** (6): 913–17

Klessmann C. 1998, *Zeitgeschichte in Deutschland nach dem Ende des Ost-West-Konflikts*. Klartext Verlag, Essen

Klessmann C., Sabrow M. 1997, 'Contemporary History in Germany after 1989', *Contemporary European History*, **6** (2): 221–43

Klinger F. 1985, 'Soziale Statik und Dynamik in der DDR: zum Leistungsverhalten von Industriearbeiterschaft und wissenschaftlich-technischer Intelligenz', *Aus Politik und Zeitgeschichte*, 16 November, no. 46–7: 19–35

Klonovsky M., von Flocken J. 1991, *Stalins Lager in Deutschland 1945–1960. Dokumentation, Zeugenberichte*. Deutscher Taschenbuch Verlag, Munich

Knabe H. 1990, 'Politische Opposition in der DDR. Ursprünge, Programmatik, Perspektiven', *Aus Politik und Zeitgeschichte*, 22 January, no. 1–2: 21–32

Knabe H. 1993, 'Die geheimen Lager der Stasi', *Aus Politik und Zeitgeschichte*, 22 January, no. 4: 22–34

Knabe H. 1997, 'Die Stasi als Problem des Westens', *Aus Politik und Zeitgeschichte*, 5 December, no. 50: 17–34

Knecht W. Ph 1999, 'Die schwierigen Wandlungen der KJS zu Elitenschulen des Sports', *Deutschland Archiv*, **32** (1): 74–9

Knoll V., Kölm L. (eds) 1993, *Der Fall Berija. Protokoll einer Abrechnung. Das Plenum des ZK der KPdSU Juli 1953. Stenographischer Bericht*. Aufbau Taschenbuch Verlag, Berlin

Kocka J. 1995, *Vereinigungskrise. Zur Geschichte der Gegenwart*. Vandenhoeck and Rupprecht, Göttingen

Kocka J., Sabrow M. (eds) 1994, *Die DDR als Geschichte. Fragen – Hypothesen – Perspektiven*. Akademie Verlag, Berlin

Koop V. 1996, *'Den Gegner vernichten'. Die Grenzversicherung der DDR*. Bouvier Verlag, Bonn

Köhler A., Ronge V. 1984, '"Einmal BRD-einfach": die DDR-Ausreisewelle im Frühjahr 1984', *Deutschland Archiv*, **17** (12): 1280–86

Kopstein J. 1994, 'Ulbricht Embattled: The Quest for Socialist Modernity in the Light of New Sources', *Europe-Asia Studies*, **46** (4): 597–615

Korte K.-R. 1994, *Die Chance genutzt? Die Politik zur Einheit Deutschlands*. Campus Verlag, Frankfurt/Main and New York

Kotschemassow W. 1994, *Meine letzte Mission: Fakten, Erinnerungen, Überlegungen*. Dietz Verlag, Berlin

Kowalczuk I.-S. 1995, 'Von der Freiheit, Ich zu sagen. Widerständiges Verhalten in der DDR', in Poppe U., Eckert R., Kowalczuk I.-S. (eds), *Zwischen Selbstbehauptung und Anpassung*. Ch. Links Verlag, Berlin, pp. 85–115

[316] Krakat K. 1990, 'Schlußbilanz der elektronischen Datenverarbeitung in der früheren DDR', *FS-Analysen*, **17** (5): 1–59

Krakat K. 1996, 'Probleme der DDR-Industrie im letzten Fünfjahrplanzeitraum (1986–1989/1990)', in Kuhrt E., Buck H. F., Holweißig G. (eds), *Am Ende des realen Sozialismus (2). Die wirtschaftliche und ökologische Situation in den achtziger Jahren*. Opladen, Leske + Budrich, pp. 137–72

Krenz E. 1990, *Wenn Mauern fallen*. Paul Neff Verlag, Vienna

Krusch H.-J., Malycha A. 1990, *Einheitsdrang oder Zwangsvereinigung? Die Sechziger Konferenz von KPD und SPD 1945 und 1946*. Dietz Verlag, Berlin

Küchenmeister D. (ed.) 1993, *Honecker-Gorbatschow: Vieraugengespräche*. Dietz Verlag, Berlin

Kuhn E. 1992, *Der Tag der Entscheidung. Leipzig, 9. Oktober 1989*. Ullstein, Berlin and Frankfurt/Main

Kuhn E. 1993, *Gorbatschow und die deutsche Einheit. Aussagen wichtigsten russischen und deutschen Beteiligten*. Bouvier Verlag, Bonn

Kühnel W., Sallmon-Metzner C. 1991, 'Grüne Partei und Grüne Liga', in Müller-Enbergs H., Schulz M., Wielgohs J. (eds), *Von der Illegalität ins Parlament. Werdegang und Konzepte der neuen Bürgerbewegungen*. Ch. Links Verlag, Berlin, pp. 166–220

Kusch G., Montag R., Specht G., Wetzker K. 1991, *Schlußbilanz-DDR. Fazit einer verfehlten Wirtschafts- und Sozialpolitik*. Duncker and Humblot, Berlin

Kusmin I. 1995, 'Die Verschwörung gegen Honecker', *Deutschland Archiv*, **28** (3): 286–90

Lapp P. J. 1990, *Die DDR geht – die Länder kommen*. Friedrich-Ebert Stiftung, Bonn-Bad-Godesberg

Lapp P. J. 1998, 'Die Grenztruppen der DDR (1961–1989)', in Diedrich T., Ehlert H., Wenzke R. (eds), *Im Dienste der Partei. Handbuch der bewaffneten Organe der DDR*. Ch. Links Verlag, Berlin, pp. 225–52

Laqueur W. 1994, *The Dream That Failed*. Oxford University Press, New York and Oxford

Larres K. 1994, 'Neutralisierung oder Westintegration? Churchill, Adenauer, die USA und der 17. Juni 1953', *Deutschland Archiv*, **27** (6): 568–85

Lemke M. 1995a, *Die Berlinkrise 1958 bis 1963. Handlungsspielräume der SED im Ost-West-Konflikt*. Akademie Verlag, Berlin

Lemke M. 1995b, 'Kampagne gegen Bonn. Die Systemkrise der DDR und die West-Propaganda der SED 1960–1963', *Vierteljahreshefte für Zeitgeschichte*, **41** (2): 153–74

Lemke M. 1997, 'Als Otto Grotewohl noch von der Einheit der deutschen Nation sprach', *Das Parlament*, 8–15 August: 17

Leonhard W. 1979, *Child of the Revolution* (trans. C. M. Woodhouse). Ink Links, London

Leptin G., Melzer M. 1978, *Economic Reform in East German Industry*. Oxford University Press, Oxford, London and New York

Lindenberger T. 1999, 'Die Diktatur der Grenzen. Zur Einleitung', in Lindenberger [317]
T. (ed.), *Herrschaft und Eigen-Sinn in der Diktatur. Studien zur Gesellschaftsgeschichte der DDR*. Böhlau Verlag, Cologne, Weimar and Vienna, pp. 13–44

Linz J. J., Stepan A. 1996, *Problems of Democratic Transition and Consolidation. Southern Europe, South America, and Post-Communist Europe*. Johns Hopkins University Press, Baltimore and London

Loth W. 1994, *Stalins ungeliebtes Kind. Warum Moskau die DDR nicht wollte*. Rowohlt, Berlin

Löwenthal F. 1950, *News from Soviet Germany* (trans. E. Fitzgerald). Victor Gollancz, London

Lüdtke A. 1998, 'Die DDR als Geschichte. Zur Geschichtsschreibung über die DDR', *Aus Politik und Zeitgeschichte*, 28 August, no. 36: 3–16

Ludz P. C. 1970, *The German Democratic Republic from the sixties to the seventies*. AMS, New York

Mählert U. 1998a, *Kleine Geschichte der DDR*. Verlag C. H. Beck, Munich

Mählert U. 1998b, '"Die Partei hat immer recht!" Parteisäuberungen als Kaderpolitik in der SED (1948–1953)', in Weber H., Mählert U. (eds), *Terror. Stalinistische Parteisäuberungen 1936–1953*. Schöningh, Paderborn and Munich, pp. 351–457

Malycha A. 1993, 'Die SED auf dem Weg zur Staatspartei; Wandlungen in ihrem Charakter und Selbstverständnis', in Scherstjanoi E. (ed.), *'Provisorium für längstens ein Jahr'. Protokoll des Kollegiums Die Gründung der DDR*. Akademie Verlag, Berlin, pp. 279–85

Malycha A. 1996, *Partei von Stalins Gnaden? Die Entwicklung der SED zur Partei neuen Typs in den Jahren 1946 bis 1950*. Dietz Verlag, Berlin

Maximytschew I. F., Hertle H.-H .1994, 'Die Maueröffnung. Eine russisch-deutsche Trilogie. Teil 1', *Deutschland Archiv*, **27** (11): 1145–58

McAdams A. J. 1996, 'The Honecker Trial: The East German Past and the German Future', *Review of Politics*, **58** (1): 53–80

McCardle A. W., Boenau A. B. (eds) 1984, *East Germany. A New Nation Under Socialism?* University Press of America, Lanham, New York and London

McCauley M. 1983, *The German Democratic Republic since 1945*. Macmillan, London and Basingstoke

McElvoy A. 1992, *The Saddled Cow. East Germany's Life and Legacy*. Faber and Faber, London and Boston

Meckel M., Gutzeit M. 1994, *Opposition in der DDR. Zehn Jahre kirchliche Friedensarbeit – kommentierte Quellentexte*. Bund-Verlag, Cologne

Merson A. 1985, *Communist Resistance in Nazi Germany*. Lawrence and Wishart, London

Meuschel S. 1992, *Legitimation und Parteiherrschaft in der DDR. Zum Paradox von Stabilität und Revolution in der DDR 1945–1989*. Suhrkamp Verlag, Frankfurt/Main

Michnik A. 1985, *Letters from Prison and Other Essays* (trans. M. Latynski). University of California Press, Berkeley, Los Angeles and London

[318]   Mittag G. 1991, *Um jeden Preis. Im Spannungsfeld zweier Systeme.* Aufbau-Verlag, Berlin and Weimar

Mitter A. 1991, 'Die Ereignisse im Juni und Juli 1953 in der DDR. Aus den Akten des Ministeriums für Staatssicherheit', *Aus Politik und Zeitgeschichte*, 25 January, no. 5: 31–41

Mitter A., Wolle S. 1990, *Ich liebe euch doch alle! Befehle und Lageberichte des MfS Januar– November 1989.* BasisDruck, Berlin

Mitter A., Wolle S. 1993, *Untergang auf Raten. Unbekannte Kapitel der DDR-Geschichte.* Bertelsmann, Munich

Möller H. 1994, 'Die Geschichte des Nationalsozialismus und der DDR: ein (un)möglicher Vergleich?' in Suhl K. (ed.), *Vergangenheitsbewältigung 1945 und 1989.* Verlag Volk und Welt, Berlin, pp. 127–38

Müller K.-D. 1997, '"Jeder kriminelle Mörder ist mir lieber . . ." Haftbedingungen für politische Häftlinge in der Sowjetischen Besatzungszone und der Deutschen Demokratischen Republik und ihre Veränderungen von 1945–1989', in Gedenkstätte für die Opfer politischer Gewalt Moritzplatz Magdeburg (ed.), *'Die Vergangenheit läßt uns nicht los . . .' Haftbedingungen politischer Gefangener in der SBZ / DDR und deren gesundheitliche Folgen.* Oktoberdruck, Berlin, pp. 7–127

Müller-Enbergs H. 1991, *Der Fall Rudolf Herrnstadt. Tauwetterpolitik vor dem 17. Juni.* LinksDruck Verlag, Berlin

Müller-Enbergs H. 1995, 'Warum wird einer IM? Zur Motivation bei der inoffiziellen Zusammenarbeit mit dem Staatssicherheitsdienst', in Behnke K., Fuchs J. (eds), *Zersetzung der Seele. Psychologie und Psychiatrie im Dienst der Stasi.* Rotbuch Verlag, Hamburg, pp. 102–29

Müller-Enbergs H. 1996, *Inoffizielle Mitarbeiter des Ministeriums für Staatssicherheit. Richtlinien und Durchführungsbestimmungen.* Ch. Links Verlag, Berlin

Murphy D. E., Kondrashev S. A., Bailey G. 1997, *Battleground Berlin. CIA vs KGB in the Cold War.* Yale University Press, New Haven and London

Naimark N. M. 1995, *The Russians in Germany. A History of the Soviet Zone of Occupation.* Harvard University Press, Cambridge, Massachusetts, and London

Nakath D. 1995, *Erfurt und Kassel* hefte zur ddr-geschichte, no. 24, 'Helle Panke', Berlin

Nakath D., Stephan G.-R. (eds) 1995, *Von Hubertusstock nach Bonn. Eine dokumentierte Geschichte der deutsch-deutschen Beziehungen auf höchster Ebene 1980–1987.* Dietz Verlag, Berlin

Nakath D., Stephan G.-R. (eds) 1996, *Countdown zur Deutschen Einheit. Eine dokumentierte Geschichte der deutsch-deutschen Beziehungen 1987–1990.* Dietz Verlag, Berlin

Nakath D., Stephan G.-R. 1999, 'Aufstieg und Fall des Herbert Häber', *Deutschland Archiv*, **32** (2): 199–209

Narinskii M. N. 1996, 'The Soviet Union and the Berlin Crisis, 1948–9', in Gori F., Pons S. (eds), *The Soviet Union and Europe in the Cold War, 1949–53.* Macmillan, Basingstoke and London, and St Martin's Press, New York, pp. 57–75

Naumann G., Trümpler E. 1990, *Von Ulbricht zu Honecker. 1970 – ein Krisenjahr der DDR*. Dietz Verlag, Berlin [319]

Neske N. 1998, 'Versorgung, Krankheit, Tod in den Speziallagern', in von Plato A. (ed.), *Sowjetische Speziallager in Deutschland 1945 bis 1950. Studien und Berichte.* Akademie Verlag, Berlin, pp. 189–223

Neubert E. 1991, 'Protestantische Kultur und DDR-Revolution', *Aus Politik und Zeitgeschichte*, 3 May, no. 19: 21–9

Neubert E. 1993, *Vergebung oder Weißwäscherei. Zur Aufarbeitung des Stasiproblems in den Kirchen.* Herderbücherei, Freiburg im Breisgau

Neubert E. 1997, *Geschichte der Opposition in der DDR 1949–1989.* Ch. Links Verlag, Berlin

Neue Gesellschaft für Bildende Kunst (ed.) 1996, *Wunderwirtschaft. DDR-Konsumkultur in den 60er Jahren.* Böhlau-Verlag, Cologne, Weimar and Vienna

Niemann H. 1993, *Meinungsforschung in der DDR. Die geheimen Berichte des Instituts für Meinungsforschung an das Politbüro der SED.* Bund-Verlag, Cologne

Niemann H. 1995, *Hinterm Zaun. Politische Kultur und Meinungsforschung in der DDR – die geheimen Berichte an das Politbüro der SED.* edition ost, Berlin

von Nesselrode F. 1963, *Germany's Other Half.* Abelard-Schuman, London, New York and Toronto

Oleschinski B., Pampel B. 1997, *'Feindliche Elemente sind in Gewahrsam zu halten'. Die sowjetische Speziallager Nr. 8 und 10 in Torgau 1945–1948.* Gustav Kiepenheuer Verlag, Leipzig

Opp K.-D., Voß P., Gern C. 1995, *Origins of a Spontaneous Revolution. East Germany, 1989.* University of Michigan Press, Ann Arbor

Otto W. 1991, 'Sowjetische Deutschlandnote 1952. Stalin und die DDR. Bisher unveröffentliche handschriftliche Notizen Wilhelm Piecks', *Beiträge zur Geschichte der Arbeiterbewegung*, **33** (3): 374–5

Philipsen D.1993, *We Were the People. Voices from East Germany's Revolutionary Autumn of 1989.* Duke University Press, Durham, N. C., and London

Pirker T., Lepsius R., Weinert R., Hertle H.-H. 1995, *Der Plan als Befehl und Fiktion. Wirtschaftsführung in der DDR. Gespräche und Analysen.* Westdeutscher Verlag, Opladen

von Plato A. 1998, 'Zur Geschichte des sowjetischen Speziallagersystems in Deutschland. Einführung', in von Plato A. (ed.), *Sowjetische Speziallager in Deutschland 1945 bis 1950. Studien und Berichte.* Akademie Verlag, Berlin, pp. 19–75

Plenzdorf U. 1979, *The New Sufferings of Young W* (trans. K. P. Wilcox). Frederick Ungar, New York

Pollack D. 1990, 'Außenseiter oder Repräsentanten? Zur Rolle der politisch alternativen Gruppen im gesellschaftlichen Umbruchsprozeß der DDR', *Deutschland Archiv*, **23** (8): 216–23

Pollack D. 1993, 'Religion und gesellschaftlicher Wandel. Zur Rolle der evangelischen Kirche im Prozeß des gesellschaftlichen Umbruchs', in Joas H.,

[320]   Kohli M. (eds), *Der Zusammenbruch der DDR*. Suhrkamp Verlag, Frankfurt/Main, pp. 246–66

Poltergeist im Politbüro. Siegfried Prokop im Gespräch mit Alfred Neumann 1996, Frankfurter Oder Editionen, Frankfurt/Oder

Poppe U. 1995, '"Der Weg ist das Ziel". Zum Selbstverständnis und der politischen Rolle oppositioneller Gruppen der achtziger Jahre', in Poppe U., Eckert R., Kowalczuk I.-S. (eds), *Zwischen Selbstbehauptung und Anpassung. Formen des Widerstandes und der Oppostion in der DDR*. Ch. Links Verlag, Berlin, pp. 244–72

Poppe U., Eckert R., Kowalczuk I.-S. 1995, 'Opposition, Widerstand und widerständiges Verhalten in der DDR. Forschungsstand – Grundlinien – Probleme', in Poppe U., Eckert R., Kowalczuk I.-S. (eds), *Zwischen Selbstbehauptung und Anpassung. Formen des Widerstandes und der Opposition in der DDR*. Ch. Links Verlag, Berlin, pp. 9–26

Potthoff H. 1995, *'Koalition der Vernunft'. Deutschlandpolitik in den 80er Jahren*. Deutscher Taschenbuch Verlag, Munich

Prieß B. 1992, *Unschuldig in den Todeslagern des NKWD 1946–1954. Torgau, Bautzen, Sachsenhausen, Waldheim*. Author's own publication, Calw

Prieß L., Kural V., Wilke M. 1996, *Die SED und der 'Prager Frühling' 1968. Politik gegen einen 'Sozialismus mit menschlichem Antlitz'*. Akademie Verlag, Berlin

Priller E. 1999, 'Demokratieentwicklung und gesellschaftliche Mitwirkung', in Winkler G. (ed.), *Sozialreport 1999. Daten und Fakten zur sozialen Lage in den neuen Bundesländern*. Verlag am Turm, Berlin, pp. 327–77

Probst L. 1996, 'The Round Table Model. Reflections on a Political Experiment', in Gerber M., Woods R. (eds), *Studies in GDR Culture and Society 14/15. Changing Identities in East Germany*. University Press of America, Lanham, New York and Boston, pp. 169–78

Protokoll der Verhandlungen des V. Parteitages der Sozialistischen Einheitspartei Deutschlands 10. bis 16. Juli 1958 in der Werner Seelenbinder-Halle zu Berlin 1959. Dietz Verlag, Berlin (East)

Przybylski P. 1991, *Tatort Politbüro. Die Akte Honecker*. Rowohlt, Berlin

Przybylski P. 1992, *Tatort Politbüro. Band 2: Honecker, Mittag und Schalck-Golodkowski*. Rowohlt, Berlin

Pulzer P. 1995, *German Politics, 1945–1995*. Oxford University Press, Oxford

Rehlinger L. A. 1991, *Freikauf. Die Geschäfte der DDR mit politisch Verfolgten 1963–1989*. Ullstein, Frankfurt/Main

Reich J. 1990, 'Reflections on becoming an East German dissident, on losing the Wall and a country', in Prins G. (ed.), *Spring in Winter. The 1989 revolutions*. Manchester University Press, Manchester, pp. 67–97

Rein G. 1989, *Die Opposition in der DDR: Entwürfe für einen anderen Sozialismus*. Wichern-Verlag, Berlin

Rein G. 1990, *Die protestantische Revolution 1987–1990. Ein deutsches Lesebuch*. Wichern-Verlag, Berlin

Reuth R. G. 1992, *IM Sekretär. Die 'Gauck-Recherche' und die Dokumente zum 'Fall Stolpe'*. Ullstein, Berlin [321]

Rexin M. 1993, 'Der 16. und 17. Juni in West-Berlin', *Deutschland Archiv*, **25** (8): 985–94

Richie A. 1998, *Faust's Metropolis. A History of Berlin*. HarperCollins, London

Richter J. 1993, 'Re-examining Soviet Policy Towards Germany in 1953', *Europe-Asia Studies*, **45** (4): 671–91

Riecker A., Schwarz A., Schneider D. 1990, *Stasi intern. Gespräche mit ehemaligen MfS-Angehörigen*. Forum Verlag, Leipzig

Roesler J. 1991, 'The Rise and Fall of the Planned Economy in the German Democratic Republic, 1945–1989', *German History*, **9** (1): 46–61

Roesler J. 1993a, *Das Neue Ökonomische System − Dekorations- oder Paradigmwechsel?* hefte zur ddr-geschichte, no. 3, 'Helle-Panke', Berlin

Roesler J. 1993b, 'Der Einfluß der Außenhandelspolitik auf die Beziehungen DDR-Bundesrepublik. Die achtziger Jahre', *Deutschland Archiv*, **26** (5): 558–72

Sa'adah A. 1998, *Germany's Second Chance. Trust, Justice, and Democratization*. Harvard University Press, Cambridge, Massachusetts, and London

Sandford J. 1983, *The Sword and the Ploughshare: Autonomous Peace Initiatives in East Germany*. Merlin Press and European Nuclear Disarmament, London

Sarotte M. E. 1993, 'Elite Intransigence and the End of the Berlin Wall', *German Politics*, **2** (2): 270–87

Schabowski G. 1990, *Das Politbüro. Ende eines Mythos. Eine Befragung*. Rowohlt Taschenbuch Verlag, Reinbek bei Hamburg

Schabowski G. 1992, *Der Absturz*. Rowohlt Taschenbuch Verlag, Reinbek bei Hamburg

Schell M., Kalinka W. 1991, *Stasi und kein Ende. Die Personen und Fakten*. Ullstein, Frankfurt/Main and Berlin

Scherstjanoi E. 1994, 'Die DDR im Frühjahr 1952. Sozialismuslosung und Kollektivierungsbeschluß in sowjetischer Perspektive', *Deutschland Archiv*, **27** (4): 354–63

Schirdewan K. 1994, *Aufstand gegen Ulbricht. Im Kampf um politische Kurskorrektur gegen stalinistische, dogmatische Politik*. Aufbau Taschenbuch Verlag, Berlin

Schmidt W. 1996, *Das Zwei-Nationen-Konzept der SED und sein Scheitern. Nationsdiskussion in der DDR in den 70er und 80er Jahren* hefte zur ddr-geschichte, no. 38, 'Helle Panke', Berlin

Schneider G. 1996, 'Lebensstandard und Versorgungslage', in Kuhrt E., Buck H. F., Holzweißig G. (eds), *Am Ende des realen Sozialismus (2). Die wirtschaftliche und ökologische Situation der DDR in den achtziger Jahren*. Opladen, Leske + Budrich, pp. 111–30

Schroeder K. 1998, *Der SED-Staat. Partei, Staat und Gesellschaft 1949–1990*. Munich and Vienna, Carl Hauser Verlag

Schulz D. 1993, *Der Weg in die Krise 1953* hefte zur ddr-geschichte, no. 6, 'Helle Panke', Berlin

[322] Schulz M. 1991, 'Neues Forum', in Müller-Enbergs H., Schulz M., Wielgohs J. (eds), *Von der Illegalität ins Parlament. Werdegang und Konzept der neuen Bürgerbewegungen*. Linksdruck Verlag, Berlin, pp. 11–104

Schürer G. 1996, *Gewagt und verloren. Eine deutsche Biographie*. Frankfurter Oder Editionen, Frankfurt/Oder

Schürers Krisen-Analyse 1992, *Deutschland Archiv*, **25** (10): 1112–20

Schwan H. 1997, *Erich Mielke. Der Mann, der die Stasi war*. Droemer Knaur, Munich

Schwarze H. W. 1973, *The GDR today. Life in the 'other' Germany*. Oswald Wolf, London

Schweigler G. 1975, *National Consciousness in Divided Germany*. Sage, London

Shears D. 1970, *The Ugly Frontier*. Chatto and Windus, London

Sills D. (ed.) 1968, *International Encyclopedia of the Social Sciences*, vol. 9. Collier, New York

Simmons M. 1989, *The Unloved Country. A Portrait of East Germany Today*. Abacus, London

Smith H. W. 1991, 'Socialism and nationalism in the East German Revolution, 1989–1990, *East European Politics and Society*, **5** (2): 234–46

Spittmann I. 1984, *Der 17. Juni im Wandel der Legenden*. Verlag Wissenschaft und Politik, Cologne

Staadt J. 1996, 'Walter Ulbrichts letzter Machtkampf?' *Deutschland Archiv*, **29** (5): 686–700

Staritz D. 1995, *Die Gründung der DDR. Von der sowjetischen Besatzungsherrschaft zum sozialistischen Staat* (3rd edn). Deutscher Taschenbuch Verlag, Munich

Staritz D. 1996, *Geschichte der DDR* (2nd edn). Suhrkamp Verlag, Frankfurt/Main

Statistisches Amt der DDR (ed.) 1990, *Statistisches Jahrbuch der Deutschen Demokratischen Republik '90*. Rudolf Haufe Verlag, Berlin

Statistisches Bundesamt (ed.) 1992, *Datenreport 1992. Zahlen und Fakten über die Bundesrepublik Deutschland*. Bundesanstalt für politische Bildung, Bonn

Steele J. 1977, *Socialism with a German Face: The State that came in from the Cold*. Jonathan Cape, London

Steininger R. 1984, 'Ein vereintes, unabhängiges Deutschland? Winston Churchill, der Kalte Krieg und die deutsche Frage im Jahre 1953', *Militärgeschichtliche Mitteilungen*, **36** (2): 105–44

Stelkens J. 1997, 'Machtwechsel in Ost-Berlin. Der Sturz Walter Ulbrichts', *Vierteljahrshefte für Zeitgeschichte*, **45** (4): 503–33

Stephan G.-R. 1994, *'Vorwärts immer, rückwärts nimmer!' Interne Dokumente zum Verfall von SED und DDR 1988/89*. Dietz Verlag, Berlin

Stephan G.-R. 1995, '"Wir brauchen Perestroika und Glasnost für die DDR". Zur Reflexion des Zustands der Gesellschaft durch die Leipziger Jugendforschung', *Deutschland Archiv*, **28** (7): 721–33

Stöckigt R. 1990, 'Ein Dokument von großer historischer Bedeutung vom Mai 1953', *Beiträge zur Geschichte der Arbeiterbewegung*, **32** (5): 648–54

Stulz-Herrnstadt N. (ed.) 1990, *Das Herrnstadt-Dokument, das Politbüro der SED und die* [323]
Geschichte des 17. Juni 1953. Rowohlt Taschenbuch Verlag, Reinbek bei Hamburg

Suckut S. 1994, 'Die DDR-Blockparteien im Lichte neuer Quellen', in Weber J. (ed.)
Der SED-Staat: Neues über eine vergangene Diktatur. Olzog Verlag, Munich, pp. 99–107

Suckut S. 1996, 'Die Bedeutung der Akten des Staatssicherheitsdienstes für die
Erforschung der DDR-Geschichte', in Helwig G. (ed.) *Rückblicke auf die DDR.*
Verlag Wissenschaft und Politik, Opladen, pp. 67–74

Sudaplatov P., Sudaplatov A. 1994, *Special Tasks. Memoirs of an Unwanted Witness – A
Soviet Spymaster.* Little, Brown and Company, London

Süß W. 1997a, 'Politische Taktik und institutioneller Zerfall. MfS und SED in der
Schlußphase des Regimes', in Suckut S., Süß W. (eds), *Staatspartei und Staatssicherheit.
Zum Verhältnis von SED und MfS.* Ch. Links Verlag, Berlin, pp. 249–69

Süß W. 1997b, 'Zum Verhältnis von SED und Staatssicherheit', in Herbst A.,
Stephan G.-R., Winkler J. (eds), *Die SED. Geschichte-Organisation-Politik. Ein
Handbuch.* Dietz Verlag, Berlin, pp. 215–40

Teltschik H. 1991, *329 Tage. Innenansichten der Einigung.* Siedler Verlag, Berlin

Templin W., Weißhuhn R. 1991, 'Initiative Frieden und Menschenrechte. Die erste
unabhängige DDR-Oppositionsgruppe', in Müller-Enbergs H., Schulz M.,
Wielgohs J. (eds), *Von der Illegalität ins Parlament. Werdegang und Konzepte der neuen
Bürgerbewegungen.* Ch. Links Verlag, Berlin, pp. 148–65

Thomaneck J. K. A., Mellis J. (eds) 1989, *Politics, Society and Government in the German
Democratic Republic. Basic Documents.* Berg, Oxford, New York and Munich

Torpey J. C. 1995, *Intellectuals, Socialism and Dissent. The East German Opposition and Its
Legacy.* University of Minnesota Press, Minnesota and London

Ulbricht W. 1968, *On Questions of Socialist Construction in the GDR.* Verlag Zeit im
Bild, Dresden

Uschner M. 1993, *Die zweite Etage. Funktionsweise eines Machtapparates.* Dietz Verlag,
Berlin

Vinke H. (ed.) 1993, *Akteneinsicht Christa Wolf. Zerrspiegel und Dialog. Eine
Dokumentation.* Luchterhand Literaturverlag, Hamburg

Vollnhals C. 1994, 'Das Ministerium für Staatssicherheit. Ein Instrument totalitärer
Herrschaftsübung', in Kaelbe H., Kocka J., Zwahr H. (eds), *Sozialgeschichte der
DDR.* Klett-Cotta, Stuttgart, pp. 498–518

Vollnhals C. 1996, 'Die kirchenpolitische Abteilung des Ministeriums für
Staatssicherheit', in Vollnhals C. (ed.), *Die Kirchenpolitik von SED und
Staatssicherheit. Eine Zwischenbilanz.* Ch. Links Verlag, Berlin, pp. 79–119

Vollnhals C. 1998, *Der Fall Havemann. Ein Lehrstück politischer Justiz.* Ch. Links Verlag,
Berlin

Volze A. 1996, 'Ein großer Bluff. Die Westverschuldung der DDR', *Deutschland
Archiv,* **29** (5): 701–13

Vortmann H. 1990, 'DDR: Verteilungswirkungen von Verbraucherpreissubven-
tionen und indirekten Steuern', *FS-Analysen,* **17** (2): 29–50

[324]   Wagner H. 1993, 'Kirchen, Staat und politisch alternative Gruppen', in Dähn H. (ed.), *Die Rolle der Kirchen in der DDR. Eine erste Bilanz.* Olzog Verlag, Munich, pp. 104–26

Wagner M. 1998, *DDR-Witze: Walter schützt vor Torheit nicht. Erich währt am längsten.* Dietz Verlag, Berlin

Waibel H. 1996, *Rechtsextremismus in der DDR bis 1989.* PapyRossa Verlag, Cologne

Wallace I. 1994, 'Writers and the Stasi', *German Monitor*, no. 33: 115–28

Walther J. 1996, *Sicherungsbereich Literatur. Schriftsteller und Staatssicherheit in der Deutschen Demokratischen Republik.* Ch. Links Verlag, Berlin

Weber H. 1985, *Geschichte der DDR.* Deutscher Taschenbuch Verlag, Munich

Weber H. 1990, *'Weiße Flecken' in der Geschichte. Die KPD-Opfer der Stalinschen Säuberungen und ihre Rehabilitierung.* LinksDruck Verlag, Berlin

Weber H. 1991, *DDR. Grundriß der Geschichte 1945–1990* (revised edn). Fackelträger, Hannover

Weber H. 1993, *Die DDR 1945–1990* (2nd edn). R Oldenbourg Verlag, Munich

Wegmann B. 1997, *Entstehung und Vorläufer des Staatsicherheitsdienstes der DDR*, hefte zur ddr-geschichte, no. 46, 'Helle Panke', Berlin

Wendel E. 1996, *Ulbricht als Richter und Henker – Stalinistische Justiz im Parteiauftrag.* Aufbau-Verlag, Berlin

Wendt H. 1991, 'Die deutsch-deutschen Wanderungen – Bilanz einer 40jährigen Geschichte von Flucht und Ausreise', *Deutschland Archiv*, **24** (4): 386–95

Wengst U. 1993, 'Der Aufstand am 17. Juni 1953 in der DDR Aus den Stimmungsberichten der Kreis- und Bezirksverbände der Ost-CDU im Juni und Juli 1953', *Vierteljahrshefte für Zeitgeschichte*, **41** (2): pp. 277–321

Wenzel S. 1996, 'Die DDR-Wirtschaft im Spannungsfeld zwischen objektiven Bedingungen und Politik der SED', in Elm L., Keller D., Mocek R. (eds), *Ansichten zur Geschichte der DDR*, vol. 6. Verlag Matthias Kirchner, Eggersdorf, pp. 89–164

Wenzel S. 1998, *Plan und Wirklichkeit. Zur DDR-Ökonomie. Dokumentation und Erinnerungen.* Scriptura Mercaturae Verlag, St. Katherinen

Wenzke R. 1995, *Die NVA und der Prager Frühling 1968. Die Rolle Ulbrichts und der DDR-Streitkräfte bei der Niederschlagung der tschechoslowakischen Reformbewegung.* Ch. Links Verlag, Berlin

Werkentin F. 1995, *Politische Strafjustiz in der Ära Ulbricht.* Ch. Links Verlag, Berlin

Werkentin F. 1997, 'Zur Dimension politischer Inhaftierungen in der DDR 1949–1989', in Gedenkstätte für die Opfer politischer Gewalt Moritzplatz Magdeburg (ed.), *'Die Vergangenheit läßt uns nicht los . . .' Haftbedingungen politischer Gefangener in der SBZ/DDR und deren gesundheitliche Folgen.* Oktoberdruck, Berlin, pp. 129–43

Wettig G. 1993, 'Zum Stand der Forschung über Berijas Deutschland-Politik im Frühjahr 1953', *Deutschland Archiv*, **26** (6): 674–82

Wettig G. 1994, 'Die KPD als Instrument der sowjetischen Deutschland-Politik. Festlegungen 1949 und Implementierung 1952', *Deutschland Archiv*, **27** (8): 816–29

Wettig G. 1997, 'Die sowjetische Politik während der Berlinkrise 1958 bis 1962. [325]
Der Stand der Forschungen', *Deutschland Archiv*, **30** (3): 383–98

Wielgohs J., Schulz M. 1990, 'Reformbewegung und Volksbewegung. Politische
und soziale Aspekte im Umbruch der DDR-Gesellschaft', *Aus Politik und
Zeitgeschichte*, 13 April, no. 16–17: 15–24

Wilke M., Kubina M. 1993, ' "Die Lage in Polen ist schlimmer als 1968 in der
CSSR . . ." Die Forderung des SED-Politbüros nach einer Intervention in Polen
im Herbst 1980', *Deutschland Archiv*, **26** (3): 335–40

Wille M. 1993, *Entnazifizierung in der Sowjetischen Besatzungszone Deutschlands 1945–
48*. Helmuth-Block-Verlag, Magdeburg

Winkler G. (ed.) 1989, *Geschichte der Sozialpolitik der DDR 1945–1985*. Akademie
Verlag, Berlin (East)

Winkler G. (ed.) 1990, *Sozialreport '90. Daten und Fakten zur sozialen Lage in der DDR*.
Verlag Die Wirtschaft, Berlin (East)

Winkler G. 1997, 'Leben in Ostdeutschland', in Winkler G. (ed.), *Sozialreport
1997. Daten und Fakten zur sozialen Lage in den neuen Bundesländern*. Sozialwis-
senschaftliches Forschungszentrum Berlin-Brandenburg, Berlin, pp. 11–63

Wolf H. 1991, *Hatte die DDR je eine Chance?* VSA-Verlag, Hamburg

Wolle S. 1998, *Die heile Welt der Diktatur. Alltag und Herrschaft in der DDR 1971–1989*.
Ch. Links Verlag, Berlin

Zelikow P., Rice C. 1995, *Germany Unified and Europe Transformed. A Study in State-
craft*. Harvard University Press, Cambridge, Massachusetts, and London

Zille C. 1997, *Ostalgie? National and Regional Identifications in Germany after Unification*.
Discussion Papers in German Studies No. IG97/10, Institute for German Studies,
University of Birmingham, Birmingham

Zimmermann M. (ed.) 1994, *Was macht eigentlich . . . ? 100-DDR-Prominente heute*.
Ch. Links Verlag, Berlin

Zubok V., Pleshakov C. 1996, *Inside the Kremlin's Cold War. From Stalin to Khrushchev*.
Harvard University Press, Cambridge, Massachusetts, and London

INDEX